Taking SIDES

Clashing Views on Controversial Issues in Race and Ethnicity

Third Edition

Edited, Selected, and with Introductions by

Richard C. Monk
Coppin State College

Dushkin/McGraw-Hill
A Division of The McGraw-Hill Companies

To the memory of my father, Daniel R. Monk (1913–1995), who taught his children to tell the truth and to stand up for their beliefs, and to the brave student writers and researchers of Kaleidoscope: VSC's Journal of Criminal Justice, *who virtually alone stood up for the sororities, both Black and white, and tried to tell the truth.*

Photo Acknowledgments

Cover image: © 2000 by PhotoDisc, Inc.

Cover Art Acknowledgment

Charles Vitelli

Library of Congress Cataloging-in-Publication Data

Main entry under title:
    Taking sides: clashing views on controversial issues in race and ethnicity/edited, selected, and with introductions by Richard C. Monk.—3rd ed.
    Includes bibliographical references and index.
    1. Race awareness. 2. Ethnicity. I. Monk, Richard C., *comp.*

305.8

0-697-39142-6

95-83858

Printed on Recycled Paper

PREFACE

*Do not at the outset of your career make the all too common error of mistaking names for things. Names are only conventional signs for identifying things....
If a thing is despised, either because of ignorance or because it is despicable, you will not alter matters by changing its name. If men despise Negroes, they will not despise them less if Negroes are called "colored" or "Afro-American."*
... Your real work ... does not lie with names. It is not a matter of changing them, losing them, or forgetting them.

—W. E. B. Du Bois (1928)

When you control a man's thinking, you do not have to worry about his actions.

—Carter G. Woodson, *The Mis-Education of the Negro* (1933)

I have sworn upon the altar of God, eternal hostility against every form of tyranny over the mind of man.

—Thomas Jefferson (1800)

This volume contains 21 controversial issues in race and ethnicity debated in a pro and con format. Each issue is expressed as a single question in order to draw the lines of debate more clearly. The authors of the essays—sociologists, political commentators, historians, and others—reflect a broad range of disciplines and perspectives. For each issue I have provided an issue *introduction*, which provides some background information and sets the stage for the debate as it is argued in the YES and NO selections, and a *postscript* that summarizes the debate, considers other views on the issue, and suggests additional readings on the topics raised in the issue. In addition, Internet site addresses (URLs) have been provided on the *On the Internet* page that accompanies each part opener, which should prove useful as starting points for further research.

In part, this work grew out of the prodding of my former student Deputy U.S. Marshal Barrett Gay. As a Black American, he wanted to know where he could find a challenging book on controversial issues on racial and ethnic minorities. He challenged me to edit such a work, and he provided many outstanding suggestions. I was delighted both by his encouragement and the opportunity to work in my favorite area of sociology: ethnic and racial studies.

The reception of the first two editions of *Taking Sides: Clashing Views on Controversial Issues in Race and Ethnicity* by both students and professors has been gratifying. This third edition reflects my continuing commitment as a teacher to generating vigorous but informed student dialogue about racial and ethnic issues. As we enter the twenty-first century, ethnic and racial understandings and interactions remain highly fluid and increasingly violent in many areas. Just as the patterns of interaction between minorities and the majority groups shift, so do the ways in which sociologists and other scholars as well as the media, politicians, and the general public conceptualize, think about, and evaluate them change. Often the changes are dramatic and surprising.

I have attempted to capture as much as possible the shifting empirical realities of increasing ethnic and racial conflicts and the theoretical developments among scholars who are trying to comprehend them. On the one hand, new developments in the mosaic of minority relations around the world as well as how these developments are thought about and taught represent a veritable intellectual feast. On the other hand, there is great angst and a sense of tragedy in many recent minority developments and in some of the current approaches to minority relations. A specific tragedy that has reemerged in the 1990s is genocide. This development has caught the scholarly community so off guard that many race relations and sociological texts only have a page, footnote, or less devoted to this reality, which claimed over 1 million lives since the publication of the first edition of *Taking Sides* and possibly another million since the publication of the second edition.

There are many different issues to explore, think about, and debate in this volume. My primary concern is to get the authors' ideas up front so that you can be immersed in them, fight with them, embrace some of them, and then make your own decisions about the issues. However, now and then my own disdain for or support of certain ideas may be more manifest than on other occasions. Do not be bashful about debating the authors and their ideas, or your editor as well. My students frequently remind me that I could be wrong and need their (and your) critical evaluation. Indeed, it was my students as well as my colleagues who encouraged me to include more of what might be called "contrarian" issues and articles. These reflect ideas that are challenging, logical, and empirically based but, in spite of their relevancy, may be peripheral to or even excluded from mainstream social scientific dialogue. A few may even be on the cutting edge of what scholars and others will be arguing about or framing debates with in the twenty-first century.

Taking Sides: Clashing Views on Controversial Issues in Race and Ethnicity is a tool to encourage critical thinking on important issues concerning racial and ethnic minorities. Although students may find themselves supporting one side of an issue or the other, readers should not feel confined to the views expressed in the selections. Some readers may see important points on both sides of an issue and may construct for themselves a new and creative approach to the issue, which may incorporate the best of both sides or provide an entirely new vantage point for understanding.

I feel that the issues and articles found in *Taking Sides* are representative of what is currently going on in the area of race and ethnic relations. They also allow students to get into this important area of sociology without having old prejudices reinforced or new doctrines internalized. My hope is that students will find these debates stimulating and will use them to clarify their own thinking about issues that are all vital and frequently emotional as well as controversial.

Changes to this edition   In response to changes in ethnic and racial controversies, and on the helpful suggestions of those who have used the first two editions, considerable modifications were made to this edition. There are 10 completely new issues: *Is Judging Thomas Jefferson and Others Chronocentrically Unfair?* (Issue 3); *Do Industrialization and Capitalism Cause Racial and Ethnic Inequalities?* (Issue 5); *Have Scholars Ignored the Willing Participation of Germans in Killing Jews During the Holocaust?* (Issue 6); *Do the Identities of Blacks Lie in Africa?* (Issue 7); *Does Rap Music Contribute to Violent Crime?* (Issue 11); *Are Arabs and Other Muslims Portrayed Unfairly in American Films?* (Issue 12); *Is Racial Segregation Necessarily Bad?* (Issue 13); *Should Race Be a Consideration in College Admissions?* (Issue 17); *Should Sovereignty for American Indians Be Increased?* (Issue 18); and *Is the Drug War Harming Blacks?* (Issue 21). In addition, the NO selection in Issue 1 (*Can Outsiders Successfully Research Insiders?*) has been replaced to bring a fresh perspective to the debate. In all, there are 21 new selections in this edition. All issue introductions and postscripts have been revised and updated where necessary.

The organization and sections of this book have been changed to reflect emerging intellectual and empirical realities. Part 1 deals with Research, Theory, and Basic Concepts; Part 2, Social Identities and Cultural Conflict; Part 3, Immigration, Segregation, and Leadership; and Part 4, Affirmative Action, Legal Issues, and New Policies.

A word to the instructor   An *Instructor's Manual With Test Questions* (multiple-choice and essay) is available through the publisher for the instructor using *Taking Sides* in the classroom. A general guidebook, *Using Taking Sides in the Classroom,* which discusses methods and techniques for using the pro-con approach in any classroom setting, is also available. An online version of *Using Taking Sides in the Classroom* and a correspondence service for Taking Sides adopters can be found at http://www.dushkin.com/usingts/. For students, we offer a field guide to analyzing argumentative essays, *Analyzing Controversy: An Introductory Guide,* with exercises and techniques to help them to decipher genuine controversies.

Taking Sides: Clashing Views on Controversial Issues in Race and Ethnicity is only one title in the Taking Sides series. If you are interested in seeing the table of contents for any of the other titles, please visit the Taking Sides Web site at http://www.dushkin.com/takingsides/.

Acknowledgments   Many people contribute to any worthwhile project. Among those more directly involved in this project whom I would like to thank are the authors of these excellent and stimulating selections. Also, my thanks to the many students over the years who have contributed to the social scientific dialogue. At Coppin State College, these students include Andrew C. Brezinski, Sandra Ben-Avraham, Mark A. Garnes, Laquisha Harvey, Tom Francis Mwaura, and Vaughan L. James.

Several colleagues, scholars, and others provided comments and/or support that were immensely helpful and are greatly appreciated. Thanks are extended to John Hudgins and Elias Taylor, in Social Sciences; Genevieve Knight, in Mathematics and Computer Sciences; Judith Willner, chairperson of Fine and Communication Arts; Shaun Gabbidon and Ralph Hughes, in Criminal Justice; and Mary Wanza, director of Parlett Moore Library, and her staff, all at Coppin State College. Also helpful were Kurt Finsterbusch, of the University of Maryland; Alex Hooke, of Villa Julie College; Tom Gitchoff and Joel Henderson, of San Diego State University; Mike Lynch, of the University of South Florida; Harv Greisman, of Westchester State University; Rick Collum, of Cleveland, Ohio; Daniel B. Monk, of Arlington, Virginia; Kevin Bowman, of Warner Robin, Georgia; Daria Capps, of the Magothy River Middle School in Anne Arundel County, Maryland; Martha Mercer, of San Diego, California; Megan Pedersen, of Silver Spring, Maryland; Rudy Faller, of the Inter-American Development Bank; and Horst Senger, of Simi Valley, California. And, once again, to Goober and Midnight, who, when we dwelled in the land of deceit and duplicity, taught me to love and laugh again, and now to little Tommy, who makes everyone love and laugh.

A special thanks goes to those professors who responded to the questionnaire with specific suggestions for the third edition:

John P. Deluca
State University of New York
   at Albany

Hirosi Fukurai
University of California,
   Santa Cruz

Donald Haydu
El Camino College

Guinevere Hodges
Cypress College

Virginia Juffer
Century College

Antonio Menendez
Butler University

Finally, someone must have once said that an author or editor is only as good as his or her publisher. Thanks are extended to Ted Knight, list manager, and David Brackley, senior developmental editor for the Taking Sides series, at Dushkin/McGraw-Hill. Naturally, I remain solely responsible for errors.

Richard C. Monk
Coppin State College

CONTENTS IN BRIEF

CONTENTS

Robert K. Merton, dean of American sociology at Columbia University, challenges the idea that superior insights automatically result from membership in a specific group. In so doing, he generates several hypotheses for researching and understanding ethnic and racial minorities. Ann Oakley, an honorary research officer at the University of London, questions whether the traditional canons of value-free science, especially when interviewing members of minority groups, are desirable or even possible.

Journalist and historian David A. Bell acknowledges some difficulties and hurdles faced by Asian Americans, but he portrays the road taken by Asian Americans as "America's greatest success story." Ronald Takaki, a historian at the University of California, Berkeley, faults the mass media and some ethnic studies scholars for perpetuating the myth that Asians are a model minority. Takaki argues that within Asian groups there are vast differences in success.

Freelance writer H. L. Goldstein briefly traces the controversy surrounding the recent disclosure that DNA evidence may confirm that Thomas Jefferson's slave Sally Hemings bore his children. Goldstein attacks the interpretations of the DNA findings as unfair chronocentrism that tells us nothing about race relations. Brent Staples, an editorial writer for the *New York Times,* argues that genetic evidence proves that Jefferson was a racist and a hypocrite who talked one game (democracy, fairness, and liberty) but played another (oppression and exploitation).

Glenn C. Loury, a professor of economics and a noted race relations writer, charges that Dinesh D'Souza's theory that racism is not an essential component of the problems of Blacks is flawed. Dinesh D'Souza, a research fellow at the American Enterprise Institute and a social critic, defends his controversial thesis that racism is a thing of the past.

Professor of arts and sciences Sheila E. Henry argues that in the United States, minorities whose ancestral nations have high prestige are allocated high prestige themselves, while African Americans and others, reflecting both institutional racism and the low status of many African societies, are forced to occupy the bottom rungs of society. Thomas Sowell, a researcher at the Hoover Institute, maintains that dominant theories of racial and ethnic inequality that are based on prejudice, oppression, exploitation, and discrimination are simply wrong.

Daniel Jonah Goldhagen, a political scientist at Harvard University, argues that most writers on the Holocaust have ignored or minimized the role of the police, soldiers, and other "ordinary" Germans as willing executioners of Europe's Jews. Pacific Lutheran University professor Christopher R. Browning rejects Goldhagen's "accusatory approach," which he contends is self-serving, promotes misunderstanding of traditional scholarship, and does little to advance society's understanding of genocide.

Assistant professor of speech communication Olga Idriss Davis links Black identity with Africa. In a moving account based on her visits to Senegal, West Africa, she reveals how she and many other African Americans have benefited from their pilgrimages to Africa. *Washington Post* correspondent Keith B. Richburg contends that it is trendy and foolish for Blacks to attempt to validate themselves through identification with Africa.

Professor of sociology John Sibley Butler briefly traces the history of the terms that Black Americans have applied to themselves and argues that it makes sense for them to be called African Americans. Professor of economics Walter E. Williams dismisses those who opt to call themselves African American (or related terms) in order to achieve cultural integrity among Blacks. He says that there are serious problems in the Black community that need to be addressed, none of which will be solved by a new name.

Scholar and former political candidate Linda Chavez argues that Hispanics are making it in America. Michigan State University social scientist Robert Aponte suggests that social scientists have concentrated on Black poverty, which has resulted in a lack of accurate data and information on the economic status of Hispanics. Aponte argues that disaggregation of demographic data shows that Hispanics are increasingly poor.

Professor of curriculum and instruction Jon Reyhner blames the high dropout rate for Native Americans on schools, teachers, and curricula that ignore the needs and potentials of North American Indian students. Educator Susan Ledlow questions the meaning of "cultural discontinuity," and she faults this perspective for ignoring important structural factors, such as employment, in accounting for why Native American students drop out of school.

Dennis R. Martin, president of the National Association of Chiefs of Police, theorizes that rising racial tensions and violence can be attributed to rock music's promotion of "vile, deviant, and sociopathic behaviors." Criminologists Mark S. Hamm and Jeff Ferrell charge that Martin's theory is based on racism and ignorance of both music and broader cultural forces.

Author and *CBS News* consultant Jack G. Shaheen contends that Hollywood's long history of denigrating Arabs as villains and terrorists continues in the film *The Siege*. He maintains that portrayals of Arabs as thugs significantly increases attacks on Muslims in the United States. Lawrence Wright, a staff writer for the *New Yorker* and coauthor of *The Siege*, asserts that the producers of *The Siege* were supportive of Arabs and that the movie's depiction of a heroic Muslim police officer as well as of dangerous, unfair treatment of Arabic Americans indicate that the movie was anything but denigrating.

Paul Ruffins, executive editor of *Crisis*, rejects three arguments supporting school segregation in the 1990s and asserts that efforts to achieve school integration should be increased. Glenn C. Loury, director of the Institute on Race and Social Division at Boston University, contends that school racial integration is an untenable goal because schools are more segregated now than they were 30 years ago, the courts and public sentiment no longer support school busing, and enforced integration implies Black inferiority.

Peter Brimelow, senior editor of *Forbes* and *National Review*, links the recent increase in immigration to many of America's major problems, including crises in health care, education, and pollution. David Cole, a professor at the Georgetown University Law Center, maintains that, throughout history, immigrants to the United States have been perceived as a threat by U.S. citizens but that they are beneficial to America.

The editors of *Social Justice* aim to "reclaim the true history" of the continent, which, they say, is one of enslavement, torture, and repression of people of color, who are now in revolt against lies and exploitation. Harvard University historian Arthur M. Schlesinger, Jr., argues that the genius of the United States lies in its unity—the ability of its citizens to embrace basic, common values while accepting cultural diversity.

Eugene F. Rivers III, founder and pastor of the Azusa Christian Community, notes the many social and economic problems of Black youth in the United States and argues that three types of Black leaders have contributed to the problems rather than the solutions. Emeritus professor of psychology Edmund W. Gordon and researcher Maitrayee Bhattacharyya maintain that intentional neglect and racism by all of society are responsible for the poor state of Black development.

William G. Bowen, president of the Andrew W. Mellon Foundation, and Derek Bok, former president of Harvard University, contend that the high rate of success of the Black college graduates that they studied would not have happened if they had attended lesser schools. Because admission to the elite schools for many of these students resulted from affirmative action, Bowen and Bok argue that the policy of considering race should be continued. Dinesh D'Souza, the John M. Olin Scholar at the American Enterprise Institute, dismisses the conclusions of Bowen and Bok and asserts that admission to any organization should always be based on merit, not preferential treatment.

Joseph P. Kalt, codirector of the Harvard Project on American Indian Economic Development, and Jonathan B. Taylor, director of Indian Projects at the Economics Resource Group, Inc., in Cambridge, Massachusetts, argue that increasing sovereignty (freedom from external control) will give Native Americans the ability to help themselves. Hendrik Mills, a writer and teacher, maintains that since the 1960s, Indian militants and their allies have received increased federal monies to fight poverty and recognition of their increasing sovereignty but that mismanagement botched these opportunities while legitimizing absurd victim excuses based on a mythical heroic past.

Paul Butler, an associate professor at the George Washington University Law School, argues that Black jurors should acquit Black defendants of certain crimes, regardless of whether or not they perceive the defendant to be guilty, to make up for inequities in the criminal justice system. Randall Kennedy, a professor at the Harvard Law School, in examining the acquittal of O. J. Simpson, finds it tragic that Black jurors would pronounce a murderer "not guilty" just to send a message to white people. He maintains that allowing Black criminals to go free does not help minorities.

Florida International University criminology professor William Wilbanks advances the thesis that the criminal justice system is not now racist. Indiana
University criminologist Coramae Richey Mann argues that at almost every
point in the criminal justice system, racism persists.

Psychiatrist and psychoanalyst Thomas Szasz maintains that the current drug
war harms almost all people, especially Blacks, and that its main function is to
increase the power of the medical and criminal justice establishments. James
A. Inciardi, director of the Center for Drug and Alcohol Studies at the University of Delaware, surveys several arguments supporting the legalization
of drugs and rejects them all, insisting that Blacks and others would be hurt
by legalization.

INTRODUCTION

Issues in Race and Ethnicity

Richard C. Monk

Modern man finds himself confronted not only by multiple options of possible courses of action, but also by multiple options of possible ways of thinking about the world.

—Peter Berger, *The Heretical Imperative* (1979)

The world is a giant lab waiting for your exploration.

—Robert Park

Bienvenidos (Welcome)! Your intellectual voyage into controversial issues in race and ethnicity is bound to be an exciting one. Some ancient ethnic groups would wish their members: "May you live in interesting times." Every person entering the twenty-first century seems to be a direct recipient of this benediction. This is especially true for students both experiencing and studying the rapidly changing and controversial mosaic of ethnic and racial relations.

Since the publication in 1996 of the second edition of this reader, many changes have occurred in race and ethnic relations both in the United States and around the world. While some changes are encouraging, many are not. Indeed, long before the dissolution of the Marxian experiment that was the former Soviet Union in the early 1990s, sociologists and others argued that the greatest flaw in Marx's theory was that he completely underestimated the continued importance of race and ethnicity in both modern and developing societies. Media reports, for example, indicate that Chinese in Indonesia are still scapegoats for that country's troubles and that rioters openly attack ethnic Chinese businesspeople and their families.

A February 1999 government report in Britain concludes that British society is also tainted by racism. In one incident in 1993, several white racists beat to death a Black teenager. Police seemed to make little effort to solve the crime. Also, British tabloids routinely use ethnic slurs, such as *Paki* and *Jap*. In Spain, fans booed the winning Barcelona soccer team because it consists of several Dutch players, whose presence offends many Spaniards.

The ethnic and religious carnage in the former Yugoslavia has escalated, and as NATO forces bomb Serbians, Albanians and others are being driven out of Kosovo by the Serbs. As many as 400,000 women, children, and men are leaving Kosovo and other areas to escape being massacred. Meanwhile, over 50 years after the destruction of Nazi Germany and the subsequent Nuremberg trials, which established the international legal condemnation of genocide, thousands of bodies of human beings subject to "ethnic cleansing" have been found throughout villages in central Europe. Though greatly abated for the time being, some slaughters continue in central Europe. Recent reports indicate that 100,000 or more Hutu participated in the extermination of some 2 million Tutsi, about half of Rwanda's Tutsi citizens.

While the world's eyes seem glued upon Kosovo and central Europe, many ignore the plight of Africans fleeing the internal war in Sierra Leone. The UN estimates that 440,000 refugees have escaped to neighboring African nations. Critics are appalled that while relief funds are springing up for European victims of ethnic attacks, few, including Black U.S. leaders, are publicly worried about Sierra Leone.

In Borneo (between Indonesia and Malaysia) ethnic Malay, Dayak, and Bugis men attacked immigrants from adjoining Madura; the military ignored the events. Recently, a Russian general who is also a communist member of Parliament, advocated immediately arresting all Jews. He used traditional Russian derogatory terms such as *zhid* (yid). In theory, Marxian and communist doctrine is vehemently opposed to such jingoism.

On a more positive note, for the first time in 500 years, Jews in Spain can now publicly celebrate Hanukkah. Also, although only a handful of alleged war criminals responsible for recent genocides in Asia, Europe, and Africa have been captured and charged, efforts are underway to bring more to justice. If a precedent is set, future racial and ethnic minority repressions might be deterred. The NATO bombings of central Europe, with strong U.S. support, are at least ostensibly being carried out to eliminate and punish the documented attacks on ethnic and religious minority groups. Defenders of the NATO attacks insist that in terms of ethnic and racial protection, the war is a noble one. Others, especially the Serbs, have a distinctly different perspective. However, the point is that both the *meanings* and *control* of ethnic and racial conflicts, notably those that include efforts at genocide, are changing dramatically. A few years ago most sociology texts made little or no mention of genocide. Intellectuals around the world, for the most part, ignored horrible racial and ethnic slaughters in Asia, Africa, and central Europe until the late 1990s. World events have forced a change in this former ethnic and racial parochialism.

Within the United States, some minority-related events have been as dramatic as those that have been unfolding around the world. On the negative side are tragedies: the ruthless murder in Jasper, Texas, of James Byrd, Jr., by white racist John King; the sodomizing of a Black immigrant by New York police with a club; and the homophobic murder of Matthew Sheppard, a gay youth in Wyoming. Equally tragic but far more confusing are the April 1999 murders of high school students in Littleton, Colorado, by two students who also killed themselves. Apparently, these teenage killers had specifically targeted Christians, Blacks, and athletes. Moreover, preparations for this attack appear to have been made on computers and discussed via e-mail. Many are concerned that an increasing number of hate sites are emerging on the Internet. While the Anti-Defamation League and other organizations are vigilantly trying to alert the public about these sites, their effects on minority relations are unclear.

In California and other states, massive legal changes are occurring. Legislation has been passed blocking social services to illegal immigrant families (see Issue 14), banning college admissions based on race (see Issue 17), banning bilingual education, and stepping up deportations of immigrants. Yet significant legislation and court rulings have also sided with racial and ethnic minorities. These include huge monetary judgments against those engaged in mortgage-lending discrimination and against restaurant chains that refuse to serve Blacks, awards to Black farmers, and the extension of benefits to Native Americans (see Issue 18), to mention a few.

At another level of analysis, conceptualizations of minority relations by both scholars and minorities themselves have been reworked. The trinity over the past 10 years or so of gender, race, and class emphasis is being increasingly challenged within various disciplines, several of which now have divided professional organizations (e.g., the newly formed Historical Society, the Association of Literary Scholars and Critics, and the Sociological Research Association). Members of emerging organizations often complain that their disciplines have become too ideological because traditional theories are being rejected allegedly on the grounds that their formulators were members of the dominant group (i.e., white European males). Others reject the new thinking's alleged overemphasis on gender and class aspects of minority problems. While naysayers worry that all of this signifies the demise of the social sciences and humanities, others argue that such conflicts are healthy. Indeed, so goes this argument, the academic factionalism merely reflects changing ethnic and racial minority realities (see Issue 1).

The emergence of outstanding thinkers who are minority members is also significantly changing traditional conceptualizations. For instance, radical rejection of traditional knowledge of minority problems and solutions is flowering. These include challenges to the economic discrimination and racism models to account for inequities (see Issues 2, 4, and 5); challenges to the traditional views of the African homeland and African American leaders (see Issues 7 and 16); and the goal of the civil rights movement itself.

At a more local level, there has been a tremendous amount of support for families of victims of discrimination. These include support for the Byrd family in Texas, Jewish families harassed by anti-Semites, and others.

Some examples of positive ethnic relations with which you might more closely identify would be if you were to invite a foreign student home for Thanksgiving or Christmas (extremely lonely times for "outsiders") or if you were to take the time to learn about and appreciate holidays and ceremonies of a culture or religion that is different from yours.

At another level of analysis, the pervasiveness of ethnicity, in spite of assimilation in the United States, remains both bold and subtle. Countless news articles and electronic media reports document the integration of racial and ethnic minorities into the sports and entertainment worlds. Achievements in other sectors, such as education, government, medicine, and law, are also noted. Thus, it is obvious that we exist in a world of racial and ethnic minority interactions. However, some would maintain that the fact that only 1 of the 166 Academy Award nominees in 1996 was Black, as well as other apparent indications of blatant racism, suggest that these interactions are as yet still limited.

It is also obvious from the few examples cited above, as well as from your own experiences growing up in the modern world, that the types, meanings or interpretations, and consequences of minority-based actions and the majority's responses are complex. Moreover, as contemporary sociologist Peter Berger notes, you are confronted not only by different ways of responding to your world, including your interactions with minority members and majority ones, but you also face "multiple options of possible ways of thinking about the world." This includes how you view ethnic and racial groups and the controversies related to their presence, their actions, and the ways in which other members of society respond to them.

THE STUDY OF RACIAL AND ETHNIC RELATIONS

For generations many social scientists, as trained "people watchers" (a term coined by Berger), have found minority relations to be among the most fascinating aspects of social life. Initially, sociologists and anthropologists tended to have an intellectual monopoly on the formal, systematic study of this area. More recently, historians, economists, and political scientists have increased significantly their studies of minority group relations. Although the work of these people is generally narrower and more focused than that of sociologists (typical subjects for study would be the historical treatment of one region's slave system in a specific time period, attitudes of Italian American voters, or the consumption and marketplace behavior of selected Asian groups), their gradual inclusion of minorities in their research is a welcome addition to the scholarship.

Sociologists and anthropologists have energized research methods, theories, and perspectives within minority scholarship, but the process has been painful and the source of acrimonious controversies among sociologists about proper scholarly work *vis-à-vis* ethnic and racial minorities. Two major events sparked this critical examination of the foundations of concepts and studies: (1) the civil rights movement in the 1960s and the rapid changes that resulted from it; and (2) breakthroughs in the philosophy of science that increased understanding of science, theories, and methods.

The civil rights movement in the United States politicized minority groups, especially Blacks, and moved them onto the public stage. Articulate and militant, they were finally listened to by the majority, including sociologists. Moreover, agents of social control, especially the federal government, assumed a direct role in supporting increasing changes for minorities.

The antiwar protest against the Vietnam War of the same period functioned to undermine both social science characterizations of uniformity and the consensus of American society, as well as the government's claims of fairness and veracity in its justification for the war. Both the civil rights movement and the antiwar protest generated a radical cohort of social scientists who were suspicious of both the political-military and the educational-university establishments, including the establishment teachers and their graduate programs.

Two areas within ethnic and racial minority theories and research that were bitterly attacked during this time were the standard minorities relations cyclical model, which was originally formulated in the 1920s by sociologist Robert Park (1864–1944) and his students at the University of Chicago (hereinafter referred to as "Chicago sociologists"), and the studies that were generated in the 1950s and 1960s by structural functionalists such as Talcott Parsons and Robert Merton and their students. The Chicago model consists of a series of stages that ethnic and racial minorities pass through in their contacts with the dominant group. Partially based on models from plant ecology and from Park's newspaper days—as well as on ideas he learned during the time he was a secretary for Booker T. Washington, founder of the Tuskegee Institute—the model identifies several minority-majority relations processes, such as conflict, accommodation, and eventual assimilation. The latter stage reflects the turn-of-the-century emphasis on the American "melting pot." Up through the 1950s major U.S. institutions simply assumed for the most part that racial and ethnic minorities wanted to and tried to "blend in" with American society. Minorities were encouraged to Anglicize their names, learn and speak English, embrace Anglo middle-class customs and norms, and so on.

Although pluralism (a stage in which a cultural, ethnic, or racial minority group coexists equally within a nation-state while maintaining harmoniously its own values, attitudes, language, and customs) was identified by the Chicago sociologists, it remained a relatively undeveloped concept until the 1940s and 1950s. Then anthropologists and others (such as F. J. Furnival and M. G. Smith) utilized pluralism but primarily to depict social processes in the Caribbean and other areas outside of the United States. However, since conflict, oppression, and exploitation were viewed by radical sociologists in the 1960s and 1970s (and currently) as areas ignored by Park and his followers, the Chicago sociologists' model was dismissed.

Many standard, or liberal, sociologists were horrified at what they viewed as the desecration of Park and his memory. They were especially incensed by the charges of racism against Park and the Chicago race relations theory and research. These supporters argued that the Chicago sociologists were very progressive for their time. The Chicago model clearly allowed for conflict, although Park generally viewed conflict in terms of prejudice and discrimination at the interpersonal level. Because it tended to focus on influences of the individual, Chicago sociology was often more like social psychology. Oppressive institutions and structurally induced and maintained inequalities simply were not part of the vocabulary of most sociologists in the United States until the 1960s. Two important exceptions were the turn-of-the-century writings of black intellectual W. E. B. Du Bois and the later writings of Professor Oliver Cox (e.g., *Caste, Class, and Race,* 1948), but their work was largely ignored by both the public and sociology.

Structural functionalist theory, which originated at Harvard and Columbia Universities and generally dominated sociology throughout the 1960s, was also bitterly attacked. Structural functionalist theory basically states that a society acquires the characteristics that it does because they meet the particular needs of that society. This theory stresses cohesion, conformity, and integration among the society's members. Some of the charges against this theory were that it was inherently conservative, it celebrated middle-class values while ignoring the pains of the minority status, it excluded contributions of minority scholars, and it relied unduly on the natural science model, omitting systematic efforts to understand the subjective experiences of human beings —including ethnic and racial minorities.

These criticisms (and I only mentioned selected salient points) resulted in a reexamination of sociological work, including ethnic and racial minorities scholarship. Unfortunately, although some of this investigation was infused with sociology of knowledge concepts—that is, sociologists attempted to systematically trace the origins of ideas to the positions that intellectuals held within groups—much of it was largely reduced to name-calling. Many social scientists would argue that hunting down ideological biases in research and theory does not necessarily advance understanding, especially if strengths in the existing work are ignored or no alternative programs are developed. A few would even claim that the social sciences have not advanced significantly in ethnic and racial minority theories beyond the Chicago sociology of the 1920s and 1930s or some of the essays of the structural functionalists of the 1960s, such as Talcott Parsons's *The Negro American* (1968).

Another factor that stimulated change in minority research and theorizing is less direct but possibly as important: breakthroughs in the philosophy of science that occurred in the 1950s and that have continued to occur up to the present. The philosophy of science is generally narrower than the sociology of knowledge. It aims to rigorously identify and explicate the criteria that scientists use to develop and evaluate theory, concepts, and methods. The structures of scientific work and the standards used to accept or reject it are carefully delineated by the philosophy of science.

Before the 1960s the philosophy of science had eschewed "mere" ideology hunting that characterized some variants of the sociology of knowledge. It was considerably more formal and analytic. However, beginning with the works of Thomas Kuhn, especially his *Structure of Scientific Revolutions* (1961), as well as the writings of British philosopher Sir Karl Popper and his student Imre Lakatos, physical and social scientists became sensitized to the importance of both formal analytical aspects of scholarship *and* communal elements.

Links between variants of the philosophy of science and ethnic-racial minorities issues include analyses of schools of thought within which particular race relations scientific research programs have emerged; the basic terms and their utilizations (e.g., pluralism, and whether or not it is being observed); conflict; and styles of operationalization (how terms are measured). In addition, the kinds of data (information) that are collected—attitudes, consumption patterns, behaviors (observed, implied, elicited from questionnaires, income levels, and so on)—who collects the facts, and how the facts are analyzed (through narrative summaries, tabular presentations, and statistics) have all been subject to scrutiny drawing from the methods of the philosophy of science.

Part of the philosophy of science's influence is expressed directly in some of the more current and influential discussions of theory and theory formation, such as the writings of sociologists George Ritzer and Edward A. Tiryakian. Ritzer combines the sociology of knowledge and the philosophy of science concerns in studying the underlying structure of sociological theory. Tiryakian, taking a tack somewhat closer to traditional sociology of knowledge, has argued for the importance of systematically examining hegemonic, or dominant, schools of thought within the social sciences. Such an examination includes social influences on theory development and the methodological agenda. The former is primarily a sociology of knowledge concern, and the latter is a philosophy of science concern.

Thus far, most contemporary ethnic and racial minority researchers and theorists do not directly draw from Ritzer, Tiryakian, and others; at least not in a systematic, comprehensive fashion. However, they do routinely acknowledge these concerns and often attack other researchers and studies on philosophy of science grounds. Moreover, most introductory racial minorities textbooks raise and briefly discuss underlying assumptions of studies they survey, though frequently in a simplistic manner. Most of the issues in this book indirectly touch on these concerns, and some grapple with them directly.

ADDITIONAL BASIC CONCEPTS AND TERMS

Many definitions and typologies (classificatory schemes) of minority groups exist. At the very least, it would seem, a scientifically adequate conceptualization ought to take into account both subjective aspects (attitudes, definitions of the situation, and assignment of meanings) and objective ones (proportion, ratio, and quantity of minority members; their income, amount of education, and percentage in specific occupations; and so on).

One definition of *minority* that seems to have hung on since its inception 50 years ago and that remains vital and remarkably serviceable was provided by sociologist Louis Wirth. According to Wirth, a minority is a "group of people who, because of their physical or cultural characteristics, are singled out from the others ... for differential and unequal treatment and who therefore regard themselves as objects of collective discrimination. [This] implies the existence of a corresponding dominant group enjoying social status and greater privileges ... the minority is treated and regards itself as a people apart." This definition clearly includes ethnic and racial minorities. It does not mean *nu-*

merical minority since, as Wirth points out, frequently a sociological minority group could be a numerical majority (e.g., Blacks in South Africa). The point is that minority members are systematically excluded from certain societal privileges and that they have less power than others.

Although ethnic and racial minorities can be included in Wirth's 50-year-old definition, ethnicity and racism are relatively new concepts. Strict biological classifications of groups by race are scientifically untenable. However, the social construction of images and stereotypes of categories of people based upon attributed racial characteristics are quite real. Although individuals of different racial origins may dress like you do, speak like you do, and have the same attitudes as you, if you view them in terms of their race, then they will be so defined. This is true even if there is absolutely no discernable trait or behavioral characteristic that can be accurately traced to race, as opposed to class, nationality, or region, for example. Unfortunately, while sociologically fascinating, the construction of the myth of race and its perpetuation in terms of attitudes and treatment has had frequently devastating consequences. Ironically, such world-taken-for-granted classifications, along with the concomitant attribution of all kinds of behaviors (often perceived as quite different and negative), are relatively unique to recent history and to the West. Among the ancients there was little or no understanding of the differences of peoples based on race. Nor were there objectionable connotations placed upon peoples of different physiological appearances.

Groups arranged in terms of ethnicity, however, have far more empirical accuracy than those arranged by race. Although negative attributes have been inaccurately and unfairly fixed to different ethnic groups, ethnicity does imply common characteristics such as language, religion, custom, and nationality. Wirth would identify ethnic minority groups as those with distinguishable characteristics who have less power than the dominant group and who are singled out for negative differential treatment.

This reader is restricted to selected controversial issues pertaining to ethnic and racial minorities. I acknowledge that other, equally important minorities exist. Indeed, some argue that the original minority groups were women and children! Certainly they were known to be mistreated and discriminated against long before racial, national, ethnic, or religious groups were on the scene. Nevertheless, the controversial issues in this reader emphasize ethnic and racial minority membership.

Another useful term that students of minority relations will draw from frequently is *ethnocentrism*, which was coined by sociologist William Graham Sumner. He introduced the concept of ethnocentrism in his delightful book *Folkways* (1907). To be ethnocentric is to be group-centered, to take the attitudes, values, customs, and standards of one's group and impose them on the members of another group. To the extent that the latter's behavior differs from the behavior or norms of one's own group, negative connotations are attached to the others' actions. The opposite of this is reverse ethnocentrism, which means to deprecate one's own group and embrace the behaviors and norms of the members of another group, possibly with a blind eye to the problems of that group. An interesting variant of this term is *chronocentrism*, which entails judging people who lived at a different time by the standards of one's own time. See Issue 3 and decide if this concept is useful.

The purpose of much of your training in the social sciences, especially in sociology and minority relations, is to liberate you from ethnocentrism as well as reverse ethnocentrism. In the first issue of the *Journal of Negro History* (1916), Carter G. Woodson, a founder of Black history, warned against controversies that, in the treatment of Blacks, either "brands him as a leper of society" or treats him "as a persecuted saint."

Your goal in reading these controversies, writing about them, criticizing them, and perhaps reformulating them or even eventually resolving them is to learn how to think about and understand major ethnic and racial minority issues.

Part 1, Research, Theory, and Basic Concepts, consists of six controversial issues pertaining to research, theory, and basic concepts. Before they can think clearly, scholars must first do conceptual work. This means learning what the key ideas are, what myths and conceptual baggage exist and need to be weeded out before knowledge can grow, and what the core problems of researching and theorizing about minorities are. Part 1 will assist you in this endeavor.

Part 2, Social Identities and Cultural Conflict, first addresses the ancient Greek query "Who am I?" from a minority standpoint. Next, the abstract but vital cultural level of analysis is tackled. The culture of any group has been likened to a societal blueprint or template for behavior. It consists of ideas, values, beliefs, conceptions of the good and bad, symbols and so on.

Often when members of minority and majority groups are battling it out either verbally or physically, each group's culture is clashing with that of the other. Selected debates pertain to an important conduit for cultural transmission, the public schools; the influence of rap music on certain kinds of behavior; and cultural conflict as a product of commercial films. The empirical case that is debated in the latter is whether or not Arabs are unfairly portrayed in films.

Part 3, Immigration, Segregation, and Leadership, reflects some of the most controversial racial and ethnic processes currently being experienced in the United States and elsewhere. Immigration continues to be a hotly contested issue, as Americans debate eliminating services, jailing more illegal immigrants, and restricting the numbers of newcomers. For some, this and other issues indicate that the United States does not really want to integrate some minorities and has never been a true "melting pot." Instead, they insist, the United States has always been a racist, imperialistic society bent on exploiting and oppressing others. The contentious issue of leadership among minorities also addresses these charges, as both a growing number of Black leaders and social scientists contend that the dissenters are not really analyzing social relations but are simply mapping out their own personal agendas. These agendas, they argue, are frequently linked with cries of victimization.

The issues in Part 4, Affirmative Action, Legal Issues, and New Policies, represent for some the "payoff" of social scientific theories and research. That is, what policies toward minorities are the most likely to be helpful for both them and others? Does the presence of racial minorities on all college campuses necessarily help society, and should such a goal be pursued? Has the policy of increasing sovereignty for Native Americans really been a rational policy, or is it generating increasing problems? Meanwhile, for some, one of the most unfair charges against minorities is that they are responsible for fueling the crime problem. To others, this is a case of blaming the victims themselves for unfair treatment and discrimination. They argue that existing crime control policies, especially the so-called drug war, are actually harmful to minorities.

From these arguments, you will learn how to look at controversial issues in a new way. Not only will you learn these new debates and facts pertaining to minorities and society's responses to them, but you will learn—to paraphrase Peter Berger—new ways of thinking about these issues, problems, and possible solutions.

On the Internet . . .

Asian Community Online Network

The links on this page of the Asian Community Online Network provide information on the political, historical, legal, and other concerns and interests of a wide variety of Asian American groups.
http://www.igc.apc.org/acon/links/index.html

The Truth About the Thomas Jefferson DNA Study

Herbert Barger, the Jefferson family historian, here addresses the issue of the Thomas Jefferson–Sally Hemings DNA study and provides a list of updated links to other sites on Jefferson, including an online resource on the Jefferson-Hemings DNA testing.
http://www.angelfire.com/va/TJTruth/

Holocaust—Understanding and Prevention

This site, sponsored by Holocaust survivor Alexander Kimel, provides some first-hand accounts of the horror of the Holocaust. Among other things, Kimel explores post-Holocaust issues, offers memoirs and poetry related to the Holocaust, and lists a handful of links to other sites related to the Holocaust.
http://haven.ios.com/~kimel19/index.html#top

PART 1

Research, Theory, and Basic Concepts

What are minority groups? How should research on minority groups be conducted? Are standard sociological theories on ethnicity and race still valid? How do theories and research generate as well as maintain myths about minority groups? The debates in this section explore how to study racial and ethnic relations and some of the basic sociological terminology and concepts.

■ Can Outsiders Successfully Research Insiders?

■ Are Asian Americans a "Model Minority"?

■ Is Judging Thomas Jefferson and Others Chronocentrically Unfair?

■ Is the "End of Racism" Thesis Badly Flawed?

■ Do Industrialization and Capitalism Cause Racial and Ethnic Inequalities?

■ Have Scholars Ignored the Willing Participation of Germans in Killing Jews During the Holocaust?

ISSUE 1

Can Outsiders Successfully Research Insiders?

YES: Robert K. Merton, from "Insiders and Outsiders: A Chapter in the Sociology of Knowledge," *American Journal of Sociology* (July 1972)

NO: Ann Oakley, from "Interviewing Women: A Contradiction in Terms," in Helen Roberts, ed., *Doing Feminist Research* (Routledge Kegan Paul, 1981)

ISSUE SUMMARY

YES: Robert K. Merton, dean of American sociology at Columbia University, challenges the idea that superior insights automatically result from membership in a specific group. In so doing, he generates several hypotheses for researching and understanding ethnic and racial minorities.

NO: Ann Oakley, an honorary research officer at the University of London, questions whether the traditional canons of value-free science, especially when interviewing members of minority groups, are desirable or even possible. Based on her extensive, in-depth research of females before and after their giving birth, she asserts that being a mother herself—as well as a researcher —precludes any pretense at maintaining an outsider position.

Scientific research, including sociological, anthropological, and psychological, has traditionally been held to standards of objectivity. Such research must be rational, value free, detached, and apolitical. Early sociologists and other researchers of race and ethnicity took pride in their ability to transcend stereotyping, prejudices, and ignorance while much of the rest of the population were denouncing others simply because of their race, ethnicity, and other minority characteristics.

Until after World War II, most Americans took for granted what many now realize were stereotypical views of minorities, often because on the surface, these views "made sense." Some examples of these attitudes include "Women can never be doctors or soldiers because they are too frail"; "Jews cannot be good farmers because they are city dwellers who cannot function in rural areas"; and "Blacks could never run a business or be real leaders because they prefer to allow others to think for them."

Sociologists, anthropologists, and others approached minorities scientifically in order to objectively understand them as well as to understand members of dominant groups. Such studies almost always transcended the unfair and inaccurate depictions of racial, religious, ethnic, and gender minorities.

For example, studies showed that when women were given the same opportunities as men, they could perform as well as men in the roles of police officer, college professor, and leader. Also, when Blacks and Hispanics had the opportunities, they could perform as well as whites and Anglos economically, socially, and politically. Such findings helped to bring about significant changes in public attitudes, influence legal and economic changes, and legitimize the civil rights movement in the 1960s.

Social scientists were proud of their work, partly because of the contributions that their studies made to reducing misunderstandings and conflict among different racial and ethnic groups. In disseminating their findings, these scientists felt that they had destroyed the mean-spirited myths, superstitions, and ignorance upon which many Americans had based their attitudes toward racial, ethnic, and gender minorities.

Almost all early researchers in sociology, psychology, and anthropology were white males, although the latter discipline did produce several distinguished female scholars early on, such as Ruth Benedict and Margaret Mead. The scientific assumption was that "outsiders" (nonmembers of the group under study) who were properly trained, regardless of their race, gender, or background, could successfully research "insiders," such as members of radically different minority groups. Indeed, Robert K. Merton suggests in the following selection, insiders will sometimes divulge personal information to sympathetic strangers that they would not share with members of their own group.

By contrast, in the second selection, Ann Oakley rejects the contention that objectivity, detachment, and neutrality in social research are worthy goals. Drawing from the research of others and her own extensive studies of pregnant women, she condemns the idea of demarcating one's role as an observer from one's role as a human being. As a woman and a mother, Oakley suggests it would be monstrous for her not to bond with her subjects, especially the many who are desperately seeking information on child care or who simply need consensual validation that as mothers they are doing the right things.

As you read the selections, consider Oakley's and Merton's ideas as they apply to other minorities (e.g., Blacks directing or assisting research of other Blacks, Hispanic farm workers being researched, or gay researchers studying other gay people). Is it necessarily advantageous to maintain the insider/outsider perspective? Note that this debate is not only about researching minorities but that it is also a squaring off of the sociology of knowledge perspective represented by Merton (who significantly shaped its original contours) and the emerging feminist epistemology. Oakley herself has played a key role in bringing this relatively new approach to knowledge to life and, some say, has injected a badly needed vitality into the social sciences in general and minority theorizing and research in particular. Whose epistemology do you prefer? Why?

YES
Robert K. Merton

INSIDERS AND OUTSIDERS:
A CHAPTER IN THE SOCIOLOGY
OF KNOWLEDGE

The sociology of knowledge has long been regarded as a complex and esoteric subject, remote from the urgent problems of contemporary social life. To
some of us, it seems quite the other way. Especially in times of great social
change, precipitated by acute social conflict and attended by much cultural
disorganization and reorganization, the perspectives provided by the various
sociologies of knowledge bear directly upon problems agitating the society.
It is then that differences in the values, commitments, and intellectual orientations of conflicting groups become deepened into basic cleavages, both
social and cultural. As the society becomes polarized, so do the contending
claims to truth. At the extreme, an active reciprocal distrust between groups
finds expression in intellectual perspectives that are no longer located within
the same universe of discourse. The more deep-seated the mutual distrust,
the more does the argument of the other appear so palpably implausible or
absurd that one no longer inquires into its substance or logical structure to
assess its truth claims. Instead, one confronts the other's argument with an
entirely different sort of question: how does it happen to be advanced at all?
Thought and its products thus become altogether functionalized, interpreted
only in terms of their presumed social or economic or psychological sources
and functions.... In place of the vigorous but intellectually disciplined mutual checking and rechecking that operates to a significant extent, though
never of course totally, within the social institutions of science and scholarship, there develops a strain toward separatism, in the domain of the intellect
as in the domain of society. Partly grounded mutual suspicion increasingly
substitutes for partly grounded mutual trust. There emerge claims to group-
based truth: Insider truths that counter Outsider untruths and Outsider truths
that counter Insider untruths.

In our day, vastly evident social change is being initiated and funneled
through a variety of social movements. These are formally alike in their
objectives of achieving an intensified collective consciousness, a deepened
solidarity and a new or renewed primary or total allegiance of their members

From Robert K. Merton, "Insiders and Outsiders: A Chapter in the Sociology of Knowledge,"
American Journal of Sociology, vol. 78 (July 1972). Copyright © 1972 by University of Chicago
Press. Reprinted by permission. References and some notes omitted.

to certain social identities, statuses, groups, or collectivities. Inspecting the familiar list of these movements centered on class, race, ethnicity, age, sex, religion, and sexual disposition, we note two other instructive similarities between them. First, the movements are for the most part formed principally on the basis of ascribed rather than acquired statuses and identities, with eligibility for inclusion being in terms of who you are rather than what you are.... And second, the movements largely involve the public affirmation of pride in statuses and solidarity with collectivities that have long been socially and culturally downgraded, stigmatized, or otherwise victimized in the social system. As with group affiliations generally, these newly reinforced social identities find expression in various affiliative symbols of distinctive speech, bodily appearance, dress, public behavior patterns and, not least, assumptions and foci of thought.

THE INSIDER DOCTRINE

Within this context of social change, we come upon the contemporary relevance of a long-standing problem in the sociology of knowledge: the problem of patterned differentials among social groups and strata in access to certain types of knowledge. In its strong form, the claim is put forward as a matter of epistemological principle that particular groups in each moment of history have *monopolistic access* to particular kinds of knowledge. In the weaker, more empirical form, the claim holds that some groups have *privileged access*, with other groups also being able to acquire that knowledge for themselves but at greater risk and cost.

Claims of this general sort have been periodically introduced.... [T]he Nazi *Gauleiter* of science and learning, Ernest Krieck, expressed an entire ideology in contrasting the access to authentic scientific knowledge by men of unimpeachable Aryan ancestry with the corrupt versions of knowledge accessible to non-Aryans. Krieck could refer without hesitation to "Protestant and Catholic science, German and Jewish science."... Nobel laureate in physics, Johannes Stark, could castigate... his... scientific contemporaries... for accepting what Stark described as "the Jewish physics of Einstein."

... [W]e need not review the array of elitist doctrines which have maintained that certain groups have, on biological or social grounds, monopolistic or privileged access to new knowledge. Differing in detail, the doctrines are alike in distinguishing between Insider access to knowledge and Outsider exclusion from it....

SOCIAL BASES OF INSIDER DOCTRINE

... [W]hite male Insiderism in American sociology during the past generations has largely been of the tacit or de facto rather than doctrinal or principled variety. It has simply taken the form of patterned expectations about the appropriate selection of specialties and of problems for investigation. The handful of Negro sociologists were in large part expected... to study problems of Negro life and relations between the races just as the handful of women sociologists were expected to study problems of women, principally as these related to marriage and the family.

In contrast to this de facto form of Insiderism, an explicitly doctrinal form has in recent years been put forward most clearly and emphatically by some black intellectuals.... The argument holds that, as a matter of social epistemology, *only* black historians can truly understand black history, *only* black ethnologists can understand black culture, *only* black sociologists can understand the social life of blacks, and so on.... [T]he Insider doctrine maintains that there is a body of black history, black psychology, black ethnology, and black sociology which can be significantly advanced only by black scholars and social scientists.

... [T]his represents... the balkanization of social science, with separate baronies kept exclusively in the hands of Insiders bearing their credentials in the shape of one or another ascribed status. Generalizing the specific claim, it would appear to follow that if only black scholars can understand blacks, then only white scholars can understand whites. Generalizing further from race to nation, it would then appear, for example, that only French scholars can understand French society and, of course, that only Americans, not their external critics, can truly understand American society. Once the basic principle is adopted, the list of Insider claims to a monopoly of knowledge becomes indefinitely expansible to all manner of social formations based on ascribed (and, by extension, on some achieved) statuses. It would thus seem to follow that only women can understand women—and men, men. On the same principle, youth alone is capable of understanding youth.... [O]nly Catholics, Catholics; Jews, Jews, and to halt the inventory of socially atomized claims to knowledge with a limiting case that on its face would seem to have some merit, it would then plainly follow that only sociologists are able to understand their fellow sociologists.

In all these applications, the doctrine of extreme Insiderism represents a new credentialism. This is the credentialism of ascribed status, in which understanding becomes accessible only to the fortunate few or many who are to the manner born. In this respect, it contrasts with credentialism of achieved status that is characteristic of meritocratic systems.

Extreme Insiderism moves toward a doctrine of *group* methodological solipsism. [The belief that all one *really* knows is one's subjective experience is sometimes described as the "egocentric predicament."] In this form of solipsism, each group must in the end have a monopoly of knowledge about itself.... The Insider doctrine can be put in the vernacular with no great loss in meaning: you have to be one in order to understand one....

We can quickly pass over the trivial version of that rationale; the argument that the Outsider may be incompetent, given to quick and superficial forays into the group or culture under study and even unschooled in its language. That this kind of incompetence can be found is beyond doubt but it holds no principled interest for us. Foolish men (and women) or badly trained men (and women) are to be found everywhere.... But such cases of special ineptitude do not bear on the Insider *principle*. It is not merely that Insiders also have their share of incompetents. The Insider principle does not refer to stupidly designed and stupidly executed inquiries that happen to be made by stupid Outsiders; it maintains a more fundamental position. According to the doctrine of the Insider, the Outsider, no matter how careful and talented, is excluded in principle from gaining access to the social and cultural truth.

In short, the doctrine holds that the Outsider has a structurally imposed incapacity to comprehend alien groups, statuses, cultures, and societies. Unlike the Insider, the Outsider has neither been socialized in the group nor has engaged in the run of experience that makes up its life, and therefore cannot have the direct, intuitive sensitivity that alone makes empathic understanding possible.... [T]o take a specific expression of this thesis by Ralph W. Conant: "Whites are not and never will be as sensitive to the black community precisely because they are not part of that community." ...

A somewhat less stringent version of the doctrine maintains only that Insider and Outsider scholars have significantly different foci of interest.... [T]his weaker version argues only that they will not deal with the same questions and so will simply talk past one another. With the two versions combined, the extended version of the Insider doctrine can also be put in the vernacular: one must not only be one in order to understand one; one must be one in order to understand what is most worth understanding.

Clearly, the social epistemological doctrine of the Insider links up with what Sumner long ago defined as ethnocentrism: "the technical name for [the] view of things in which one's own group is the center of everything, and all others are scaled and rated with reference to it." ...

Theodore Caplow ... examined 33 different kinds of organizations—ranging from dance studios to Protestant and Catholic churches, from skid row missions to ... university departments—and found that members overestimated the prestige of their organization some "eight times as often as they underestimated it" (when compared with judgments by Outsiders).... [W]hile members tended to disagree with Outsiders about the standing of their own organization, they tended to agree with them about the prestige of the other organizations in the same set. These findings can be taken as something of a sociological parable. In these matters at least, the judgments of "Insiders" are best trusted when they assess groups other than their own; that is, when members of groups judge as Outsiders rather than as Insiders.... Ethnocentrism... becomes intensified under specifiable conditions of acute social conflict. When a nation, race, ethnic group, or any other powerful collectivity has long extolled its own admirable qualities and, expressly or by implication, deprecated the qualities of others, it invites and provides the potential for counterethnocentrism. And when a once largely powerless collectivity acquires a socially validated sense of growing power, its members experience an intensified need for self-affirmation. Under such circumstances, collective self-glorification, found in some measure among all groups, becomes a predictable and intensified counterresponse to long-standing belittlement from without.... What is being proposed here is that the epistemological claims of the Insider to monopolistic or privileged access to social truth develop under particular social and historical conditions. Social groups or strata on the way up develop a revolutionary élan. The new thrust to a larger share of power and control over their social and political environment finds various expressions, among them claims to a unique access to knowledge about their history, culture, and social life.

On this interpretation, we can understand why this Insider doctrine does not argue for a Black Physics, Black Chemistry, Black Biology, or Black Technology. For the new will to control their fate deals with the social environment, not the environment of nature.... [T]he black Insider doctrine adopts an essentially social-environmental rationale, not a biologically genetic one....

With varying degrees of intent, groups in conflict want to make their interpretation the prevailing one of how things were and are and will be. The critical measure of success occurs when the interpretation moves beyond the boundaries of the ingroup to be accepted by Outsiders. At the extreme, it then gives rise, through identifiable processes of reference-group behavior, to the familiar case of the converted Outsider validating himself, in his own eyes and in those of others, by becoming even more zealous than the Insiders in adhering to the doctrine of the group with which he wants to identify himself, if only symbolically. He then becomes more royalist than the king, more papist than the pope. Some white social scientists, for example, vicariously and personally guilt ridden over centuries of white racism, are prepared to outdo the claims of the group they would symbolically join. They are ready even to surrender their hard-won expert knowledge if the Insider doctrine seems to require it....

The black Insider doctrine links up with the historically developing social structure in still another way. The dominant social institutions in this country have long treated the racial identity of individuals as actually if not doctrinally relevant to all manner of situations in every sphere of life. For generations, neither blacks nor whites, though with notably differing consequences, were permitted to forget their race. *This treatment of a social status (or identity) as relevant when intrinsically it is functionally irrelevant constitutes the very core of social discrimination.* As the

once firmly rooted systems of discriminatory institutions and prejudicial ideology began to lose their hold, this meant that increasingly many judged the worth of ideas on their merits, not in terms of their racial pedigree.

What the Insider doctrine of the most militant blacks proposes on the level of social structure is to adopt the salience of racial identity in every sort of role and situation, a pattern so long imposed upon the American Negro, and to make that identity a total commitment issuing from within the group rather than one imposed upon it from without. By thus affirming the universal saliency of race and by redefining race as an abiding source of pride rather than stigma, the Insider doctrine in effect models itself after doctrine long maintained by white racists.

Neither this component of the Insider doctrine nor the statement on its implications is at all new. Almost a century ago, Frederick Douglass hinged his observations along these lines on the distinction between collective and individual self-images based on ascribed and achieved status:

One of the few errors to which we are clinging most persistently and, as I think, most mischievously has come into great prominence of late. It is the cultivation and stimulation among us of a sentiment which we are pleased to call race pride. I find it in all our books, papers, and speeches. For my part I see no superiority or inferiority in race or color. Neither the one nor the other is a proper source of pride or complacency. Our race and color are not of our own choosing. We have no volition in the case one way or another. The only excuse for pride in individuals or races is in the fact of their own achievements.... I see no benefit to be derived from this everlasting exhortation of speakers and writers among us to the cultivation of race pride. On the contrary, I see in it a positive evil. It is building on a false foundation....

Just as conditions of war between nations have long produced a strain toward hyperpatriotism among national ethnocentrics, so current intergroup conflicts have produced a strain toward hyperloyalty among racial or sex or age or religious ethnocentrics. Total commitment easily slides from the solidarity doctrine of "our group, right or wrong" to the morally and intellectually preemptive doctrine of "our group, always right, never wrong." ...

SOCIAL STRUCTURE OF INSIDERS AND OUTSIDERS

... In structural terms, we are all, of course, both Insiders and Outsiders, members of some groups and, sometimes derivatively, not of others; occupants of certain statuses which thereby exclude us from occupying other cognate statuses. Obvious as this basic fact of social structure is, its implications for Insider and Outsider epistemological doctrines are apparently not nearly as obvious. Else, these doctrines would not presuppose, as they typically do, that human beings in socially differentiated societies can be sufficiently located in terms of a single social status, category, or group affiliation— black or white, men or women, under 30 or older—or of several such categories, taken seriatim [in a series] rather than conjointly. This neglects the crucial fact of social structure that individuals have not a single status but a status set: a complement of variously interrelated statuses

which interact to affect both their behavior and perspectives.

The structural fact of status sets, in contrast to statuses taken one at a time, introduces severe theoretical problems for total Insider (and Outsider) doctrines of social epistemology. The array of status sets in a population means that aggregates of individuals share some statuses and not others; or, to put this in context, that they typically confront one another simultaneously as Insiders and Outsiders. Thus, if only whites can understand whites and blacks, blacks, and only men can understand men, and women, women, this gives rise to the paradox which severely limits both premises: for it then turns out, by assumption, that some Insiders are excluded from understanding other Insiders with white women being condemned not to understand white men, and black men, not to understand black women, and so through the various combinations of status subsets....

This symptomatic exercise in status-set analysis may be enough to indicate that the idiomatic expression of total Insider doctrine—one must be one in order to understand one—is deceptively simple and sociologically fallacious (just as ... is the case with the total Outsider doctrine). For, from the sociological perspective of the status set, "one" is not a man *or* a black *or* an adolescent *or* a Protestant, *or* self-defined and socially defined as middle class, and so on. Sociologically, "one" is, of course, all of these and, depending on the size of the status set, much more.... [T]he greater the number and variety of group affiliations and statuses distributed among individuals in a society, the smaller, on the average, the number of individuals having precisely the same social configuration....

[I]t is precisely the individual differences among scientists and scholars that are often central to the development of the discipline. They often involve the differences between good scholarship and bad; between imaginative contributions to science and pedestrian ones; between the consequential ideas and stillborn ones. In arguing for the monopolistic access to knowledge, Insider doctrine can make no provision for individual variability that extends beyond the boundaries of the ingroup which alone can develop sound and fruitful ideas....

Yet sociologically, there is nothing fixed about the boundaries separating Insiders from Outsiders. As situations involving different values arise, different statuses are activated and the lines of separation shift. Thus, for a large number of white Americans, Joe Louis was a member of an outgroup. But when Louis defeated the Nazified Max Schmeling, many of the same white Americans promptly redefined him as a member of the (national) ingroup. National self-esteem took precedence over racial separatism. That this sort of drama in which changing situations activate differing statuses in the status set is played out in the domain of the intellect as well is the point of Einstein's ironic observation in an address at the Sorbonne: "If my theory of relativity is proved successful, Germany will claim me as a German and France will declare that I am a citizen of the world. Should my theory prove untrue, France will say that I am a German and Germany will declare that I am a Jew."...

INSIDERS AS "OUTSIDERS"

... [W]hat some Insiders profess as Insiders they apparently reject as Outsiders. For example, when advocates of black Insider doctrine engage in analysis of "white society," trying to assay its power structure or to detect its vulnerabilities, they seem to deny in practice what they affirm in doctrine. At any rate, their behavior testifies to the assumption that it is possible for self-described "Outsiders" to diagnose and to understand what they describe as an alien social structure and culture....

The strong version of the Insider doctrine, with its epistemological claim to a monopoly of certain kinds of knowledge, runs counter, of course, to a long history of thought....

[First Georg] Simmel and then... Max Weber... adopted the memorable phrase: "one need not be Caesar in order to understand Caesar." In making this claim, they rejected the extreme Insider thesis which asserts in effect that one *must* be Caesar in order to understand him just as they rejected the extreme Outsider thesis that one must *not* be Caesar in order to understand him.... The Insider argues that the authentic understanding of group life can be achieved only by those who are directly engaged as members in the life of the group. Taken seriously, the doctrine puts in question the validity of just about all historical writing.... If direct engagement in the life of a group is essential to understanding it, then the only authentic history is contemporary history, written in fragments by those most fully involved in making inevitably limited portions of it. Rather than constituting only the raw materials of history, the documents prepared by engaged Insiders become all there is to history. But once the historian elects to write the history of a time other than his own, even the most dedicated Insider, of the national, sex, age, racial, ethnic, or religious variety, becomes the

Outsider, condemned to error and mis-understanding.

Writing some 20 years ago in another connection, Claude Lévi-Strauss noted the parallelism between history and ethnography. Both subjects, he observed,

> are concerned with societies *other* than the one in which we live. Whether this *otherness* is due to remoteness in time (however slight) or to remoteness in space, or even to cultural heterogeneity, is of secondary importance compared to the basic similarity of perspective. All that the historian or ethnographer can do, and all that we can expect of either of them, is to enlarge a specific experience to the dimensions of a more general one, which thereby becomes accessible as *experience* to men of another country or another epoch. And in order to succeed, both historian and ethnographer, must have the same qualities: skill, precision, a sympathetic approach and objectivity.

... Simmel develops the thesis that the stranger, not caught up in commitments to the group, can more readily acquire the strategic role of the relatively objective inquirer. "He is freer, practically and theoretically," notes Simmel, "he surveys conditions with less prejudice; his criteria for them are more general and more objective ideals: he is not tied down in his action by habit, piety, and precedent." ... It is the stranger, too, who finds what is familiar to the group significantly unfamiliar and so is prompted to raise questions for inquiry less apt to be raised at all by Insiders.

... Outsiders are sought out to observe social institutions and cultures on the premise that they are more apt to do so with detachment. Thus, in the first decade of this century, the Carnegie Foundation for the Advancement of Teaching, in its search for someone

to investigate the condition of medical schools, reached out to appoint Abraham Flexner, after he had admitted never before having been inside a medical school. It was a matter of policy to select a total Outsider who, as it happened, produced the uncompromising Report which did much to transform the state of American medical education at the time.

Later, casting about for a scholar who might do a thoroughgoing study of the Negro in the United States, the Carnegie Corporation searched for an Outsider, ... with the quest ending ... with the selection of Gunnar Myrdal [a Swedish social scientist]. In the preface to *An American Dilemma,** Myrdal (pp. xviii–xix) reflected on his status as an Outsider who, in his words, "had never been subject to the strains involved in living in a black-white society" and who "as a stranger to the problem ... has had perhaps a greater awareness of the extent to which human valuations everywhere enter into our scientific discussion of the Negro problem."

Reviews of the book repeatedly alluded to the degree of detachment from entangling loyalties that seemed to come from Myrdal's being an Outsider. J. S. Redding (1944), for one, observed that "as a European, Myrdal had no American sensibilities to protect. He hits hard with fact and interpretation." Robert S. Lynd (1944), for another, saw it as a prime merit of this Outsider that he was free to find out for himself "without any side glances as to what was politically expedient." And for a third, Frank Tannenbaum (1944) noted that Myrdal brought "objectivity in regard to the special foibles and shortcomings in American life. As

---

*[*An American Dilemma* (1944) was a benchmark study of race relations.—Ed.]

an outsider, he showed the kind of objectivity which would seem impossible for one reared within the American scene." Even later criticism of Myrdal's work—for example, the comprehensive critique by Cox (1948, chap. 23)—does not attribute imputed errors in interpretation to his having been an Outsider.

Two observations should be made on the Myrdal episode. First, in the judgment of critical minds, the Outsider, far from being excluded from the understating of an alien society, was able to bring needed perspectives to it. And second, that Myrdal, wanting to have both Insider and Outsider perspectives, expressly drew into his circle of associates in the study such Insiders, engaged in the study of Negro life and culture and of race relations, as E. Franklin Frazier, Arnold Rose, Ralph Bunche, Melville Herskovits, Otto Klineberg, J. G. St. Clair Drake, Guy B. Johnson, and Doxey A. Wilkerson....

The cumulative point of this variety of intellectual and institutional cases is not—and this needs to be repeated with all possible emphasis—is *not* a proposal to replace the extreme Insider doctrine by an extreme and equally vulnerable Outsider doctrine. The intent is, rather, to transform the original question altogether.... Just as with the process of competition generally, so with the competition of ideas. Competing or conflicting groups take over ideas and procedures from one another, thereby denying in practice the rhetoric of total incompatibility. Even in the course of social polarization, conceptions with cognitive value are utilized all apart from their source. Concepts of power structure, co-optation, the dysfunctions of established institutions and findings associated with these concepts have for some time been utilized by social

scientists, irrespective of their social or political identities.... Such diffusion of ideas across the boundaries of groups and statuses has long been noted. In one of his more astute analyses, Mannheim (1952) states the general case for the emergence and spread of knowledge that transcends even profound conflicts between groups:

> Syntheses owe their existence to the same social process that brings about polarization; groups take over the modes of thought and intellectual achievements of their adversaries under the simple law of 'competition on the basis of achievement.'... In the socially-differentiated thought process, even the opponent is ultimately forced to adopt those categories and forms of thought which are most appropriate in a given type of world order. In the economic sphere, one of the possible results of competition is that one competitor is compelled to catch up with the other's technological advances. In just the same way, whenever groups compete for having their interpretation of reality accepted as the correct one, it may happen that one of the groups takes over from the adversary some fruitful hypothesis or category—anything that promises cognitive gain....

FROM SOCIAL CONFLICT TO INTELLECTUAL CONTROVERSY

... Insider and Outsider perspectives can converge, in spite of such differences, through reciprocal adoption of ideas and the developing of complementary and overlapping foci of attention in the formulation of scientific problems. But these intellectual potentials for synthesis are often curbed by social processes that divide scholars and scientists. Internal divisions and polarizations in the society at large often stand in the way of realizing those potentials....

When a transition from social conflict to intellectual controversy is achieved, when the perspectives of each group are taken seriously enough to be carefully examined rather than rejected out of hand, there can develop trade-offs between the distinctive strengths and weaknesses of Insider and Outsider perspectives that enlarge the chances for a sound and relevant understanding of social life. . . .

If indeed we have distinctive contributions to make to social knowledge in our roles as Insiders or Outsiders— and it should be repeated that all of us are both Insiders and Outsiders in various social situations—then those contributions probably link up with a long-standing distinction between two major kinds of knowledge, a basic distinction that is blurred in the often ambiguous use of the word "understanding." In the language of William James (1932, pp. 11–13), . . . this is the distinction between "acquaintance with" and "knowledge about." The one involves direct familiarity with phenomena that is expressed in depictive representations; the other involves more abstract formulations which do not at all "resemble" what has been directly experienced (Merton 1968, p. 545). . . .

These distinct and connected kinds of understanding may turn out to be distributed, in varying mix, among Insiders and Outsiders. The introspective meanings of experience within a status or a group may be more readily accessible, for all the seemingly evident reasons, to those who have shared part or all of that experience. But authentic awareness, even in the sense of acquaintance with, is not guaranteed by social affiliation, as the concept of false consciousness is designed to remind us. Determi-

nants of social life—for an obvious example, ecological patterns and processes— are not necessarily evident to those directly engaged in it. In short, sociological understanding involves much more than acquaintance with. It includes an empirically confirmable comprehension of the conditions and often complex processes in which people are caught up without much awareness of what is going on. To analyze and understand these requires a theoretical and technical competence which, as such, transcends one's status as Insider or Outsider. The role of social scientist concerned with achieving knowledge about society requires enough detachment and trained capacity to know how to assemble and assess the evidence without regard for what the analysis seems to imply about the worth of one's group. . . .

The acceptance of criteria of craftsmanship and integrity in science and learning cuts across differences in the social affiliations and loyalties of scientists and scholars. Commitment to the intellectual values dampens group-induced pressures to advance the interests of groups at the expense of these values and of the intellectual product.

The consolidation of group-influenced perspectives and the autonomous values of scholarship is exemplified in observations by John Hope Franklin who, for more than a quarter-century, has been engaged in research on the history of American Negroes from their ancient African beginnings to the present. . . . Franklin's application of exacting, autonomous and universalistic standards culminates in a formulation that, once again, transcends the statuses of Insiders and Outsiders:

> . . . It takes a person of stout heart, great courage, and uncompromising honesty

to look the history of this country squarely in the face and tell it like it is.... And when this approach prevails, the history of the United States and the history of the black man can be written and taught by any person, white, black, or otherwise. For there is nothing so irrelevant in telling the truth as the color of a man's skin.

NO

Ann Oakley

INTERVIEWING WOMEN: A CONTRADICTION IN TERMS

Despite the fact that much of modern sociology could justifiably be considered 'the science of the interview,' very few sociologists who employ interview data actually bother to describe in detail the process of interviewing itself.... Some issues on which research reports do not usually comment are: social/personal characteristics of those doing the interviewing; interviewees' feelings about being interviewed and about the interview; interviewers' feelings about interviewees; and quality of interviewer-interviewee interaction; hospitality offered by interviewees to interviewers; attempts by interviewees to use interviewers as sources of information; and the extension of interviewer-interviewee encounters into more broadly-based social relationships.

I shall argue [here] that social science researchers' awareness of those aspects of interviewing which are 'legitimate' and 'illegitimate' from the viewpoint of inclusion in research reports reflect their embeddedness in a particular research protocol. This protocol assumes a predominantly masculine model of sociology and society. The relative undervaluation of women's models has led to an unreal theoretical characterisation of the interview as a means of gathering sociological data which cannot and does not work in practice. This lack of fit between the theory and practice of interviewing is especially likely to come to the fore when a feminist interviewer is interviewing women (who may or may not be feminists).

INTERVIEWING: A MASCULINE PARADIGM?

Let us consider first what the methodology textbooks say about interviewing. First, and most obviously, an interview is a way of finding out about people. 'If you want an answer, ask a question.... The asking of questions is the main source of social scientific information about everyday behaviour.' ...

The motif of successful interviewing is 'be friendly but not too friendly'. For the contradiction at the heart of the textbook paradigm is that interviewing necessitates the manipulation of interviewees as objects of study/sources of data, but this can only be achieved via a certain amount of humane treatment. If the interviewee doesn't believe he/she is being kindly and sympathetically treated by the interviewer, then he/she will not consent to be studied and will not come up with the desired information. A balance must then be struck between the warmth required to generate 'rapport' and the detachment necessary to see the interviewee as an object under surveillance; walking this tightrope means, not surprisingly, that 'interviewing is not easy' (Denzin, 1970, p. 186), although mostly the textbooks do support the idea that it *is* possible to be a perfect interviewer and both to get reliable and valid data and make interviewees believe they are not simple statistics-to-be. It is just a matter of following the rules.

A major preoccupation in the spelling out of the rules is to counsel potential interviewers about where necessary friendliness ends and unwarranted involvement begins....

C. A. Moser... advises of the dangers of 'over rapport'.

> ... [T]here is something to be said for the interviewer who, while friendly and interested does not get too emotionally involved with the respondent and his problems. Interviewing on most surveys is a fairly straightforward job.... Pleasantness and a business-like nature is the ideal combination.

'Rapport', a commonly used but ill-defined term, does not mean in this context what the dictionary says it does ('a sympathetic relationship', *O.E.D.*) but the acceptance by the interviewee of the interviewer's research goals and the interviewee's active search to help the interviewer in providing the relevant infor-mation. The person who is interviewed has a passive role in adapting to the definition of the situation offered by the person doing the interviewing. The person doing the interviewing must actively and continually construct the 'respondent' (a telling name) as passive. Another way to phrase this is to say that both interviewer and interviewee must be 'socialised' into the correct interviewing behaviour (Sjoberg and Nett, 1968, p. 210)....

One piece of behaviour that properly socialised respondents do not engage in is asking questions back.... 'Never provide the interviewee with any formal indication of the interviewer's beliefs and values. If the informant poses a question... parry it' (Sjoberg and Nett, 1968, p. 212). 'When asked what you mean and think, tell them you are here to learn, not to pass any judgement, that the situation is very complex' (Galtung 1967, p. 161). 'If he (the interviewer) should be asked for his views, he should laugh off the request with the remark that his job at the moment is to get opinions, not to have them' (Selltz *et al.*, 1965, p. 576)...

Of course the reason why the interviewer must pretend not to have opinions (or to be possessed of information the interviewee wants) is because behaving otherwise might 'bias' the interview....

[T]wo separate typifications of the interviewer are prominent in the literature.... In one the interviewer is 'a combined phonograph and recording system'; the job of the interviewer 'is fundamentally that of a reporter, not an evangelist, a curiosity-seeker, or a debater' (Selltiz *et al.*, 1965, p. 576). It is important to note that while the interviewer must treat the interviewee as an object or data-producing machine which, when handled correctly will function properly, the interviewer herself/himself has the same status from the point of view of the person/people, institution or corporation conducting the research. Both interviewer and interviewee are thus depersonalised participants in the research process.

The second typification of interviewers in the methodology literature is that of the interviewer as psychoanalyst. The interviewer's relationship to the interviewee is hierarchical and it is the body of expertise possessed by the interviewer that allows the interview to be successfully conducted. Most crucial in this exercise is the interviewer's use of non-directive comments and probes to encourage a free association of ideas which reveals whatever truth the research has been set up to uncover. Indeed, the term 'nondirective interview' is derived directly from the language of psychotherapy and carries the logic of interviewer-impersonality to its extreme (Selltiz *et al.*, 1965, p. 268)....

It seems clear that both psychoanalytic and mechanical typifications of the interviewer and, indeed, the entire paradigmatic representation of 'proper' interviews in the methodology textbooks, owe a great deal more to a masculine social and sociological vantage point than to a feminine one. For example, the paradigm of the 'proper' interview appeals to such values as objectivity, detachment, hierarchy and 'science' as an important cultural activity which takes priority over people's more individualised concerns. Thus the errors of poor interviewing comprise subjectivity, involvement, the 'fiction' of equality and undue concern with the ways in which people are not statistically comparable. This polarity of 'proper' and 'improper' interviewing is an almost classical representation of the widespread gender stereotyping which has been shown, in countless studies, to occur in modern industrial civilisations.... Women are characterised as sensitive, intuitive, incapable of objectivity and emotional detachment and as immersed in the business of making and sustaining personal relationships. Men are thought superior through their capacity for rationality and scientific objectivity and are thus seen to be possessed of an instrumental orientation in their relationships with others. Women are the exploited, the abused; they are unable to exploit others through the 'natural' weakness of altruism—a quality which is also their strength as wives, mothers and housewives. Conversely, men find it easy to exploit, although it is most important that any exploitation be justified in the name of some broad political or economic ideology ('the end justifies the means').

Feminine and masculine psychology in patriarchal societies is the psychology of subordinate and dominant social groups. The tie between women's irrationality and heightened sensibility on the one had and their materially disadvantaged position on the other is, for example, also to be found in the case of ethnic minorities. The psychological characteristics of subordinates 'form a certain familiar cluster: submissiveness, passivity, docility, dependency, lack of initiative, inability to act, to decide, to think and the like. In general, this cluster includes qualities more characteristic of children than adults— immaturity, weakness and helplessness. If subordinates adopt these characteristics, they are considered well adjusted'. It is no accident that the methodology textbooks ... refer to the interviewer as male. Although not all interviewees are referred to as female, there are a number of references to 'housewives' as the kind of people interviewers are most likely to meet in the course of their work (for example Goode and Hatt, 1952, p. 189). Some of what Jean Baker Miller has to say about the relationship between dominant and subordinate groups would appear to be relevant to this paradigmatic interviewer–interviewee relationship:

A dominant group, inevitably, has the greatest influence in determining a culture's overall outlook—its philosophy, morality, social theory and even its science. The dominant group, thus, legitimizes the unequal relationship and incorporates it into society's guiding concepts....

Inevitably the dominant group is the model for 'normal human relationships'. It then becomes 'normal' to treat others destructively and to derogate them, to obscure the truth of what you are doing by creating false explanations and to oppose actions toward equality. In short, if one's identification is with the dominant group, it is 'normal' to continue in this pattern....

It follows from this that dominant groups generally do not like to be told about or even quietly reminded of the existence of inequality. 'Normally' they can avoid awareness because their explanation of the relationship becomes so well integrated *in other terms*; they can even believe that both they and the subordinate group share the same interests and, to some extent, a common experience....

Dominants are usually convinced that the way things are is right and good, not only for them but especially for the subordinates. All morality confirms this view and all social structure sustains it.

To paraphrase the relevance of this to the interviewer–interviewee relationship we could say that: interviewers define the role of interviewees as subordinates; extracting information is more to be valued than yielding it; the convention of the interviewer–interviewee hierarchy is a rationalisation of inequality; what is good for interviewers is not necessarily good for interviewees....

Getting involved with the people you interview is doubly bad: it jeopardises the hard-won status of sociology as a science and is indicative of a form of personal degeneracy.

WOMEN INTERVIEWING WOMEN: OR OBJECTIFYING YOUR SISTER

... [T]he case I want to make is that when a feminist interviews women: (1) use of prescribed interviewing practice is morally indefensible; (2) general and irreconcilable contradictions at the heart of the textbook paradigm are exposed; and (3) it becomes clear that, in most cases, the goal of finding out about people through interviewing is best achieved when the relationship of interviewer and interviewee is non-hierarchical and when the interviewer is prepared to invest his or her own personal identity in the relationship.

... I have interviewed several hundred women over a period of some ten years, but it was the most recent research project, one concerned with the transition to motherhood, that particularly highlighted problems in the conventional interviewing recipe. Salient features of this research were that it involved repeated interviewing of a sample of women during a critical phase in their lives (in fact 55 women were interviewed four times; twice in pregnancy and twice afterwards and the average total period of interviewing was 9.4 hours.) ... Although I had a research assistant to help me, I myself did the bulk of the interviewing—178 interviews over a period of some 12 months. The project was my idea and the analysis and writing up of the data was entirely my responsibility. . . .

Asking Questions Back

Analysing the tape-recorded interviews I had conducted, I listed 878 questions that interviewees had asked me at some point in the interviewing process. Three-quarters of these were requests for information (e.g. 'Who will deliver my baby?' 'How do you cook an egg for a baby?') Fifteen per cent were questions about me, my experiences or attitudes in the area of reproduction ('Have you got any children?' 'Did you breast feed?'); and 4 per cent were more directly requests for advice on a particular matter ('How long should you wait for sex after childbirth?' 'Do you think my baby's got too many clothes on?'). . . . The largest category of questions concerned medical procedures: for example, how induction of labour is done, and whether all women attending a particular hospital are given episiotomies. The second-largest category related to infant care or development: for example, 'How do you clean a baby's nails?' . . . Last, there were questions about the physiology of reproduction; for example, 'Why do some women need caesareans?' and (from one very frightened mother-to-be) 'Is it right that the baby doesn't come out of the same hole you pass water out of?'

It would be the understatement of all time to say that I found it very difficult to avoid answering these questions as honestly and fully as I could. I was faced, typically, with a woman who was quite anxious about the fate of herself and her baby, who found it either impossible or extremely difficult to ask questions and receive satisfactory answers from the medical staff with whom she came into contact, and who saw me as someone who could not only reassure but inform. . . . I *was* asking a great deal—not only 9.4 hours of interviewing time but confidences on highly personal matters such as sex and money and 'real' (i.e. possibly negative or ambivalent) feelings about babies, husbands, etc. I was, in addition, asking some of the women to allow me to witness them in the highly personal act of giving birth. . . .

The Transition to Friendship?

. . . I found that interviewees very often took the initiative in defining the interviewer–interviewee relationship as something which existed beyond the limits of question-asking and answering. For example, they did not only offer the minimum hospitality of accommodating me in their homes for the duration of the interview: at 92 per cent of the interviews I was offered tea, coffee or some other drink; 14 per cent of the women also offered me a meal on at least one occasion. . . . [T]here was also a certain amount of interest in my own situation. What sort of person was I and how did I come to be interested in this subject?

. . . Sixty two per cent of the women expressed a sustained and quite detailed interest in the research; they wanted to know its goals, any proposed methods for disseminating its findings, how I had come to think of it in the first place, what the attitudes of doctors I had met or collaborated with were to it and so forth. . . . Several rang up to report particularly important pieces of information about their antenatal care—in one case a distressing encounter with a doctor who told a woman keen on natural childbirth that this was 'for animals: in this hospital we give epidurals'....

[S]ome four years after the final interview I am still in touch with more than a third of the women I interviewed. Four have become close friends, several others I visit occasionally, and the rest write or telephone when they have something salient to report such as the birth of another child.

A FEMINIST INTERVIEWS WOMEN

Such responses as I have described on the part of the interviewees to participation in research, particularly that involving repeated interviewing, are not unknown, although they are almost certainly under-reported. It could be suggested that the reasons why they were so pronounced in the research project discussed here is because of the attitudes of the interviewer —i.e. the women were reacting to my own evident wish for a relatively intimate and non-hierarchical relationship. While I was careful not to take direct initiatives in this direction, I certainly set out to convey to the people whose co-operation I was seeking the fact that I did not intend to exploit either them or the information that they gave me. For instance, if the interview clashed with the demands of housework and motherhood I offered to, and often did, help with the work that had to be done....

The practice I followed was to answer all personal questions and questions about the research as fully as was required.... On the emotive issue of whether I experienced childbirth as painful (a common topic of conversation) I told them that I did find it so but that in my view it was worth it to get a baby at the end.... When asked for information I gave it if I could or... referred the questioner to an appropriate medical or non-medical authority. Again, the way I responded to interviewee's questions probably encouraged them to regard me as more than an instrument of data-collection.

Dissecting my practice of interviewing further, there were three principal reasons why I decided not to follow the textbook code of ethics with regard to interviewing women. First, I did not regard it as reasonable to adopt a purely exploitative attitude to interviewees as sources of data. My involvement in the women's movement in the early 1970s and the re-birth of feminism in an academic context had led me, along with many others, to re-assess society and sociology as masculine paradigms and to want to bring about change in the traditional cultural and academic treatment of women. 'Sisterhood'... certainly demanded that women re-evaluate the basis of their relationships with one another.

The dilemma of a feminist interviewer interviewing women could be summarised by considering the practical application of some of the strategies recommended in the textbooks for meeting interviewee's questions. For example, these advise that such questions as 'Which hole does the baby come out of?' 'Does an epidural ever paralyse women?' and 'Why is it dangerous to leave a small baby alone in the house?' should be met with such responses from the interviewer as 'I guess I haven't thought enough about it to give a good answer right now,' or 'a head-shaking gesture which suggests "that's a hard one."' Also recommended is laughing off the request with the remark that 'my job at the moment is to get opinions, not to have them' (Selltiz *et al.*, quoted above).

A second reason for departing from conventional interviewing ethics was that I regarded sociological research as an essential way of giving the subjective situation of women greater visibility not only in sociology, but, more importantly, in society, than it has traditionally had. Interviewing women was, then, a strategy for documenting women's own accounts of their lives. What *was* important was not taken-for-granted sociological assumptions about the role of the interviewer but a new awareness of the interviewer as an instrument for promoting a sociology for women—that is, as a tool for making possible the articulated and recorded commentary of women on the very personal business of being female in a patriarchal capitalist society. Note that the formulation of the interviewer role has changed dramatically from being a data-collecting instrument for researchers to being a data-collecting instrument for those whose lives are being researched. Such a reformulation is enhanced where the interviewer is also the researcher. It is not coincidental that in the methodological literature the paradigm of the research process is essentially disjunctive, i.e. researcher and interviewer functions are typically performed by different individuals.

A third reason why I undertook the childbirth research with a degree of skepticism about how far traditional percepts of interviewing could, or should, be applied in practice was because I had found, in my previous interviewing experiences, that an attitude of refusing to answer questions or offer any kind of personal feedback was not helpful in terms of the traditional goal of promoting 'rapport'. A different role, seemed especially important in longitudinal in-depth interviewing. Without feeling that the interviewing process offered some personal satisfaction to them, interviewees would not be prepared to continue after the first interview. This involves being sensitive not only to those questions that are asked (by either party) but to those that are not asked. The interviewee's definition of the interview is important.

... On the question of the rapport established in the Transition to Motherhood research I offer the following cameo:

A.O.: 'Did you have any questions you wanted to ask but didn't when you last went to the hospital?'
M.C.: 'Er, I don't know how to put this really. After sexual intercourse I had some bleeding, three times, only a few drops and I didn't tell the hospital because I didn't know how to put it to them. It worried me first off, as soon as I saw it I cried. I don't know if I'd be able to tell them. You see, I've also got a sore down there and a discharge and you know I wash there lots of times a day. You think I should tell the hospital; I could never speak to my own doctor about it. You see I feel like this but I can talk to you about it and I can talk to my sister about it.'

... Nearly three quarters of the women said that being interviewed had affected them and the three most common forms this influence took were in leading them to reflect on their experiences more than they would otherwise have done; in reducing the level of their anxiety and/or in reassuring them of their normality; and in giving a valuable outlet for the verbalisation of feelings... There were many references to the 'therapeutic' effect of talking... [A] process of emotional recovery is endemic in the normal transition to motherhood and there is a general need for some kind of 'therapeutic listener' that is not met within the usual circle of family and friends.

On the issue of co-operation, only 2 out of 82 women contacted initially about the research actually refused to take part in it, making a refusal rate of 2 per cent which is extremely low....

IS A 'PROPER' INTERVIEW EVER POSSIBLE?

... Sweig, in his study of *Labour, Life and Poverty,*

> dropped the idea of a questionnaire or formal verbal questions ... instead I had causal talks with working-class men on an absolutely equal footing ...
>
> I made many friends ... Some of them confided their troubles to me and I often heard the remark: 'Strangely enough, I have never talked about that to anybody else'....

Marie Corbin, the interviewer for the Pahls' study of *Managers and their Wives,* commented:

> ... simply because I am a woman and a wife I shared interests with the other wives and this helped to make the relationship a relaxed one.

... [E]thical dilemmas are generic to all research involving interviewing.... But they are greatest where there is least social distance between the interviewer and interviewee. Where both share the same gender socialisation and critical life-experiences, social distance can be minimal. Where both interviewer and interviewee share membership of the same minority group, the basis for equality may impress itself even more urgently on the interviewer's consciousness. [Alexander] Mamak's comments apply equally to a feminist interviewing women:

> I found that my academic training in the methodological views of Western social science and its emphasis on 'scientific objectivity' conflicted with the experiences of my colonial past. The traditional way in which social science research is conducted proved inadequate for an understanding of the reality, needs and desires of the people I was researching.

Some of the reasons why a 'proper' interview is a masculine fiction are illustrated by observations from another field in which individuals try to find out about other individuals—anthropology....

A poignant example is the incident related in Elenore Smith Bowen's *Return to Laughter* when the anthropologist witnesses one of her most trusted informants dying in childbirth:

> I stood over Amara. She tried to smile at me. She was very ill. I was convinced these women could not help her. She would die. She was my friend but my epitaph for her would be impersonal observations scribbled in my notebook, her memory preserved in an anthropologist's file: 'Death (in childbirth)/Cause: witchcraft/Case of Amara.' A lecture from the past reproached me: 'The anthropologist cannot, like the chemist or biologist, arrange controlled experiments.... His claim to science must therefore rest on a meticulous accuracy of observations and on a cool, objective approach to his data.' ...

An anthropologist has to 'get inside the culture'; participant observation means 'that ... the observer participates in the daily life of the people under study, either openly in the role of researcher or covertly in some disguised role' (Becker and Geer, 1957, p. 28). A feminist interviewing women is by definition both 'inside' the culture and participating in that which she is observing. However, in these respects the behaviour of a feminist interviewer/researcher is not extraordinary....

A feminist methodology of social science requires that this rationale of research be described and discussed not only in feminist research but in social science research in general. It requires, further, that the mythology of 'hygienic' research with its accompanying mystification of the researcher and the researched as objective instruments of data production be replaced by the recognition that personal involvement is more than dangerous bias—it is the condition under which people come to know each other and to admit others into their lives.

REFERENCES

Becker, H.S. and Geer, B. (1957), 'Participant Observation and Interviewing: A Comparison? *Human Organisation*, vol. XVI, pp. 28–32.

Bell, C. and Newby, H. (1977), *Doing Sociological Research*, Allen & Unwin, London.

Bowen, E.S. (1956), *Return to Laughter*, Gollancz, London.

Corbin, M. (1971), 'Appendix 3' in J.M. and R.E. Pahl, *Managers and their Wives*, Allen Lane, London.

Denzin, N.K. (1970) (ed.), *Sociological Methods: A Source Book*, Butterworth, London.

Galtung, J. (1967), *Theory and Methods of Social Research*, Allen & Unwin, London.

Goode, W.J. and Hatt, P.K. (1952), *Methods in Social Research*, McGraw Hill, New York.

Mamak, A.F. (1978), *Nationalism, Race-Class Consciousness and Social Research on Bougainville Island, Papua, New Guinea*, in C. Bell and S. Encel (eds), *Inside the Whale*, Pergamon Press, Oxford.

Miller, J.B. (1976), *Toward a New Psychology of Women*, Beacon Press, Boston.

Mitchell, J. and Oakley A. (1976), 'Introduction' in J. Mitchell and A. Oakley (eds), *The Rights and Wrongs of Women*, Penguin, Harmondsworth.

Moser, C. A. (1958), *Survey Methods in Social Investigaiton*, Heinemann, London.

Oakley, A. (1972), *Sex, Gender and Society*, Maurice Temple Smith, London.

Oakley, A. (1979), *Becoming a Mother*, Martin Robertson, Oxford.

Oakley, A. (1980), *Women Confined: Towards a Sociology of Childbirth*, Martin Robertson, Oxford.

Oakley, A. (1981a), *Subject Women*, Martin Robertson, Oxford.

Selltiz, C., Jahoda, M., Deutsch, M. and Cook, S.W. (1965), *Research Methods in Social Relations*, Methuen, London.

Sjoberg, G. and Nett, R. (1968), *A Methodology for Social Research*, Harper & Row, New York.

Sweig, F. (1949), *Labour, Life and Poverty*, Gollancz, London.

POSTSCRIPT

Can Outsiders Successfully Research Insiders?

For generations North American sociologists embraced in their work Max Weber's notion of value-free sociology. That is, they contended that their research was neutral, objective, unbiased, and free of value contamination. Many in minority relations and other areas of the social sciences were caught off guard in 1944 with the publication of Gunnar Myrdal's *American Dilemma*, arguably the most significant study of its kind in the twentieth century. In this study of U.S. treatment of Blacks, Myrdal, a Swedish economist, simply said that it was wrong, that it contradicted the creed of the United States, and that he personally opposed exploitation and prejudice.

At about the same time or shortly afterward a variety of "radical" sociologists, such as Robert Lynd, C. Wright Mills, Howard Becker, and Alvin Gouldner, partially following Myrdal, elected to take stands on issues. Moreover, they contended that a value-free science of human beings was impossible. Just the fact that one elected to research the discriminated against instead of the discriminators, for instance, automatically implied a value position.

Mills and Gouldner insisted that not only did sociological research and theory contain implicit values (generally conservative and in support of the status quo), it was impossible for this not to be the case. Moreover, Mills sharply attacked the dominant perspective in the 1950s in American sociology: structural functionalism.

To a large extent, Oakley and other feminist scholars reflect the ideas of Mills and also go considerably beyond them. Much of the emerging feminist epistemology is profound and challenging, and it has enormous implications for minority research.

The sociology of knowledge (which Merton's selection is largely an explication of) can be traced to German philosopher Karl Marx's assertion that the "ruling ideas of any age are the ideas of the ruling class." The sociology of knowledge pays less attention to formal validity of knowledge claims and pays more attention to the location of intellectuals and their schools within society to account for their research problems, their theories and methods, their findings and interpretations, and how their interpretations are used. The sociology of knowledge parallels the fundamental insight that a person's location within a social structure influences his or her actions. That location also entails occupying several positions based on group memberships that together influence behaviors and attitudes. People who occupy the same or similar locations tend to have similar attitudes.

By combining this sociological insight with Marx's assertion about the ruling class, minority scholars have charged that minority relations theories and methods have been used to maintain racist, sexist, and patriarchal domination. To be consistent, some say, analysis of any group would have to trace the believed causes of behavior to the group's position in the social structure. This exercise, the new sociology insists, will show that most social science research was performed by white, middle- to upper-middle-class males. Hence, this work is contaminated by those scientists' group attachments.

How might Merton and other traditional sociologists respond to this new intellectual situation? Merton suggests that the ideal research combines both insider and outsider knowledge. Would Oakley view this as a realistic compromise? How would one transcend one's own group attributes (e.g., age, gender, race, and religion) in order to develop a foundation of knowledge that wouldn't be considered "contaminated" by one's position? Is this possible? Are there any situations in which an outsider might better understand the problems of the insiders? For example, do you ever feel that you understand your friends' families better than your friends do?

A recent work by Merton is *On Social Structure and Science* (University of Chicago Press, 1996), and a recent work about Merton is Carlo Mongardini and Simonetta Tabboni, eds., *Robert K. Merton and Contemporary Sociology* (Transaction Publishers, 1998). Among Oakley's recent books is *Who's Afraid of Feminism?* (New Press, 1997). A sample of excellent discussions of the insider/outsider issue can be found in "New Scientific Method: Reach Out to the Community," by Paul Van Slambrouck, *Christian Science Monitor* (March 30, 1999) and *The Culture and Psychology Reader* edited by Nancy Rule Goldberger and Jody Veroff (New York University Press, 1995). A critique of science largely from an anthropological view is *Taboo: Sex, Identity, and Erotic Subjectivity in Anthropological Fieldwork* edited by Don Kulick and Margaret Willson (Routledge, 1995).

Two books dealing with the ethnographic issues raised by Oakley are Jaber F. Gubrium and James A. Holstein, *The New Language of Qualitative Method* (Oxford University Press, 1997) and Norman K. Denzin, *Interpretive Ethnography: Ethnographic Practices for the Twenty-First Century* (Sage Publications, 1997). An interesting article on teaching race issues is "Teaching About Race and Ethnicity: A Message of Despair or a Message of Hope?" by Frances Moulder, *Teaching Sociology* (April 1997). Philosophically relevant aspects of the issue are in *Virtuous Persons, Vicious Deeds: An Introduction to Ethics* edited by Alexander E. Hooke (Mayfield, 1999) and *The Philosophy of Science: Science and Objectivity* by G. Couvalis (Sage Publications, 1997).

Earlier works critiquing studies of Blacks are Joyce A. Ladner, ed., *The Death of White Sociology* (Vintage Books, 1973) and *Race and Ethnicity in Research Methods* edited by John H. Stanfield II and Rutledge M. Dennis (Sage Publications, 1993). More recently, Bruce DiCristina, in *Method in Criminology: A Philosophical Primer* (Harrow & Heston, 1995), rejects scientists who hold a "privileged status" over minorities.

ISSUE 2

Are Asian Americans a "Model Minority"?

YES: David A. Bell, from "America's Greatest Success Story: The Triumph of Asian-Americans," *The New Republic* (July 15 and 22, 1985)

NO: Ronald Takaki, from *Strangers from a Different Shore: A History of Asian Americans* (Little, Brown, 1989)

ISSUE SUMMARY

YES: Journalist and historian David A. Bell reflects on the current, frequently expressed enthusiasm for the successes of Asian Americans that appears in the mass media. Although he acknowledges some difficulties and hurdles faced by Asian Americans, Bell nevertheless portrays the road taken by Asian Americans as "America's greatest success story."

NO: Historian Ronald Takaki faults the mass media and some ethnic studies scholars for misunderstanding the statistics and examples used as proof that Asians are a model minority. Takaki argues that within Asian groups there are vast differences in success, and he reviews the prejudice and exploitation experienced by Asian Americans.

In the study of ethnic and racial minorities, myths play a fantastically important role. They enter society in many ways and forms. Frequently, oppressed peoples develop myths about a distant past when they were in a better situation or were the dominant group. Members of dominant or oppressor groups also create myths. These range from myths that extoll their own so-called superiority (and hence justify the exploitation of others) to mythical images of subordinate peoples. The latter are almost inevitably negative and sometimes form the basis of stereotypes.

Throughout the twentieth century, science has been frequently used to create and maintain negative myths about people. For example, Nazi biology imputed superiority to Aryans and inferiority to others (e.g., Gypsies and Jews) based on genes and race. The terrible ways in which the physiological and biological sciences were used to generate mythical theories of ethnic and racial superiorities and inferiorities is well known. However, the possible use of the social sciences for the same purposes is considerably more complicated and controversial. One current example of science being used to create negative images or myths about minorities is the controversy over the 15-point IQ gap between Blacks and others alleged in *The Bell Curve* by Richard J.

Herrnstein and Charles Murray (Free Press, 1994). This allegation has been attacked bitterly.

Other myth constructions that tend to be more neutral or even benign and that more closely resemble the issue of ethnic groups' creating tenuous ties to a rapidly receding "homeland" include creations of festivals and holidays to commemorate ethnic or racial solidarity. Some Black leaders and intellectuals find it functional to create elaborate myths of African ties. For many outsiders the "Sun People" delineation is neutral, even silly. However, others are concerned that the pattern of Black ethnocentrism (being group-centered) is tragically moving from generating group pride and solidarity to becoming anti-others (e.g., whites or Jews). Many worry that unscrupulous leaders are intentionally fanning racial and religious hatreds to gain popularity.

In this issue, the problems associated with mythmaking and minority status assume a new and more abstract twist. Citing abundant sources and studies, including professional scholarship and the mass media, David A. Bell argues that Asian Americans are a model minority. He is not the creator of this label, but he summarizes it, presents facts to support it, and clearly adds to it.

By contrast, Ronald Takaki, frequently citing the same sources as Bell, insists that the public as well as social scientists have created the myth of Asian Americans as a "model minority" or an American success story. He sees continuing prejudice, often backed by violence, against Asian Americans. He is also disturbed by the indiscriminate grouping of Asian Americans. Southeast Asians as well as Hindus and others have had very different experiences, often less happy, than the Chinese and Japanese (in spite of the horrible treatment of the Chinese in the 1800s and the fact that Japanese Americans were interned as enemy aliens during World War II).

As you read Bell's selection, carefully note the many examples he cites to show that Asian Americans are a model minority. As you read Takaki's selection, note the many examples he gives to show that it is wrong to label them a model minority. Who is correct? If both social scientists and the public, particularly the mass media, have created a myth, why do you think this is so? What might be its functions?

Essential to the manufacturing of stereotypes, myths, and prejudices about others is the language that is used to label them. What negative labels are mentioned by Bell and Takaki? What terms have you heard? What information in these two selections might you use to point out to those who use derogatory terms just how terrible, unfair, and empirically inaccurate they are?

Both Bell and Takaki mention films that each one thinks have been grossly unfair to Asian Americans. Which have you seen? What were your reactions? What current films pertaining to Asian minorities are being shown? Exactly how do they portray Asians?

YES

David A. Bell

AMERICA'S GREATEST SUCCESS STORY: THE TRIUMPH OF ASIAN-AMERICANS

It is the year 2019. In the heart of downtown Los Angeles, massive electronic billboards feature a model in a kimono hawking products labeled in Japanese. In the streets below, figures clad in traditional East Asian peasant garb hurry by, speaking to each other in an English made unrecognizable by the addition of hundreds of Spanish and Asian words. A rough-mannered policeman leaves an incongruously graceful calling card on a doorstep: a delicate origami paper sculpture.

This is, of course, a scene from a science-fiction movie, Ridley Scott's 1982 *Blade Runner*. It is also a vision that Asian-Americans dislike intensely. Hysterical warnings of an imminent Asian "takeover" of the United States stained a whole century of their 140-year history in this country, providing the backdrop for racial violence, legal segregation, and the internment of 110,000 Japanese-Americans in concentration camps during World War II. Today integration into American society, not transformation of American society, is the goal of an overwhelming majority. So why did the critics praise *Blade Runner* for its "realism"? The answer is easy to see.

The Asian-American population is exploding. According to the Census Bureau, it grew an astounding 125 percent between 1970 and 1980, and now stands at 4.1 million, or 1.8 percent of all Americans. Most of the increase is the result of immigration, which accounted for 1.8 million people between 1973 and 1983, the last year for which the Immigration and Naturalization Service has accurate figures (710,000 of these arrived as refugees from Southeast Asia). And the wave shows little sign of subsiding. Ever since the Immigration Act of 1965 permitted large-scale immigration by Asians, they have made up over 40 percent of all newcomers to the United States. Indeed, the arbitrary quota of 20,000 immigrants per country per year established by the act has produced huge backlogs of future Asian-Americans in several countries, including 120,000 in South Korea and 336,000 in the Philippines, some of whom, according to the State Department, have been waiting for their visas since 1970.

The numbers are astonishing. But even more astonishing is the extent to which Asian-Americans have become prominent out of all proportion to their share of the population. It now seems likely that their influx will have as important an effect on American society as the migration from Europe of 100 years ago. Most remarkable of all, it is taking place with relatively little trouble.

The new immigration from Asia is a radical development in several ways. First, it has not simply enlarged an existing Asian-American community, but created an entirely new one. Before 1965, and the passage of the Immigration Act, the term "Oriental-American" (which was then the vogue) generally denoted people living on the West Coast, in Hawaii, or in the Chinatowns of a few large cities. Generally they traced their ancestry either to one small part of China, the Toishan district of Kwantung province, or to a small number of communities in Japan (one of the largest of which, ironically, was Hiroshima). Today more than a third of all Asian-Americans live outside Chinatowns in the East, South, and Midwest, and their origins are as diverse as those of "European-Americans." The term "Asian-American" now refers to over 900,000 Chinese from all parts of China and also Vietnam, 800,000 Filipinos, 700,000 Japanese, 500,000 Koreans, 400,000 East Indians, and a huge assortment of everything else from Moslem Cambodians to Catholic Hawaiians. It can mean an illiterate Hmong tribesman or a fully assimilated graduate of the Harvard Business School.

Asian-Americans have also attracted attention by their new prominence in several professions and trades. In New York City, for example, where the Asian-American population jumped from 94,500 in 1970 to 231,500 in 1980, Korean-Americans run an estimated 900 of the city's 1,600 corner grocery stores. Filipino doctors—who outnumber black doctors—have become general practitioners in thousands of rural communities that previously lacked physicians. East Indian-Americans own 800 of California's 6,000 motels. And in parts of Texas, Vietnamese-Americans now control 85 percent of the shrimp-fishing industry, though they only reached this position after considerable strife (now the subject of a film, *Alamo Bay*).

Individual Asian-Americans have become quite prominent as well. I. M. Pei and Minoru Yamasaki have helped transform American architecture. Seiji Ozawa and Yo Yo Ma are giant figures in American music. An Wang created one of the nation's largest computer firms, and Rocky Aoki founded one of its largest restaurant chains (Benihana). Samuel C. C. Ting won a Nobel prize in physics.

* * *

Most spectacular of all, and most significant for the future, is the entry of Asian-Americans into the universities. At Harvard, for example, Asian-Americans ten years ago made up barely three percent of the freshman class. The figure is now ten percent—five times their share of the population. At Brown, Asian-American applications more than tripled over the same period, and at Berkeley they increased from 3,408 in 1982 to 4,235 only three years later. The Berkeley student body is now 22 percent Asian-American, UCLA's is 21 percent, and MIT's 19 percent. The Julliard School of Music in New York is currently 30 percent Asian and Asian-American. American medical schools had only 571 Asian-American students in 1970, but in 1980 they had

1,924, and last year 3,763, or 5.6 percent of total enrollment. What is more, nearly all of these figures are certain to increase. In the current, largely foreign-born Asian-American community, 32.9 percent of people over 25 graduated from college (as opposed to 16.2 percent in the general population). For third-generation Japanese-Americans, the figure is 88 percent.

By any measure these Asian-American students are outstanding. In California only the top 12.5 percent of high school students qualify for admission to the uppermost tier of the state university system, but 39 percent of Asian-American high school students do. On the SATs, Asian-Americans score an average of 519 in math, surpassing whites, the next highest group, by 32 points. Among Japanese-Americans, the most heavily native-born Asian-American group, 68 percent of those taking the math SAT scored above 600 —high enough to qualify for admission to almost any university in the country. The Westinghouse Science Talent search, which each year identified 40 top high school science students, picked 12 Asian-Americans in 1983, nine last year, and seven this year. And at Harvard the Phi Beta Kappa chapter last April named as its elite "Junior Twelve" students five Asian-Americans and seven Jews.

* * *

Faced with these statistics, the understandable reflex of many non-Asian-Americans is adulation. President Reagan has called Asian-Americans "our exemplars of hope and inspiration." *Parade* magazine recently featured an article on Asian-Americans titled "The Promise of America," and *Time* and *Newsweek* stories have boasted headlines like "A For-

mula for Success," "The Drive to Excel," and "A 'Model Minority.'" However, not all of these stories come to grips with the fact that Asian-Americans, like all immigrants, have to deal with a great many problems of adjustment, ranging from the absurd to the deadly serious.

Who would think, for example, that there is a connection between Asian-American immigration and the decimation of California's black bear population? But Los Angeles, whose Korean population grew by 100,000 in the past decade, now has more than 300 licensed herbal-acupuncture shops. And a key ingredient in traditional Korean herbal medicine is *ungdam*, bear gallbladder. The result is widespread illegal hunting and what *Audubon* magazine soberly called "a booming trade in bear parts."

As Mark R. Thompson recently pointed out in *The Wall Street Journal*, the clash of cultures produced by Asian immigration can also have vexing legal results. Take the case of Fumiko Kimura, a Japanese-American woman who tried to drown herself and her two children in the Pacific. She survived but the children did not, and she is now on trial for their murder. As a defense, her lawyers are arguing that parent-child suicide is a common occurrence in Japan. In Fresno, California, meanwhile, 30,000 newly arrived Hmong cause a different problem. "Anthropologists call the custom 'marriage by capture,'" Mr. Thompson writes. "Fresno police and prosecutors call it 'rape.'"

A much more serious problem for Asian-Americans is racial violence. In 1982 two unemployed whites in Detroit beat to death a Chinese-American named Vincent Chin, claiming that they wanted revenge on the Japanese for hurting the automobile industry. After pleading

ASIANS AND JEWS

Comparing the social success of Asian-Americans with that of the Jews is irresistible. Jews and Asians rank number one and number two, respectively, in median family income. In the Ivy League they are the two groups most heavily "over-represented" in comparison to their shares of the population. And observers are quick to point out all sorts of cultural parallels. As Arthur Rosen, the chairman of (appropriately) the National Committee on United States–China Relations, recently told *The New York Times*, "There are the same kind of strong family ties and the same sacrificial drive on the part of immigrant parents who couldn't get a college education to see that their children do."

In historical terms, the parallels can often be striking. For example, when Russian and Polish Jews came to this country in the late 19th and early 20th centuries, 60 percent of those who went into industry worked in the garment trade. Today thousands of Chinese-American women fill sweatshops in New York City doing the same work of stitching and sewing. In Los Angeles, when the Jews began to arrive in large numbers in the 1880s, 43 percent of them became retail or wholesale proprietors, according to Ivan Light's essay in *Clamor at the Gates*. One hundred years later, 40 percent of Koreans in Los Angeles are also wholesale and retail proprietors. The current controversy over Asian-American admission in Ivy League colleges eerily recalls the Jews' struggle to end quotas in the 1940s and 1950s.

In cultural terms, however, it is easy to take the comparison too far. American Jews remain a relatively homogeneous group, with a common religion and history. Asian-Americans, especially after the post-1965 flood of immigrants, are exactly the opposite. They seem homogeneous largely because they share some racial characteristics. And even those vary widely. The label "Chinese-American" itself covers a range of cultural and linguistic differences that makes those between German and East European Jews, or between Reform and Orthodox Jews, seem trivial in comparison.

The most important parallels between Jews and the various Asian groups are not cultural. They lie rather in the sociological profile of Jewish and Asian immigration. The Jewish newcomers of a hundred years ago never completely fit into the category of "huddled masses." They had an astonishing high literacy rate (nearly 100 percent for German Jews, and over 50 percent for East European Jews), a long tradition of scholarship even in the smallest shtetls, and useful skills. More than two-thirds of male Jewish immigrants were considered skilled workers in America. Less than three percent of Jewish immigrants had worked on the land. Similarly, the Japanese,

Box continued on next page.

Korean, Filipino, and Vietnamese immigrants of the 20th century have come almost exclusively from the middle class. Seventy percent of Korean male immigrants, for example, are college graduates. Like middle-class native-born Americans, Asian and Jewish immigrants alike have fully understood the importance of the universities, and have pushed their children to enter them from the very start.

Thomas Sowell offers another parallel between the successes of Asians and Jews. Both communities have benefited paradoxically, he argues, from their small size and from past discrimination against them. These disadvantages long kept both groups out of politics. And, as Sowell writes in *Race and Economics:* "those American ethnic groups that have succeeded best politically have not usually been the same as those who succeeded best economically ... those minorities that have pinned their greatest hopes on political action—the Irish and the Negroes, for example—have made some of the slower economic advances." Rather than searching for a solution to their problems through the political process, Jewish, Chinese, and Japanese immigrants developed self-sufficiency by relying on community organizations. The combination of their skills, their desire for education, and the gradual disappearance of discrimination led inexorably to economic success.

—D.A.B.

guilty to manslaughter, they paid a $3,000 fine and were released. More recently, groups of Cambodians and Vietnamese in Boston were beaten by white youths, and there have been incidents in New York and Los Angles as well.

Is this violence an aberration, or does it reflect the persistence of anti-Asian prejudice in America? By at least one indicator, it seems hard to believe that Asian-Americans suffer greatly from discrimination. Their median family income, according to the 1980 census, was $22,713, compared to only $19,917 for whites. True, Asians live almost exclusively in urban areas (where incomes are higher), and generally have more people working in each family. They are also better educated than whites. Irene Natividad, a Filipino-American active in the Democratic Party's Asian Caucus, states bluntly that "we are underpaid for the high level of education we have achieved." However, because of language difficulties and differing professional standards in the United States, many new Asian immigrants initially work in jobs for which they are greatly overqualified.

Ironically, charges of discrimination today arise most frequently in the universities, the setting generally cited as the best evidence of Asian-American achievement. For several years Asian student associations at Ivy League universities have cited figures showing that a smaller percentage of Asian-American students than others are accepted. At

Harvard this year, 12.5 percent of Asian-American applicants were admitted, as opposed to 16 percent of all applicants; at Princeton, the figures were 14 to 17 percent. Recently a Princeton professor, Uwe Reinhardt, told a *New York Times* reporter that Princeton has an unofficial quota for Asian-American applicants.

The question of university discrimination is a subtle one. For one thing, it only arises at the most prestigious schools, where admissions are the most subjective. At universities like UCLA, where applicants are judged largely by their grades and SAT scores, Asian-Americans have a higher admission rate than other students (80 percent versus 70 percent for all applicants). And at schools that emphasize science, like MIT, the general excellence of Asian-Americans in the field also produces a higher admission rate.

Why are things different at the Ivy League schools? One reason, according to a recent study done at Princeton, is that very few Asian-Americans are alumni children. The children of alumni are accepted at a rate of about 50 percent, and so raise the overall admissions figure. Athletes have a better chance of admission as well, and few Asian-Americans play varsity sports. These arguments, however, leave out another admissions factor: affirmative action. The fact is that if alumni children have a special advantage, at least some Asians do too, because of their race. At Harvard, for instance, partly in response to complaints from the Asian student organization, the admissions office in the late 1970s began to recruit vigorously among two categories of Asian-Americans: the poor, often living in Chinatowns; and recent immigrants. Today, according to the dean of admissions, L. Fred Jewett, roughly a third of Harvard's Asian-American applicants come from

these groups, and are included in the university's "affirmative action" efforts. Like black students, who have a 27 percent admission rate, they find it easier to get in. And this means that the *other* Asian-Americans, the ones with no language problem or economic disadvantage, find things correspondingly tougher. Harvard has no statistics on the two groups. But if we assume the first group has an admissions rate of only 20 percent (very low for affirmative action candidates), the second one still slips down to slightly less than nine percent, or roughly half the overall admissions rate.

Dean Jewett offers two explanations for this phenomenon. First, he says, "family pressure makes more marginal students apply." In other words, many Asian students apply regardless of their qualifications, because of the university's prestige. And second, "a terribly high proportion of the Asian students are heading toward the sciences." In the interests of diversity, then, more of them must be left out.

* * *

It is true that more Asian-Americans go into the sciences. In Harvard's class of 1985, 57 percent of them did (as opposed to 29 percent of all students) and 71 percent went into either the sciences or economics. It is also true that a great many of Harvard's Asian-American applicants have little on their records except scientific excellence. But there are good reasons for this. In the sciences, complete mastery of English is less important than in other fields, an important fact for immigrants and children of immigrants. And scientific careers allow Asian-Americans to avoid the sort of large, hierarchical organization where their unfamiliarity with America, and management's resistance to putting them into highly visible positions, could hinder their advancement. And so the admissions problem comes down to a problem of clashing cultural standards. Since the values of Asian-American applicants differ from the universities' own, many of those applicants appear narrowly focused and dull. As Linda Matthews, an alumni recruiter for Harvard in Los Angeles, says with regret, "We hold them to the standards of white suburban kids. We want them to be cheerleaders and class presidents and all the rest."

The universities, however, consider their idea of the academic community to be liberal and sound. They are understandably hesitant to change it because of a demographic shift in the admissions pool. So how can they resolve this difficult problem? It is hard to say, except to suggest humility, and to recall that this sort of thing has come up before. At Harvard, the admissions office might do well to remember a memorandum Walter Lippmann prepared for the university in 1922. "I am fully prepared to accept the judgment of the Harvard authorities that a concentration of Jews in excess of fifteen per cent will produce a segregation of cultures rather than a fusion," wrote Lippmann, himself a Jew and a Harvard graduate. "They hand on unconsciously and uncritically from one generation to another many distressing personal and social habits...."

* * *

The debate over admissions is abstruse. But for Asian-Americans, it has become an extremely sensitive issue. The universities, after all, represent their route to complete integration in American society, and to an equal chance at the advantages that enticed them and their parents to immigrate in the first place. At the same time, discrimination, even very slight discrimination, recalls the bitter prejudice and discrimination that Asian-Americans suffered for their first hundred years in this country.

Few white Americans today realize just how pervasive legal anti-Asian discrimination was before 1945. The tens of thousand of Chinese laborers who arrived in California in the 1850s and 1860s to work in the goldfields and build the Central Pacific Railroad often lived in virtual slavery (the words ku-li, now part of the English language, mean "bitter labor"). Far from having the chance to organize, they were seized on as scapegoats by labor unions, particularly Samuel Gompers's AFL, and often ended up working as strikebreakers instead, thus inviting violent attacks. In 1870 Congress barred Asian immigrants from citizenship, and in 1882 it passed the Chinese Exclusion Act, which summarily prohibited more Chinese from entering the country. Since it did this at a time when 100,600 male Chinese-Americans had the company of only 4,800 females, it effectively sentenced the Chinese community to rapid decline. From 1854 to 1874, California had in effect a law preventing Asian-Americans from testifying in court, leaving them without the protection of the law.

Little changed in the late 19th and early 20th centuries, as large numbers of Japanese and smaller contingents from Korea and the Philippines began to arrive on the West Coast. In 1906 San Francisco made a brief attempt to segregate its school system. In 1910 a California law went so far as to prohibit marriage between Caucasians and "Mongolians," in flagrant defiance of the Fourteenth Amendment. Two Alien Land Acts in

1913 and 1920 prevented noncitizens in California (in other words, all alien immigrants) from owning or leasing land. These laws, and the Chinese Exclusion Act, remained in effect until the 1940s. And of course during the Second World War, President Franklin Roosevelt signed an Executive Order sending 110,000 ethnic Japanese on the West Coast, 64 percent of whom were American citizens, to internment camps. Estimates of the monetary damage to the Japanese-American community from this action range as high as $400,000,000, and Japanese-American political activists have made reparations one of their most important goals. Only in Hawaii, where Japanese-Americans already outnumbered whites 61,000 to 29,000 at the turn of the century, was discrimination relatively less important. (Indeed, 157,000 Japanese-Americans in Hawaii at the start of the war were *not* interned, although they posed a greater possible threat to the war effort than their cousins in California.)

* * *

In light of this history, the current problems of the Asian-American community seem relatively minor, and its success appears even more remarkable. Social scientists wonder just how this success was possible, and how Asian-Americans have managed to avoid the "second-class citizenship" that has trapped so many blacks and Hispanics. There is no single answer, but all the various explanations of the Asian-Americans' success do tend to fall into one category: self-sufficiency.

The first element of this self-sufficiency is family. Conservative sociologist Thomas Sowell writes that "strong, stable families have been characteristic of ... successful minorities," and calls Chinese-Americans and Japanese-Americans the most stable he has encountered. This quality contributes to success in at least three ways. First and most obviously, it provides a secure environment for children. Second, it pushes those children to do better than their parents. As former Ohio state demographer William Petersen, author of *Japanese-Americans* (1971), says, "They're like the Jews in that they have the whole family and the whole community pushing them to make the best of themselves." And finally, it is a significant financial advantage. Traditionally, Asian-Americans have headed into family businesses, with all the family members pitching in long hours to make them a success. For the Chinese, it was restaurants and laundries (as late as 1940, half of the Chinese-American labor force worked in one or the other), for the Japanese, groceries and truck farming, and for the Koreans, groceries. Today the proportion of Koreans working without pay in family businesses is nearly three times as high as any other group. A recent *New York* magazine profile of one typical Korean grocery in New York showed that several of the family members running it consistently worked 15 to 18 hours a day. Thomas Sowell points out that in 1970, although Chinese median family income already exceeded white median family income by a third, their median personal income was only ten percent higher, indicating much greater participation per family.

Also contributing to Asian-American self-sufficiency are powerful community organizations. From the beginning of Chinese-American settlement in California, clan organizations, mutual aid societies, and rotating credit associations gave many Japanese-Americans a start in business, at a time when most banks would only lend to whites. Throughout the first half of this century, the strength of community organizations was an important reason why Asian-Americans tended to live in small, closed communities rather than spreading out among the general population. And during the Depression years, they proved vital. In the early 1930s, when nine percent of the population of New York City subsisted on public relief, only one percent of Chinese-Americans did so. The community structure has also helped keep Asian-American crime rates the lowest in the nation, despite recently increasing gang violence among new Chinese and Vietnamese immigrants. According to the 1980 census, the proportion of Asian-Americans in prison is one-fourth that of the general population.

The more recent immigrants have also developed close communities. In the Washington, D.C., suburb of Arlington, Virginia, there is now a "Little Saigon." Koreans also take advantage of the "ethnic resources" provided by a small community. As Ivan Light writes in an essay in Nathan Glazer's new book, *Clamor at the Gates*, "They help one another with business skills, information, and purchase of ethnic commodities; cluster in particular industries; combine easily in restraint of trade; or utilize rotation credit associations." Light cites a study showing that 34 percent of Korean grocery store owners in Chicago had received financial help from within the Korean community. The immigrants in these communities are self-sufficient in another way as well. Unlike the immigrants of the 19th century, most new Asian-Americans come to the United States with professional skills. Or they come to obtain those skills, and then stay on. Of 16,000 Taiwanese who came to the

U.S. as students in the 1960s, only three percent returned to Taiwan.

* * *

So what does the future hold for Asian-Americans? With the removal of most discrimination, and with the massive Asian-American influx in the universities, the importance of tightly knit communities is sure to wane. Indeed, among the older Asian-American groups it already has: since the war, fewer and fewer native-born Chinese-Americans have come to live in Chinatowns. But will complete assimilation follow? One study, at least, seems to indicate that it will, if one can look to the well-established Japanese-Americans for hints as to the future of other Asian groups. According to Professor Harry Kitano of UCLA, 63 percent of Japanese now intermarry.

But can all Asian-Americans follow the prosperous, assimilationist Japanese example? For some, it may not be easy. Hmong tribesmen, for instance, arrived in the United States with little money, few valuable skills, and extreme cultural disorientation. After five years here, they are still heavily dependent on welfare. (When the state of Oregon cut its assistance to refugees, 90 percent of the Hmong there moved to California.) Filipinos, although now the second-largest Asian-American group, make up less than ten percent of the Asian-American population at Harvard, and are the only Asian-Americans to benefit from affirmative action programs at the University of California. Do figures like these point to the emergence of a disadvantaged Asian-American underclass? It is still too early to tell, but the question is not receiving much attention either. As Nathan Glazer says of Asian-Americans, "When they're already above average, it's very hard to pay much attention to those who fall below." Ross Harano, a Chicago businessman active in the Democratic Party's Asian Caucus, argues that the label of "model minority" earned by the most conspicuous Asian-Americans hurt less successful groups. "We need money to help people who can't assimilate as fast as the superstars," he says.

Harano also points out that the stragglers find little help in traditional minority politics. "When blacks talk about a minority agenda, they don't include us," he says. "Most Asians are viewed by blacks as whites." Indeed, in cities with large numbers of Asians and blacks, relations between the communities are tense. In September 1984, for example, *The Los Angeles Sentinel,* a prominent black newspaper, ran a four-part series condemning Koreans for their "takeover" of black businesses, provoking a strong reaction from Asian-American groups. In Harlem some blacks have organized a boycott of Asian-American stores.

Another barrier to complete integration lies in the tendency of many Asian-American students to crowd into a small number of careers, mainly in the sciences. Professor Ronn Takaki of Berkeley is a strong critic of this "maldistribution," and says that universities should make efforts to correct it. The extent of these efforts, he told *The Boston Globe* last December, "will determine whether we have our poets, sociologists, historians, and journalists. If we are all tracked into becoming computer technicians and scientists, this need will not be fulfilled."

Yet it is not clear that the "maldistribution" problem will extend to the next generation. The children of the current immigrants will not share their parents' language difficulties. Nor will they worry as much about joining large institutions where subtle racism might once have barred them from advancement. William Petersen argues, "As the discrimination disappears, as it mostly has already, the self-selection will disappear as well.... There's nothing in Chinese or Japanese culture pushing them toward these fields." Professor Kitano of UCLA is not so sure. "The submerging of the individual to the group is another basic Japanese tradition," he wrote in an article for *The Harvard Encyclopedia of American Ethnic Groups.* It is a tradition that causes problems for Japanese-Americans who wish to avoid current career patterns: "It may only be a matter of time before some break out of these middleman jobs, but the structural and cultural restraints may prove difficult to overcome."

* * *

In short, Asian-Americans face undeniable problems of integration. Still, it takes a very narrow mind not to realize that these problems are the envy of every other American racial minority, and of a good number of white ethnic groups as well. Like the Jews, who experienced a similar pattern of discrimination and quotas, and who first crowded into a small range of professions, Asian-Americans have shown an ability to overcome large obstacles in spectacular fashion. In particular, they have done so by taking full advantage of America's greatest civic resource, its schools and universities, just as the Jews did 50 years ago. Now they seem poised to burst out upon American society.

* * *

The clearest indication of this course is in politics, a sphere that Asian-Americans traditionally avoided. Now this is changing. And importantly, it is *not* changing just because Asian-Americans want government to solve their particular problems. Yes, there are "Asian" issues: the loosening of immigration restrictions, reparations for the wartime internment, equal opportunity for the Asian disadvantaged. Asian-American Democrats are at present incensed over the way the Democratic National Committee has stripped their caucus of "official" status. But even the most vehement activists on these points still insist that the most important thing for Asian-Americans is not any particular combination of issues, but simply "being part of the process." Unlike blacks or Hispanics, Asian-American politicians have the luxury of not having to devote the bulk of their time to an "Asian-American agenda," and thus escape becoming prisoners of such an agenda. Who thinks of Senator Daniel Inouye or former senator S. I. Hayakawa primarily in terms of his race? In June a young Chinese-American named Michael Woo won a seat on the Los Angeles City Council, running in a district that is only five percent Asian. According to *The Washington Post*, he attributed his victory to his "links to his fellow young American professionals." This is not typical minority-group politics.

Since Asian-Americans have the luxury of not having to behave like other minority groups, it seems only a matter of time before they, like the Jews, lose their "minority" status altogether, both legally and in the public's perception. And when this occurs, Asian-Americans will have to face the danger not of discrimination but of losing their cultural identity. It is a problem that every immigrant group must eventually come to terms with.

For Americans in general, however, the success of Asian-Americans poses no problems at all. On the contrary, their triumph has done nothing but enrich the United States. Asian-Americans improve every field they enter, for the simple reason that in a free society, a group succeeds by doing something better than it had been done before: Korean grocery stores provide fresher vegetables; Filipino doctors provide better rural health care; Asian science students raise the quality of science in the universities, and go on to provide better medicine, engineering, computer technology, and so on. And by a peculiarly American miracle, the Asian-Americans' success has not been balanced by anyone else's failure. Indeed, as successive waves of immigrants have shown, each new ethnic and racial group adds far more to American society than it takes away. This Fourth of July, that is cause for hope and celebration.

NO
Ronald Takaki

THE MYTH OF THE "MODEL MINORITY"

Today Asian Americans are celebrated as America's "model minority." In 1986, NBC *Nightly News* and the *McNeil/Lehrer Report* aired special news segments on Asian Americans and their success, and a year later, CBS's *60 Minutes* presented a glowing report on their stunning achievements in the academy. "Why are Asian Americans doing so exceptionally well in school?" Mike Wallace asked, and quickly added, "They must be doing something right. Let's bottle it." Meanwhile, *U.S. News & World Report* featured Asian-American advances in a cover story, and *Time* devoted an entire section on this meteoric minority in its special immigrants issue, "The Changing Face of America." Not to be outdone by its competitors, *Newsweek* titled the cover story of its college-campus magazine "Asian-Americans: The Drive to Excel" and a lead article of its weekly edition "Asian Americans: A 'Model Minority.'" *Fortune* went even further, applauding them as "America's Super Minority," and the *New Republic* extolled "The Triumph of Asian-Americans" as "America's greatest success story."

The celebration of Asian-American achievements in the press has been echoed in the political realm. Congratulations have come even from the White House. In a speech presented to Asian and Pacific Americans in the chief executive's mansion in 1984, President Ronald Reagan explained the significance of their success. America has a rich and diverse heritage, Reagan declared, and Americans are all descendants of immigrants in search of the "American Dream." He praised Asian and Pacific Americans for helping to "preserve that dream by living up to the bedrock values" of America—the principles of "the sacred worth of human life, religious faith, community spirit and the responsibility of parents and schools to be teachers of tolerance, hard work, fiscal responsibility, cooperation, and love." "It's no wonder," Reagan emphatically noted, "that the median incomes of Asian and Pacific-American families are much higher than the total American average." Hailing Asian and Pacific Americans as an example for all Americans, Reagan conveyed his gratitude to them: we need "your values, your hard work" expressed within "our political system."

But in their celebration of this "model minority," the pundits and the politicians have exaggerated Asian-American "success" and have created a new myth. Their comparisons of incomes between Asians and whites fail to recognize the regional location of the Asian-American population. Concentrated in California, Hawaii, and New York, Asian Americans reside largely in states with higher incomes but also higher costs of living than the national average: 59 percent of all Asian Americans lived in these three states in 1980, compared to only 19 percent of the general population. The use of "family incomes" by Reagan and others has been very misleading, for Asian-American families have more persons working per family than white families. In 1980, white nuclear families in California had only 1.6 workers per family, compared to 2.1 for Japanese, 2.0 for immigrant Chinese, 2.2 for immigrant Filipino, and 1.8 for immigrant Korean (this last figure is actually higher, for many Korean women are unpaid family workers). Thus the family incomes of Asian Americans indicate the presence of more workers in each family, rather than higher incomes.

Actually, in terms of personal incomes, Asian Americans have not reached equality. In 1980 the mean personal income for white men in California was $23,400. While Japanese men earned a comparable income, they did so only by acquiring more education (17.7 years compared to 16.8 years for white men twenty-five to forty-four years old) and by working more hours (2,160 hours compared to 2,120 hours for white men in the same age category). In reality, then, Japanese men were still behind Caucasian men. Income inequalities for other men were more evident: Korean men earned only $19,200, or 82 percent of the income of white men, Chinese men only $15,900 or 68 percent, and Filipino men only $14,500 or 62 percent. In New York the mean personal

income for white men was $21,600, compared to only $18,900 or 88 percent for Korean men, $16,500 or 76 percent for Filipino men, and only $11,200 or 52 percent for Chinese men. In the San Francisco Bay Area, Chinese-immigrant men earned only 72 percent of what their white counterparts earned, Filipino-immigrant men 68 percent, Korean-immigrant men 69 percent, and Vietnamese-immigrant men 52 percent. The incomes of Asian-American men were close to and sometimes even below those of black men (68 percent) and Mexican-American men (71 percent).

The patterns of income inequality for Asian men reflect a structural problem: Asians tend to be located in the labor market's secondary sector, where wages are low and promotional prospects minimal. Asian men are clustered as janitors, machinists, postal clerks, technicians, waiters, cooks, gardeners, and computer programmers; they can also be found in the primary sector, but here they are found mostly in the lower-tier levels as architects, engineers, computer-systems analysts, pharmacists, and schoolteachers, rather than in the upper-tier levels of management and decision making. "Labor market segmentation and restricted mobility between sectors," observed social scientists Amado Cabezas and Gary Kawaguchi, "help promote the economic interest and privilege of those with capital or those in the primary sector, who mostly are white men."

This pattern of Asian absence from the higher levels of administration is characterized as "a glass ceiling"—a barrier through which top management positions can only be seen, but not reached, by Asian Americans. While they are increasing in numbers on university campuses as students, they are virtually nonexistent as administrators: at Berkeley's University of California campus where 25 percent of the students were Asian in 1987, only one out of 102 top-level administrators was an Asian. In the United States as a whole, only 8 percent of Asian Americans in 1988 were "officials" and "managers," as compared to 12 percent for all groups. Asian Americans are even more scarce in the upper strata of the corporate hierarchy: they constituted less than half of one percent of the 29,000 officers and directors of the nation's thousand largest companies. Though they are highly educated, Asian Americans are generally not present in positions of executive leadership and decision making. "Many Asian Americans hoping to climb the corporate ladder face an arduous ascent," the *Wall Street Journal* observed. "Ironically, the same companies that pursue them for technical jobs often shun them when filling managerial and executive positions."

Asian Americans complain that they are often stereotyped as passive and told they lack the aggressiveness required in administration. The problem is not whether their culture encourages a reserved manner, they argue, but whether they have opportunities for social activities that have traditionally been the exclusive preserve of elite white men. "How do you get invited to the cocktail party and talk to the chairman?" asked Landy Eng, a former assistant vice president of Citibank. "It's a lot easier if your father or your uncle or his friend puts his arm around you at the party and says, 'Landy, let me introduce you to Walt.'" Excluded from the "old boy" network, Asian Americans are also told they are inarticulate and have an accent. Edwin Wong, a junior manager at Acurex, said: "I was given the equivalent of an ultimatum: 'Either you improve your accent or your future in get-

ting promoted to senior management is in jeopardy.'" The accent was a perceived problem at work. "I felt that just because I had an accent a lot of Caucasians thought I was stupid." But whites with German, French, or English accents do not seem to be similarly handicapped. Asian Americans are frequently viewed as technicians rather than administrators. Thomas Campbell, a general manager at Westinghouse Electric Corp., said that Asian Americans would be happier staying in technical fields and that few of them are adept at sorting through the complexities of large-scale business. This very image can produce a reinforcing pattern: Asian-American professionals often find they "top out," reaching a promotional ceiling early in their careers. "The only jobs we could get were based on merit," explained Kumar Patel, head of the material science division at AT&T. "That is why you find most [Asian-Indian] professionals in technical rather than administrative or managerial positions." ...

Asian-American "success" has emerged as the new stereotype for this ethnic minority. While this image has led many teachers and employers to view Asians as intelligent and hardworking and has opened some opportunities, it has also been harmful. Asian Americans find their diversity as individuals denied: many feel forced to conform to the "model minority" mold and want more freedom to be their individual selves, to be "extravagant." Asian university students are concentrated in the sciences and technical fields, but many of them wish they had greater opportunities to major in the social sciences and humanities. "We are educating a generation of Asian technicians," observed an Asian-American professor at Berkeley, "but the communities also need their historians and poets." Asian Americans find themselves all lumped together and their diversity as groups overlooked. Groups that are not doing well, such as the unemployed Hmong, the Downtown Chinese, the elderly Japanese, the old Filipino farm laborers, and others, have been rendered invisible. To be out of sight is also to be without social services. Thinking Asian Americans have succeeded, government officials have sometimes denied funding for social service programs designed to help Asian Americans learn English and find employment. Failing to realize that there are poor Asian families, college administrators have sometimes excluded Asian-American students from Educational Opportunity Programs (EOP), which are intended for *all* students from low-income families. Asian Americans also find themselves pitted against and resented by other racial minorities and even whites. If Asian Americans can make it on their own, pundits are asking, why can't poor blacks and whites on welfare? Even middle-class whites, who are experiencing economic difficulties because of plant closures in a deindustrializing America and the expansion of low-wage service employment, have been urged to emulate the Asian-American "model minority" and to work harder.

Indeed, the story of the Asian-American triumph offers ideological affirmation of the American Dream in an era anxiously witnessing the decline of the United States in the international economy (due to its trade imbalance and its transformation from a creditor to a debtor nation), the emergence of a new black underclass (the percentage of black female-headed families having almost doubled from 22 percent in 1960 to 40 percent in 1980), and a collapsing white middle class

(the percentage of households earning a "middle-class" income falling from 28.7 percent in 1967 to 23.2 percent in 1983). Intellectually, it has been used to explain "losing ground"—why the situation of the poor has deteriorated during the last two decades of expanded government social services. According to this view, advanced by pundits like Charles Murray, the interventionist federal state, operating on the "misguided wisdom" of the 1960s, made matters worse: it created a web of welfare dependency. But his analysis has overlooked the structural problems in society and our economy, and it has led to easy cultural explanations and quick-fix prescriptions. Our difficulties, we are sternly told, stem from our waywardness: Americans have strayed from the Puritan "errand into the wilderness." They have abandoned the old American "habits of the heart." Praise for Asian-American success is America's most recent jeremiad—a renewed commitment to make America number one again and a call for a rededication to the bedrock values of hard work, thrift, and industry. Like many congratulations, this one may veil a spirit of competition, even jealousy.

Significantly, Asian-American "success" has been accompanied by the rise of a new wave of anti-Asian sentiment. On college campuses, racial slurs have surfaced in conversations on the quad: "Look out for the Asian Invasion." "M.I.T. means Made in Taiwan." "U.C.L.A. stands for University of Caucasians Living among Asians." Nasty anti-Asian graffiti have suddenly appeared on the walls of college dormitories and in the elevators of classroom buildings: "Chink, chink, cheating chink!" "Stop the Yellow Hordes." "Stop the Chinese before they flunk you out." Ugly racial incidents have broken out on college campuses. At the University of Connecticut, for example, eight Asian-American students experienced a nightmare of abuse in 1987. Four couples had boarded a college bus to attend a dance. "The dance was a formal and so we were wearing gowns," said Marta Ho, recalling the horrible evening with tears. "The bus was packed, and there was a rowdy bunch of white guys in the back of the bus. Suddenly I felt this warm sticky stuff on my hair. They were spitting at us! My friend was sitting sidewise and got hit on her face and she started screaming. Our boy friends turned around, and one of the white guys, a football player, shouted: 'You want to make something out of this, you Oriental faggots!'"

Asian-American students at the University of Connecticut and other colleges are angry, arguing that there should be no place for racism on campus and that they have as much right as anyone else to be in the university. Many of them are children of recent immigrants who had been college-educated professionals in Asia. They see how their parents had to become greengrocers, restaurant operators, and storekeepers in America, and they want to have greater career choices for themselves. Hopeful a college education can help them overcome racial obstacles, they realize the need to be serious about their studies. But white college students complain: "Asian students are nerds." This very stereotype betrays nervousness —fears that Asian-American students are raising class grade curves. White parents, especially alumni, express concern about how Asian-American students are taking away "their" slots—admission places that should have gone to their children. "Legacy" admission slots reserved for children of alumni have come to function as a kind of invisible affirmative-action program for whites. A college education has always represented a valuable economic resource, credentialing individuals for high income and status employment, and the university has recently become a contested terrain of competition between whites and Asians. In paneled offices, university administrators meet to discuss the "problem" of Asian-American "over-representation" in enrollments.

Paralleling the complaint about the rising numbers of Asian-American students in the university is a growing worry that there are also "too many" immigrants coming from Asia. Recent efforts to "reform" the 1965 Immigration Act seem reminiscent of the nativism prevalent in the 1880s and the 1920s. Senator Alan K. Simpson of Wyoming, for example, noted how the great majority of the new immigrants were from Latin America and Asia, and how "a substantial portion" of them did not "integrate fully" into American society. "If language and cultural separatism rise above a certain level," he warned, "the unity and political stability of the Nation will—in time—be seriously eroded. Pluralism within a united American nation has been our greatest strength. The unity comes from a common language and a core public culture of certain shared values, beliefs, and customs, which make us distinctly 'Americans.'" In the view of many supporters of immigration reform, the post-1965 immigration from Asia and Latin America threatens the traditional unity and identity of the American people. "The immigration from the turn of the century was largely a continuation of immigration from previous years in that the European stock of Americans was being maintained," explained Steve Rosen, a member of an organization lobbying for changes in the current law. "Now, we are having a large influx of third-world people, which could be potentially disruptive of our whole Judeo-Christian heritage." Significantly, in March 1988, the Senate passed a bill that would limit the entry of family members and that would provide 55,000 new visas to be awarded to "independent immigrants" on the basis of education, work experience, occupations, and "English language skills."

Political concerns usually have cultural representations. The entertainment media have begun marketing Asian stereotypes again: where Hollywood had earlier portrayed Asians as Charlie Chan displaying his wit and wisdom in his fortune cookie Confucian quotes and as the evil Fu Manchu threatening white women, the film industry has recently been presenting images of comic Asians (in *Sixteen Candles*) and criminal Asian aliens (in *Year of the Dragon*). Hollywood has entered the realm of foreign affairs. *The Deer Hunter* explained why the United States lost the war in Vietnam. In this story, young American men are sent to fight in Vietnam, but they are not psychologically prepared for the utter cruelty of physically disfigured Viet Cong clad in black pajamas. Shocked and disoriented, they collapse morally into a world of corruption, drugs, gambling, and Russian roulette. There seems to be something sinister in Asia and the people there that is beyond the capability of civilized Americans to comprehend. Upset after seeing this movie, refugee Thu-Thuy Truong exclaimed: "We didn't play Russian roulette games in Saigon! The whole thing was made up." Similarly *Apocalypse Now* portrayed lost innocence: Americans enter the heart of darkness in Vietnam and become possessed by madness (in the persona played by Marlon Brando) but are saved in the end by their own technology and violence (represented by Martin Sheen). Finally, in movies celebrating the exploits of Rambo, Hollywood has allowed Americans to win in fantasy the Vietnam War they had lost in reality. "Do we get to win this time?" snarls Rambo, our modern Natty Bumppo, a hero of limited conversation and immense patriotic rage.

Meanwhile, anti-Asian feelings and misunderstandings have been exploding violently in communities across the country, from Philadelphia, Boston, and New York to Denver and Galveston, Seattle, Portland, Monterey, and San Francisco. In Jersey City, the home of 15,000 Asian Indians, a hate letter published in a local newspaper warned: "We will go to any extreme to get Indians to move out of Jersey City. If I'm walking down the street and I see a Hindu and the setting is right, I will just hit him or her. We plan some of our more extreme attacks such as breaking windows, breaking car windows and crashing family parties. We use the phone book and look up the name Patel. Have you seen how many there are?" The letter was reportedly written by the "Dotbusters," a cruel reference to the *bindi* some Indian women wear as a sign of sanctity. Actual attacks have taken place, ranging from verbal harassments and egg throwing to serious beatings. Outside a Hoboken restaurant on September 27, 1987, a gang of youths chanting "Hindu, Hindu" beat Navroz Mody to death. A grand jury has indicted four teenagers for the murder.

Five years earlier a similarly brutal incident occurred in Detroit. There, in July, Vincent Chin, a young Chinese American, and two friends went to a bar in the late afternoon to celebrate his upcoming wedding. Two white autoworkers,

Ronald Ebens and Michael Nitz, called Chin a "Jap" and cursed: "It's because of you ... that we're out of work." A fistfight broke out, and Chin then quickly left the bar. But Ebens and Nitz took out a baseball bat from the trunk of their car and chased Chin through the streets. They finally cornered him in front of a McDonald's restaurant. Nitz held Chin while Ebens swung the bat across the victim's shins and then bludgeoned Chin to death by shattering his skull. Allowed to plead guilty to manslaughter, Ebens and Nitz were sentenced to three years' probation and fined $3,780 each. But they have not spent a single night in jail for their bloody deed. "Three thousand dollars can't even buy a good used car these days," snapped a Chinese American, "and this was the price of a life." "What kind of law is this? What kind of justice?" cried Mrs. Lily Chin, the slain man's mother. "This happened because my son is Chinese. If two Chinese killed a white person, they must go to jail, maybe for their whole lives.... Something is wrong with this country." ...

The murder of Vincent Chin has aroused the anger and concern of Asian Americans across the country. They know he was killed because of his racial membership. Ebens and Nitz perceived Chin as a "stranger," a foreigner, for he did not look like an American. But why was Chin viewed as an alien? Asian Americans blame the educational system for not including their history in the curricula and for not teaching about U.S. society in all of its racial and cultural diversity. Why are the courses and books on American history so Eurocentric? they have asked teachers and scholars accusingly.

POSTSCRIPT

Are Asian Americans a "Model Minority"?

Which point of view do you support? An increasing number of social scientists are beginning to question the model minority label, and some are rejecting it as inaccurate, as Takaki does. Yet there are a number of achievements by Asian Americans that on the surface would appear to set them apart from other ethnic minorities.

A serious problem for many Asian Americans, especially newcomers, is their experiences as so-called middleman minorities. That is, like Chinese in parts of Asia outside of China, many first-generation Asian Americans, especially Koreans, provide food and other services for the inner-city poor through the small businesses they run. This is an important function. The poor need these services desperately. For the merchant, rents are cheap. Initial capital for stock is relatively small. The market is there. Required skills are minimal (counting and shelving, for example). Thus, a disproportionately high number of immigrants have seized the advantage and opened stores in ghetto areas. Many poorer or less skilled Eastern European Jews, Italians, and others have followed this pattern.

These merchants are considered middlemen because they are not fully members of the poor neighborhoods in which they locate their businesses, but neither are they accepted into the dominant society. In order to keep expenses down, many such middleman merchants staff their stores with members of their own families. They rarely live in the area, and they close their stores at night to return home, often to an equally poor area but in another neighborhood.

There is enormous stress between lower-class, frequently first-generation Asian Americans and poorer urban Blacks and, to a lesser extent, Hispanics. If a merchant has limited mastery of English, customers sometimes experience this as rudeness or disrespect. The close scrutiny and matter-of-fact efficiency of middleman minorities can be seen by customers as suspicious and unfriendly behavior. Charging higher prices for items because of the high cost of insurance for inner-city businesses is viewed as ripping off poor neighborhood people. The hiring of only family members is proof to some that these merchants do not like the locals; that, and their living in other areas.

At another level of analysis, if the model minority notion of Asian Americans is a myth, what might its functions be? How might claiming that one group is a model minority tie into blaming other groups for their particular problems, such as unemployment and poverty? Drawing from Takaki and your own thinking, what might be some of the unanticipated negative consequences of a positive myth, such as Asian Americans being a model minority?

Among the many works of Takaki on this subject are *Strangers at the Gates Again: Asian American Immigration After 1965* (Chelsea House, 1995) and *Breaking Silences: Asian Americans Today* (Chelsea House, 1995). An interesting account of one Asian group that has recently arrived in America, the Hmong, is Wendy Walker-Moffat's *The Other Side of the Asian American Success Story* (Jossey-Bass, 1995). An analysis of the largest Asian group in the United States is Maria P. Root, ed., *Filipino Americans: Transforming Identity* (Sage Publications, 1998). Studies that contrast Asians with other minorities include E. Kim, " 'At Least You're Not Black': Asian Americans in U.S. Race Relations," *Social Justice* (Fall 1998); Pamela Constable, "Misperceived Minorities: 'Good' and 'Bad' Stereotypes Saddle Hispanics and Asian Americans," *Washington Post National Weekly Edition* (October 23–29, 1995); and Jonathan Tilove, "Asian-American History Rises Above Pitfalls for Trail of Success," in Paula S. Rothenberg, ed., *Race, Class, and Gender in the United States: An Integrated Study*, 4th ed. (St. Martin's Press, 1998). Christopher G. Ellison and W. Allen Martin's edited book *Race and Ethnic Relations in the United States: Readings for the Twenty-First Century* (Vipassana, 1997) contains a helpful study that directly addresses the issue, W. Hurh and Kwang Kim's "The 'Success' Image of Asian Americans," and an empirical analysis of one Asian group, I. Yoon's "The Growth of Korean Immigrant Entrepreneurship in Chicago."

Another article that reviews stereotyping is "Stereotyping by the Media: Framing Asian Americans," by T. Nakayama, in Coramae R. Mann and Marjorie S. Zatz, *Images of Color, Images of Crime* (Roxbury, 1998).

Comparisons of Asian groups with other minorities include "Differences in the Process of Self-Employment Among Whites, Blacks, and Asians," by J. Tang, *Sociological Perspectives* (vol. 18, no. 2, 1995); "Ethnicity and Political Participation: A Comparison Between Asian and Mexican Americans," *Political Behavior* (June 1, 1994); P. Abrantes, "The Impact of Race and Culture on Adolescent Girls: Four Perspectives," *Women's Health Issues* (Summer 1994); and K. Park, "The Re-Invention of Affirmative Action: Korean Immigrants' Changing Conceptions of African Americans and Latin Americans," *Urban Anthropology* (vol. 24, nos. 1–2, 1995).

For discussions somewhat paralleling that of Bell, see A. Allen's "To Be Successful You Have to Deal With Reality," *Vital Speeches of the Day* (February 15, 1993) and the essay "Asians" in Jared Taylor's *Paved With Good Intentions: The Failure of Race Relations in Contemporary America* (Carroll & Graf, 1992). Also see P. Kim's "Myths and Realities of the Model Minority," *Public Manager* (Fall 1994). An interesting film on the "success" story of one Asian society is *South Korea: Inside the Miracle*, produced by Films for the Humanities and Science.

For an outstanding though somewhat more general discussion of middleman minorities, see Edna Bonacich, "A Theory of Middleman Minorities," *American Sociological Review* (vol. 38, 1983).

ISSUE 3

Is Judging Thomas Jefferson and Others Chronocentrically Unfair?

YES: H. L. Goldstein, from "Thomas Jefferson, Sally, DNA and Cuckoldry," *The Baltimore Chronicle* (January 1999)

NO: Brent Staples, from "Revelations Add to Mystery of Jefferson," *The Baltimore Sun* (November 5, 1998)

ISSUE SUMMARY

YES: Freelance writer H. L. Goldstein briefly traces the controversy surrounding the recent disclosure that DNA evidence may confirm that Thomas Jefferson's slave Sally Hemings bore his children. Goldstein attacks the interpretations of the DNA findings as unfair chronocentrism that legitimizes a feeding frenzy on a former icon and that tells us nothing about race relations.

NO: Brent Staples, an editorial writer for the *New York Times*, argues that genetic evidence proves that Jefferson was a racist and a hypocrite who talked one game (democracy, fairness, and liberty) but played another (oppression and exploitation). Although he acknowledges that Jefferson's behavior probably was similar to that of other slave owners, Staples finds Jefferson's attacks on Blacks appalling.

Sexual access to those in subordinate status positions has served several functions throughout history, whether the contact was heterosexual or (less common) homosexual. In the latter case, when the act resulted because of unequal power relations among men—such as currently sometimes occurs in prisons where tougher or better organized inmates "have a go" at a weaker one—the act defiles the weaker person. In the past the victim became the "woman" of the aggressor. When women in subordinate positions were used by dominant males, the relations were considerably more complex. Not only were subordinate peoples whose females were sexually exploited insulted and humiliated, but such easy access reinforced the traditional low status of females in all societies. To survive, female slaves in the antebellum South often attempted to use the relations to better themselves and any children that resulted from their encounters.

The offspring from slave-master relations in most of the South technically and legally had *no status* other than that of slaves. Yet, socially, relations are almost always complicated, especially those pertaining to sex and resulting offspring. They may be infused with intense affection; they may informally bind (in this case) Black and white families whose blood runs together; and they may be a source of pride and advantage for the mistress, her children, and her family. However, such relations might also be a source of extreme cruelty, such as when the master elects to sell his own children or their mother. They could also result in conflict and envy among other slaves, who might ridicule resulting children as "high yellow" and other demeaning terms. At best, at least by 1990s standards, the legitimate wife and her children would experience an ambivalent relationship with the usually open knowledge that their father and husband had relations, if not bonded, with a slave whose children were their half siblings. Meanwhile, the dominant white male in that system would have his wife and legitimate family as well as a slave mistress (almost always young and attractive), who could be, unlike his wife, exchanged for another almost instantly.

While Thomas Jefferson was ridiculed by his enemies in his lifetime for his alleged relation with his slave Sally Hemings, on many plantations it was generally understood that planters and especially their teenage sons (as well as other whites, such as overseers) could take sexual advantage of female slaves at will. The fact that a slave's brothers, father, mother, the slave that she loved, and possibly her own children had to acquiesce to such an arrangement functioned to further maintain Blacks in an ontologically inferior status position (a term used by sociologist Peter Berger, meaning people whose very existence was considered less than human).

For over 150 years historians and others have debated the Jefferson/Hemings relationship. Was she his mistress? Were some or all of her children his as well? Recently DNA testing on a sample of known descendants of Hemings and Jefferson's uncle revealed a match between the Jefferson line and Sally's youngest son, Eston (1808–1852). This, however, is not proof that Jefferson fathered any of her children, including Eston. Yet many are willing to attack Jefferson as a liar and a hypocrite. His many political and scientific achievements are now under attack. After all, who wants to look up to a racist who sexually abused a powerless Black female for dozens of years?

However, according to H. L. Goldstein in the following selection, the morality play generated by seemingly conclusive scientific proof (DNA evidence) linked with contemporary society's sensitivity to minority issues may merely be one myth replacing another. For generations people were taught to—and indeed many *wanted* to—believe in white superiority and Black inferiority. Goldstein suggests that people are exchanging that conceptual baggage for the far more subtle but equally absurd myth that most of what happened in the past was bad, especially when it involved powerful figures in U.S. history. Brent Staples counters that Jefferson did terrible things and lied about them. To him, revealing this is not unfair.

As you read this particular variant of the debate, consider the idea of "chronocentrism" (to be centered in time or one's own generation). To be chronocentric is to judge those in different times with your time's or generation's standards. Is this fair?

YES

H. L. Goldstein

THOMAS JEFFERSON, SALLY, DNA AND CUCKOLDRY

Media pundits, talk show philistines, Black scholars, minority group hustlers, savvy politicians, the perpetually morally outraged, and the just plain angry—along with the other usual suspects filled with diffuse grievances—have rounded up to attack yet another icon and legend, speculating on the Thomas Jefferson-Sally Hemings relationship. Yet that story is infused with contradictions and paradoxes. The fact that half-truths are being 'legitimized' by DNA evidence makes the use of reason especially important.

Thomas Jefferson (1743–1826), third president of the U.S. (1800–1808), author of the Declaration of Independence and numerous other political and scientific documents that remain the envy of the world, has been 'proved beyond a reasonable doubt' to have fathered at least one son with his alleged slave-mistress, Sally Hemings (1772–1836). "I cannot tell a lie," scream recent DNA tests performed on several groups of people who logically might be related to Jefferson.

At least, that is what the deaf want to hear. But the DNA tests, while impressive and lending credence to the oft-repeated tale of Tom and Sally, remain inconclusive and prove nothing.

THE RESEARCH

Retired University of Virginia pathology professor Dr. Eugene A. Foster decided to research the Jefferson-Sally connection through DNA testing. The results appear in a recent issue of *Nature* magazine. Foster ingeniously compared five different groups of males to determine if their sampled DNA was similar or the same.

Since Thomas Jefferson himself had no known legitimate male descendants (his wife Martha bore six children between 1772 and her death in 1782, but only two daughters lived to adulthood), Foster sampled direct descendants of Jefferson's uncle, Field Jefferson.

Next he sampled male descendants of Thomas, Sally Hemings' first child (1790–1879), and those of Eston, Sally's last child (1808–1852). Her other five children either died early or 'disappeared' by passing as white.

Descendants of Jefferson's nephews, long thought to have been responsible for Sally's children, were tested. For good measure, a passel of white descendants of Monticello's neighbors were also tested, in case their forefathers might have contaminated the Monticello flock.

The results were surprising. First, the nephews' heirs did not match any of the others. Neither did the neighbors' descendants, or even Tom, the first-born son. However, Foster found that there *was* a match between the male descendants of Uncle Field Jefferson and those of Sally's youngest son, Eston. (The latter, by the way, live in New York and have long since passed for white. Indeed, they had no knowledge until recently that they were related to either Jefferson or his slave.)

This is all most interesting, as a European detective might say. Next to fingerprints, one of the greatest breakthroughs in criminal identification is DNA testing. If there's a match, you did it.

In the matter of DNA genetic tracing, it is also clear-cut, but with some qualifications. First, such linkages have to be traced through males in the family to determine if the Y chromosomes of the groups being tested match. Frequently in doing such scientific work the hardest part is obtaining samples of the Y chromosome (present in blood). Because Thomas Jefferson's only legitimate male child died in infancy, a *direct* comparison between his and Sally's offspring could not be made.

Foster, as indicated, analyzed DNA from *other* male members of the Jefferson clan (Uncle Field's descendants) and compared them with samples from Sally's male descendants to see if a *Jefferson* fathered them.

The fact that Field Jefferson's descendants and those of Eston matched, along with the historical fact of Thomas Jefferson and Sally's 'closeness' for almost 40 years, logically points to his having sired at least Eston. Yet—and this is both important and utterly ignored by the mob—there still is *no conclusive proof.* Not even close to it.

Reached at his home in Charlottesville on Nov. 19, Dr. Foster candidly said, "I do not claim conclusively that Thomas Jefferson was the father."

He maintains that while the probability is high of Jefferson's being the father of Eston (and the other children), other explanations are possible for the link between Eston's descendants and those of Field Jefferson.

DISREGARDING FINDINGS

Unfortunately, many so-called social science scholars, journalists, and others are not so cautious. Perhaps one should not expect those with either a commercial or political (or both) agenda to even feign fairness.

There has been almost complete disregard of the tentative nature of the DNA findings. For example, in a lengthy and often excellent article in *U.S. News & World Report*, the reader is misled with dubious assertions such as "one can say with certainty" or "now that it is proven beyond any reasonable doubt" that Jefferson fathered Sally's son.

Mixed with the incredible media bandwagoning is the embarrassing ignorance displayed by writers of even assumedly first-rate publications. For instance, a *New*

York Times columnist misinforms us in his lead sentence that "geneticists have turned up a match between a descendant of Thomas Jefferson and an offspring of Sally Hemings..." But they did no such thing. They found a match between his relatives and Sally's last son. Jefferson had no known male descendants; hence they could not find a match taken directly from him.

The *Times'* sloppy writer continues, "The case shows that Jefferson lied about sex..." *Jefferson did no such thing.* His well-known stance was simply to refuse to discuss the issue. Maybe he and Sally felt it was no one's business.

In another spate of misinformation, the columnist informs us that Sally bore at least five children. The correct figure is at least seven (Tom, Eddy, Harriet, Beverly, another Harriet, Madison and Eston). His pathetic inaccuracies and half truths quickly descend into historical slander. For example, the writer—now playing psychiatrist—says Jefferson's "lust was being satisfied with Sally Hemings."

Even a freshman editor would have pointed out the sheer ugliness of such claims stated in the 'lust' context. But what the hell, it's a hot story, we've got a dead hero to attack with virtual moral and intellectual impunity, the 'writer' is 'just a columnist,' and the publication is only the NY *Times.*

BLATANT RACISM

There is also blatant racism implicit in the 'explanation' for why Tom, Sally's oldest son, has no known descendants whose DNA samples match Field Jefferson's. As one writer tried to explain, "Tom... still may have been Jefferson's son... The negative may have resulted from an unknown male—an illegitimate father— breaking the Y chromosome chain."

Yes, but this is equally true for Jefferson's male relatives—e.g., his nephews, Peter and Samuel Carr, who could have had access to Sally and were apparently known to be rakes. Dr. Foster found that the nephews' descendants' DNA did not match that of Eston's descendants. But while their white Virginia husbands were off amusing themselves, the Jefferson wives would have had plenty of time to break the DNA chain. Why do the media pundits willingly hypothesize that Tom—Sally the slave's son—and/or his descendants' spouses might have had 'an illegitimate father,' but do not apply this same logic to white women?

CHRONO-CENTRISM

Our 'reporters' here are superimposing the standards of our own time and circumstances upon the actions and attitudes of people in other historical periods. Examples of this chrono-centrism abound. One is the absurd chorus of chants that love between Tom and Sally was not 'possible' because of her legal/political status. It would seem that each generation works out in its own way partial resolutions of the universal conditions of love and loneliness. Hence to judge Sally and Tom by what spews from our daytime TV sit-coms and talk shows is curious.

Another example of chrono-centrism is the constant reference to Sally as a "Black woman" or "Black slave." In spite of her legal status, factually Sally was at least 'one half white' and possibly even more. Her father was Jefferson's wife's father, known as a white man, and her mother was a slave who may have been partially white. Several of Sally's children and/or their descendants passed as white. The charges that Jefferson was a hypocrite because of his later tirades against racial 'amalgamation,' as horrid by today's standards as they are, may simply reflect not inconsistencies or lies, but his viewing Sally as white, though a slave.

None of this is meant to excuse any aspect of slavery or racial inequality, but simply to try to understand it in context. Scholars and journalists in the 1990s have no such categories by which to make sense out of this aspect of life in the 1700s.

Jefferson was approximately 66 and Sally was 36 when their alleged son, Eston, was born in 1808. This may put to lie the charge that Sally was his child mistress.

Scholars from Harvard U. to Howard U. comment bitterly and freely on Jefferson's hypocrisy. Yet they conveniently ignore the same problem existing in 1998 in Sudan in Africa and part of Asia, among other areas. Human beings are *currently* being sold and purchased. Now. Period.

Vigorously attacking Jefferson while remaining oblivious to the same—or possibly even worse problems—in the world today is totally unconscionable. If the Jefferson-baiting 'scholar' at Harvard or Hopkins or Howard also is "Black," then the hypocrisy might even be worse, since he or she may very well be building a career with attacks on historical racism and slavery, living *off* Blacks and other minorities, not *for* them.

(To some extent, this particular irony applies equally to scholars of the Holocaust, who commendably collect monies, grants, and funds for research on WWII genocide and worthwhile memorials, but remain mysteriously silent about genocide in Europe, Asia and Africa in the 1990s.)

We have not even attempted here to delineate the possible meanings that Tom and Sally 'really' had for each other. We do, though, sharply question the constructed meanings assigned to Jefferson by the many who suffer from bad history, bad science, and worse, chrono-centric naiveté, if not shameless hypocrisy.

NO

Brent Staples

REVELATIONS ADD TO MYSTERY OF JEFFERSON

Historians are spinning in their armchairs over the news that geneticists have turned up a match between a descendant of Thomas Jefferson and an offspring of Sally Hemings, the slave rumored for two centuries to have had a long-running affair with America's most celebrated president. Hero worshipers argued violently that the affair had not taken place, seeing Jefferson as pristine and above sex—not just with a slave, but with anyone other than his wife. Faced with rumor and innuendo—and no physical evidence—even historians who believed in the affair took the position that we would never know the truth.

The case shows that Jefferson lied about sex in the last century just as William Jefferson Clinton did in this one. It also vindicates people like the historian Fawn Brodie and the novelist Barbara Chase-Riboud who were scorned as lust peddlers for thinking the master and the slave had an affair. But from a historical standpoint, the proof that Jefferson slept with Sally Hemings brings almost nothing to our understanding of Jefferson, Hemings or the system of plantation slavery that brought them into contact.

JEFFERSON IN PARIS

The Jefferson-Hemings story begins in the 1780s in Paris, when Jefferson, bereaved at the death of his wife, accepted the post of ambassador to France. Dashing Sally, as visitors called her at Monticello, arrived in Paris in 1786 accompanying Jefferson's daughter. But once back at Monticello, Sally bore at least five children, beginning with Tom in 1790 and ending with Eston in 1808.

Historians argued that Jefferson's "basic character" made him immune to illicit sex. Joseph Ellis suggested in his most recent book that Jefferson sublimated his sex drive into architecture, making Monticello a perpetual work in progress that was built and rebuilt almost up to the day he died. Mr. Ellis and others also note that none of Jefferson's many thousands of letters mentioned Hemings or contained even a hint of lust. What we now know is that this lust was being satisfied with Sally Hemings.

Bear in mind as well that Hemings and Jefferson's wife were half-sisters, fathered by the same plantation owner. Raised in the same household, they would have had similar tastes, and they may have had similar features. It is easy to imagine Jefferson, widowed and lonely, cleaving to a young replica of his dead wife. That he reached out to Sally is understandable. But it makes him neither better nor worse than his father-in-law, and thousands of other slave masters (and slave mistresses, too) who took slave lovers within plain view of the neighboring gentry.

Some modern observers assume that Sally was a passive victim of forced intercourse. Rape was a constant hazard on the plantation. But well-positioned slave women who crossed racial lines often did so to improve their children's chances of survival. Mulatto children often prospered during and after slavery because they were literate, professionally aggressive and thought themselves the equals of whites—all of which they acquired through close proximity to the plantation elite. Hemings would have known these tactics well.

If the utilitarian version of this relationship does not suit you, consider the loving quasi-marriage depicted by Ms. Chase-Riboud or in the Merchant Ivory film "Jefferson in Paris." If we assume that Hemings loved Jefferson, she got some of what she wanted: a loving relationship and valuable education and trades for her children. What she could never have was full stature as a partner.

But this version introduces a riddle about Jefferson's racism, which grew coarser and more intractable over time. Jefferson started out as a cautious believer in abolition, but retreated steadily from the position, thinking that slavery needed to be kept intact in part to preclude race mixing. The notion that he developed and hardened these attitudes while having a truly loving relationship with a black woman seems implausible. If this is what happened, Jefferson was more conflicted and self-deceptive than we knew.

BIGOTED VIEWS

A few people will see something redemptive in the fact that Jefferson fathered children with a black woman. But nothing done in bed would atone for the fiercely bigoted views of black people put forth in "Notes on the State of Virginia." The most committed racists reveled in illicit sex in the slave quarters.

Among our presidents, Thomas Jefferson has been the most controversial and paradoxical. When Americans speak of him, they elaborate a personal relationship with the founding father who conjured democracy out of nothing—or the mere mortal who failed to break the chains of slavery, poisoning the Republic's future. [The recent] disclosure adds to the mystery of Jefferson but does nothing to solve it.

POSTSCRIPT

Is Judging Thomas Jefferson and Others Chronocentrically Unfair?

This controversial issue touches on several aspects of both the sociology of knowledge and historiography (methods and theory of writing history). On one hand, why are so many so willing to assume the worst about someone who arguably provided America with the most passionate defenses of liberty and free speech? Even if Hemings were Jefferson's mistress and she bore him at least one child, is it silly to judge him by contemporary standards, let alone pretend to know what the *meaning* of their relationship was to them? Or is iconoclasm functional in that it can ensure that such behavior can never happen again and that those who abuse minorities will never again be viewed as noble?

The historiographical issue concerns the emerging novel use of biology to resolve historical questions. In the O. J. Simpson murder trial, for example, DNA evidence was introduced, but the jury apparently ignored it. Is such evidence being properly used here, or, as Dr. Eugene A. Foster told Goldstein, has his research been badly misunderstood? Do we want to enshrine any minority member or situation to make us somehow feel superior to those whose conduct we judge by our standards to be wrong? As a corollary of this, can the classic sociologist Emile Durkheim's thesis that crime is functional because it makes the rest of us feel morally superior to criminals be extended to say that condemnation of others' behavior, especially that occurring in the past, is functional because it makes us feel morally superior?

Another relevant sociology of knowledge and historiographical question is, why did so many historians bitterly reject the notion that Jefferson might have had a relationship with someone who was Black? Many such scholars termed such assertions "filth" and maintained that Jefferson was a "gentleman," implying that he would not "stoop" to such behavior. Others insisted that the rumors were lies spread by Blacks to "make themselves elevated." Why did American historians, independent of the veracity of the rumors, allow such racism in their profession? Moreover, as Goldstein asks, why do so many assume that if the DNA link were broken, making it impossible to trace descendants to Jefferson, that the break occurred because Black mothers had extramarital relations but white mothers did not?

Staples implies that Hemings might have entered freely into a relationship with Jefferson to advance herself. Many feminists would be scandalized by this assertion and would insist that because Hemings was owned by Jefferson, nothing about their relationship was voluntary. Who is right? Goldstein is bothered that many who attack Jefferson are tragically silent about slavery in Sudan or genocide in Europe, Asia, and parts of Africa. Why might this be so? If you could travel back to 1800 to interview Jefferson, what would you ask him? Hemings? Her children? Jefferson's "legitimate" daughter? What might you discover that would indicate that your initial thinking was chronocentric? How might your descendants 150 years from now judge you in terms of minority relations? How can we strive—or should we strive—to transcend chronocentrism?

A good account that was published almost immediately following the disclosure of the alleged DNA link is the series of articles in *U.S. News and World Report* (November 8, 1998), especially "Did the Author of the Declaration of Independence Take a Slave for a Mistress? DNA Tests Say Yes," by M. Murray and B. Duffy. Also see "Grand Illusion," by Richard Cohen, *The Washington Post Magazine* (December 13, 1998) and "Three Perspectives on America's Jefferson Fixation," by Andrew Burstein, Nancy Isenberg, and Annette Gordon-Reed, *The Nation* (November 30, 1998). An interesting feminist view is voiced in Ellen Goodman's "The Key Issue Remains That He Owned Her," *The Baltimore Sun* (November 5, 1998). A shocking new take is "Did Jefferson Also Father Children by Sally Hemings' Sister?" by L. Randolph, *Ebony* (February 1999). For an update that largely supports Goldstein's concerns, see "Journal Editors Clarify, Defend DNA Study of Jefferson's Descendants," *The Washington Post* (January 6, 1999).

For radically different views of the Founders and slavery, see "Slavery and the Founders: Telling the Truth During Black History Month," by Dinesh D'Souza, *Weekly Standard* (February 3, 1997) and N. E. Magnis, "Thomas Jefferson and Slavery," *Journal of Black Studies* (March 1999).

ISSUE 4

Is the "End of Racism" Thesis Badly Flawed?

YES: Glenn C. Loury, from "The End of Relativism," *The Weekly Standard* (September 25, 1995)

NO: Dinesh D'Souza, from "Let Me Say What the Book Is About," *The Weekly Standard* (October 2, 1995)

ISSUE SUMMARY

YES: Glenn C. Loury, a professor of economics and a noted race relations writer, charges that Dinesh D'Souza's theory that racism is not an essential component of the problems of Blacks is flawed and dangerously close to being racist itself.

NO: Dinesh D'Souza, a research fellow at the American Enterprise Institute and a social critic, defends his controversial thesis that racism is a thing of the past and argues that Loury has misunderstood his ideas.

In 1903 the preeminent Black sociologist W. E. B. Du Bois (1868–1963) stated, "The problem of the twentieth century will be the problem of the color line." Since then, many scholars have attributed whites' mistreatment of Blacks to the pervasiveness of racism. Racism is a highly developed ideological system legitimizing and, until recently, legally codifying highly negative attitudes toward and actions against a race of people. Racism has existed as both a blatant set of customs—such as forced segregation, miscegenation laws, and "proper" racial etiquette—and a subtle mind-set that is fervently maintained.

Undoubtedly, most of the blatant legal and other institutional supports of overt discrimination in the United States have been reduced significantly since the 1960s. Yet liberals and radicals maintain that the pernicious results of almost 400 years of racism still linger in America's institutions and social structures. A growing number of intellectuals argue, for example, that countless Black females are trapped inside inner cities due to ineffective and misguided welfare programs, lack of training, and continuing discrimination.

Historically, racism is a relatively new mind-set. Although differing groups of people have competed, fought, hurt, and disliked each other because they were different, it wasn't until the 1600s that northern Europeans produced an elaborate conceptual frame of reference that functioned to symbolically deny the humanity of Black people. At that time, many scientists and ministers conspired with slave traders and plantation owners to define Blacks as "heathens," "biologically inferior," and so on. Initially, this helped to justify in the Europeans' minds the horrible acts committed against the Blacks. Entire African tribes, as well as families, were torn apart as slave hunters rounded up, transported, and then auctioned off Black human beings in America. The slaves were transported across the Atlantic Ocean on unsanitary, crowded ships, and up to one-third of them perished during the journey. Although no group had a monopoly on this savage conduct, it was the Europeans who developed racism as a doctrine.

After 1865, when the slaves in the United States were freed, racism led to the legal segregation of, discrimination against, and sometimes the lynching of Black people. Even the definition of the word *Negro* became more narrow, reflecting the new racism. Many states in the 1800s adopted different categories of Blacks reflecting different degrees of privileges and rights. These ranged from "slave" (virtually no rights) to "free colored," "mulatto," and "octoroon" (a person of mixed ancestry). In some states, whites were allowed to marry individuals who had up to one-eighth "Negro blood" and who were free. However, in the 1920s, some southern states made it illegal for a white person to marry an individual with even a "drop of Negro blood." Miscegenation laws such as this were not declared unconstitutional until the 1960s.

Despite an extensive history of racism against Blacks in the United States, Dinesh D'Souza, in his provocative 1995 book *The End of Racism: Principles for a Multiracial Society*, argues that racism does not exist in the 1990s. He maintains that problems of the Black community that are commonly attributed to racism are in fact rooted in Blacks' cultural defects. In a purported effort to promote a race-neutral society, D'Souza supports abandoning programs based on multiculturalism and affirmative action and confronting Black cultural pathologies so that Blacks can become more competitive with other groups in society.

In the following selections, Glenn C. Loury takes D'Souza to task for what he considers to be racist ideas in themselves. D'Souza responds with a defense of his book and his thesis, arguing that Loury misrepresents the book's arguments. It is interesting to note the similarities between the opposing authors. Both Loury and D'Souza are conservative intellectuals, both are highly critical of affirmative action programs and Blacks who do not try to help themselves, and both are critical of Black crime and violence as well as liberals who attempt to "excuse" black criminal behavior as a result of racism. In addition, both are racial minorities (Loury is African American, and D'Souza is a native of Bombay, India, who characterizes himself as a "person of color").

As you read these selections, identify areas of agreement between Loury and D'Souza. At what point do their ideologies deviate from one another? Can the problems of Blacks and whites be understood independently of racism?

YES

Glenn C. Loury

THE END OF RELATIVISM

Dinesh D'Souza is sure to generate controversy with his new book, *The End of Racism: Principles for a Multiracial Society* (Free Press, 724 pages, $30). His dismissive attack on "liberal antiracism" will drive civil rights advocates and their political sympathizers to apoplexy. It will be denounced as a dangerously racist tract by every Afrocentrist demagogue still able to draw a crowd.

The publisher's publicity calls *The End of Racism* a "sweeping" and "bold" book that "challenges the last taboo" about racism. And the book is laced with incendiary sentences, like this one: "If America as a nation owes blacks as a group reparations for slavery, what do blacks as a group owe America for the abolition of slavery?" And this: "It is hard not to hear the triumphant roar of the white supremacist: 'Forget about the legacy of racism and discrimination: these people are naturally stupid.'" Chapter titles, too. One section on behavioral problems among poor blacks is entitled "Uncle Tom's Dilemma: Pathologies of Black Culture." Another discusses race and IQ under the heading "The Content of Our Chromosomes."

The controversy will not be limited to turns of phrase; the ideas, too, are explosive. D'Souza claims that most middle class blacks owe their prosperity to affirmative action, and then speculates they must suffer "intense feelings of guilt" because "they have abandoned their poor brothers and sisters, and realize that their present circumstances became possible solely because of the heart-wrenching sufferings of the underclass." And in a pithy turn of phrase that really ought not to have got past his editors, he ridicules those who are afraid that Nazi-like crimes could result if belief in the biological inferiority of blacks were to become widespread: such people, he writes, "employ the *reductio ad Hitlerum*—an argument is necessarily false if Hitler happened to share the same view."

If one were to adopt the voice used by D'Souza throughout the book, one might speculate that he actually longs to hear those "triumphant roars," from black and white racists alike, because such vitriolic discussion sells books. But *ad hominem* (or is it *ad Hitlerum*?) rhetoric like that is unbecoming. Suffice it to say that, by examining this book's reception—how it is attacked and by whom it is defended—one will learn a great deal about the true, and unbearably sad, nature of race relations in our society. More, perhaps, than can be learned from a careful study of its pages.

Which is not to say the book has no argument. But much that is compelling in it has been said before, more carefully, and with greater dignity. D'Souza restates the devastating critique of civil rights orthodoxy developed by Thomas Sowell in a number of books starting two decades ago. Sowell noted that, because ethnic groups are endowed with unequal cultures, histories, and temperaments, group disparities per se do not prove the existence of discrimination. He argued that racism need not lead to discrimination; that segregation did not necessarily connote a belief in racial inferiority or redound to the detriment of blacks; and that in any case, belief in the innate inferiority of a group is neither necessary nor sufficient for the existence of inter-group conflict. Sowell observed that the use of group stereotypes is a universal, rational, human behavior, and refuted a host of assertions about the relevance to contemporary moral debates of American slavery. He emphasized the self-serving character of much civil rights advocacy. And, most important, he exposed, and rejected as incoherent, the implicit assumptions—what he called "the vision"—underlying the legal and policy claims of civil rights proponents.

What is best in The End of Racism updates and embellishes these Sowellian themes. But D'Souza aspires to be a social thinker in his own right; indeed, his title recalls the Hegelian tone of Francis Fukuyama's The End of History and the Last Man, the acclaimed volume on the deeper meaning of the collapse of communism. D'Souza, also looking for broad historical forces, reasons that if we can understand how racism came into the modern world,

then perhaps, as with communism, we can envision its end.

He finds that racism originated five centuries ago, when Europe emerged as the world's dominant economic and technological civilization. At the same time, Europeans encountered the more backward peoples of Asia, the Americas, and especially sub-Saharan Africa. The obvious disparity of accomplishment between different peoples led many Europeans to explain their dominance as the result of their biological superiority. Thus was racism born, a product of Western reason, the result of a rational effort to account for certain conspicuous facts. As historian Winthrop Jordan has put it, "racism developed in conjunction with Enlightenment, not in resistance to it."

So much the worse for Enlightenment, one might say, but D'Souza does not think so. He really believes this obvious historical point is relevant to contemporary racial debates. How? Because it gives the lie to the liberal claim that racism must be the result of ignorance, fear, or superstition. Quoting Hume ("I... suspect the Negroes... to be naturally inferior to the whites"), Kant ("The Negroes... have received from nature no intelligence that rises above the foolish"), and Hegel ("The Negro race has perfect contempt for humanity"), D'Souza declares: "These views pose a problem to mainstream scholars today... because they call the widely shared premises of modern antiracism into question." Unlike those liberals, D'Souza see nobility in historic racism: "[It] reflected the highest ethical ideals of the most enlightened sectors of society. It was a progressive view. Opposition to it was considered to be a sign of ignorance or religious dogmatism." This would make the old liberal epithet, "ignorant racist," an oxymoron.

Never mind that one after another of these "enlightened" racial claims proved to be wrong, and that, across the globe and over the centuries, great crimes against humanity were perpetrated because of these claims, crimes denounced by "religious dogmatists" even as they were being carried out. The Enlightenment was not an unqualified success for humanism, as John Paul II never tires of saying, and as the tortuous history of scientific racism makes clear. But D'Souza is too concerned with the shortcomings of "liberal antiracism" to dwell on a simple ethical truth: the intellectual, military, or economic achievements of a civilization do not confer moral worth, or moral wisdom, on its constituents.

* * *

Curiously, given its subject, this book is devoid of serious moral argument. D'Souza has discovered that slavery was not a racist institution, as today's liberals charge. Why? Because there were black slaveholders (a fact he finds "morally disturbing"); because only the West made the ethics of slavery an issue; and because the belief in black inferiority arose, in part, to justify a practice inconsistent with cherished American ideals. Though these points are not without interest, stating them only begins an argument; many issues remain unresolved,

If a tiny fraction of all slaveholders, but every one of the millions of slaves, were black, how is the notion that slavery was a system of racial domination thereby refuted? Which is more compelling—that Western ideals existed, or that they went unrealized? After all, the issue is not whether America is morally superior to Saudi Arabia, but whether America is all

it can and should be. If belief in black inferiority arose for complex reasons, it is nonetheless a pernicious doctrine that has never been strictly scientific in character. Moreover, it is a doctrine with far-reaching and genuinely disturbing moral implications. What, pray tell, is wrong with a strong presumption against it?

* * *

It is inarguably the case that absent the deeply committed, religiously motivated protests of abolitionists, slavery might well have survived into the 20th century. It is also inarguable that without the moralistic efforts of the liberal antiracists who founded the NAACP, fought the Ku Klux Klan, and laid the foundation for the modern civil rights movement, the caste-like subordination of blacks might still be a fact of life in America. D'Souza knows all of this, but he is not moved by it. What excites him is the chance to score points against his political enemies, the contemporary civil rights establishment.

To this end, he advances a peculiar (and weak) anthropological argument. According to D'Souza, the dual racial scourges of our day—affirmative action and black social pathology—share a common intellectual heritage with the ideology of antiracism. This heritage is rooted in the idea of "cultural relativism," made popular by the anthropologist Franz Boas and his students in the early decades of this century. Mr. D'Souza refers to this purportedly bankrupt perspective as "Boasian relativism." Because of its attachment to these ideas, the civil rights movement and its liberal allies have failed their black constituents and, D'Souza fears, now threaten to ruin American civilization. If ever we are to see the end of racism, we must first abandon the doctrine of Boasian relativism.

D'Souza's reasoning goes like this: Boasian relativism is the idea that all cultures are inherently equal, and in particular, that Western culture is neither better nor worse than any other. Hence, a true relativist expects people from different groups to succeed equally in American society, unless they are artificially held back. Since blacks have not succeeded to the same extent as whites and Asians, the relativist simply must conclude that blacks are the victims of racism, and that American society must be reformed, by coercion if necessary, to secure the just outcome. And the relativist cannot believe that pathological social behavior among blacks reflects their lack of culture and civilization, since it is axiomatic to him that all cultures are equal. Hence, the relativist cannot condemn such behavior as uncivilized; he can only view it as the result of failures in American society.

Complaining about Boasian relativism, D'Souza writes: "Other cultures are automatically viewed on the same plane as the West; minority groups are entitled to a presumption of moral and intellectual equality with whites; no group, whether blacks in America or aborigines in Australia, can be considered inferior."

D'Souza makes a horrific error by suggesting that blacks in an urban ghetto are part of a culture separate from the rest of America. By likening them to aborigines in the outback of Australia, he denies the truth and tragedy of their existence: Inner-city blacks are intimately connected to the culture of American society, influencing it and being influenced by it in turn.

But D'Souza is utterly determined to place poor urban blacks outside the orbit of American civilization. Their lives

are governed by barbarism; they are the enemy within. This is wrongheaded. The sociologist Elijah Anderson, reporting on the moral life of poor urban blacks, has stressed again and again that these communities are full of decent people, with values no different from D'Souza's or my own, who struggle against long odds to live in dignity. Of course pathology lurks there—and it is a uniquely *American* pathology.

The youth movement of the 1960s, with its celebration of drugs and sex, and its cult of irresponsibility, was no invention of black culture. For example, the huge demand for cocaine in this country can hardly be taken as an expression of the uncivilized tastes of the ghetto poor. With suburban whites buying more rap music than ghetto blacks, with the purveyors of jeans and sneakers betting billions on their ability to move the urban market this way or that, with radical feminists, gay activists, and liberal jurists exerting their influence for better or worse on the context in which all American families now function, how would the question even arise in our society as to whether "minority groups are entitled to moral equality with whites"?

*   *   *

Lest the reader misunderstand, I share D'Souza's rejection of the political program of the civil rights leadership. I agree that affirmative action must go, that behavioral problems in the ghetto must be confronted, that discrimination is no longer the primary obstacle to black progress, and that the idealism and moral authority of the historic crusade against racism have been squandered by liberal activists over the past three decades. But I reject, wholeheartedly and with intense fervor, his effort to draw a moral line down through the heart of my country, placing those he deems civilized on one side, and leaving the barbaric to the other. Is it not a measure of the quality of *American* civilization that so many of our "brothers and sisters," of all colors, live amidst squalor, in hopelessness and despair? D'Souza has not one useful word to say about how this problem will be remedied beyond urging blacks in the middle class to get busy raising the "civilizational standards" of their brethren.

As someone who has spent a decade calling for moral leadership within the black community, I find it now an even more important task to urge that responsible moral leadership come forth in the "conservative community." This book is not even close to what is required. Racial discourse in America has too often been a kind of public theater—sometimes tragedy, sometimes farce. Far from deriving the principles by means of which progress might be sought, *The End of Racism* turns out to be only the latest tragicomic performance in a seemingly endless repertory.

NO

Dinesh D'Souza

LET ME SAY WHAT THE BOOK IS ABOUT

Glenn C. Loury's review of my book, *The End of Racism* (Sept. 25), is mystifying, because it consistently misrepresents the books' argument and tone; consequently, it argues against positions which I do not hold. Let me, therefore, say what the book is about and then deal specifically with some of Loury's criticisms.

The End of Racism is a comprehensive challenge to the conventional wisdom that racism is the primary cause of black failure. I argue that the main problem faced by African Americans is neither deficient IQ, as suggested in *The Bell Curve*, nor racial discrimination, as alleged by Jesse Jackson and other civil-rights activists. Rather, the book contends that blacks have developed a culture in this country that was an adaptation to historical circumstances but one that is, in many important respects, dysfunctional today.

I point out that some pathologies, such as extremely high African-American crime rates, have the effect of legitimizing "rational discrimination," such as cabdrivers who are reluctant to pick up young black males. *The End of Racism* exposes as fatally flawed America's two contemporary policy remedies: multiculturalism and proportional representation. The book shows that liberal programs such as affirmative action have little to do with fighting racism; rather, they are aimed at camouflaging the embarrassing reality of black failure on merit standards of academic achievement and economic performance.

One of my main conclusions is that even though we now have substantial numbers of Hispanics, Asians, and Middle Easterners in this country, racism remains primarily a black-and-white problem. Many people may not like Korean or Mexican immigrants, but there is no systematic belief that holds these groups to be inferior. Yet four centuries after blacks were brought to this country against their will, the suspicion of black inferiority persists.

This suspicion helps to keep racism alive and so hinders progress toward a race-neutral society. Only by recognizing and confronting cultural pathology and becoming fully competitive with other groups, I argue, can blacks discredit racism and join whites and immigrants in claiming the fruits of the American dream.

From Dinesh D'Souza, "Let Me Say What the Book Is About," *The Weekly Standard* (October 2, 1995). Copyright © 1995 by Dinesh D'Souza. Reprinted by permission.

* * *

As for the book's tone: It is written with a view to being intellectually provocative while at the same time being morally sensitive. None of Loury's examples proves otherwise. In a chapter that disagrees with *The Bell Curve* but which takes the book seriously and explores its implications, I point out that if the IQ theorists are right that there are biological, ineradicable differences of intelligence between races, then "it is hard not to hear the triumphant roar of the white supremacists; 'forget about the legacy of racism and discrimination —these people are naturally stupid.'"

Is there any question that this is why *The Bell Curve* stirred up such angry condemnation? Yet Loury quotes the line as if it represents my personal jubilation: "One might speculate that [D'Souza] actually longs to hear those triumphant roars." This is an outrageous misrepresentation of my views. One of the explicit theses of my book is that the genetic explanation for group differences in performance is misconceived.

Loury takes angry exception to my use of the phrase *"reductio ad Hitlerum."* Actually, this term is not original with me but was coined by philosopher Leo Strauss in *Natural Right and History,* published in 1953. Strauss defines it thus: "A view is not refuted by the fact that it happens to have been shared by Hitler." This is precisely the sense in which I use the term. Anyone who reads *The End of Racism* will see that Loury's other examples are equally misleading.

According to Loury, my discussion of racism's origins as an ideology of European superiority leads to an unambiguous defense of the Enlightenment. This is not so; indeed, I express decidedly mixed feelings about the Enlightenment project, and firmly condemn the consequences of its evolution into the scientific racism of the 19th century. Moreover, I point out that the main opposition to social and racial Darwinism came from evangelical Christians.

My reason for examining the origins of racism is to challenge the view, publicized by Andrew Hacker in *Two Nations* and Derrick Bell in *Faces at the Bottom of the Well,* that racism may be a staple of the human, or at least Western psyche, so that we can never be rid of it. I conclude my discussion by noting that "painful though we may find it to read what people in earlier centuries had to say about others, it remains profoundly consoling to know that racism had a beginning, because then it becomes possible to envision its end."

Loury attributes to me the view that "slavery was not a racist institution." What in fact I do say (citing Orlando Patterson, Bernard Lewis, David Brion Davis, and others) is that historically, slavery has proven to be a universal institution, practiced in ancient Egypt, Mesopotamia, Greece, Rome, China, India, the Arab world, the Americas, and virtually all of sub-Saharan Africa. I point out that even in America, between 1830 and 1860, there were some 3,500 free blacks who owned more than 10,000 black slaves—a historical fact known to scholars, but carefully kept out of public view because it confuses the morality tale of slavery as a racist crime inflicted by white masters on black slaves.

Despite such anomalies, I go on to argue that slavery strengthened American racism, which flourished not because of simple white "ignorance, fear and hate" but because of the contradiction between the principles of the founding and the practice of human bondage. After all, if you believe that "all men are created equal" and at the same time own slaves, then in order to be consistent you are compelled to hold, at some level, that blacks are somehow less than human.

Loury charges me with asserting that "most middle class blacks owe their prosperity to affirmative action." Wrong again. What I write is much more nuanced and entirely defensible: "The effect of affirmative action has been to accelerate the growth of the first sizable middle class in the history of African Americans.... This group constituted a distinct social phenomenon by the 1960s, as desegregation and antidiscrimination laws went into effect. Yet although scholars debate their precise effect, racial preferences have undoubtedly helped to solidify the black middle class."

Loury accuses me of calling poor blacks barbarians who are incapable of civilization. He cites Elijah Anderson's remark: "these communities are full of decent people with values no different from D'Souza's or my own." I argue— citing Anderson—that "the inner city is characterized by two rival cultures; a hegemonic culture of pathology and a besieged culture of decency."

My whole point is to call for a social policy that strengthens black people's "culture of decency" and works to end the dominant inner-city culture of irresponsibility. Here is the moral line that needs to be drawn. In an omission that is both hurtful and surprising, Loury omits my crucial distinction between competing inner-city African American cultures; this allows him to saddle me with a view that is a profound distortion of my precisely stated position.

The most serious complaint of Loury's review is that I fail to recognize that black cultural failings are *American* cultural failings (his emphasis). Has he read the book?

Discussing cultural breakdown, here is what I do say: "This is not merely an African American problem; it is a national problem. The American crime rate has risen dramatically over the past few decades, and juvenile homicide has reached catastrophic proportions. Alarming numbers of high school students use drugs, get pregnant, or carry weapons to class.... Cultural relativism now prevents liberals from publicly asserting and enforcing civilizational standards for everyone, not just African Americans."

At the same time, I argue that just as African-American culture has distinctive strengths, it also has distinctive strengths, it also has developed identifiable weaknesses. These cultural pathologies are most concentrated among the underclass but in some respects they also extend to the black middle class.

After all, if this is a purely American problem without distinctive ethnic dimensions, then why do blacks who come from families earning more than $60,000 a year score lower on the SAT and many other measures of academic performance than whites and Asians who come from families earning less than $20,000 a year? Why is the illegitimacy rate for poor blacks vastly higher than that for poor whites, and why are college-educated black women between eight and ten times more likely to bear children out of wedlock than college-educated white women? Loury does not dispute my analysis of these problems; he simply writes as though they haven't been raised.

* * *

Pointing to the hopelessness and squalor of many American lives, Loury charges that I have "not one useful word to say" beyond urging middle-class blacks to take responsibility for the lives of poor blacks. In fact, I point to the work of Charles Ballard, Kimi Gray, Jesse Peterson, and others who are setting up teen-pregnancy programs, family-support initiatives, community job-training, instruction in language and social demeanor, resident supervision of housing projects, and privately-run neighborhood schools.

I cite black scholar John Sibley Butler about the importance of strengthening entrepreneurial institutions in the inner city, perhaps modeled on the rotating credit associations that have helped poor Koreans accumulate capital and become successful capitalists. And I say that society has an obligation to help as well.

Like Loury, I believe that black cultural restoration depends on strengthening three vital institutions—family, church, and small business. "If blacks can achieve such a cultural renaissance," I conclude, "they will teach other Americans a valuable lesson in civilizational restoration... solve the American dilemma, and become the truest and noblest exemplars of Western civilization."

Why Loury has chosen to portray this position as not only mistaken but destructive and dangerous, I do not know. *The End of Racism* is a tough book which faces painful facts, yet it is ultimately a hopeful book that is aimed at building a secure intellectual and moral foundation for a multiracial America. In this project Loury has played a central role, so whatever he thinks of my work, I will continue to benefit from many of his excellent writings.

POSTSCRIPT

Is the "End of Racism" Thesis Badly Flawed?

Much of the historical debate on racism centers on the fact that there were some Black slave owners. Loury contends that, unlike other minority members, Blacks were viewed as less than human, a group that was clearly distinct and whose actions and attitudes were directly attributed to their race. This, to Loury, is racism. Similarly, Loury views discussions of Blacks in the 1990s in terms of their alleged moral inferiority based on their "cultural pathologies" as transparent racism. Neither Loury nor D'Souza points out that, other than indentured servants, whites were never enslaved in the United States.

Loury criticizes D'Souza for attacking the theories of "cultural relativism" of anthropologist Franz Boas (1858–1942) in order to show that inner-city Blacks are culturally different from the rest of society. Boas delineated cultural relativism to counter the widespread ethnocentrism of Western scholars and missionaries, who viewed non-Westerners, particularly Africans and South Americans, as having inferior religious institutions, families, values, and so on. Cultural relativism states that all cultures are inherently equal and that any group of people's patterns of behavior must be identified as structures that may or may not be functional for their society. Polygamy, for example, may not be functional in the United States, but it may be functional elsewhere. In D'Souza's view (according to Loury), different cultures *can* be judged inferior, and urban Blacks embrace a culture that deviates from the rest of America. Blacks' lives, suggests D'Souza, "are governed by barbarism."

For a moving analysis of a white man who dyed his skin to pass as a Black and was confronted by racism, see "Skin Deep," by J. Solomon, *The Washington Post* (October 30, 1994). Additional discussions of racism include Michel Wieviorka, *The Arena of Racism* (Sage Publications, 1995); bell hooks, *Killing Rage: Ending Racism* (Henry Holt, 1995); and Michael P. Smith and Joseph R. Feagin, eds., *The Bubbling Cauldron* (University of Minnesota Press, 1995). Two works that deal with politics and race are *Creating Boundaries: The Politics of Race and Nation* by Kathryn A. Manzo (Lynne Rienner, 1995) and *Beyond Black and White* by Manning Marable (Verso, 1996).

An important work on race as a concept is Audrey Smedley's *Race in North America: Origin and Evolution of a World View* (Westview Press, 1993). A widely praised book that documents structural causes of urban blight is Douglas S. Massey and Nancy A. Denton's *American Apartheid: Segregation and the Making of the Underclass* (Harvard University Press, 1993). Finally, an ethnography that qualitatively analyzes racism is *Living to Tell About It: Young Black Men in America Speak Their Piece* by Darrell Dawsey (Bantam Doubleday, 1995).

ISSUE 5

Do Industrialization and Capitalism Cause Racial and Ethnic Inequalities?

YES: Sheila E. Henry, from "Ethnic Identity, Nationalism, and International Stratification: The Case of the African American," *Journal of Black Studies* (January 1999)

NO: Thomas Sowell, from "Race, Culture and Equality," *Forbes* (October 5, 1998)

ISSUE SUMMARY

YES: Professor of arts and sciences Sheila E. Henry argues that ethnic and racial inequalities can be understood only in the context of global stratification. She holds that in the United States, minorities whose ancestral nations have high prestige are allocated high prestige themselves, while African Americans and others, reflecting both institutional racism and the low status of many African societies, are forced to occupy the bottom rungs of society.

NO: Thomas Sowell, a researcher at the Hoover Institute, maintains that dominant theories of racial and ethnic inequality that are based on prejudice, oppression, exploitation, and discrimination are simply wrong. He develops an alternative explanation based on geography, which he indicates also has meaningful policy implications.

In all societies some people are better off than others. However, the basis for how society's valued resources (e.g., money, prestige, power, and opportunities) are distributed varies greatly, as does the amount of inequality. Traditional explanations of inequality have been based on genetics (some are born superior to others), theology (it is God's way), and custom (people from one tribe are considered better—or worse—than people from the others).

Most social scientists (and a growing number of laypersons) categorically reject such reasons for inequality. Instead, structural or sociological explanations as well as social psychological factors, such as attitudes and values, are embraced. That is, the environment or social situation within which groups exist accounts for much inequality. For instance, people born in poverty obviously have far less wealth, opportunities, and power than others. Moreover, their speech, body language, clothing, consumption patterns, recreational activities, and even health are sometimes visibly different from those who are better off. This makes it "natural" for others to discriminate against the poor. Prejudice develops, and members of the victimized group often come to agree with the dominant group's definition of them. Quickly, the whole thing becomes a cruel spiral of cumulative causation. Unemployment, lack of formal education, "nonstandard" behavior, and so on are reflected, which reinforces both the low status of the minority group and the perceptions of the dominant group. Even those attempting to be fair sometimes decide that there must be some fault in the poor themselves because they are so different.

While almost all scholars reject the notion that inequality results from biological or religious inferiority, there remains much disagreement about the actual causes. Marxists, for instance, maintain that class or economic factors based on the control of a society's wealth by its elites create social inequalities. Others insist that race and ethnicity are important contributors (that there is discrimination against those with different racial and ethnic backgrounds). Some more recent work has included gender along with race and class as a basis for inequality. Many other variables, such as age and language, also partially account for social differences.

Sheila E. Henry's analysis in the following selection draws heavily from race-based theories and the world-system perspective. Following that model, she divides nations into core and peripheral ones. She asserts that the core, or developed, capitalist societies more or less colonize and exploit less developed nations, or those that are peripheral to the world economy. Henry finds parallels between the position of nations within the world economic system and the status of its citizens within the United States. Blacks, for example, were snatched from Africa to function as slaves in the West, and for generations their disadvantaged status has been maintained and even magnified through racism. In the 1990s these chains are still in existence, Henry argues. Moreover, the low international market position of Africa in general helps to reinforce the low status of African Americans.

In the second selection Thomas Sowell, drawing from once-popular geopolitical theories, contends that it is geography, not race or discrimination, that is destiny. Simply put, folks who are isolated from others are bound to be deprived of cultural stimulation as well as excluded from trade routes. It is not just natural resources that may be lacking but also location. Most African societies, for instance, had a shortage of natural harbors, waterways that were easily navigable, and land routes that were easy to create and use. Thus, they were automatically excluded from contact with others. He cites several similar geographic handicaps among Europeans and others and argues that when these people migrated to the United States, they too could not compete with many other minority members.

Both Henry and Sowell reflect a broad, macrostructural approach to the problem of inequality. Henry considers it self-evident that capitalism and industrialization create inequality. Sowell sharply questions this thesis. Which position seems to have the most empirical validity? Which has the most analytical or theoretic validity? What might the policy implications be for minority members if one or the other viewpoint is accepted?

YES

ETHNIC IDENTITY, NATIONALISM, AND INTERNATIONAL STRATIFICATION

Insofar as Western European nations—in particular Britain, France, and Germany—were among the earliest to industrialize, the imposition of their hegemony on Africa and Asia created a new basis for status allocation within a global stratification system. This article will attempt to explore the relationship between contemporary levels of ethnic or racial inequality within the United States and the global status of country of origin for a number of ethnic groups.

... It will be argued that there are at least two major systemic factors involved: (a) the status of the nation of origin within the global stratification system so that the higher its international status on the criteria of economic, political, and military dominance, the higher the social status accorded group members by the dominant group within the United States; and (b) changes in the international status of the country of origin will be reflected in revisions of status level for such ethnic/racial groups....

THEORETICAL EXPLANATION OF THE U.S. STRATIFICATION SYSTEM

The characteristics of social stratification and its bases are well established and documented in the literature. Among scholars, Gerth and Mills (1946), Davis and Moore (1945), Bendix and Lipset (1958), and Kerbo (1983) speak to the institutionalization of unequal access to scarce resources and the differential allocation of rank and prestige to groups bearing specific "valued" characteristics, real or imagined, physical or intellectual. Similarly, proponents of the elitist view of American social structure have demonstrated not only the importance of shared social background and values among the "power elite" but also the degree to which such inherited advantages contribute to the maintenance of elite social status and the opportunity for its members to control the social, political, and economic institutions. The critical contribution of the ascribed status of race/ethnicity is inadequately examined, the privileges of "whiteness" being invisible to those so endowed. Among stigmatized

From Sheila E. Henry, "Ethnic Identity, Nationalism, and International Stratification: The Case of the African American," *Journal of Black Studies*, vol. 29, no. 3 (January 1999). Copyright © 1999 by Sage Publications, Inc. Reprinted by permission. Some references omitted.

ethnics, Jews have used the survival technique of changing the family name, but African or Asian ancestry with visibly distinguishing characteristics of skin color and texture of hair cannot be so simply discarded or disguised.

These realities contradict or discredit theories of assimilation or the "melting pot" theory, whose basic assumptions held that abandonment of ancestral culture and traditions was the key to entry into mainstream America and access to social, economic, and political opportunity.

EUROPEAN IMMIGRATION AND SOCIAL STRATIFICATION

... National status will be shown to be allocated, imposed, and created by the economic relations inherent in imperialism, colonialism, and industrialization. Just as the upper class within a class-based system determines the norms and values of a society—exploiting the labor of the working class for the benefit of the upper classes—so within the international stratification system, the imperial power determines the position of the colonized by exploiting the latter's resources. Informal United States immigration policy has always reflected a preference for immigrants from northwestern Europe, that is, Anglo-Saxons....

Before 1880, about 80% of all immigrants came from the United Kingdom, Ireland, Germany, and Scandinavia. By 1900, immigrants from Italy, Russia, and the Austro-Hungarian Empire accounted for more than one half of the total number of immigrants....

The demand for labor by a rapidly expanding industrial economy and a determination to crush the growing strength of labor unions, the drying up of labor from the preferred countries, together with the effects of World War I had overridden nativism and anti-Popist sentiments and opened the door to previously "undesirable" immigrants from southern and eastern European countries. The "whitening" of southern Europeans had begun, both in response to the freeing of African slaves and the fear of working-class coalitions being formed between former African slaves and the cheap imported European factory laborers and steel and coal mine workers. The possibility of a class struggle evolving was real. The concept of being "White" and privileged took root, yet the preference for immigrants from northwestern Europe persisted with periodic eruptions of nativism at the increasingly visible presence of the "new" immigrants....

CHINESE IMMIGRATION AND THE CHINESE EXCLUSION ACT OF 1882

Although the East Coast and the Midwest were inundated with European immigrants, the West Coast drew its labor from the Pacific Rim, specifically China and Japan. Between 1851 and 1858, more than 200,000 Chinese had emigrated to work on the railroads in California. Ethnic hostility and exclusion took many forms. In 1852, the governor of California wanted restrictions placed on the Chinese on the grounds that Chinese "coolies" were unassimilable, lowered the standard of living, were heathens, and were economic opportunists who would eventually overrun the state. In 1854, a California Supreme Court decision effectively disenfranchised Chinese immigrants by denying them the right to testify against a White man. Violence against Chinese became commonplace. In 1871, some 22 Chinese were lynched in Los Angeles, and in 1885 in Wyoming, 29 Chinese were murdered and their property looted and destroyed....

Chinese immigrants had no recourse, neither could they expect protection from the Chinese Emperor for a number of reasons. As was the case with central and southern Europe, China in the 1840s and until the fall of the Manchu dynasty was [not] a politically united empire.... Chinese identity was framed by family, kinship group, and clan. China's weak political position and low international status is... evidenced by the military defeats she suffered....

THE JAPANESE AND THE GENTLEMEN'S AGREEMENT: 1908

Japanese immigration followed Chinese, and between 1890 and 1900 approximately 20,000 had arrived on the mainland from Japan and Hawaii where they had already emigrated to work on the sugar cane plantations. Although initially welcomed because of their industry, compliant nature, and willingness to accept low wages, their attempts to improve their economic positions soon aroused the ire of the White American community. Newspaper editorials and legislation record the intensity of anti-Japanese sentiment. The *San Francisco Chronicle* (1910) comments,

Japanese ambition is to progress beyond mere servility to the plane of the better class of American workman and to own a home with him. The moment that this position is exercised, the Japanese ceases to be an ideal laborer....

Despite [many] obstacles, the Japanese succeeded in securing a significant share of the truck farming market. Their economic success was met with the passing of a more serious restriction, the California Alien Land Act of 1913. Now, as persons ineligible for citizenship, they were prevented from land ownership and could only lease agricultural land up to a period of 3 years.... Although state law and local custom persecuted the Japanese and their children, at the national level an entirely different picture emerges. Attempts to force Japanese children into segregated schools as had been done to the Chinese children were unsuccessful largely as a result of presidential intervention. The furor in Japan at this serious racial insult had the potential to provoke an international incident. President Theodore Roosevelt's concern not to offend the emperor and the Japanese nation could fairly be related to Japan's recent demonstration of its military strength—a convincing defeat of the Russian army in 1904 (an event that had stunned all of Western Europe and the United States)—followed by the conquest of Korea and Manchuria in 1905. Japan had effectively claimed a place within the higher levels of the international stratification system by its military prowess.... And so... the Gentlemen's Agreement of 1908 between the governments of Japan and the United States was a bilateral agreement between political and military equals. Japan agreed to halt immigration to the United States, whereas the United States undertook to ensure that Japanese citizens in the United States would be protected from discriminatory acts. Unlike China, Japan remained a fully independent nation during the flowering of Western imperialism....

AFRICA, COLONIALISM, AND THE SLAVE TRADE

The history of Africans in the United States as slaves is inextricably tied to the colonization of both the United States and Africa and Britain's rise to supremacy among mercantilist nations in the 17th century.... British ships were supreme on the high seas and had a 30-year monopoly to supply slaves to the Spanish colonies in the West Indies. In West Africa, from which the majority of slaves were brought, kidnapped, or stolen, political structures in 17th and 18th century West Africa broadly resembled that of much of eastern and southern Europe and China—monarchical empires and fragmented communities bound together by traditional tribal social organizations in which tribute was owed and paid to the most powerful military overlord.... Ethnic rivalry fueled continuous raiding parties and warfare, and as was traditional, prisoners were sold as slaves to any willing buyer. Invitations from indigenous chiefs for armed support against an ethnic rival or entry into a temporary strategic alliance with British or French traders were transformed into opportunities for widening economic and political control....

COLONIALISM AND THE INTERNATIONAL STRATIFICATION SYSTEM

In colonial Africa, the imperialists systematically denigrated and partially destroyed indigenous social and political institutions. Most significantly, the economy of the nations in the periphery were distorted to serve those of the core nations, thus the "underdevelopment" of former colonies.... Histo-

rians have concluded that whereas in 1879 approximately 90% of the continent was still formally under traditional African sovereignty, by 1900 almost the entire continent was under European rule (Burns, 1929; Oliver & Atmore, 1969)....

The bases for the current system of international and ethnic stratification can be seen to derive from the process of emergent capitalism, the creation and consolidation of nation states in Europe, and imperial expansionism, colonialism, and competition among European nations. The scramble for Africa that occurred between 1880 and 1900 in which Britain, France, and Germany partitioned Africa into spheres of influence resulted in a tumultuous overturning of African sovereignty....

AFRICAN AMERICANS, ETHNIC IDENTITY, AND GROUP STATUS

What are the consequences of colonialism for Americans of African ancestry or Africans in the diaspora in general? It would appear that the most extreme case of the negative impact of low international status of a country on its members is that of African states for Africans in the diaspora and on African Americans in particular. African Americans find themselves in a qualitatively different situation from either Chinese or Japanese Americans. Arriving as slaves beginning in the 17th century, African slaves and their descendants were not free until the 19th century with the passage of the 13th Amendment (1865). Despite this, they were denied the actual enjoyment of the rights and privileges as evidenced by a series of amendments and Supreme Court decisions—the 14th and 15th Amendments (1868, 1870); *Plessy v. Ferguson* (1892); *Brown v. the Board of Ed-*

ucation, Topeka, Kansas (1954); the Civil Rights Act of 1964; and the Voting Rights Act of 1965. With little authentic knowledge of their ancestral homelands, culture(s), or traditions, they instead widely rejected Africa as ancestral home, with the exception of one state, Ethiopia. The reasons for the rejection should be obvious in the light of the foregoing. On the other hand, Ethiopia was the exception because it was the single African nation that had a long and illustrious history reflected in its international status. It bears comparison with Japan in that it was a politically independent nation that had successfully fended off European intrusion and, in 1896, had inflicted a military defeat on Italy in the decisive battle of Adowa....

The colonial status of Africa continued until the 1950s when political independence was granted or won by most states. But decades of underdevelopment and economic exploitation have made it increasingly difficult to bridge the ever-widening technological gap that reinforces the core/periphery relationship. "Divide and conquer" colonial strategies have sharpened interethnic rivalry into deep political cleavages. In Nigeria, for example, typical of former colonies, the task of creating a single nation with shared values, goals, and a sense of peoplehood from collectivities of linguistically and ethnically diverse peoples (among whom are traditional rivalries) has proved elusive. Rather, the territory has devolved into a myriad of ethnic provinces, a contemporary reversion to precolonial geographic and ethnic homelands. Economic growth resulting from the discovery of extensive oil fields has led to her becoming a significant player in the world market and has had a recognizable psychological impact during the 1960s and 1970s on African Americans, seen in a growth of ethnic pride and awareness. The civil rights movement in the 1960s owed much to the explosion of political and budding economic independence among Africa nations....

INTERNATIONAL STATUS, ETHNIC GROUP STATUS IN THE UNITED STATES

How are these sociopolitical historical events and processes reflected in the relationship between the international status of a nation and that of its members within American society? Primacy of place for the British in particular has already been explored. Its imperial power deriving from the resources of its colonial dependents enabled it to confer the highest social status on its members. As "White" came to replace European national origin, all persons of European ancestry have enjoyed a social status higher than those whose origins are non-European. The principle of global economic dominance nevertheless still operates as in the modern-day decline in the status of Britain with loss of empire and economic superiority and its replacement first by Germany during the 1960s and 1970s when the German economy dominated the world market, then by Japan in the 1970s and 1980s. Although Japan's adversarial role in World War II had negative effects for Japanese Americans, its rapid postwar modernization and later domination of the global economy not only restored its status but led to the imitation of its business management strategies....

Chinese Americans, on the other hand, are highly endogamous and retain strong local ethnic communities and associations. Although the two Chinas

—mainland China and Taiwan—exist in different relationships with the United States, nevertheless each confers national status benefits on its citizens as a result of its peculiar location within the world system.... Chinese Americans benefit from both sources of international status. African nations, however, have not been able to sustain their initial promise and have, for the most part, declined into a new state of political instability and economic dependency. Today they remain on the periphery of the global economy, of minor strategic interest to the new world system. Despite social and political gains by the African American population, their status as a group remains lower than that of any other ethnic group, even including the most recent immigrants from southeast Asia.

CONCLUSIONS

Viewing stratification systems within nations as a reflection of the global economic stratification system offers a perspective that provides greater insight into the origins of internal stratification systems, particularly that of a multiethnic society such as the United States. The case studies seem to support the main arguments of this article. The high status held by Britain and other imperial European nations was conferred on their immigrant representatives in the United States, and the possibility of class revolution in the United States led to the inclusion of all persons of European descent under a "White" umbrella. Although some European immigrants were initially excluded, their treatment was still muted compared with that meted out to those who originated from China and Africa. The reasons have been presented. In contemporary times, Japan

ranks among the leading capitalist nations of the world, and Japanese Americans may be said to have achieved the status of "honorary" Whites, as Andrew Hacker recently opined. China (mainland, including Hong Kong today and Taiwan) is generally speculated to replace Japan as the next economic giant in the global economy due to the raw potential of its massive populations, its military threat, and the remarkable success (Taiwan and Hong Kong) as semiperipheral societies, and as manufacturers of finished goods for the global market, albeit using the cheap "sweatshop" labor of its citizens. Thus, Chinese Americans as an ethnic group now enjoy a relatively respectable status, although it is by comparison lower than that of Japanese Americans. Africa, by comparison, remains largely noncompetitive within the postindustrial global economy (a peripheral economy in the world system). Its constituent nations remain mired in interethnic wars and unstable political systems reminiscent of mid-19th-century Europe rather than contemporary industrialized societies. Given that the likelihood of any individual African state achieving economic global dominance in the near future appears slim, no revision of ethnic group status appears imminent for African Americans.

REFERENCES

Bendix, R., & Lipset, S. M. (Eds.). Class, status and power: A reader in social stratification. Glencoe, IL: Free Press.

Burns, A. (1929). History of Nigeria. London: Allen & Unwin.

Chase-Dunn, C., & Hall, T. D. (Eds.). (1991). Core-periphery relations in a pre-capitalist world. Oxford: Blackwell.

Davis, K., & Moore, W. E. (1945). Some principles of stratification. American Sociological Review, 10, 243–248.

Gerth H., & Mills, C. W. (1946). *From Max Weber: Essays in sociology.* New York: Oxford University Press.

Kerbo, H. R. (1983). *Social stratification and inequality: Conflict in the U.S.* New York: McGraw-Hill.

Oliver, R., & Atmore, A. (1969). *Africa since 1800.* Cambridge, UK: Cambridge University Press.

Omi, M., Winant, H. (1986). *Racial formation in the United States: From the 1960s to the 1980s.* London: Routledge & Kegan Paul.

NO

Thomas Sowell

RACE, CULTURE AND EQUALITY

During the 15 years that I spent researching and writing my recently completed trilogy on racial and cultural issues, I was struck again and again with how common huge disparities in income and wealth have been for centuries, in countries around the world—and yet how each country regards its own particular disparities as unusual, if not unique. Some of these disparities have been among racial or ethnic groups, some among nations, and some among regions, continents or whole civilizations.

In the nineteenth century real per capita income in the Balkans was about one-third that in Britain. That dwarfs intergroup disparities that many in the United States today regard as not merely strange but sinister. Singapore has a median per capita income that is literally hundreds of times greater than that in Burma.

During the recent rioting in Indonesia, much of it directed against the ethnic Chinese in that country, some commentators found it strange that the Chinese minority, which is just 5 percent of the Indonesian population, owned an estimated four-fifths of the capital in the country. But it is not strange. Such disparities have long been common in other countries in Southeast Asia, where Chinese immigrants typically entered poor and then prospered, creating whole industries in the process. People from India did the same in much of East Africa and in Fiji.

Occupational differences have been equally unequal.

In the early 1920s, Jews were just 6 percent of the population of Hungary and 11 percent of the population of Poland, but they were more than half of all the physicians in both countries, as well as being vastly over-represented in commerce and other fields. In the early twentieth century, all of the firms in all of the industries producing the following products in Brazil's state of Rio Grande do Sul were owned by people of German ancestry: trunks, stoves, paper, hats, neckties, leather, soap, glass, watches, beer, confections and carriages.

In the middle of the nineteenth century, just three countries produced most of the manufactured goods in the world—Britain, Germany, and the United

From Thomas Sowell, "Race, Culture and Equality," *Forbes* (October 5, 1998). Copyright © 1998 by Forbes, Inc. Reprinted by permission of *Forbes* magazine.

States. By the late twentieth century, it was estimated that 17 percent of the people in the world produce four-fifths of the total output on the planet.

Such examples could be multiplied longer than you would have the patience to listen.

Why are there such disparities? In some cases, we can trace the reasons, but in other cases we cannot. A more fundamental question, however, is: Why should anyone have ever expected equality in the first place?

Let us assume, for the sake of argument, that not only every racial or ethnic group, but even every single individual in the entire world, has identical genetic potential. If it is possible to be even more extreme, let us assume that we all behave like saints toward one another. Would that produce equality of results?

Of course not. Real income consists of output and output depends on inputs. These inputs are almost never equal—or even close to being equal.

During the decade of the 1960s, for example, the Chinese minority in Malaysia earned more than a hundred times as many engineering degrees as the Malay majority. Halfway around the world at the same time, the majority of the population of Nigeria, living in its northern provinces, were just 9 percent of the students attending that country's University of Ibadan and just 2 percent of the much larger number of Nigerian students studying abroad in foreign institutions of higher learning. In the Austrian Empire in 1900, the illiteracy rate among Polish adults was 40 percent and among Serbo-Croatians 75 percent—but only 6 percent among the Germans.

Given similar educational disparities among other groups in other countries —disparities in both the quantity and quality of education, as well as in fields of specialization—why should anyone expect equal outcomes in incomes or occupations?

Educational differences are just one source of economic disparities. Even at the level of craft skills, groups have differed enormously, as they have in urbanization. During the Middle Ages, and in some places long beyond, most of the population of the cities in Slavic Eastern Europe were not Slavs. Germans, Jews, and other non-Slavic peoples were the majority populations in these cities for centuries, while the Slavs were predominantly peasants in the surrounding countrysides. Prior to the year 1312, the official records of the city of Cracow were kept in German—and the transition that year was to Latin. Only decades later did Poles become a majority of the population of Cracow. Only over a period of centuries did the other cities of Slavic Eastern Europe acquire predominantly Slavic populations. As late as 1918, 97 percent of the people living in the cities of Byelorussia were not Byelorussians.

Until this long transition to urban living took place among the Slavs, how could the wide range of skills typically found in cities be expected to exist in populations that lived overwhelmingly in the countryside? Not only did they not have such skills in Eastern Europe, they did not have them when they immigrated to the United States, to Australia, or to other countries, where they typically worked in low-level occupations and earned correspondingly low incomes. In the early years of the twentieth century, for example, immigrants to the United States from Eastern and Southern Europe earned just 15 percent of the income of immigrants from Norway, Holland, Sweden, and Britain.

Groups also differ demographically. It is not uncommon to find some groups with median ages a decade younger than the median ages of other groups, and differences of two decades are not unknown. During the era of the Soviet Union, for example, Central Asians had far more children than Russians or the peoples of the Baltic republics, and so had much younger median ages. At one time, the median age of Jews in the United States was 20 years older than the median age of Puerto Ricans. If Jews and Puerto Ricans had been absolutely identical in every other respect, including their cultures and histories, they would still not have been equally represented in jobs requiring long years of experience, or in retirement homes, or in activities associated with youth, such as sports or crime.

Nothing so intractably conflicts with our desires for equality as geography. Yet the physical settings in which races, nations, and civilizations have evolved have had major impacts on the cultures developed within those settings. At its simplest and crudest, the peoples of the Himalayas have not had an equal opportunity to acquire seafaring skills. Nor have Eskimos had an equal opportunity to acquire knowledge and experience in growing pineapples or other tropical crops.

Too often the influence of geography on wealth is thought of narrowly, in terms of natural resources that directly translate into wealth, such as oil in the Middle East or gold in South Africa. But, important as such differences in natural wealth are, geography influences even more profound cultural differences among the people themselves.

Where geography isolates people, whether in mountain valleys or on small islands scattered across a vast sea, there the cultural exposures of those people to the outside world are very limited and so, typically, is their technological advancement. While the rest of the world exchanges goods, knowledge and innovations from a vast cultural universe, isolated peoples have been largely limited to what they alone have been able to develop.

Few, if any, of the great advances in human civilization have come from isolated peoples. As the eminent French historian Fernand Braudel put it, the mountains almost always lag behind the plains—even if the races in the two places are the same. Potatoes and the English language both reached the Scottish lowlands before they reached the highlands. Islam reached North Africa's Rif mountains long after the people in the plains had become Moslems.

When the Spaniards invaded the Canary Islands in the fifteenth century, they found people of a Caucasian race living at a Stone-Age level. So were the Australian aborigines when the British discovered them.

Geographically imposed cultural isolation takes many forms and exists in many degrees. Cities have long been in the vanguard of human progress, all over the world, but cities do not arise randomly in all geographic settings. Most of the great cities of the world have developed on navigable waterways—rivers or harbors—but such waterways are by no means equally or randomly distributed around the world. They are very common in Western Europe and very rare in sub-Saharan Africa. Urbanization has long been correspondingly common in Western Europe and correspondingly rare in sub-Saharan Africa. One-third of the land mass of Europe consists of islands and peninsulas but only one percent of the land mass of South America consists of islands and peninsulas.

Navigable waterways have been economically crucial, especially during the millennia of human history before the development of railroads, trucks and airplanes. Before the transcontinental railroad was built, it was both faster and cheaper to reach San Francisco from a port in China than from Saint Louis. People in the city of Tbilisi bought their kerosene from Texas—8,000 miles away across water—rather than from the Baku oil fields, less than 400 miles away across land.

Such vast differences in costs between water transport and land transport affect what can be transported and how far. Gold or diamonds can repay the costs of transport across thousands of miles of land, but grain or coal cannot. More important, the size of a people's cultural universe depends on how far they can reach out to other peoples and other cultures. No great civilization has developed in isolation. Geography in general and navigable waterways in particular set the limits of a people's cultural universe, broadly or narrowly. But these limits are by no means set equally for all peoples or all civilization.

For example, when the British first crossed the Atlantic and confronted the Iroquois on the eastern seaboard of what is today the United States, they were able to steer across that ocean in the first place because they used rudders invented in China, they could navigate on the open seas with the help of trigonometry invented in Egypt, their calculations were done with numbers invented in India, and their general

knowledge was preserved in letters invented by the Romans. But the Iroquois could not draw upon the knowledge of the Aztecs or the Incas, whose very existence they had no way of knowing. The clash was not between the culture created by the British versus the culture created by the Iroquois. It was a clash between cultural developments drawn from vast regions of the world versus cultural developments from a much more circumscribed area. The cultural opportunities were unequal and the outcomes were unequal. Geography has never been egalitarian.

A network of rivers in Western Europe flows gently through vast plains, connecting wide areas economically and culturally. The rivers of tropical Africa plunge a thousand feet or more on their way to the sea, with cascades and waterfalls making them navigable only for stretches between these natural barriers —and the coastal plain in Africa averages just 20 miles. Regular rainfall and melting snows keep the rivers of Western Europe flowing throughout the year, but African rivers have neither—and so rise and fall dramatically with the seasons, further limiting their usefulness. The two continents are at least as dramatically different when it comes to natural harbors. Although Africa is more than twice the size of Europe, it has a shorter coastline. That is because the European coastline continually twists and turns, creating innumerable harbors, while the African coastline is smooth, with few harbors. How surprising is it that international commerce has played a much smaller role in the economic history of Africa than in that of Europe in general and Western Europe in particular?

These particular geographic disparities are by no means exhaustive. But they are suggestive of some of the many ways in which physical settings have expanded or constricted the size of the cultural universe available to different peoples. One revealing indication of cultural fragmentation is that African peoples are 10 percent of the world's population but have one-third of the world's languages.

In controversies over "nature versus nurture" as causes of economic and other disparities among peoples and civilizations, nature is often narrowly conceived as genetic differences. Yet geography is also nature—and its patterns are far more consistent with history than are genetic theories. China, for example, was for many centuries the leading nation in the world—technologically, organizationally and in many other ways. Yet, in more recent centuries, China has been overtaken and far surpassed by Europe. Yet neither region of the world has changed genetically to any extent that would account for this dramatic change in their relative positions. This historic turnaround also shows that geographic limitations do not mean geographic determinism, for the geography of the two regions likewise underwent no such changes as could account for the reversal of their respective positions in the world.

Back in the fifteenth century, China sent ships on voyages of exploration longer than that of Columbus, more than half a century before Columbus, and in ships more advanced than those in Europe at the time. Yet the Chinese rulers made a decision to discontinue such voyages and in fact to reduce China's contacts with the outside world. European rulers made the opposite decision and established worldwide empires, ultimately to the detriment of China. In short, geography sets limits, but people determine what they will do within those limits. In some parts of the world, geographic limits have been set so narrowly that the peoples of these regions have never had the options available to either the Europeans or the Chinese. Isolation has left such regions not only lagging economically but fragmented culturally and politically, making them prey to larger, more prosperous and more powerful nations.

We have seen how cultural handicaps have followed Eastern Europeans as they immigrated overseas, leading to lower levels of income than among immigrants from Western Europe who settled in the same places, whether North America or Australia. If Africans had immigrated voluntarily to the Western Hemisphere, instead of in bondage, is there any reason to believe that their earnings would have achieved an equality that the Slavic immigrants failed to achieve?

There is no question that Africans and their descendants faced the additional barrier of color prejudice, but can we measure its effects by assuming that black people would have had the same income and wealth as white people in the absence of this factor—especially in view of the large disparities among different groups of white immigrants, not to mention the rise of some nonwhite groups such as Chinese Americans and Japanese Americans to incomes above the national average?

Put differently, geography has not only cheated many peoples of equal cultural opportunities, it has also cheated all of us today of a simple criterion for measuring the economic and social effects of other variables, such as prejudice and discrimination. Nothing has been more common in human history than discrimination against different groups, whether different by race, religion, caste or in innumerable other ways. Moreover, this discrimination has itself been unequal—more fierce against some groups than others and more pervasive at some periods of history than in others. If there were not so many other powerful factors creating disparities in income and wealth, it might be possible to measure the degree of discrimination by the degree of differences in economic outcomes. Even so, the temptation to do so is seductive, especially as a means of reducing the complexities of life to the simplicities of politics. But the facts will not fit that vision.

Anyone familiar with the history of race relations in the Western Hemisphere would find it virtually impossible to deny that blacks in the United States have faced more hostility and discrimination than blacks in Latin America. As just one example, 161 blacks were lynched in one year in the United States, but racial lynching was unknown south of the Rio Grande. Perhaps the strongest case against the predominance of discrimination as an explanation of economic disparities would be a comparison of blacks in Haiti with blacks in the United States. Since Haiti became independent two centuries ago, Haitian blacks should be the most prosperous blacks in the hemisphere and American blacks the poorest, if discrimination is the overwhelming factor, but in fact the direct opposite is the case. It is Haitians who are the poorest and American blacks who are the most prosperous in the hemisphere—and in the world.

None of this should be surprising. The fact that discrimination deserves moral condemnation does not automatically make it causally crucial. Whether it is or is not in a given time and place is an empirical question, not a foregone conclusion. A confusion of morality with causation may be politically convenient, but that does not make the two things one.

We rightly condemn a history of gross racial discrimination in American education, for example, but when we make that the causal explanation of educational differences, we go beyond what the facts will support. Everyone is aware of times and places when the amount of money spent educating a black child was a fraction of what was spent educating a white child, when the two groups were educated in separate systems, hermetically sealed off from one another, and when worn-out textbooks from the white schools were then sent over to the black schools to be used, while new and more up-to-date textbooks were bought for the white children. The number of days in school sometimes differed so much that a black child with nine years of schooling would have been in class the same number of days as a white child with only six years of schooling. It seems so obvious that such things would account for disparities in test scores, for example.

But is it true?

There are other groups to whom none of these factors apply—and who still have had test score differences as great as those between black and white children in the Jim Crow South. Japanese and Mexican immigrants began arriving in California at about the same time and initially worked in very similar occupations as agricultural laborers. Yet a study of a school district in which their children attended the same schools and sat side-by-side in the same classrooms found IQ differences as great as those between blacks and whites attending schools on opposite sides of town in the Jim Crow South. International studies have found different groups of illiterates—people with no educational differences because they had no education—with mental test differences larger than those between blacks and whites in the United States. Nor is this necessarily a matter of genetics. During the First World War, black soldiers from Ohio, Illinois, New York, and Pennsylvania scored higher on mental tests than did white soldiers from Georgia, Arkansas, Kentucky, and Mississippi.

What is "the" reason? There may not be any such thing as "the" reason. There are so many cultural, social, economic, and other factors interacting that there was never any reason to expect equal results in the first place. That is why plausible simplicities must be subjected to factual scrutiny.

Back in 1899, when the schools of Washington, D.C. were racially segregated and discrimination was rampant, there were four academic high schools in the city—three white and one black. When standardized tests were given that year, the black academic high school scored higher than two of the three white academic high schools.

Today, nearly a century later, even setting such a goal would be considered hopelessly utopian. Nor was this a fluke. That same high school was scoring at or above the national average on IQ tests during the 1930s and 1940s. Yet its physical plant was inadequate and its average class size was higher than that in the city's white high schools. Today, that same school has a much better physical plant, and per-pupil expenditures in the District of Columbia are among the highest in the nation. But the students' test scores are among the lowest. Nor was this school unique in having had higher academic achievements during a period when it seemingly lacked the prerequisites of achievement and yet fell far behind in a later period when these supposed prerequisites were more plentiful.

This is obviously not an argument for segregation and discrimination, nor does it deny that counter-examples might be found of schools that languished in the first period and did better in the second. The point here is much more specific—that resources have had little or nothing to do with educational quality. Numerous studies of schools in general have shown that, both within the United States and in international comparisons. It should be no surprise that the same applies to black schools.

Politically, however, the disbursement of resources is by no means inconsequential. The ability to dispense largess from the public treasury has for centuries been one of the signs and prerogatives of power in countries around the world. In electoral politics, it is vital as an element in reelection. But the ultimate question is: Does it in fact make people better off? How that question is answered is much less important than that it be asked—that we not succumb to social dogmas, even when they are intellectually fashionable and politically convenient.

It is also important that economic and other disparities be confronted, not evaded. Bestselling author Shelby Steele says that whites in America today are fearful of being considered racists, while blacks are fearful of being considered inferior. Social dogmas may be accepted because they relieve both groups of their fears, even if these dogmas neither explain the past nor prepare for the future.

It should be axiomatic that there is not unlimited time, unlimited resources, nor unlimited good will among peoples—anywhere in the world. If we are serious about wanting to enlarge opportunities and advance those who are less fortunate, then we cannot fritter away the limited means at our disposal in quixotic quests. We must decide whether our top priority is to smite the wicked or to advance the less fortunate, whether we are looking for visions and rhetoric that make us feel good for the moment or whether we are seeking methods with a proven track record of success in advancing whole peoples from poverty to prosperity.

In an era when esoteric theories can be readily turned into hard cash from the public treasury, our criteria must be higher than what can get government grants for middle-class professionals. They must instead be what will rescue that youngster imprisoned, not only in poverty, but also in a social and cultural isolation that has doomed whole peoples for centuries in countries around the world. When we promote cultural provincialism under glittering labels, we must confront the hard question whether we are throwing him a lifeline or an anchor.

History, geography, and cultures are influences but they are not predestination. Not only individuals but whole peoples have moved from the backwaters of the world to the forefront of civilization. The late Italian author Luigi Barzini asked of Britain: "How, in the first place, did a peripheral island rise from primitive squalor to world domination?" The story of Japan's rise from a backward country in the mid-nineteenth century to one of today's leading economic powers has been at least equally as dramatic. Scotland was for centuries known for its illiteracy, poverty, and lack of elementary cleanliness. Yet, from the mid-eighteenth to the mid-nineteenth century, most of the leading intellectual pioneers of Britain were Scots, and Scots also become prominent in business, banking, medicine, and engineering—not only in Britain but around the world.

These and other dramatic and heartening rises of whole peoples came from doing things that were often directly the opposite of what is being urged upon less fortunate groups in the United States today. Far from painting themselves into their own little cultural corner and celebrating their "identity," these peoples sought the knowledge and insights of other peoples more advanced than themselves in particular skills, technologies, or organizational experience. It took centuries for the English to absorb the cultural advances brought by such conquerors as the Romans and the Normans and by such immigrants as the Huguenots, Germans, Jews, and others who played a major role in developing the British economy. Their early dependence on outsiders was painfully demonstrated when the Romans pulled out of Britain in the fifth century, in order to go defend their threatened empire on the continent, and the British economy and political structure both collapsed. Yet ultimately—more than a thousand years later—the British rose to lead the world into the industrial revolution and controlled an empire containing one-fourth of the land area of the earth and one-fourth of the human race.

Japan's economic rise began from a stage of technological backwardness that was demonstrated when Commodore Perry presented them with a gift of a train. Here was their reaction: "At first the Japanese watched the train fearfully from a safe distance, and when the engine began to move they uttered cries of astonishment and drew in their breath. Before long they were inspecting it closely, stroking it, and riding on it, and they kept this up throughout the day."

A century later, the Japanese "bullet train" would be one of the technological wonders of the world, surpassing anything available in the United States. But, before this happened, a major cultural transformation had to take place among the Japanese people. A painful aware- ness of their own backwardness spread through Japan. Western nations in gen- eral and the United States in particular were held up as models to their children. Japanese textbooks urged imitation of Abraham Lincoln and Benjamin Franklin, even more so than Japanese heroes. Many laments about their own shortcomings by the Japanese of that era would today be called "self-hate." But there were no cul- tural relativists then to tell them that what they had achieved was just as good, in its own way, as what others had. Instead, the Japanese overcame their backwardness, through generations of dedicated work and study, rather than redefining it out of existence.

Both the British and the Japanese became renowned for their ability to absorb the ideas and the technology of others and to carry them forward to higher levels. So did the Scots. At one time, it was common for Scots to blindly imitate the English, even using an English plow that proved to be unsuitable for the soil of Scotland. Yet, once they had absorbed what the English had to offer, the Scots then surpassed the English in some fields, notably medicine and engineering.

History does not offer blueprints for the present but it does offer examples and insights. If nothing else, it can warn us against becoming mesmerized by the heady visions and soaring rhetoric of the moment.

POSTSCRIPT

Do Industrialization and Capitalism Cause Racial and Ethnic Inequalities?

A mere generation ago, racial and ethnic inequalities were quite peripheral to most social science courses. Efforts to link the international scene with discrimination in specific countries were rare. Now, as shown by this debate, the issue is obtaining a serious hearing. The alleged parochialism of U.S. social science, especially in matters of minority relations, may be less of a problem than it was in the past. To some, the current problem in this area is how to transcend what is seen as reverse ethnocentrism and the bashing of U.S. society. That is, most problems pertaining to racial, ethnic, and gender minorities are seen as terrible. White males of European descent are sometimes seen as the source of all structural strains, if not of evil.

This debate, it seems, considerably raises the level of discourse. Henry presents the "radical" and, some would say, "trendy" position. Yet her argument is deeply rooted in careful historical analysis, she develops meaningful analytical categories, and she leaves at least some room to acknowledge minority achievements. Sowell's ideas are fairly original, and they present a potentially stimulating alternative to most standard theories of racial and ethnic inequalities. Moreover, he attempts to use his analysis to generate meaningful policies that might help minorities.

Can the two sides be synthesized? Is it possible to reformulate Sowell's categories so that his geographical determinism could be seen as generating technological advantages for some who then, in terms of Henry's arguments, turned this achievement into instruments by which to exploit others (such as guns)? Can generations of prejudice and discrimination be discounted simply because a theory identifies initial inequalities as resulting from geographical disadvantages? In today's world, can the geopolitical argument hold up? Also, although they do not yet match the achievements of some Asian Americans in terms of economic and educational gains, haven't African Americans made many significant gains that Henry ignores?

Among Sowell's later books is *The Vision of the Annointed: Self-Congratulation as a Basis for Social Policy* (Basic Books, 1995). Among the many insightful works of world-system analyst Immanuel Wallerstein is *The Modern World-System III: The Second Era of Great Expansion of the Capitalist World-Economy* (Academic Press, 1988). One delineation of this perspective that is easy to follow is *An Introduction to the World-System Perspective*, 2d ed., by Thomas R. Shannon (Westview Press, 1996). A challenging work that links Eurocentrism, colonialism, and Western science is *Is Science Multicultural? Postcolonialisms,*

Feminisms, and Epistemologies by Sandra G. Harding (Indiana University Press, 1998).

Other works that lie somewhere between Henry's and Sowell's perspectives are *White Lies: Race and the Myths of Whiteness* by Maurice Berger (Farrar, Straus & Giroux, 1998) and Farai Chideya's *Color of Our Future* (William Morrow, 1999). Two works that address the thesis that capitalism creates racism are Carter A. Wilson's *Racism: From Slavery to Advanced Capitalism* (Sage Publications, 1996) and *How Capitalism Underdeveloped Black America: Problems in Race, Political Economy, and Society* by Manning Marable (South End Press, 1983).

ISSUE 6

Have Scholars Ignored the Willing Participation of Germans in Killing Jews During the Holocaust?

YES: Daniel Jonah Goldhagen, from "The Paradigm Challenged," *Tikkun* (May/June 1998)

NO: Christopher R. Browning, from "Victim Testimony," *Tikkun* (January/February 1999)

ISSUE SUMMARY

YES: Daniel Jonah Goldhagen, a political scientist at Harvard University, argues that most writers on the Holocaust have ignored or minimized the role of the police, soldiers, and other "ordinary" Germans as willing executioners of Europe's Jews.

NO: Pacific Lutheran University professor Christopher R. Browning rejects Goldhagen's "accusatory approach," which he contends is self-serving, promotes misunderstanding of traditional scholarship, and does little to advance society's understanding of genocide.

Human beings are remarkably ingenious at creating barriers between themselves and others. One of the most obvious results of such barrier creation, if maintained, is the classification of an entire group as a "minority." By definition, a minority will, at the very least, have less power than the majority. The actual numbers are usually irrelevant. Frequently, members of the majority are numerically a minority, although they may control the numerical majority economically, politically, and socially.

Various labels and definitions of minorities are created to legitimate their separation and unequal treatment (e.g., they are biologically or intellectually inferior, they are emotional, they are dishonest, they are heathens, and so on). In addition, institutional mechanisms emerge. The former are attitudinal or sociopsychological control variables. Institutional mechanisms include legal and other kinds of structural controls, such as apartheid, segregation, the prohibition of hiring minorities for certain jobs, and the prohibition of teaching minorities to read and write.

More extreme modalities of institutional control include enslavement and genocide. The latter means the systematic killing of the members of a particular group. Usually, efforts at genocide result in mass murder, with many, if not most, members of the targeted group escaping and surviving. Most attempts at genocide in the past, while horrible, failed to wipe out any group of people entirely. The Turks' murder of hundreds of thousands of Armenians in the early part of the twentieth century, the recent carnage in central Europe, the Rwandan and other African massacres, and the killing fields of Cambodia in the 1970s—as terrible as they were and are—fell short of their objectives.

Hitler's killing machine was far more efficient. Approximately one-third of the world's Jews—between 7 and 12 million—were systematically murdered during the years 1933–1945. If it had not been stopped by the Allied victory, there is little doubt that Germany would have come close to killing most Jews. Ironically, the Jews were arguably the most assimilated minority group in Germany, if not in all of Europe. They held positions of honor, and their scientific, political, economic, social, and legal contributions were enormous. Yet in less than a dozen years the Jews went from being friends and neighbors to pariahs who were hunted down in Germany and throughout Europe and cast into death camps and gas chambers. Women, children, and grandparents were murdered along with teenage and middle-aged males. How did this happen?

In spite of the fact that many of the Holocaust survivors (as well as Jews in other parts of the world) are among the most educated women and men in their countries, this question has not yet been answered satisfactorily to many. For over 50 years the utter surprise, horror, and enormity of the deed has generated more ink by both Jewish and non-Jewish scholars than any other efforts at minority oppression, including other cases of attempted geno-cide. Yet it remains a serious *Historikerstreit* (deep conflict between scholars) both in and out of Germany. Unlike the better-publicized Holocaust deniers controversy, in which fringe types maintain that there was no killing of Jews in Germany, the controversy over how the Holocaust could have happened at all has shaken the foundations of traditional scholarship.

As you read the following selection by Daniel Jonah Goldhagen, note the many reasons why he is angry that most scholars (in his eyes) have mis-understood or misrepresented the importance of anti-Semitism in Germany. Are such scholars functioning, however unintentionally, as apologists for the Nazis? What alternative paradigm does Goldhagen seem to provide? Consider how elements from his suggestions might be useful in researching slavery and in addressing current issues of racism and sexism in the United States.

Note how Christopher R. Browning defends his methodology in the sec-ond selection (he relied on survivors' statements in his studies). What is the disagreement between Goldhagen and Browning on the role of interviewing victims? Consider also the reasons why Browning dismisses Goldhagen for misusing facts and engaging in self-promotion. Who is right? Have scholars ignored the willing participation of many in the killing of Jews?

YES

Daniel Jonah Goldhagen

THE PARADIGM CHALLENGED

Imagine a history of American slavery whose authors assert that the testimony of slaves should not be used and where the practice is not to use it, where there is no extensive investigation of whites' conceptions of the enslaved Africans, where it is said that the whites were unwilling slave holders and that few non-slave owning southern whites supported the institutions of slavery, where it is said that those enslaving and routinely brutalizing the slaves were not at all influenced by their conceptions of the victims, where the precept and practice is not to describe the full extent and character of the slave holders' brutality, where it is said furthermore that African American scholars today are suspect because they are African American and the motivation is imputed to them of writing about slavery solely for monetary or political gain or psychological gratification. Imagine what our understanding of American slavery would look like, how skewed it would be, if even only some of these positions prevailed. We would wonder how slavery ever could have existed.

When writing about the Holocaust, many scholars and commentators routinely adopt positions analogous to one or several of these examples. Indeed, some of these positions are a never justified, seemingly unquestioned norm among those who write about the Holocaust. These positions would seem curious—methodologically, substantively, and interpretively—even absurd, if put forward about slavery or about other genocides or mass slaughters such as those in Rwanda or Bosnia. Yet when asserted about the Holocaust, barely an eyebrow is raised. The question naturally arises as to why such manifestly false positions have been frequently adopted? Why until recently were almost no studies, especially no systematic studies, of the perpetrators —namely of those who killed Jews, guarded the camps and ghettos, and deported them to their deaths—to be found among the tens of thousands of books written about the Holocaust, despite the wealth of evidence that had long been available?

The heretofore hegemonic paradigm about the Holocaust has rendered them puppet-like actors, mere pawns whose inner world need not be investigated. It denies the moral agency and assent of the perpetrators and holds

From Daniel Jonah Goldhagen, "The Paradigm Challenged," *Tikkun*, vol. 13, no. 3 (May/June 1998). Copyright © 1998 by *Tikkun*. Reprinted by permission of *Tikkun*, a bimonthly Jewish critique of politics, culture, and society.

that they were compelled to act by forces external to them, such as terror, bureaucratic strictures and modes of behaving, the logic of the system, or social psychological pressure. For a long time, this paradigm diverted attention away from the perpetrators because its logic of external compulsion meant that the perpetrators' internal lives (their beliefs and values) and anything that was sociohistorically particular to them (that they were members of a deeply anti-Semitic political culture) did not influence their actions and that, therefore, the study of them would not contribute much to explaining the Holocaust. The problems with this view and its construction can be indicated by comparing it to the hypothetical, fanciful rendering of slavery above.

The perpetrators are finally being discussed extensively, even if the number of empirical studies remains small. Yet in the last couple of years, a phalanx of scholars and commentators have adopted positions which would make the perpetrators of the Holocaust the only perpetrators of genocide who believed that their victims did not deserve to die, indeed that their victims were innocent. This strange view seems still stranger given that many of the German perpetrators knew explicitly that they had a choice not to kill, and that no German perpetrator was ever killed, sent to a concentration camp, jailed, or punished in any serious way for refusing to kill Jews. That it was possible for many perpetrators to avoid killing Jews, and that some of them availed themselves of this possibility, became known already at the Nuremberg Trials. The related, stunning fact that not a single German perpetrator was ever seriously punished for refusing to kill Jews has been known

since 1967 when the jurist Herbert Jager published his pioneering study, *Crime Under Totalitarian Domination*. (I treated both the general issue and presented the case of one man who refused to kill in "The 'Cowardly' Executioner: On Disobedience in the SS" in 1985). Yet this latter fact has remained unmentioned in virtually every work written on the perpetration of the Holocaust since Jager first established it.

Why would Martin Broszat, Raul Hilberg, Eberhard Jäckel, Hans Mommsen and other scholars who wish to explain the Holocaust not discuss these fundamental facts extensively or incorporate their significance into the explanations and interpretations which they put forward? Is it of so little import—that men and women who knew that they could avoid killing children would choose to destroy them anyway—that it is not even worth mentioning this information? Acknowledging these facts would have shaken the foundations of the paradigm to which many scholars are wedded, namely that the perpetrators were compelled by external forces to act against their will. This crucial omission of evidence, for which no justification has been offered, has for decades skewed non-experts' and the public's understanding of the Holocaust.

Similarly, when these writers depict and analyze the events of the Holocaust and particularly when they analyze the motives of the perpetrators, they rarely, if ever, use the testimony of the victims, neither their letters, diaries, memoirs, nor oral testimonies. That is not to say this testimony is never used; certainly, it is used by those writing about the lives and plight of the victims, and by scholars like Yehuda Bauer, Saul Friedlander, and Israel Gutman. But when constructing interpretations of the perpetrators of the Holocaust, it has been the unspoken practice of so many scholars to all but ignore, and certainly not to use systematically, victims' accounts of the perpetrators' actions and the victims' understanding of perpetrators' attitudes towards them. With the sometime exception of a quotation or two from Primo Levi (or some other particularly distinguished memoirist), one searches such authors' works in vain for the instances where they use such evidence seriously or even at all.

Some authors explicitly declare that victim testimony is of little value and an impediment to understanding. Raul Hilberg, who is one of the principal exponents of the conventional paradigm and practice and who often speaks authoritatively for those who are in his school, has written roughly seven pages on survivor testimony in his recent memoir, *The Politics of Memory*, which are highly distorting and almost thoroughly disparaging. He makes not a single positive statement about the victims' testimony as a historical source, except when it shows Jews in a bad light. Even though Hilberg acknowledges in passing, in a strikingly critical vein, that the survivors' "principal subjects are deportations, concentration camps, death camps, escapes, hiding, and partisan fighting"—precisely those themes relevant to learning about and analyzing the perpetrators—his practice and that of those who follow him suggests that they believe that there is little evidentiary or interpretive value in all this testimony.

This widespread devaluation of the testimony of the Jewish victims is peculiar. I know of no other historical or contemporary instance about which it is said that the victims of genocidal onslaughts, sus-

tained violence, or brutality have little of value to tell us about those who victimized and brutalized them. I know of no other crime (e.g., assault, kidnapping), no instance of large scale brutal domination (e.g., slavery, serfdom), no genocide (e.g., Rwanda, Cambodia), nor any other historical instance in which the victims— in the case of the Holocaust a group of eyewitnesses numbering in the millions —are said, as a class, to have little or nothing to tell us about the deeds and attitudes of the men and women who victimized them and whose murderousness and brutalities against others they witnessed. And not only is their testimony silently ignored by many and explicitly devalued by some but it is also sometimes deprecated by writers like Istvan Deak, who began a review of several books on the Holocaust in *The New York Review of Books* (June 26, 1997) by presenting a caricature of and an attack on survivors memoirs. He goes so far as to say that "an accurate record of the Holocaust has been endangered, in my opinion, by the uncritical endorsement, often by well-known Jewish writers or public figures, of virtually any survivor's account or related writings." How have the survivors' writings "endangered" "an accurate record of the Holocaust"? Except to say (correctly) that personal details may be inaccurate or embellished, Deak does not justify his sweeping condemnation.

The invaluable importance of survivor testimony is attested by the crucial, indeed, indispensable part that the survivors have played in the trials of thousands of perpetrators in the Federal Republic of Germany. Many of these trials could not have been held without survivor testimony. The judgment in the most famous of these trials, that of a contingent of guards and administrators of

Auschwitz held in 1963, states: "Apart from scattered and not very informative documents, the court had to rely exclusively on witness testimony to help it reconstruct the acts of the defendants" (my emphasis). One thousand three hundred witnesses (among them former guards) gave testimony for that trial.

The Germans' documentation of the killing institutions and operations never record the details of the hundreds or thousands of perpetrators' many actions. Typically, the documents contain, at most, the bare logistics and results of killing operations. So an entire killing operation that might have lasted a full day will appear in a document with nothing more than one line stating that on a given date, the German unit "resettled" (a euphemism) or "shot" some number of Jews.

The accounts of survivors afford a more transparent, more spacious window to the Nazi inferno than the often beclouded and distorting postwar testimonies of the perpetrators who, in order to escape punishment, frequently lie. (Still, some of the perpetrators are surprisingly forthcoming, especially about other perpetrators, and many unwittingly reveal a great deal. Such testimony is invaluable and should be used.) Who would expect to learn from the perpetrators or from contemporaneous German documents a full and accurate account of the texture and details of the Holocaust, of the daily living and dying, of the treatment of the prisoners by the German overlords, including their frequent gratuitous brutality, of the social life of the inmates, their thoughts and feelings, their suffering and their agony? Where can we more fully learn about the character of the perpetrators' actions —the degree to which the perpetrators tortured, brutalized, beat, degraded, and mocked the victims—about the perpetrators' demeanor and attitudes, about whether they acted zealously or reluctantly, about whether they expressed hatred for the victims, and gain insight into the perpetrators' willingness and motivation?

The answer is obvious: from the victims.

Could accurate histories of the Jewish ghettos and of the concentration camps be written without the accounts of the survivors contained in their depositions and memoirs? A perusal of three great books, H. G. Adler's *Theresienstadt, 1941–1945*, Israel Gutman's *The Jews of Warsaw 1939–1943*, and Hermann Langbein's panoramic analysis of Auschwitz, *People in Auschwitz*, shows that the authors have drawn heavily on the accounts of survivors. Are these historical works thereby vitiated? Do they imperil the accuracy of the historical record?

A comparison with the historiography of the Soviet Gulag is instructive. Its scholars do not cast aspersion on the memoirs and accounts of former inmates, whose narratives are indispensable. Aleksandr Solzhenitsyn writes in his Preface to *The Gulag Archipelago:* "This book could never have been created by one person alone. In addition to what I myself was able to take away from the Archipelago—on the skin of my back, and with my eyes and ears—material for this book was given me in reports, memoirs, and letters by 227 witnesses ... this is our common, collective monument to all those who were tortured and murdered." Evidence of the kind that Hilberg, Deak, Christopher, Browning, and others dismiss, explicitly or tacitly, as unreliable and inessential forms the foundation of Solzhenitsyn's magisterial work. Would Deak argue that Solzhenitsyn has "endangered" "an accurate record" of the Gulag? Or are only survivors of the Holocaust and those who find great value in their testimony prone to such "endangerment"?

It is not because this witness testimony is meager, imprecise, or devoid of insight that it has been ignored. It includes hundreds of memorial volumes, each one containing compilations from survivors of one destroyed Jewish community after another detailing their fates; depositions of many thousands of survivors in the trials of the perpetrators from one camp, killing unit, and ghetto after another; vast amounts of oral testimony; and thousands of memoirs. It would be hard to imagine an instance of mass slaughter, violence, or brutality that would be documented by a greater abundance of rich, detailed, often highly literate testimony that contains penetrating analyses of the events and of the people who perpetrated them. This makes the disparagement of the victims' testimony and its paltry use that much more surprising and indefensible.

Victims' accounts belie the conventional paradigm and the attendant scholarly theories about the perpetrators that have held sway, namely that the perpetrators either explicitly disapproved or at least did not approve of the mass slaughter of Jews and of other victims. The victims know differently. They have testified so again and again. If the proponents of these explanations had incorporated the voices of the victims into their own writings, then they would have undercut immediately and devastatingly their own theories, and the conventional paradigm.

The omission of the survivors' accounts has obscured, among many other aspects of the Holocaust, one of its constituent features. Scholars' failure to use victim accounts has thus, to use Deak's phraseology, "endangered" "an accurate record": the perpetrators' virtually boundless cruelty towards the Jews has been all but ignored by those who purport to explain the perpetrators' actions. If, as many authors do, one relies principally on highly partial and often unrevealing contemporaneous German documents, then, of course, one will not find frequent and detailed recitations of Germans' routine torturing of Jews. These authors construct a distorted portrait of the Holocaust in which the perpetrators' brutality—so frequent, inventive, and willful—is minimized, blurred, or absent. Consequently, it is not surprising that those few authors adhering to the conventional paradigm who do at least say something in passing about the sources of the German perpetrators' brutality to the Jews do not deem the perpetrators to have been moved by hatred of their victims.

Hilberg, for instance, in *Perpetrators, Victims, Bystanders,* puts forward the notion that the German perpetrators' brutality was "most often" an "expression of impatience" with the pace of killing operations. Browning's related view, in *Ordinary Men,* is that the perpetrators' brutality was utilitarian, the consequence of a pragmatic need to be brutal when they were under "pressure" "in terms of manpower... to get the job done," like rounding up Jews for deportation. When not under such pressure, in Browning's view, they were cruel when under the sway of cruel officers but seemingly not at other times. Hilberg and Browning have failed to present evidence which supports what are ultimately little more than speculations. (How does Hilberg know that they were impatient? He never says. And is the torture of defenseless people, including children, the invariable result of impatience, as Hilberg's quick and casual manner of presenting his speculation suggests?) But that is the least of their problems. Hilberg and Browning's empirical claims are falsified by evidence of the perpetrators' widespread, non-utilitarian cruelty in all manner of circumstances, even when they were not undermanned, even when they were not impatient, even when they were not undertaking killing operations at all.

For example: although the Germans of Police Battalion 101, during one of the ghetto roundups and deportations in Miedzyrzec, Poland, degraded and tortured Jews in the most gratuitous, willful manner, their deeds are entirely absent from their testimony and, therefore, also from Browning's analysis of the killing operation. The accounts of survivors tell a different, more accurate, and more revealing story. Survivors are adamant that the Germans' cruelty that day was anything but instrumental. It was wanton, at times turning into sadistic sport. At the marketplace the Jews, who had been forced to squat for hours, were "mocked" (khoyzek gemacht) and "kicked," and some of the Germans organized "a game" (shpil) of "tossing apples and whoever was struck by the apple was then killed." This sport was continued at the railway station, with empty liquor bottles. "Bottles were tossed over Jewish heads and whoever was struck by a bottle was dragged out of the crowd and beaten murderously amid roaring laughter. Then some of those who were thus mangled (tseharget) were shot." Afterwards, the Germans loaded the dead together with the living onto freight cars bound for Treblinka. One photograph documenting the final stage of what may be this deportation has survived.

Small wonder that in the eyes of the victims—but not in the self-serving testimony of the perpetrators, in contemporaneous German documents, or in Browning's book—these ordinary Germans appeared not as mere murderers, certainly not as reluctant killers dragged to their task against their inner opposition to genocide, but as "two-legged beasts" filled with "bloodthirstiness." (Browning claims that from survivors "we learn nothing about" Police Battalion 101 or, for that matter, about itinerant units in general.) Germans' cruelty towards Jews, as the victims (and also some of the perpetrators after the war) reveal, was voluntary, widespread, sustained, inventive, and gleeful. Such gratuitous cruelty could have been produced only by people who approved of what they were doing.

The vast corpus of the victims' testimony substantiates the conclusion that ordinary Germans degraded, brutalized, and killed Jews willingly because of their hatred of Jews. So profound and near universal was the anti-Semitism during the Nazi period that to the Jewish victims it appeared as if its hold on Germans could be captured and conveyed only in organic terms. As Chaim Kaplan, the trenchant observer and diarist of the Warsaw ghetto, concluded: "A poison of diseased hatred permeates the blood of the Nazis." Once activated, the Germans' profound hatred of Jews, which had in the 1930s by necessity lain relatively dormant, so possessed them, that it appeared to have exuded from their every pore. Kaplan observed many Germans from September 1939 until March 1940 when he penned his evaluation derived from their actions and words:

The gigantic catastrophe which has descended on Polish Jewry has no parallel, even in the darkest periods of Jewish history. First, in the depth of hatred. This is not just hatred whose source is in a party platform, and which was invented for political purposes. It is a hatred of emotion, whose source is some psychopathic malady. In its outward manifestations it functions as physiological hatred, which imagines the object of hatred to be unclean in body, a leper who has no place within the camp.

The [German] masses have absorbed this sort of qualitative hatred.... They have absorbed their masters' teachings in a concrete, corporeal form. The Jew is filthy; the Jew is a swindler and an evildoer; the Jew is the enemy of Germany, who undermines its existence; the Jew was the prime mover in the Versailles Treaty, which reduced Germany to nothing; the Jew is Satan, who sows dissension between one nation and another, arousing them to bloodshed in order to profit from their destruction. These are easily understood concepts whose effect in day-to-day life can be felt immediately.

Significantly, this characterization is based on the words and acts of Germans —of SS men, policemen, soldiers, administrators, and those working in the economy—*before* the formal genocidal program of systematic killing had begun. It is the masses, the ordinary Germans, not the Nazi ideologues and theoreticians, whom Kaplan exposes. The causal link between the Germans' beliefs and actions is palpable, so that the Jews feel the effect of their "concepts" "in day-to-day life." In the more than two-and-a-half years of subsequent concentrated observation of the Germans in Warsaw, Kaplan saw no reason to alter this evaluation, an evaluation confirmed by a German police official, who states plainly that those serving alongside him in the Cracow region

of Poland "were, with a few exceptions, quite happy to take part in shootings of Jews. They had a ball!" Their killing was motivated by "great hatred against the Jews; it was revenge...." The revenge was not for any real harm that the Jews had visited upon Germans, but for the figmental harms for which the perpetrators believed, in their anti-Semitically-inflamed minds, the Jews were responsible.

Effectively extinguishing the voices of the victims, and sometimes suggesting that they do little more than glorify themselves, is not only indefensible methodologically but also a deep affront to survivors. Most victims want to do nothing more than convey what the perpetrators did to them, their families, and to others. Victims of such crimes can never gain full restitution for their losses and suffering. What they generally seem to want is to have the truth be told, particularly so that the perpetrators will acknowledge their crimes. Survivors often express bewilderment that their experience has been generally ignored by the scholarship that treats the perpetration of the Holocaust. Many survivors have told me that they are thankful for my book, *Hitler's Willing Executioners[,]* and for its detailed analysis of the German perpetrators, including their gleeful cruelty and brutality, which the survivors attest was almost always voluntary. They say my interpretation of the Holocaust accords with what they and so many others witnessed and experienced.

* * *

A new way of approaching the study of the Holocaust is implicit in much of the unparalleled, widespread public discussion about various aspects of the Holocaust that has been taking place [recently]. The old paradigm consists of abstract, faceless structures and institutions (bureaucracy, the greatly exaggerated "terror apparatus" that was supposedly directed at ordinary Germans, the SS, the Nazi Party, the gas chambers) and allegedly irresistible external forces (totalitarian terror, the exigencies of war, social psychological pressure). This paradigm effaces the human actors and their capacity to judge what they were doing and to make moral choices. It is ahistorical. All of this implies that any people from any era with any set of beliefs about Jews (even non-anti-Semites) would have acted in exactly the same manner as the perpetrators, with the same brutality, zeal, and Mephistophelean laughter. This is being challenged by a view that recognizes that the Holocaust was brought about by human beings who had beliefs about what they were doing, beliefs which they developed within a highly specific historical context, and who made many choices about how to act within the institutions in which they worked and which brought them to their tasks in the first place. The human beings are finally at the center of the discussion. The heretofore dominant question of "What compelled them to act against their will?" is being replaced by the question of "Why did these people choose to act in the ways that they did?"

As a result, powerful myths are crumbling: the myth that the Swiss or the Swedes acted as they did only because of the German threat; the myth that the peoples in different occupied countries did not do more to thwart the Germans or less to help in the killing of the Jews merely because of their fear of the occupying Germans; the official Allied governmental myths that they could not reasonably have attempted to do much more to save the victims; the myth that those who procured Jewish property, including art, generally did so innocently; the myth that the perpetrators, by and large, disapproved of what they were doing but were coerced, were being blindly obedient, or were pressured to act as they did; and the three related myths that the German people more broadly (all the exceptions notwithstanding) did not know that their countrymen were killing Jews en masse, did not support the Nazi regime even though its many brutal policies (forced sterilization, so-called "euthanasia," the violent persecution of the Jews and others, the reintroduction of slavery into the European continent) were widely known, and did not approve of the general eliminationist persecution of the Jews.

Not surprisingly, many people who have either been comforted by such views or whose careers have been made by adopting positions that buttress them, and who find the new, powerful challenges to these views to be politically undesirable or personally threatening, are extremely unhappy and have let that be known. The frequent response is to attack, often in the most vitriolic and unprincipled ways, the messengers —whether they be scholars, institutions like the Hamburg Institute for Social Research which produced the exhibit, "War of Extermination: The Crime of the Wehrmacht, 1941–1944" that has been traveling around Germany, the World Jewish Congress for forcing the issue of Swiss gold onto the agenda, or the witnesses, namely Jewish survivors, whose testimony has always been a devastating threat to many of the myths.

It would be beneficial if certain basics could become widely accepted which the crumbling paradigm has obscured. They include:

1. The discarding of the caricature of individual Germans as having had no views of their own about the rightness of what they or their countrymen were doing, which included slaughtering children. We need to know how these views were distributed among Germans, and how they, singly or in interaction with other factors, influenced Germans' actions during these years. The same applies to the peoples of other countries, those where the Germans found many willing helpers and those where the populace worked to thwart (sometimes successfully) the program of extermination.

2. The rejection of the myth that the large scale, mass killing of Jews remained unknown to the broader German public. Germans themselves are becoming more candid: twenty-seven percent of those who were at least fourteen years old at the end of the war now admit that they knew of the extermination of the Jews *when it was taking place.* (The survey which determined this stunning new finding, which the chief pollster of the German wire service, dpa, says is still clearly a substantial underreporting of the real figure, was conducted for the German television network ZdF in September 1996. Yet in the flood of articles written about the Holocaust since then, I have seen no mention of this finding, perhaps because it explodes a central element of the conventional paradigm —even though the survey's results were announced and discussed on German national television during a

panel discussion on the Holocaust and reported by the dpa.)

3. The acknowledgment that Germans who were not members of specifically targeted groups (Jews; Gays; the Sinti and Roma peoples, who are commonly known as gypsies; the mentally infirm; the Communist and Social Democratic leadership) were not so terrorized as the totalitarian terror model posits. The enormous amount of dissent and opposition that Germans expressed against so many policies of the regime and the regime's responsiveness to public sentiment and action makes this clear. So a new understanding of the relationship between state power, regime policy, and popular consent needs to be worked out. The comparative question of why Germans expressed different degrees of dissent and opposition to different policies, yet virtually no principled dissent against the eliminationist persecution of the Jews, becomes central. More generally, all models that posit that irresistible external forces compelled people—Germans, French, Poles, Swiss, or the Allies—to act as they did need to be replaced by views that acknowledge the existence of human agency. If the vast majority of the German people had genuinely been opposed to the radical eliminationist persecution of the Jews, then Hitler would have never been able to pursue it as he did.

4. The adoption of a comparative perspective on genocide, so that those who study the Holocaust do not adopt methodological practices or causal claims that are at odds with how we study and what we know of other analogous phenomena. All available evidence (contemporaneous

documents and the testimony of perpetrators, victims, and bystanders) that is not rendered suspect according to clearly articulated, standard social scientific principles is to be used. Regarding the use of the testimony of Jewish survivors, for example, the reasons given for excluding it must be defensible if one changed the word "Jews" to Tutsis, Bosnians, Cambodians, Armenians, the victims of the Gulag, or enslaved Blacks in the American South. The methods of the social sciences present rules regarding research design and the structure of inference, including when generalization is allowed and even required. A major research project might be undertaken using all available evidence to catalogue what is known of the backgrounds, actions, and attitudes of every perpetrator in every ghetto, camp, and other institution of killing—those who victimized Jews and non-Jews—so that a general portrait and systematic analysis of them can be composed.

5. The recognition that the Holocaust had *both* universal and particular elements. Its universal aspect is that all people have the capacity to dehumanize groups of others so intensely that their hatred can impel them to commit genocide. Its particular aspect is that such views do not come to exist in equal measure in every society about every group, and when they do, it is not every society that has a state which mobilizes those who hold such views in a program of mass annihilation. The universal capacity to hate does not mean that all people actually do hate and hate all others in the same way, or that all hatreds will motivate people to treat the object of

their aggression similarly. Real existing hatreds, as opposed to the capacity to hate, are primarily socially constructed and historically particular.

* * *

The Holocaust is not "beyond human comprehension." In principle, it is as explicable as every other genocide. No one says that the Rwandan or Cambodian genocide cannot be explained. What so many people simply do not want to accept is that the victims of the Holocaust have a great deal to tell us about their victimizers (no less than do the victims in Rwanda and Bosnia); and that the German perpetrators were like the perpetrators of other mass slaughters: the vast majority of these Germans were also willing executioners. That people automatically accept these facts about non-Jewish victims of genocide and about African or Asian perpetrators but not about Jews and "civilized" white Christian Europeans respectively is disturbing. Does anyone think for a moment that the Turkish, Hutu, or Serbian perpetrators did not believe that slaughtering Armenians, Tutsis, or Muslims was right? Does anyone for a moment believe that the testimony of these genocides' victims should not be used extensively in order to learn about the texture of the genocides, including the attitudes of the perpetrators? Indeed, in the Armenian genocide, in Bosnia, Cambodia, Rwanda, and other instances of mass slaughter, such testimony is eagerly used by scholars and has provided the principal knowledge of the perpetrators' deeds and attitudes.

As ever more Germans themselves have come to realize, one can acknowledge that many Germans were virulent anti-Semites during and before the Nazi period, that many supported the brutal persecution of the Jews, and that the murderers of European Jewry came from the ranks of ordinary Germans, without it leading either to the indictment of those Germans who resisted the prevailing norms and practices of the time, or to a condemnation of today's Germany. This seems so obvious that it bears mentioning only because some commentators continue to put forward two fallacies: they pretend that demonstrating that *individual* culpability for crimes was far more widespread in Nazi Germany than had previously been presumed is the same as maintaining that Germans are guilty as a *collectivity*. They also react as if plain talk about the Germany of the past defames the Germany of the present. Such notions can be maintained only by people who themselves deny individual responsibility, are beholden to the insupportable notion of a timeless "national character" (Hilberg has declared in his recent memoir that a German "national character" exists and is critical of others for not accepting this), or believe in some kind of collective, inheritable guilt. Individual Germans during the Nazi period should be judged according to the same legal and moral principles that we use for people in our own societies. The Federal Republic of Germany, like all other countries, should be assessed in the light of its own character and practices, achievements and shortcomings, and not according to a period of Germany's history that is now over fifty years in the past.

Much of what I write here finds an echo in a private letter written in 1946 by a German to a priest, in which the author was plainly speaking his mind:

In my opinion the German people as well as the bishops and clergy bear a great guilt for the events in the concentration camps. It is perhaps true that afterwards not a lot could be done. The guilt lies earlier. The German people, including a great part of the bishops and clergy, accepted the National Socialist agitation. It allowed itself to be brought into line (*gleichgeschaltet*) [with Nazism] almost without resistance, indeed in part with enthusiasm. Therein lies its guilt. Moreover, even if one did not know the full extent of the events in the camps, one knew that personal freedom and all the principles of justice were being trampled underfoot, that in the concentration camps great atrocities were being perpetrated, and that the Gestapo and our SS and in part also our troops in Poland and Russia treated the civilian population with unexampled cruelty. The pogroms against the Jews in 1933 and in 1938 took place in full public view. The murders of the hostages in France were officially announced by us. One cannot therefore truly assert that the public did not know that the National Socialist government and army command constantly and as a matter of principle violated natural law, the Hague Convention, and the most simple laws of humanity. I believe that much could have been prevented if all the bishops together on a certain day from their pulpits had publicly protested against all this. This did not occur and for this there is no excuse. If for this the bishops had been sent to prison or concentration camp, then this would not have been a loss, on the contrary. All this did not occur, therefore it is best to be silent.

The author of this letter was no less a personage than Konrad Adenauer, the long time and, by many, revered post-War Christian Democratic Chancellor of Germany who, more than anyone else helped to reintegrate Germany into the community of nations. No one would accuse Adenauer of condemning every last German (even though he wrote of "the German people"), of being anti-German, of maintaining that Germans could never change and would therefore eternally share the views which led them to support Nazism, so why do some deem the speaking today of Adenauer's plain truths to be indications of such attitudes and to be impermissible?

Anyone who knows today's Germany, the Germany which Adenauer worked so steadfastly to forge, knows that it is remarkably different from Nazi Germany. Indeed, it is only by acknowledging the depths to which Germany had sunk, and not just that it somehow had the misfortune to have been captured by a brutal, murderous dictatorship, that one can appreciate the enormous accomplishments of Germans after the war. By denying how Germany really was, we will never fully understand the great effort Germans have made and the good that has occurred after the war. By being false to the past, the conventional, scholarly paradigm which denies the agency of the actors is also false to the present. When one acknowledges that it was culturally-constructed racist beliefs and values which led many Germans to take part in, and so many more—though decidedly not all Germans—to support, the annihilation of the Jews and the killing and brutalizing of many other Europeans deemed racially inferior, it becomes more comprehensible why Germany has been able to change so much. Political culture can be transformed.

Just as the beliefs which led American whites to enslave Blacks and then to impose legal segregation have changed profoundly, so too—as the survey data demonstrate unequivocally—have the dominant beliefs in Germany *gradually* changed about Jews, humanity, and

democracy. (In 1933, most Germans voted for parties openly dedicated to destroying the country's democratic institutions. Today, virtually everyone in what was West Germany sincerely supports democracy.) Such profound, positive changes in beliefs and values are hopeful—though, of course, both in the United States and in Germany prejudice and ethnic hatred have by no means been completely eradicated. Over the period of a generation or two, a society can greatly remake its prevailing views, making its people less bigoted and less prone to engaging in discrimination and violence. But this is not accomplished easily. How such changes occur are little studied and little understood. Perhaps people should devote more attention to examining such transformations, instead of working so hard to deny that in Germany any transformation was necessary.

My view of the mentality of the vast majority of Germans during the Nazi period is similar to that of one of the most esteemed of German historians of this century, Friedrich Meinecke (though our understandings of what produced this mentality differ). Meinecke remained in Germany but he kept his distance from the Nazi regime, retreating into "internal emigration" from which he observed the regime's policies and the people's attitudes, sentiments, and conduct. Soon after the war, he wrote a book, *The German Catastrophe*, seeking to explain the origins and character of Nazism. He was severely critical of Germans' conduct during the Nazi era and held that certain traits and traditions common in Germany had contributed to the emergence and success of the Nazi movement. His was a rare candor. Meinecke acknowledged that it is a "shocking" and "shameful" fact that a "criminal gang succeeded for twelve years in compelling the allegiance of the German people and in imparting to a great part of this people the belief that it was following a great 'Idea'." Germany had fallen, but it was not beyond redemption. Its moral corruption was curable. For "the German people had not become diseased to the core with a criminal mentality but suffered only a unique grave infection caused by a poison that had been administered to it. The case could have become hopeless if the poison would have wrought its effect in the body for long." The young generation would have then become incurably afflicted with moral degeneration. "That was the gloomiest thought that tormented me during the twelve years, that the party could remain in power in perpetuity and instill in the entire younger generation its own degenerate character."

His gloomy moments notwithstanding, Meinecke knew that Germany would be defeated. The prospect of that defeat filled him with mingled trepidation and hope. Germany would suffer grievous external, material destruction but it would be liberated spiritually and mentally. The poisons which he and the Warsaw ghetto's diarist, Kaplan, each identified as having infected so many Germans—so that each one chose to write in collective, corporeal terms—would, in Meinecke's view dissipate and Germany's "soul" and "conscience" would "breathe again." A new day could and would dawn.

Meinecke's depiction of the mentality of most Germans during the Nazi period could hardly be bettered. His prophecy could hardly have been more true.

NO

Christopher R. Browning

VICTIM TESTIMONY

In his recent TIKKUN article ("The Paradigm Challenged." July/August 1998), Daniel Goldhagen directly attacks my work as well as that of the larger community of Holocaust scholars. In doing so, he misrepresents and distorts what he attacks in order to achieve a hollow victory over his own easily demolished strawmen.

Goldhagen states that I "dismiss" survivor testimony "explicitly or tacitly, as unreliable and inessential" and that I have allegedly written that "from survivors 'we learn nothing [sic] about' Police Battalion 101 or, for that matter, about itinerant units in general. What in fact I wrote in the preface of *Ordinary Men* is the following: "... unlike survivor testimony about prominent perpetrators in the ghettos and camps, where prolonged contact was possible, survivor testimony can tell us *little* about an itinerant unit like Reserve Police Battalion 101" (xvii–xviii, emphasis added). In a subsequent panel exchange with Goldhagen, I expanded as follows:

> Jewish testimony was indispensable to my study in establishing the chronology of the fall of 1942. What became a blur of events for the perpetrators remained quite distinct days of horror for the victims. Also, while survivor testimony may be extremely valuable in many regards, it does not illuminate the internal dynamics of an itinerant killing unit. It would be difficult for the victim of such a unit to provide testimony concerning the various levels of participation of different perpetrators and any change in their character over time. Where long-term contact between victims and perpetrators did occur, survivors are able to and in fact do differentiate on such issues.

Thus Goldhagen misquotes from the preface of *Ordinary Men*, changing "little" to "nothing," and furthermore takes my remarks from our subsequent exchange entirely out of context. I do not "dismiss" survivor testimony either "explicitly or tacitly" as "unreliable and inessential." I do insist that survivor testimony, like any other evidence, be used cautiously and with due regard for what any particular witness was in a position to know. Quite simply, Goldhagen's summary of my position is a gross distortion; his misquotation violates accepted academic standards.

From Christopher R. Browning, "Victim Testimony," *Tikkun*, vol. 14, no. 1 (January/February 1999). Copyright © 1999 by *Tikkun*. Reprinted by permission of *Tikkun*, a bimonthly Jewish critique of politics, culture, and society.

Moreover, I have noted that in rare cases where survivors had worked as translators or menial laborers in German police stations they were indeed in a position to give invaluable testimony precisely on the question of the attitudes and mindset of middle-aged reserve policement like those in Reserve Police Battalion 101. Such a rare witness was Oswald Rufeisen, whose story was told by Nechama Tec in her book *In the Lion's Den*. According to Rufeisen, among the thirteen policement at Mir, one stood out as a "beast in the form of a man," three did not participate in Jewish actions at all, and most of the remainder considered the killing of Jews as something "unclean" about which they did not wish to talk. This is a far cry from Goldhagen's portrayal of middle-aged German reserve policement, according to which they were uniformly possessed of a "lethal, hallucinatory view of the Jews" and viewed their killing of Jews as a "a redemptive act" to be celebrated and enjoyed.

Tec's book was published in 1992, the same year as *Ordinary Men*, and thus Rufeisen's unique testimony was not available to me and could not be cited in my book. It was available to Goldhagen before he published *Hitler's Willing Executioners* four years later, but he did not cite it. It appears that this self-styled champion of survivor testimony can be quite selective himself when survivor testimony fails to support the hypothesis he is trying to prove.

In my opinion, Goldhagen's accusatory approach to the issue of survivor testimony disservices scholarship because it diverts attention from the real issue, namely what the historian can learn from a systematic use of concentrated survivor testimony. I am currently engaged in researching the Starachowice ghetto and

labor camps in the Ramdon district in central Poland; my work is based primarily on more than one hundred written and videotaped survivor testimonies given over a period of more than four decades. Several conclusions relevant to this discussion have already emerged.

The first concerns the itinerant unit involved in the ghetto roundup and deportation action on October 27, 1942. This was the notorious *Vernichtungsbatallion* or "destruction battalion" of Erich Kapke that travelled from ghetto to ghetto throughout the Ramdom district. When asked by German investigators desperate for witnesses and evidence, not one survivor could recognize either the name or picture of Kapke, much less anyone else in the unit. They knew that the battalion consisted of foreign auxiliaries but disagreed on nationality. Different witnesses suggested Lithuanians, Latvians, Ukrainians, or Estonians. The survivors had extremely vivid and precise memories about many aspects of that traumatic day, but not about the itinerant police unit that dispatched their families to Treblinka. Given the horrific circumstances of that brief event, it is no reproach of survivors or devaluation of their testimony to note that there are some things they cannot tell us about it.

Goldhagen's second strawman is an "old" or "hegemonic paradigm" that is now allegedly crumbling in the face of public discussion "that has been taking place for the last two years" (which is to say since the publication of *Hitler's Willing Executioners* in 1996). According to Goldhagen, this "old paradigm" consists of "abstract, faceless structures and institutions" and "irresistible external forces"; it renders perpetrators into "puppet-like actors" and "effaces" them as human beings making moral choices because it portrays these perpetrators as "compelled by external forces to act against their will."

For the past twenty years, I have been publishing various case studies about particular groups of perpetrators—the so-called "Jewish experts" of the German Foreign Office, the motor pool mechanics who designed and constructed the gas van, the military administration of occupied Serbia, the personnel of the Semlin death camp, the ghetto administrators of Lodz and Warsaw, the public health doctors of the General Government, and the men of Reserve Police Battalion 101. It has been my goal throughout to put human faces on the perpetrators and assess their motivation. Never did I suggest or conclude that they had been "compelled... to act against their will" in ways that precluded moral or legal judgment.

How has Goldhagen constructed this pernicious discourse that casts himself as the pioneer hero of a morally-sensitive history and attempts to delegitimize the generations of pre-1996 historians as morally obtuse? He does so by inventing an artificial dichotomy between actions motivated by allegedly "internal" factors permitting moral judgment (namely beliefs and values, which in effect Goldhagen limits to anti-Semitic or racist convictions) and actions "compelled" by what he terms "external" factors that, because of the compulsion, are devoid of a moral dimension involving choice. In reality, of course, there are numerous "values and beliefs" that motivate people other than racist ones, such as perceptions of authority, duty, legitimacy, and loyalty to one's unit and country in wartime. And there are other personality traits such as ambition, greed, and lack of empathy that shape people's behavior without absolving them of individual responsibility. Indeed, in the penultimate paragraph of my book, *Ordinary Men,* I conclude that "The reserve policemen faced choices, and most of them committed terrible deeds. But those who killed cannot be absolved by the notion that anyone in the same situation would have done as they did. For even among them, some refused to kill and others stopped killing. Human responsibility is ultimately an individual matter" (188).

The issue between Goldhagen and the "phalanx of scholars" whom he dismisses has never been the "willing" participation of "ordinary Germans" from virtually every segment of society, as would be clear to anyone who has read with an open mind Raul Hilberg's *The Destruction of the European Jews,* first published in 1961. Nor is it an issue that "culturally-constructed racist beliefs and values... led many Germans to take part in" the annihilation of the Jews, even though the debate over the relative roles of ideological and cultural factors on the one hand and situational, organizational, and institutional factors on the other has been continuous, spirited, and fruitful. Indeed, most elements of Goldhagen's proposed new paradigm, to say nothing of the passages from [Konrad] Adenauer and [Friedrich] Meinecke that he quotes approvingly, have been commonplace in virtually any course on modern German history or the Holocaust taught in the United States in the past two decades or more.

What then is all the fuss about, and why did Goldhagen's book arouse such a negative reaction among so many scholars? It is useful to remind ourselves of what he actually wrote and said in 1996. In several interviews promoting the book, Goldhagen flatly proclaimed that German culture was a "genocidal culture." In the book itself, he urged historians to rid themselves of the notion that Germans in the Third Reich were "more or less like us" or that "their sensibilities had remotely approximated our own" (27, 269). He recommended that scholars approach the Germans as they would the Aztecs, who believed human sacrifice was necessary to cause the sun to rise (28).

Goldhagen wrote emphatically that "with regard to the motivational cause of the Holocaust, for the vast majority of the perpetrators, a monocausal explanation does suffice"—namely "a demonological antisemitism" that "was the common structure of the perpetrators' cognition and that of German society in general" (416, 392). Accordingly, "equipped with little more than the cultural notions current in Germany," ordinary Germans "wanted to be genocidal executioners" (185, 279). And when given the chance, the vast majority killed with "gusto" and "for pleasure" (241, 451). In contrast, they killed Poles with "obvious distaste and reluctance" (241). A major transformation in German political culture after the war was duly noted, though the possibility of a similar or even greater transformation of German political culture under the impact of the Nazi regime between 1933 and 1941 was denied.

When I presented these quotations at the symposium of the U.S. Holocaust Memorial Museum in April 1996 as representing the core of his argument, Goldhagen acknowledged that I had read his book carefully and did not dispute that I had summarized his argument correctly. If he has muted his sweeping generalizations and fiery accusations and embraced the likes of Adenauer and Meinecke, we are witnessing not the crumbling of some "hegemonic paradigm," but the repositioning of Daniel Goldhagen.

POSTSCRIPT

Have Scholars Ignored the Willing Participation of Germans in Killing Jews During the Holocaust?

If Goldhagen is correct, why haven't Jewish concentration camp survivors been interviewed frequently by Holocaust scholars? Would German witnesses and perpetrators provide better information? Does Browning's contention that the oppression of Jews was largely done by ordinary men reflect psychological studies such as Stanley Milgram's obedience research, in which subjects delivered what they believed to be extreme electric shocks to Milgram's confederates, despite the screaming protests of the confederates, because an authority figure told them that they must do so? That is, is it accurate to suggest that anyone, under the right circumstances, would be willing to harm minority group members?

Many Marxists in Germany have attacked Goldhagen's thesis. They reject his assertion that post–World War II capitalist Germany has successfully reeducated Germans so that they are no longer capable of doing a Hilter's bidding or of having the entrenched hatred of Jews. Does Goldhagen's thesis strongly support the teaching of multicultural courses and diversity training?

A good place to begin further research on this issue is the many books mentioned in the selections, including Browning's *Ordinary Men: Reserve Police Battalion 101 and the Final Solution in Poland* (HarperCollins, 1992) and Goldhagen's *Hitler's Willing Executioners: Ordinary Germans and the Holocaust* (Alfred A. Knopf, 1996). In addition, an entire cottage industry has already developed attacking and defending Goldhagen. See, for example, Robert R. Shandley and Jeremiah Riemer, eds., *Unwilling Germans? The Goldhagen Debate* (University of Minnesota Press, 1998). See also Goldhagen's response to Browning, "Victim Testimony, a Debate: Daniel Goldhagen Responds to Browning," *Tikkun* (January–February, 1999). For broader discussions on the Holocaust, see Gabriel Schoenfeld, "Auschwitz and the Professors," *Commentary* (June 1998) and critics' reactions plus Schoenfeld's reply to them in "Holocaust Studies," *Commentary* (August 1998), as well as Lawrence L. Langer's "Preempting the Holocaust," *The Atlantic Monthly* (November 1998). For a moving account of historical events, read *Tomi: A Childhood Under the Nazis* by Tomi Ungerer (Roberts Rinehart, 1998). An additional scholarly book on the Holocaust is Saul Friedlander, *Nazi Germany and the Jews: The Years of Persecution, 1933–1939* (HarperCollins, 1997). Finally, important lessons can be learned from the Human Rights Watch book *Slaughter Among Neighbors: The Political Origins of Communal Violence* (Yale University Press, 1995).

On the Internet . . .

Afro-Americ@

This site, owned by the Afro-American Newspaper Company of Baltimore, Inc., offers information on African American culture, history, national news that is of interest to the African American community, and more.
http://www.afro.com/index.html

Academic Info: African American History

This is a thorough annotated directory of Internet resources on Black history. It links to meta-indexes and general directories, digital libraries, online publications, exhibits, and much more.
http://academicinfo.net/africanam.html

Council on American-Islamic Relations (CAIR)

This is the home page of the Council on American-Islamic Relations (CAIR). In addition to news releases, publications, and action alerts, CAIR provides a "media watch" page that reports on anti-Arab and anti-Muslim representations and stories in the media.
http://www.cair-net.org

PART 2

Social Identities and Cultural Conflict

The Socratic admonition "Know thyself" is easier said than understood for most minority group members. "Who they are" is often a composite of labels and definitions applied to minorities by members of the dominant group, media portrayals, and minorities' interpretations of their ancestors' descriptions. Scientifically identifying and analyzing minorities is only the first step toward understanding. What aspects of the broader culture are accepted or rejected by minorities? How and why do convenient, sometimes romantic myths harden into ideologies that result in cultural conflict, both functional and dysfunctional?

■ Do the Identities of Blacks Lie in Africa?

■ Should We Call Ourselves African Americans?

■ Are Hispanics Making Significant Progress?

■ Do Cultural Differences Between Home and School Explain the High Dropout Rates for American Indian Students?

■ Does Rap Music Contribute to Violent Crime?

■ Are Arabs and Other Muslims Portrayed Unfairly in American Films?

ISSUE 7

Do the Identities of Blacks Lie in Africa?

YES: Olga Idriss Davis, from "The Door of No Return: Reclaiming the Past Through the Rhetoric of Pilgrimage," *The Western Journal of Black Studies* (vol. 21, no. 3, 1997)

NO: Keith B. Richburg, from "Continental Divide," *The Washington Post Magazine* (March 26, 1995)

ISSUE SUMMARY

YES: Assistant professor of speech communication Olga Idriss Davis links Black identity with Africa. In a moving account based on her visits to Senegal, West Africa—the departing point to America for thousands of slaves, almost none of whom ever saw their homes again—she reveals how she and many other African Americans have benefited from their pilgrimages to Africa.

NO: *Washington Post* correspondent Keith B. Richburg contends that it is trendy and foolish for Blacks to attempt to validate themselves through identification with Africa. He is personally thankful that his forefathers were enslaved and transported to America so that he did not grow up in Africa.

Historically, the United States has been a nation of immigrants that continuously generates new Americans and new minorities. The country of origin of individual newcomers, or at least their descendants, is generally considered irrelevant. Yet most minorities frequently went through generational metamorphosis: people of the first generation worked extremely hard to make it in the "promised land," and they were very proud that their children were born U.S. citizens, spoke English, and acted like typical Americans. While the members of the first generation were not necessarily ashamed of their origins, their main interest was to be assimilated into American society. Their own children, however, were sometimes ashamed of their immigrant parents because they wore outlandish clothing, spoke broken English, or reflected customs that other children made fun of. However, by later generations, the stigma, the hardships, and the outsider status had evaporated. The initial hurts of the old country and the prejudice and bigotry of the new one became distant memories. People began to search for their roots, sometimes hiring genealogists or attending meetings of ethnically or racially based organizations. Eventually, interested people embarked on individual treks and organized pilgrimages back to the old country. Citizens of the old countries point out to these people sites known to have been frequent places of disembarkation from which the American tourists' ancestors may have begun their journeys to America. Religious sites, sometimes neglected or even shunned as pagan monuments by locals, assume new importance if they capture the interests of tourists seeking their roots.

Although many Blacks in the United States are racially mixed (as are whites), when they search for their roots, they almost always look toward the African continent. This is largely because the social (and, until recently, the legal) construction of citizens with significant African ancentrage was "Negro" citizenship status.

Historically, next to women and children, African Americans are by far the oldest minority group in the United States. In spite of the vast majority having been forced to come here as slaves beginning in 1619, and in spite of enforced segregation, some argue that Black Americans are the "most American" of all minorities. Regardless, Blacks have experienced painful ambivalences about their identity. For generations, African Americans have gone to great pains to distance themselves from all things African, partially because the media and historians negatively portray less developed countries, especially African ones. Although there have always been members of the Black avant-garde who proudly display African artifacts in their homes or who have traveled to Africa (other than as Black missionaries), the vast majority of Blacks have minimized any linkage, even historical, to Africa. This is partially a function of the stigma of Africa and partially the typical desire of most minorities to be considered American.

The situation is now quite different. Black intellectuals, the affluent, and the middle class are transcending the stigma attached to Africa. In the United States they are identifying with political liberation (and have for many generations), and in Africa they are identifying with the "homeland." Afrocentrism is very much in fashion. Over the past 30 years America's core values have been challenged by the civil rights movement, the antiwar movement, the feminist movement, and other movements. A variant of reverse ethnocentrism has been achieving prominence, if not dominance, among some. That is, what is foreign is viewed positively, while what is American, especially that associated with the elite, is viewed negatively. Accomplishments of Blacks both in the United States and elsewhere are now greatly celebrated. African American leaders, even when found corrupt, are usually forgiven. To many, such allowances are functional because the main thing is that Blacks are finally allowed to excel and to be proud.

As you look over the following very different interpretations of the African experience by Olga Idriss Davis and Keith B. Richburg, consider the relevancy for minority groups (and others) of myths. In what ways might returning to one's area of origin be similar or dissimilar for Blacks as it would be for Asians or white Europeans? Would Americans from Serbia or Bosnia, for instance, visiting after generations, experience similar disappointments to those of Richburg? Does Africa really tell African Americans who they are? Does the identity of any American lie outside of the United States?

YES

Olga Idriss Davis

THE DOOR OF NO RETURN

Abstract. Placed against the backdrop of Senegal, West Africa, this essay explores the symbolic meaning of pilgrimage as a re-encountering of self. By examining the role of social drama, Goree Island becomes a ritual site of meaning and lived experience. Employing Victor Turner's theory of pilgrimage, language serves as a framework for discussing the journey to Africa by many African-Americans. This essay enhances understanding of how African-Americans use discursive means to claim identity with Africa and locate a collective oneness with its people and cultures. The inquiry asks, what is the symbolic nature of African-American pilgrimage?

But watch, watch where you walk, forgotten stranger—this is the very depth of your roots: Black. Walk proud. Watch, listen to the calls of the ancestral spirits, prodigal son—to the call of the long-awaited soil. They welcome you home, home. In the song of birds the winds whisper the golden names of your tribal warriors, the fresh breeze blown into your nostrils floats their bones turned to dust. Walk tall. The spirits welcome their lost-son-returned.

—excerpt from **Home-Coming Son** by Tsegaye Gabre Medhen

Throughout the United States African-Americans are taking tours to a variety of countries on the continent of Africa. It is as though they are searching for something; attempting to fill a void that is not easily squelched by the celebratory month of Black history, Kwaanza rituals or holidays of slain civil rights leaders. The notion that African-Americans are reclaiming their identity by locating a cultural past informs the rhetorical dimensions of place as a symbolic representation of survival in the culture of pilgrimage.

The purpose of this essay is to examine how a rhetoric of pilgrimage reveals African Americans' search for identity and cultural collectiveness. Reclaiming the past through pilgrimage points to the slave castle of Goree Island off the coast of Senegal, West Africa, which serves as a site of sacred recollection through the symbolic means of the narrative. The narratives of African-Americans who travel to this island reveal the complexity of social and cultural performance of which social dramas of historical significance

From Olga Idriss Davis, "The Door of No Return: Reclaiming the Past Through the Rhetoric of Pilgrimage," *The Western Journal of Black Studies*, vol. 21, no. 3 (1997). Copyright © 1997 by *The Western Journal of Black Studies*. Reprinted by permission.

emanate. The metaphor of pilgrimage illuminates the social ritual of returning to Africa to claim self, redefine culture, and reclaim the social reality of life in America. First, the concepts of pilgrimage and social drama are defined. Second, the way in which language provides a framework for symbolic action of transformation and empowerment is explored. The essay concludes by discussing the implications of pilgrimage for explicating the deep structures of cultural memory and self-healing through a reclamation of the past.

The rhetoric of pilgrimage for the African-American is a language deeply rooted in the quest for self-identity. From the time of slavery the African-American has inquired, *Who am I? Why am I here? How do I return home?* According to historian John Henrik Clarke (1985):

Self-identity for African-Americans is a search for the lost identity that the slave system had destroyed. The search for an identity in America has been a search for an identity in the world... as a human being with a history, before and after slavery....(p. 157)

This search I contend, ruminates within the center of the African-American spirit. The inner conflict of what it means to be an American and at the same time what it means to be an African-American places one in a double bind both psychologically and politically. How do I negotiate my Africanness with my American character? Where do the two ideologies meet? How do they co-exist if they can at all? It is within the spiritual and cultural transformation of self through sojourning to locate the African consciousness that this secular pilgrimage becomes a unique phenomenon for study. Thus, travelling to a geographical place affectionately termed as the *homeland* or *motherland* is not the essence of the experience, but rather the process by which the African-American comes to know the self within an African context. More importantly, many African-Americans discover the place of pain and suffering deeply embedded in the spiritual consciousness through an encounter of place. They come to know and understand its legacy in the historical, cultural, sociological, and political matrix of world consciousness. It is my contention that a *return home* for African-Americans reaffirms a sense of self by recognizing Western-imposed alienation on the psyche, yet simultaneously reclaiming identity as a lost entity of African heritage.

For many African-Americans, the notion of heritage and ancestral roots are a mystery. Because of the vast pillaging of women, separation of families, and attempts to erase the culture of predominantly West African villages during the fifteenth through the seventeenth centuries by the English, Dutch, Portuguese, French, and Spanish, the African-American of contemporary day knows little if any of the familiar ties to Africa nor of the intellectual and cultural greatness the continent produced. Furthermore, the Western educational system and American culture with its varied media have corroborated extensively to present African people and iconic images as non-beings genetically predisposed to violence on one hand, or extraordinarily talented in the realm of athletics or entertainment on the other. Generationally, myths and folklore of the inferiority of the African have become internalized by African-Americans resulting in the schism of self-identity.

The popular notion of pilgrimage is one of a sacred journey to come in contact with a higher or greater spiritual source. It symbolizes a spiritual awakening elicited by a journey, an escape, a gestalt from which a higher level of consciousness is achieved. Pilgrimage serves as a guide for understanding the contours of human social behavior. Individuals disparate in age, occupation, gender, ethnicity, social class, power, and wealth temporarily come together to journey to sacred shrines. Victor Turner (1974) explains that pilgrimages "are 'functional equivalents' in complex cultures dominated by the major historical religions partly of 'rites de passage' and partly of 'rituals of affliction' in preliterate, small-scale societies." He suggests in the following statement that pilgrimages function both:

> ... as occasions on which communitas is experienced and as journeys toward a sacred source of communitas which is also seen as a source of healing and renewal. (p.203)

As a result, pilgrimages function as community-building efforts to perpetuate a sense of oneness, collectiveness, and unity. The notion of pilgrimages as social dramas enables rhetorical scholars to explain the homologies of narrative form and symbolic content within African-American experience. Such a lens informs that African-American pilgrimages claim a lost consciousness and serve the same individual and societal functions as Turner's corporeal pilgrimages do.

It is suggested here that while the Turnerian theory of pilgrimage asserts an anthropological purview, the African-American experience of pilgrimage is a re-awakening, a connection with the center of being-ness, an often-untapped space of yesterday in the subconsciousness of the here and now. In the poem by Tsegaye Gabre Medhen, homecoming of Africa's children is depicted much differently. It is a return to self, hidden in the mysteries of pre-slavery, slave castles, the middle passage, and the rich culture of the African heritage of which there is gross miseducation (Clarke, 1985). The pilgrimage is a recognition of the psyche, a replenishing of the reality of Blackness not celebrated in the Westernized conception of its banality, but rather Blackness as pride, strength, revelation of traditions, and recognition of greatness within.

The idea of returning to self is reflected by the late educational theorist Paulo Freire's experience of "being at home on African soil" expressed as he first stepped on African soil in Tanzania:

> ... I make this reference to underline how important it was for me to step for the first time on African soil, and to feel myself to be one who was returning and not one who was arriving. In truth, five years ago, as I left the airport of Dar es Salaam, going toward the university campus, the city opened before me as something I was seeing again and in which I re-encountered myself. The color of the skies; the blue-green of the sea; the coconut, the mango and the cashew trees; the perfume of flowers; the smell of the earth; the bananas and, among them, my very favorite, the apple-banana; the fish cooked in coconut oil; the locusts hopping in the dry grass; the sinuous body movements of the people as they walked in the streets, their smiles so ready for life; the drums sounding in the depths of night; bodies dancing and, as they did so, expressions of their culture that the colonialists, no matter how hard they tried, could not stamp out—all of this took possession of me and made me realize that I was more African than I had thought. Naturally,

it was not only these aspects, considered by some people merely sentimental, that affected me. There was something else in that encounter: a re-encounter with myself. There is so much I could say of the impressions that continue and of the learning I have done on successive visits to Tanzania only to emphasize the importance for me of stepping on African soil and feeling as though I were returning somewhere, rather than arriving. (Freire, 1974)

Re-encountering self is the foundation to the social reality of African-American pilgrimage. Language shapes the meaning of the past and provides a symbolic discourse for liberating and empowering self of an historical past.

On the island of Goree, social dramas create a language of pilgrimage where place is fused with past and present horrors.

PILGRIMAGE AS SOCIAL DRAMA

According to Turner, social dramas are created out of an urgency to become reflexive about the cause and motive of action damaging to the social fabric (Turner, 1988). Reflexivity refers to the way in which a sociocultural group reflects back upon themselves or other sociocultural components which make up their public selves (p. 24). As African-Americans at the end of the twentieth century reflect back upon the actions, symbols, meanings, roles, social structures, and ethical and legal rules of the peculiar institution of slavery and subsequent ramifications, there still remains a plethora of questions surrounding the damaging effects of such a social system. That history prior to slavery serves as a source for cultural identity illuminates the symbolic meaning of self and provides a context for exploring the

socio-political continuum of Black struggle in American society.

As a rhetorical critic, I am intrigued by the way in which symbolic discourse reveals the dynamics of culture and identity in the process of altering reality. In narrative, rhetoric locates a self of the past by revealing an identity of oppression. Through identification with oppression, the self of the present is empowered by the past. Experiencing the place in which Africans were brutally taken from their land never to return, and setting foot at the very spot from which they left, is a chilling realization of the resilience of the human spirit and of one's place in the historical continuum. The symbolic nature of social dramas point to the rhetorical situation in African-American pilgrimage.

Bitzer (1968) contends that a situation is rhetorical when discourse comes into existence as a response to an obstacle, a defect, an exigency. The exigence of slavery and a coming to terms with the historical implications of past and present invites the creation of discourse in the form of social dramas. Rhetoric provides a symbolic means of altering reality. The narratives of African-American visitors reveal the four phases of social dramas in the creation of public action identified by Turner as breach, crisis, redressive action, and reintegration (Turner, 1974).

For many African-Americans, the reality of oppression, domination, and control continue to plague their definition of national character and racial identity. Often, the rhetorical response is to travel to Africa, particularly Goree Island, to redefine the rhetorical situation of slavery. Crafted within the ritual of the African-African-American Summit, pilgrimage becomes a public discourse of social dramas and a symbolic action of claiming identity. As a delegate to the Third African-African-American Summit, the social drama began as a community of one, preparing me to redefine community through self-reclamation.

THE BREACH

Turner (1988) identifies this phase of social drama as a breach of regular norm-governed social relations. Leaving from a small, predominately-white midwestern town in which I live, to travel to a continent embellished with people diverse in color, hues, and cultures, without knowing the language nor other travellers presents a challenge for social coordination and situational adjustment.

As I departed from my home and family, it struck me quite emphatically, how it must have felt for the African women to be taken from their families. While I was not forced to board the airplane and leave, I still experienced the sorrow of leaving my family, being separated from them across a continent, and the fear of not knowing what to expect in Africa; *Would it be safe? Will I return to my family?* I knew I would be seeing from the eyes of a different culture and would connect to something deeply rooted within me. Yet, I had no expectations, only that I knew I would be transformed in such a way that I would never be the same.

Later that day, I arrived in Philadelphia, the place of our departure. The Concourse for international departures was a place of hustle-and-bustle of approximately 1200 African-American "delegates" checking baggage, obtaining boarding passes, showing passports,

and greeting former acquaintances who attended the first two African-African-American Summits in Cote D'Ivoire and Gabon, respectively. I was struck by the number of students preparing to attend and their excitement to see such dignitaries as the Reverend Jesse Jackson, comedian and social activist Dick Gregory, former United States Secretary of Agriculture Mike Espy, former President of the NAACP Benjamin Chavis, Mayors Marion Berry and Johnny Ford, and United States Secretary of Commerce, the late Ron Brown.

Such an event was history in the making. The Summit was to be a symbolic reunion to unify Africa's "children" around a common ideal. That common ideal was to build a bridge of connectedness between the cultures of Africa and of African-Americans and Friends of Africa.... [T]he children of slaves were returning to build bridges of economic, cultural, and human development in Africa for the twenty-first century and beyond. A personal journal entry reveals such sentiment:

We boarded the plane for SENEGAL! What a wonderful experience—meeting all new people, some with whom I've already made a warm connection in Philadelphia. We are going to see our HOME; A home we have never known —YET WE KNOW. An anticipation like this I've *never* felt before....

As the door opened at Dakar International Airport, we were greeted from the airplane by dignitaries from several of the African countries to be represented at the Summit. From the moments of descending the ramp, there was a sense of meeting family. Hugs, embraces, handshakes, and loving smiles were exchanged and a sense of returning rather than a sense of arrival accompanied these early moments in, for many of us, our first trip to Africa. The Summit in Dakar, Senegal, brought together persons of African ancestry and of American nationality, many of whom did not know each other, yet we were embraced such as are cousins whom one knows of but has never met. Thus, new social relationships were born out of an identity with world history of being separated from the land and the peoples of Africa.

. . . By redefining the social relations between Africans and African-Americans, the breach becomes a symbolic transgression from the contradictions of a lack of cohesiveness between the two cultures.

THE CRISIS

Social drama in the crisis phase stresses the dialectic between the temporalization of space and the spacialization of process (Turner, 1988). Framed within the postmodern turn in anthropology, Turner suggests that performance of the self in everyday life moves to the center of observation and hormeneutical observation (p. 77). In so doing, the factors which bring about inner conflict and sociocultural crises are revealed through the human communication process of symbolic action. Rhetorical discourse, then, provides the vehicle by which African-Americans come to know the meaning of identity and find a context in which to talk about their experience as orphans, pilgrims, children of Africa, dispersed of Ethiopia. The crisis of African-American pilgrimage is a dialectic between the political realities of past and present oppression and locating self-identity within the symbolic reality of both. Turner's notion of the temporalization of space points to a

return to the past to an island off the coast of Senegal; Goree Island's slave castle:

> At the dawn of the 16th century, a small strip of land on the tip of the West African coast became a bustling shipping port. Humans were the main export. They were weighted, chained, dehydrated, sold, and forced to suffer the final indignity of walking through the door of no return. (Martin, 1995)

The limitations of time and space are collapsed as African-Americans are transported back in time as they explore cave dungeons which held thousands of African men, women, children, and infants in preparation for their Transatlantic voyage known as The Middle Passage.

The island of Goree, was a re-encountering of myself in a very emotional way. Here is where an estimated 15 to 20 million Africans were held captive before being shipped to America and other parts of the world. I re-encountered myself as I stood alone in the slave caves, as I touched the stones surrounding me and the earth beneath me; as I stood and gazed out of a little slither of a opening in the wall of rocks. I thought of the many African women my ancestors who also gazed out of the same slither only to be assured they would never return to their tribe, their families again. Not to know what lay beyond the vastness of the Atlantic Ocean is an emotional and psychological turmoil one can only contemplate upon the visit to Goree Island.

I re-encountered myself when I stood in "The Door of No Return" and thought of my ancestors who were forced to either go through the door and walk the plank to the slave ship, or meet his or her death among sharks. Knowing I was standing in the very place sent chills up my spine.

As I looked at the foamy waves crashing beneath the door, I realized in essence, I was standing on holy ground.

Many African-Americans return yearly to the last piece of Africa their ancestors ever saw, Goree Island. I experienced grown men and women after more than 400 years, pay their respects to their ancestors by grieving for their suffering and rejoicing in their strength to survive. Of his trip to Goree Island, an African-American respondent from Ohio comments:

I stood in the door of no return. When a man went through this door, he would either go to America and become a slave or meet his death among the sharks. Nothing can describe the feeling of knowing our ancestors had to walk through that door.

Perhaps for the first time, this journey can begin to heal the wounds of slavery. For African-Americans, a return to the slave castle presents an inner crisis to negotiate the inconsistencies of Western history with an ancestral identity in the dungeons of yesteryear.

Several narratives of African-Americans returning to Goree Island reveal the crisis phase of pilgrimage. Selma Dodson, a radio sales manager explains:

There is still the impression among many Americans, she said, that Africa is mostly jungles, filled with primitive people and a chest-thumping Tarzan. . . . We had our history and our heritage stripped from us. But as a saying I read goes: "I am African, not because I was born in Africa, but because Africa was born in me. I'm going back to find that Africa born in me." (Martin, 1995)

. . . Ferdinand Dennis, a Jamaican-born, British-educated writer/broadcaster who lives in London spoke of the inner crisis faced by African-Americans to find identity thus:

The enslaved Africans lost their myths, their gods, their rituals of celebration, their languages, their names. . . . A search for those things lost, to cease feeling like orphans of history—that's why some of us come back to Africa again and again. But sometimes I do fear that these losses are irretrievable. (Charles, 1993)

African-Americans are attempting to re-claim their African identity while redefining their American identity through the narrative discourse of pilgrimage.

REDRESSIVE ACTION

The redressive action to resolve the historical crises of African identity and the socio-political crises of being Black in America is ritualized in the symbolic action of pilgrimage. The call to heal African-Americans of this lost identity is being addressed in Senegal. Here, Goree Island stands as a place for healing, and as a sacred site for memorializing those who because of their indomitable spirit, endured for the hope of tomorrow's children.

At the Third African-African-American Summit, the host country's President Abdou Diouf of the Republic of Senegal eluded to a redressive action in his opening address to the Summit:

Goree, an island present like a burning ember in our collective memory. Goree, an island of history, a witness to a time when man chose to silence the calling of his higher destiny, and denied his own humanity through the suffering and humiliation he inflicted on his fellow beings. If Goree is to preserve that memory for present and future generations, it is also the symbol of an Africa resolutely turned towards the future. Hopefully, a future world of justice and solidarity. A world which will transcend the prejudices of race and murderous tribalism.

The hope for tomorrow is ever-present in the rhetorical discourse of African culture. . . .

REINTEGRATION

The delegation to the Third African-African-American Summit experienced reintegration into American society with a social recognition of the tenacity of their ancestors and through a legitimation of the human character and spirit revealed on Goree Island. It is my contention that the reintegration phase signifies a process of empowerment occurring during pilgrimage. Empowerment was the recognition that healing took place and transcended us to another level of resilience upon returning to America.

Connecting with others who grieve the past atrocities and look for an escape from the pain of slavery through the knowledge of cultural and self identity is an empowering experience. My personal narrative states that:

This journal is a chronicle, a compilation, and a "journeying" back to the Africa of my past. The Summit is an opportunity to reconnect with the ancestors whose spirits provide the linkages of Africans throughout the Diaspora. (Davis, 1995)

Throughout the week-long experiences filled with workshops, plenary sessions, and visits to markets and historical sites, a spiritual connection between and among African-Americans and Africans became more and more pronounced. It was as though a presence was around us continuously. We were told it was the ancestral spirits welcoming us home and protecting us during our stay.

As the Summit was nearing its closing ceremony, we prepared for our journey back to the United States. Many brothers and sisters from many countries implored us to return to Africa saying, *You are not a stranger, you are one of us. Senegal is your home now, Come back soon.* We said our goodbyes to many of our African family and reflected on the week-long experiences as our plane entered the beautiful blue skies. As we took leave for our journey back to America, the cabin was quiet, some were weeping, others were in silent reflection. All of us however, had been transformed. We would never be the same.

REFERENCES

Bitzer, Lloyd F. (1968). "The Rhetorical Situation." *Philosophy and Rhetoric.* Vol 1:1, 1–14.

Charles, Nick. (1993). "Back to Africa: Call is Deep-Rooted in Blacks Worldwide." January 31. *The Plain Dealer*, p. G1.

Clarke, John Henrik. (1985). "African-American Historians and the Reclaiming of African History," In *African Culture: The Rhythms of Unity.* Asante, Molefi K. and Kariamu W. Asante. Westport: Greenwood Press.

Davis, Olga I. (1995). *Personal Journal.*

Diouf, Abdou. (1995). *Opening Ceremonial Address to the Third African/African-American Summit.* Senegal, West Africa.

Freire, Paulo. (1974). *The Pedagogy of Liberation.* South Hadley: Bergin and Garvey.

Martin, Norma. (1995). African-Americans Plan Trip to Africa for Heritage, Healing. February 13. *The Houston Chronicle*, p. A13.

Turner, Victor. (1974). *Dramas, Fields, and Metaphors.* Ithaca: Cornell UP.

—— (1988). *The Anthropology of Performance.* Baltimore: John Hopkins UP.

NO

Keith B. Richburg

CONTINENTAL DIVIDE

I watched the dead float down a river in Tanzania.

Of all the gut-wrenching emotions I wrestled with during three years of covering famine, war and misery around Africa, no feeling so gripped me as the one I felt that scorching hot day [of] April [1994], standing on the Rusumo Falls bridge, in a remote corner of Tanzania, watching dozens of discolored, bloated bodies floating downstream, floating from the insanity that was Rwanda.

The image of those bodies in the river lingered in my mind long after that, recurring during interminable nights in desolate hotel rooms without running water, or while I walked through the teeming refugee camps of eastern Zaire. And the same feeling kept coming back too, as much as I tried to force it from my mind. How can I describe it? Revulsion? Yes, but that doesn't begin to touch on what I really felt. Sorrow, or pity, at the monumental waste of human life? Yes, that's closer. But the feeling nagging at me was—is— something more, something far deeper. It's a sentiment that, when uttered aloud, might come across as callous, self-obsessed, maybe even racist.

But I've felt it before, that same nagging, terrible sensation. I felt it in Somalia, walking among the living dead of Baidoa and Baardheere—towns in the middle of a devastating famine. And I felt it again in those refugee camps in Zaire, as I watched bulldozers scoop up black corpses, and trucks dump them into open pits.

I know exactly the feeling that haunts me, but I've just been too embarrassed to say it. So let me drop the charade and put it as simply as I can: *There but for the grace of God go I.*

Somewhere, sometime, maybe 400 years ago, an ancestor of mine whose name I'll never know was shackled in leg irons, kept in a dark pit, possibly at Goree Island off the coast of Senegal, and then put with thousands of other Africans into the crowded, filthy cargo hold of a ship for the long and treacherous journey across the Atlantic. Many of them died along the way, of disease, of hunger. But my ancestor survived, maybe because he was strong, maybe stubborn enough to want to live, or maybe just lucky. He was ripped away from his country and his family, forced into slavery somewhere in the Caribbean. Then one of his descendants somehow made it up to South Carolina, and one of those descendants, my father, made it to Detroit during the Second World War, and there I was born, 36 years ago. And if that original ancestor hadn't been forced to make that horrific voyage, I would not have been standing there that day on the Rusumo Falls bridge, a journalist—a mere spectator—watching the bodies glide past me like river logs. No, I might have instead been one of them—or have met some similarly anonymous fate in any one of the countless ongoing civil wars or tribal clashes on this brutal continent. And so I thank God my ancestor made that voyage.

Does that sound shocking? Does it sound almost like a justification for the terrible crime of slavery? Does it sound like this black man has forgotten his African roots? Of course it does, all that and more. And that is precisely why I have tried to keep the emotion buried so deep for so long. But as I sit before the computer screen, trying to sum up my time in Africa, I have decided I cannot lie to you, the reader. After three years traveling around this continent as a reporter for The Washington Post, I've become cynical, jaded. I have covered the famine and civil war in Somalia; I've seen a cholera epidemic in Zaire (hence the trucks dumping the bodies into pits); I've interviewed evil "warlords," I've encountered machete-wielding Hutu mass murderers; I've talked to a guy in a wig and a shower cap, smoking a joint and holding an AK-47, on a bridge just outside Monrovia. I've seen some cities in rubble because they had been bombed, and some cities in rubble because corrupt leaders had let them rot and decay. I've seen monumental greed and corruption, brutality, tyranny and evil.

I've also seen heroism, honor and dignity in Africa, particularly in the stories of small people, anonymous people —Africans battling insurmountable odds to publish an independent newspaper, to organize a political party, usually just to survive. I interviewed an opposition leader in the back seat of a car driving around the darkened streets of Blantyre, in Malawi, because it was then too dangerous for us even to park, lest we be spotted by the ubiquitous security forces. In Zaire, I talked to an opposition leader whose son had just been doused with gasoline and burned to death, a message from dictator Mobutu Sese Seko's henchmen. And in the Rift Valley of central Kenya, I met the Rev. Festus Okonyene, an elderly African priest with the Dutch Reformed Church who endured terrible racism under the Afrikaner settlers there, and who taught me something about the meaning of tolerance, forgiveness, dignity and restraint.

But even with all the good I've found here, my perceptions have been hopelessly skewed by the bad. My tour in Africa coincided with two of the world's worst tragedies, Somalia and Rwanda. I've had friends and colleagues killed, beaten to death by mobs, shot and left to bleed to death on a Mogadishu street.

Now, after three years, I'm beaten down and tired. And I'm no longer even going to pretend to block that feeling from my mind. I empathize with Africa's pain. I recoil in horror at the mindless waste of human life, and human potential. I salute the gallantry and dignity and sheer perseverance of the Africans. But most of all, I feel secretly glad that my ancestor made it out—because, now, I am not one of them.

* * *

... I grew up as a black kid in 1960s white America, not really poor, but not particularly rich either. Like most blacks who settled in Detroit, my father had come up from the South because of the opportunities offered in the automobile plants. ...

There were actually two black Detroits while I was growing up, the east side and the west. The dividing line was Woodward Avenue, our own version of Beirut's infamous Green Line. But the division was more psychological than geographic, centering mainly on black attitudes, the strange caste system in black America at the time, and where you could place your roots in the South. Roughly put, the split was between South Carolina blacks on the west side and Alabama blacks on the east. These were, in a way, our "tribes."

It sounds strange even to me as I look back on it. But those divisions were very real to the black people living in Detroit when I was young, at a time when the city was transforming itself from predominantly white to predominantly black. It was drummed into me that South Carolina blacks, like my family, owned their homes and rarely rented. They had small patches of yard in the front and kept their fences mended. They came from Charleston, Anderson, Greenville, sometimes Columbia. They saved their money, went to church on Sunday, bought their kids new clothes at Easter and for the start of the school year. They kept their hair cut close, to avoid the nappy look. They ate turkey and ham and grits and sweet potato pie. They were well-brought-up, and they expected their children to be the same.

Don't cross Woodward Avenue, we were told, because those blacks over there came up from Alabama. They talked loudly, they drank heavily, and they cursed in public. They had darker skin and nappier hair. They didn't own homes, they rented, and they let the grass in the front run down to dirt, and their fences were all falling apart. They ate pigs' feet, and often had more than a dozen relatives, all from Alabama, stacked up in a few small rooms. They were, as my father would have called them back then, "niggers"— South Carolina blacks being good colored people. The greatest insult was: "He ain't nothin'—he just came up here from Alabama!"

Detroit can get oppressively hot in the summers, and those little houses that black families owned then didn't have anything like air conditioning. So to stay cool, my brother and I would walk (you could walk in those days) down Grand River Avenue to the Globe Theater, where for less than a buck you could sit all day, watching the same movie over and over in air-conditioned splendor until it was time for dinner. I especially remember when the movie "Zulu" was playing, and we watched Michael Caine lead a group of British soldiers against attacking Zulu tribesmen in what is now South Africa. We took turns cheering for the British side and the Zulus. But neither of us really wanted to cheer for the losers. Whoever was rooting for the Africans would usually sit sullenly, knowing what fate held in store. Then came the credits and the heady knowledge that when the movie played again, after a cartoon break, you would be able to cheer for the British once more.

Beyond what I learned from "Zulu," I can't say I had much knowledge of

Africa as a kid. I probably couldn't have named a single African country until high school. The word "black" came into vogue in the 1960s, thanks to, among others, James Brown. In 1967, Detroiters burned a large part of the city to the ground, and then all the white people I knew in my neighborhood starting moving out to suburbs that seemed really far away. A lot of the people my father called "black radicals" took to wearing African-style dashikis, and stocking caps in red, black and green, the colors of African liberation. But, when you were a kid from a quiet, South Carolina family growing up on the west side, these seemed like frightening symbols of militancy, defiance, even violence. Any connection to a strange and unknown continent seemed tenuous.

* * *

... What does Detroit more than a quarter-century ago have to do with contemporary Africa? Maybe I'm hoping that bit of personal history will help explain the attitude of many black Americans to the concept of their own blackness, their African-ness.

You see? I just wrote "black Americans." I couldn't even bring myself to write "African Americans." It's a phrase that, for me, still doesn't roll easily off the tongue, or look natural on the screen of the computer terminal. Going from "colored" to "black" took some time to get used to. But now "African American"? Is that what we really are? Is there anything African left in the descendants of those original slaves who made that long journey over? Are white Americans whose ancestors came here as long ago as the slaves did "English Americans" or "Dutch Americans"? Haven't the cen-

turies erased all those connections, so that we are all now simply "Americans"?

But I am digressing. Let's continue with the story at hand.

Somewhere along the line, I decided to become a journalist. It was during my undergraduate years at the University of Michigan, while working on the school newspaper, the Michigan Daily. My father would have preferred that I study law, then go into politics. Blacks in the 1970s were just coming into their own in politics, taking over city halls across the country and winning congressional seats in newly defined black districts. And that's what articulate, well-educated black kids did: They became lawyers and politicians.

But I wanted to write, and to travel. The travel urge, I think—a longing to cross an ocean—is shared by a lot of midwesterners. I became a reporter for The Post, and would take trips overseas whenever I could save up the money and vacation time. Paris. Morocco. Brazil. London for a year of graduate school. Train journeys across Europe. Trips to Hong Kong, Taiwan, later Japan and China.

But never sub-Saharan Africa (defined as "black Africa"). Whenever friends asked me why, in all my travels, I had avoided the continent of my ancestry, I would usually reply that it was so big, so diverse, that it would take many weeks if not months. I had studied African politics in school, even written a graduate school thesis on the problem of single-party states in Africa. I considered myself a wide-eyed realist, not given to any romantic notions about the place.

The real reason I avoided Africa had more to do with my personal reaction —or, more accurately, my fear of how I would react. I knew that Africa was a continent with much poverty and despair. But what would it be like, really like, to see it as a black person, knowing my ancestors came from there? What if I found myself frightened or, worse, disgusted or repulsed?

And what would it be like, for once in my life, not to stand out in a crowd? To be just one of a vast number of anonymous faces? For better or for worse, a black man in America, or a black man in Asia, stands out.

A friend of mine in Hawaii, a fourth-generation Japanese American, told me once of her fear of traveling to Japan. "I don't know what it would be like to be just another face in the crowd," she said rather innocently. It was a sentiment I immediately shared. When, in early 1991, my editors at The Post asked me if I wanted to cover Africa, that same feeling welled up inside me. I was in Asia on vacation when I got the assignment, and I sought out a Reuter reporter named Kevin Cooney, who was based in Bangkok but had spent several months working in Nairobi. He put it to me bluntly. "In Africa," he said, after we both had a few too many beers, "you'll be just another nigger."

It was a well-intentioned warning, I would find myself recalling often over three sometimes-tumultuous years.

* * *

"Where are you from?" the Zairian immigration officer asked suspiciously in French, fingering through the pages of my passport.

I found the question a bit nonsensical, since he was holding proof of my nationality in his hand. I replied in French, "United States."

"I think you are a Zairian," he said, moving his eyes from the passport photo to me to the photo again. "You look like a Zairian."

"I'm not a Zairian," I said again. I was tired, it was late, I had just spent the day in the Rwandan border town of Cyangugu, just across from Bukavu in Zaire. And all I wanted to do was get back to my room at the Hotel Residence, where, at least if the water was running, a shower awaited. "Look," I said, trying to control my temper, "that's an American passport. I'm an American."

"What about your father—was he Zairian?" The immigration man was not convinced.

"My parents, my grandparents, everybody was American," I said, trying not to shout. "Maybe, 400 years ago, there was a Zairian somewhere, but I can assure you, I'm American."

"You have the face of a Zairian," he said, calling over his colleague so they could try to assess which tribe, which region of Zaire, I might spring from.

Finally, I thought of one thing to convince him. "Okay," I said, pushing my French to its limit. "Suppose I was a Zairian. And suppose I did manage to get myself a fake American passport." I could see his eyes light up at the thought. "So, I'm a Zairian with a fake American passport. Tell me, why on earth would I be trying to sneak back into Zaire?"

The immigration officer pondered this for a moment, churning over in his mind the dizzying array of possibilities a fake U.S. passport might offer; surely, using it to come into Zaire was not among the likely options. "You are right," he concluded, as he picked up his rubber stamp and pounded in my entry. "You are American—black American."

And so it went around Africa. I was constantly met with raised eyebrows and suspicions upon explaining that I really was, really am, an American. "I know you're a Kenyan," said one woman in a bar—a hooker, I think, in retrospect. "You're just trying to pretend you don't speak Swahili."

"Okay," I told her, "you found me out. I'm really a Kenyan."

"Aha!" she said. "I knew it!"

Being able to pass for an African had some advantages. In Somalia, for example, when anti-Americanism was flaring as U.S. Cobra helicopters were bombing militia strongholds of Gen. Mohamed Farah Aideed, I was able to venture into some of the most dangerous neighborhoods without attracting undue attention. I would simply don a pair of sunglasses and ride in the back seat of my beat-up white Toyota, with my Somali driver and AK-47-toting bodyguard up front. My biggest worry was getting caught in the cross hairs of some U.S. Army marksman or helicopter gunner who would only see what, I suppose, we were: three African-looking men riding around Mogadishu's mean streets in a car with an automatic weapon sticking out one of the windows.

But mostly, I concluded, being black in Somalia was a disadvantage. This came home to me late in 1993. I was one of the reporters at the first public rally Aideed had held since coming out of four months of hiding. The arrest order on him had been lifted, and the Clinton administration had called off the humiliating and futile manhunt that had earlier left 18 U.S. soldiers dead in a single encounter. The mood at the rally was, predictably, euphoric. I was among a group of reporters standing on the stage awaiting Aideed's arrival.

Suddenly, one of the Somali gunmen guarding the stage raced up to me and shoved me hard in the chest, forcing me down onto my back. I looked up, stunned, into his wild eyes, and he seemed to be pulling his AK-47 off his shoulder to take aim at me. He was shouting in Somali, and I couldn't understand him. A crowd gathered, and there was more shouting back and forth. Finally, one of Aideed's aides, whom I recognized, helped me to my feet. "I apologize," the aide said, as others hustled my attacker away. "You look like a Somali. He thought you were someone else."

Being black in Africa: I had to fight myself to keep my composure, to keep from bursting into tears.

* * *

Many months later, I found out it wasn't only black Americans who felt the way I did. That was when I ran across Sam Msibi, a black South African cameraman for Britain-based Worldwide Television News....

Msibi knew better than I what it was like to be a black journalist amid Africa's violence; he had been shot five times, in Tokoza township, and managed to live to tell the tale. "It's a problem in Africa," he said, as he navigated the winding mountain road. "When you're black, you have to worry about black-on-black violence."

"Sometimes I want to stop to take pictures," he said, surveying the scene of refugees on the move toward the border, often with their herds of cattle and goats in front, always with small children trailing behind. "But I don't know how these people will react." I explained to him, naively, that I had just traveled the same road a week or so earlier with a Belgian TV crew that had no problem filming along the highway. "Yeah, but they're white," Msibi said. "These people might think I'm a Hutu or something."

I grew quite fond of Msibi during that nearly four-hour drive; I found that he, a black South African, and I, a black American, were thinking many of the same thoughts, venturing together into the heart of an African tragedy that was about as different from downtown Johannesburg as it was from Detroit or Washington, D.C.

"Africa is the worst place—Somalia, Zaire," Msibi said, more to himself than to me. "When you see something like this, you pray your own country will never go this way. Who wants to see his children walking like that?" ...

* * *

Are you black first, or a journalist first?

The question succinctly sums up the dilemma facing almost every black journalist working for the "mainstream" (read: white) press. Are you supposed to report and write accurately, and critically, about what you see and hear? Or are you supposed to be pushing some kind of black agenda, protecting black American leaders from tough scrutiny, treating black people and black issues in a different way?

Many of those questions were at the heart of the debate stirred up a decade ago by my Post colleague, Milton Coleman, when he reported remarks of Jesse Jackson referring to Jews as "Hymie." Coleman was accused of using material that was off the record; more troubling, he was accused of betraying his race. For being a hard-nosed journalist, he suffered the wrath of much of the black community, and even had to endure veiled threats from Louis Farrakhan's henchmen.

I have had to deal with many of the same questions over the years, including those asked by family members during Thanksgiving or Christmas gatherings in Detroit. "Let me ask you something," my favorite cousin, Loretta, began once. "Why does the media have to tear down our black leaders?" She was referring to Marion Barry and his cocaine arrest, and to Coleman Young, the longtime Detroit mayor who was always under a cloud for something or other. I tried to explain that journalists only do their job and should expose wrongdoing no matter if the wrongdoer is black or white. My cousin wasn't convinced. "But they are the only role models we have," she said.

It was an argument that couldn't be won. And it was an argument that trailed after me as a black reporter covering black Africa. Was I supposed to travel around looking for the "good news" stories out of the continent, or was I supposed to find the kind of compelling, hard-hitting stories that I would look for any other place in the world? Was I not to call a dictator a dictator, just because he happened to be black? Was I supposed to be an apologist for corrupt, ruthless, undemocratic, illegitimate black regimes?

Apparently so, if you subscribe to the kind of Pan Africanism that permeates much of black American thinking. Pan Africanism, as I see it, prescribes a kind of code of political correctness in dealing with Africa, an attitude that says black America should bury its head in the sand to all that is wrong in Africa, and play up the worn-out demons of colonialism, slavery and Western exploitation of minerals. Anyone who does, or writes, otherwise is said to be playing into the old "white conspiracy." That attitude was confirmed to me in Gabon, in

May 1993, when I first met C. Payne Lucas of Africare, a Washington-based development and relief organization. "You mean you're a *black* man writing all of that stuff about Africa?" he said.

Lucas was in Gabon for the second African-American Summit, a meeting bringing black American civil rights activists and business leaders together with African government officials and others. It was an odd affair, this "summit," for at a time of profound change across Africa—more and more African countries struggling to shed long-entrenched dictatorships—not one of the American civil rights luminaries ever talked about "democracy" or "good governance" or "political pluralism" in my hearing. These same American leaders who were so quick off the mark to condemn injustice in South Africa, when the repression was white-on-black, suddenly lost their voices when the dictatorships were black.

Instead, what came out was a nauseating outpouring of praise from black Americans for a coterie of some of Africa's most ruthless strongmen and dictators. There were such famous champions of civil rights as Jesse Jackson heaping accolades on the likes of Nigeria's number one military thug at the time, Gen. Ibrahim Babangida, who had just shut down a critical newspaper and was about to renege on his pledge to transfer his country to democratic rule. There was speaker after speaker on the American side complimenting the host, Omar Bongo, a corrupt little dictator in platform shoes who at that very moment was busy shutting down his country's only private (read: opposition) radio station.

But the most sickening spectacle of all came when the baby dictator of Sierra Leone entered the conference hall. Capt.

Valentine Strasser, a young tough in Ray-Ban sunglasses, walked in to swoons and cheers from the assembled American dignitaries, who were obviously more impressed by the macho military figure he cut than by the knowledge that back home Strasser was summarily executing former government officials and opponents of his new military regime.

I had seen that kind of display before around Africa: black Americans coming to the land of their ancestors with a kind of touchy-feely sentimentality straight out of Roots. The problem is, it flies smack into the face of a cold reality.

[In] March [1994] in the Sudanese capital of Khartoum, I ran into a large group of black Americans who were also staying at the Khartoum Hilton. They were there on some kind of a fact-finding trip, and being given VIP treatment by the Sudanese regime. Some of the men went all-out and dressed the part, donning long white Sudanese robes and turbans. Several of the women in the group covered themselves in Muslim wrap.

The U.S. ambassador in Khartoum had the group over to his house, and the next day, the government-controlled newspaper ran a front-page story on how the group berated the ambassador over U.S. policy toward Sudan. Apparently, some members of the group told the ambassador that it was unfair to label the Khartoum regime as a sponsor of terrorists and one of the world's most violent, repressive governments. After all, they said, they themselves had been granted nothing but courtesy, and they had found the dusty streets of the capital safer than most crime-ridden American cities.

I was nearly shaking with rage. Couldn't they see they were being used, manipulated by one of the world's most oppressive regimes? Human Rights Watch/Africa—hardly a water carrier for U.S. policy—had recently labeled Khartoum's human rights record as "abysmal," and reported that "all forms of political opposition remain banned both legally and through systematic terror." And here were these black Americans, these willing tools, heaping praise on an unsavory clique of ruling thugs. I wanted to confront them, but instead I deliberately avoided them....

Do I sound cynical? Maybe I am. Maybe that's because, unlike some of the African American tourists who have come out here on a two-week visit to the land of their roots, I've *lived* here.

Do you think I'm alone in my view? Then meet Linda Thomas-Greenfield, and hear her story.

* * *

Thomas-Greenfield is a black American diplomat at the U.S. Embassy in Nairobi, her third African posting; she spent three years in Gambia and 2 1/2 in Nigeria. After completing her studies at the University of Wisconsin, she had spent time in Liberia, and she remembers how elated she felt then making her first voyage to her ancestral homeland. "I remember the plane coming down," she said. "I couldn't wait to touch down."

But when I talked to Thomas-Greenfield last summer, she had just finished nine months in Kenya. And she was burned out, fed up and ready to go home.

Her house in Nairobi had been burglarized five times. She had had an electric fence installed. "When they put up the electric fence, I told them to put in enough volts to barbecue anybody who came over." When she continued to complain that even the fence didn't stop the intruders, the local Kenyan police station posted two officers on her grounds. But then the police began extorting payment for their services. "I've gotten to the point where I'm more afraid not to give them money," she said. "They're sitting outside with automatic weapons." ...

In April, Thomas-Greenfield traveled to Rwanda for an embassy assignment. She had been in the country only a day when the presidential plane was shot down and an orgy of tribal bloodletting began. Most of the victims were Tutsi, and Thomas-Greenfield, a towering 6-foot-plus black woman, was immediately mistaken for a Tutsi. She recalls cowering in fear with machine guns pointed in her face, pleading repeatedly: "I don't have anything to do with this. I'm not a Rwandan. I'm an American."

In the end, it was not just the crime and her close call in Rwanda but the attitude of the Africans that wore down even this onetime Africa-lover. Thomas-Greenfield had never been invited into a Kenyan home. And doing the daily chores of life, she had been met constantly with the Kenyans' own perverse form of racism, under which whites are granted preferential treatment over blacks.

"There's nothing that annoys me more than sitting in a restaurant and seeing two white people getting waited on, and I can't get any service," she said....

"I think it's an absolute disadvantage" being black in Africa, said Thomas-Greenfield, who, at the time we talked, said she was considering cutting short her assignment. "Here, as anywhere else in Africa, the cleavages are not racial, they are ethnic. People think they can tell what ethnic group you are by looking at you. And if there's any conflict going on between the ethnic groups, you need to let them know you're an American."

She added, "I'd rather be black in South Africa under apartheid than to go through what I'm going through here in Kenya."

* * *

This is not the story I sat down to write. Originally, I had wanted to expound on Africa's politics, the prospects of freedom and development, the hopes for the future. My tour in Africa, after all, came during what was supposed to be the continent's "decade of democracy"—after the fall of one-party communist states of Eastern Europe, the argument went, and the consolidation of democracy in Latin America, could Africa's one-party dictatorships and military regimes be far behind? At least this was the view of many Africa analysts, and of hopeful African democrats themselves, when I began the assignment.

But three years of following African elections, in countries as diverse as Nigeria, Cameroon, Kenya, Ethiopia, Malawi and Mozambique, has left me—and many of those early, hopeful African democrats—far less than optimistic. I've seen elections hijacked or stolen outright, elections canceled, elections bought and elections that have proved to be essentially meaningless. How can you talk about elections in countries where whole chunks of territory are under the sway of armed guerrillas? Where whole villages get burned down because of competing political loyalties? And where traditional belief runs so deep that a politician can be charged in public with casting magic spells over poor villagers to force them to vote for him?

African autocrats are proving far more entrenched, far more brutal and far more adept at the manipulation of state machinery than their Eastern European communist counterparts. Africa's militaries —as compared with those in, say, South America—are proving less willing to return to the barracks and bow to the popular will. In country after country, even oppositionists demonstrate themselves to be grasping, quarrelsome and in most cases incapable of running things if they ever do manage to make it to power. Politics in Africa is about lucrative spoils and fresh opportunities for corruption, and much of opposition politics across the continent consists of an out group wanting its turn at the feeding trough.

It's become a cliche to call tribalism the affliction of modern Africa, but, unfortunately, my years of covering African politics has convinced me that it is true. Tribalism is a corrosive influence impeding democratic change and development....

Even in places where opposition parties have managed to overcome the odds and win power in democratic elections, the results so far have been mixed. In Zambia's case, the 1991 election of Frederick Chiluba was supposed to herald a beginning of a new democratic era. But what I found there last year was a country reeling from corruption and incompetence. Government officials have been implicated in drug dealing, others have resigned in disgust claiming the old democratic movement has lost its direction....

And finally, finding hope becomes even more difficult when you look at the basket cases—places like Zaire, which is in perpetual meltdown; Liberia, still carved up between competing armies; Sudan, ground down by seemingly endless civil war; Rwanda, which was convulsed by one of the worst episodes of tribal genocide in modern times; and Somalia, poor Somalia, which has virtually ceased to exist as a nation-state.

My final journey in Africa was to Somalia—fittingly, I thought, because it was the place I spent most of my time over the past three years. I found it fascinating to cover a country in which all forms of government had collapsed....

* * *

In trying to explain Africa to you, I needed first to try to explain it to myself. I want to love the place, love the people. I can tell you I see hope amid the chaos, and I do, in places like Malawi, even Mozambique. But the Rwandas and Somalias and Liberias and Zaires keep intruding into my mind. Three years—three long years—have left me cold and heartless. Africa is a killing field of good intentions, as Somalia alone is enough to prove.

And where does that leave the black man who has come "home" to Africa? I write this surrounded by my own high fence, protected by two large dogs, a paid security guard, a silent alarm system and a large metal door that I bolt shut at night to keep "Africa" from coming across the yard and bashing in my brains with a panga knife for the $200 in my desk drawer. I am tired and, like Linda Thomas-Greenfield, ready to go.

Another black American, writer Eddy L. Harris, the author of *Native Stranger*, ventured into the dark continent, to discover that the place where he felt most at home was South Africa, that most modern, most Western of African countries....

So, do you think I'm a cynic? An Africa-basher? A racist even, or at least a self-hating black man who has forgotten his African roots? Maybe I am all that and more. But by an accident of birth, I am a black man born in America, and everything I am today—culture, attitudes, sensitivities, loves and desires—derives from that one simple and irrefutable truth.

POSTSCRIPT

Do the Identities of Blacks Lie in Africa?

It is worth noting that Richburg's selected case studies were all of war-torn societies or those recovering from difficult political turmoil (e.g., South Africa). Davis, meanwhile, bases her glowing discussion on a pilgrimage to a single country (Senegal) that might be considered remarkable and unusual anywhere. Does Richburg provide enough data to establish his case? Does Davis's rich and moving experience in a single society establish her case that Black identities may lie in Africa?

Scholars theorize that when groups experience sharp ambiguities, disjunctions, and changes, their identities may become problematic. One logical response is to look outside for understanding. For example, prior to and during the breakup of the former Soviet Union into competing ethnic groups, reports of flying saucer sightings were widespread. Some speculated that these reports reflected a search for some higher intelligence to somehow structure the chaotic, ambiguous situation in the former Soviet Union.

Are the many Black influentials who praise African leaders and societies self-serving hypocrites? Or are they acting on the realization that African Americans, like all people, need a sense of the past to provide continuity into the future and to make sense out of the present? Considering the hideous efforts to obliterate Blacks' ties with their families, religions, and institutions, might the identities of Black Americans at least partially lie in Africa?

What ties, perceived or otherwise, do your friends, relatives, and fellow students seem to have to their countries of origin? What does it mean for them to be an American? What does it mean for them to be a member of the racial, gender, or ethnic majority or minority?

Among the many excellent, recently published books highlighting the continuing racism in the United States and justifying, at least indirectly, Davis's position, are Maurice Berger's *White Lies: Race and the Myths of Whiteness* (Farrar, Straus & Giroux, 1999); Leonard Steinhorn's *By the Color of Our Skin: The Illusion of Integration and the Reality of Race* (Dutton, 1999); and Farai Chideya's *The Color of Our Future* (William Morrow, 1999). For a helpful sociopolitical history of Africa on disk, see Microsoft's *Encarta Africana* (1999).

Two articles bearing on the issue at hand is "Interrogating 'African Development' and the Diaspora Reality," by G. Dei, *Journal of Black Studies* (November 1998) and "Understanding Genocide," by D. Newsbury, *African Studies Review* (April 1998). A book-length update of Richburg's thesis is his *Out of America: A Black Man Confronts Africa* (Basic Books, 1998). For a biography of a pioneering Black journalist, see K. Hauke, *Ted Poston: Pioneer American Journalist* (University of Georgia Press, 1998).

ISSUE 8

Should We Call Ourselves African Americans?

YES: John Sibley Butler, from "Multiple Identities," *Society* (May/June 1990)

NO: Walter E. Williams, from "Myth Making and Reality Testing," *Society* (May/June 1990)

ISSUE SUMMARY

YES: Professor of sociology John Sibley Butler briefly traces the history of the terms that Black Americans have applied to themselves, and he contrasts their ethnic-racial identities with those of other Americans. He argues that it makes sense for them to be called African Americans.

NO: Professor of economics Walter E. Williams acknowledges the baggage contained in the labels that people select for themselves. He dismisses those who opt for African American (or related terms) in order to achieve cultural integrity among Blacks. He says that there are serious problems in the Black community that need to be addressed, none of which will be solved by a new name.

For over 200 years (1620 through the early 1800s), the ancestors of most Black Americans were brought to North America as slaves. They were first hunted, captured, and packaged, often by West Africans, who were engaged in dividing and conquering peoples and their territories. Thus, members of captured tribes were mixed together indiscriminately. Sometimes a slave was sold several times over to other slave dealers, with each transaction netting new profits and removing the captured victim one step further from his or her tribe of origin.

Many, but certainly not all, were eventually sold to European slave dealers and then later to American slave dealers, primarily New England Yankee seafarers and merchants. The slave dealers quickly learned how to handle their human chattel: they separated as much as possible members of a tribe or language group from each other and mixed slaves together in an attempt to isolate those with a common background. This obviously minimized coalition formation. They also isolated women and children so that many male slaves would comply with their new owners in the hopes of being reunited with their families. During transport across the Atlantic, 50 percent or more of all slaves would die or commit suicide, resulting in even more fragmentation. Upon arrival, separate members of tribes and families would be sold to different slave owners, although this was not always the case for family members. Over time, a significant portion of a plantation's slaves, or their descendants, would be returned to the slave auction block to be sold yet again, sometimes to new owners residing hundreds of miles away. All of this functioned to increase slaves' separation from their tribes of origin and Africa itself.

This obliteration of identity and culture for Black Americans was unlike the experiences of other racial and ethnic groups, who could draw a certain amount of psychic support and relief from the artifacts, the myths, the oral traditions, and the ancestry of their places of origin.

The situation for Blacks in the United States, especially when the many years of slavery are factored in, goes beyond Frantz Fanon's description in *The Wretched of the Earth*: "Colonialism is not satisfied merely with holding a people in its grip and emptying the native's brain of all form and content. By a kind of perverted logic, it turns to the past of the oppressed people, and distorts, disfigures, and destroys it."

To many in the United States whose ancestors suffered these horrors and who themselves cannot claim with any comfort specific ethnic or tribal heritage, the symbolic stakes in this debate are high. Although not particularly militant on the issue, John Sibley Butler clearly concurs with Jesse Jackson's statement, "To be called black is baseless. To be called African American has cultural integrity." Butler acknowledges that even before the Revolutionary War, Blacks disagreed among themselves about what name to use. During the Civil War period (shortly before and after 1861–1865), prominent Blacks such as Frederick Douglas and Martin R. Delany bitterly disagreed on the proper term for Black Americans (Douglas favored *Negro*).

Walter E. Williams agrees that people may call themselves anything they wish. However, he has a problem with the term *African American*. Williams argues that there is no single African culture; Blacks generally have no knowledge of what part of Africa and what tribes they may be from; Black Americans share little or nothing of significance with any groups in Africa, either in the present or past; and Black Americans have little to gain by discovering (or inventing) myths about affinities with the continent of Africa.

It is interesting to note that, with important exceptions (e.g., Marcus Garvey and W. E. B. Du Bois in his later years), most Black leaders until recently wanted to distance themselves from Africa. America was seen as their home and where their destinies were.

As you read the following selections, decide if creating a myth is necessarily bad. How might such a "myth" be functional, even if history is somewhat distorted? On the other hand, could playing fast and loose with facts have possible unanticipated negative consequences? What customs would you like to be part of your life if you could pick them?

YES

John Sibley Butler

MULTIPLE IDENTITIES

During the aftermath of the 1989 Presidential election, the Rev. Jesse Jackson announced that *gens de couleur* (people of color) with an African flavor should redefine themselves. Instead of referring to themselves as Black Americans or Afro-Americans (the most frequently used names for the group in recent times), they should use exclusively the term African-Americans. Because the country, and especially Mr. Jackson, was just winding down from discussions of serious campaign issues such as poverty, jobs, the homeless, inflation, and the arms race, the sudden emergence of name identification issue seemed out of place. But the distribution of his comments about name identification for blacks by the national news media prompted a series of debates and general discussions throughout the land. This Pope-like proclamation was made, Jackson said, in order to create among Black-Americans more of an identity with the original homeland of Africa. The Rev. Jackson's comments raise old issues and give us an opportunity to explore the relationship among origin of country, identification with that country, and the American experience.

THE ISSUE IN COMPARATIVE PERSPECTIVE

There have been few, if any, countries in the history of the world that developed as America has in terms of the diversity of racial and ethnic groups. Bringing diverse cultures from all parts of the world, these groups have influenced the nature of everything "American." Although some Africans came as indentured servants and later gained their "freedom," the great majority of the group was forced to leave their homeland and they worked in America as slaves and made "cotton King." Other racial and ethnic groups came to find employment in the developing country while others created entrepreneurial niches to create group economic stability. From this ethnic and racial mixture, the country developed military manpower in order to engage in war and conflict, elected U.S. Senators and Congressmen and women, developed professional sports teams, and sent people to the moon. Over the years, although the country's history contains a record of racial and ethnic conflict, members of the racial and ethnic mixtures have come to refer to themselves as Americans.

Although this is true, under certain conditions groups have hyphenated themselves so as to reflect an identification with their original homeland, thus making name identification conditional on certain historical circumstances. The identification as strictly American is very strong during times of international conflict. During the World Wars all ethnic groups were quick to assert their identification exclusively with America, despite the amount of time that they had been in the country. Italian-Americans, German-Americans, and Japanese-Americans simply identified themselves as Americans. During World War II, German-Americans were not celebrating Wurstfest and Japanese-Americans were not celebrating the greatest of the Japanese Empire. More recently, international events (*e.g.*, the bombing of a plane or restaurant, or the plight of hostages) have generated the same kind of identification with the term American that was present during the World Wars.

Groups that become hyphenated Americans usually have a history of racial or ethnic conflict and inequality. For groups that trace their origins to Europe, it is plausible to say that the more hostility they received when first adjusting to America, the more likely they are to be hyphenated Americans. This can be seen in the cases of Italian-Americans and Irish-Americans, two groups that faced systematic hostility when first entering the country. On the other hand, the terms English-American and Scandinavian-American are seldom if ever used to identify a common history of discrimination in America. In some cases, religious identity, which is usually associated with historical oppression, appears before the hyphenation. Although Jews were his-torically found in many countries in Europe, in America they refer to themselves mainly as Jewish-Americans rather than German-Americans, English-Americans, or Polish-Americans. Although ethnic groups of European origin get along rather well in America, and see themselves as white Americans, events within the country that divide the issue along ethnic lines (such as elections) have the effect of resurrecting the importance of the hyphenation. It should also be pointed out that at one time in America ethnic conflict was the result of internal competition over jobs and other resources that helped to develop economic stability. At this point in history, conflict among ethnic groups in America can be the result of tension or war in the international market. What goes on in Europe and the Middle-East can cause ethnic groups from those regions to rally around their hyphenation. Throughout the years, ethnic identification among Europeans has been conditional and is influenced by their ethnic history in America and conflicts outside of America.

Racial groups of non-European origin carry with them an almost built-in hyphenation which relates to a continent rather than to a specific country on a continent. The issue before us does not raise the question of which country on the continent of Africa should be the source of identification for black Americans. The debate is not whether they should be called Nigerian-Americans, Zaire-Americans, or Gabon-Americans, but simply African-Americans. Unlike Europeans, who identify with a specific country on the European continent, it is impossible for Americans who are black to identify with their specific country (we can say that most slaves came from West Africa) of origin because of the slave experience, which included the stripping of national identification and thus the inability to pass down one's country of identification through the years. With all due respect given to an argument which specifies that this question is exactly like the question for European ethnic groups, we must recognize that the issue is not exactly the same. If it were the same, whites would refer to themselves as Euro-Americans rather than Irish-Americans, Italian-Americans, Polish-Americans, etc. Identifying the hyphenation with a continent can also be seen in the case of Japanese-Americans, Mexican-Americans, and Cuban-Americans. As we explore the issue of identification and the Afro-American experience, we will draw on the ethnic experience for comparative purposes.

THE AFRO-AMERICAN EXPERIENCE

Before the Revolutionary War period, free blacks engaged in a general debate about what to call themselves. In the middle of this debate was James Forten, a self-made millionaire from Philadelphia who made his fortune producing sails for vessels on the high seas. After much debate, officially they agreed to call themselves Negro-Americans rather than African-Americans or Afro-Americans. They made this decision because they wished to identify with the New World rather than with the Old World. Although this decision was made, historical records indicate that not all people of African descent agreed with the term Negro-Americans; this can be seen by examining the names of some of their most cherished institutions which carried, and continue to carry, the designation "Africa." The African Episcopal Church was founded after the Rev-

olutionary War, and the African Blood Brothers was organized after World War II.

As years progressed from the Revolutionary War period, for the most part blacks called themselves names that were not directly identifiable with the African continent, the most frequent being Negroes and "Colored People." Early black scholars argued that this was the result of the almost total annihilation of the African culture in America. Consider the following quotation taken from *Race, Radicalism, and Reform*, by Abram Harris, a noted economist of his day. It is interesting that he argues that in no way can "African Negroes" in America (another name identification) be considered African:

> It is not infrequent that the economic and social subjugation of one race or class of another has led the subordinated group to adopt the culture of the dominant. This has happened to the Negro in the United States. If the first African Negroes who came to America brought with them concepts of social institutions or culture typically African they could not practice them in America. Moreover, we have no attempts by Negroes to establish African culture in the United States. Nor can the American Negro be considered in any logical way African. The assimilation of the Negro to American culture has been so complete that one [white] observer remarked: with most marvelous certainty, the Negro in the South could be trusted to perpetuate our political ideas and institutions if our republic fell, as surely as the Gaul did his adopted institutions.

Although Harris acknowledged the growing research at that time that attempted to link elements of African culture with the culture of black Americans (Harris noted the work of George Schuyler, "The Negro Art Hokum," in *The Nation* and the reply by Langston Hughes; and Milton Sampson's "Race Consciousness and Race Relations" in *Opportunity*), he concluded that blacks in America cannot be considered in any logical way African. It is plausible that many analyses of the black American situation squared with the ideas of Harris during this time period.

SOCIAL MOVEMENTS

The development of name identification that links blacks to the Motherland Africa has historically been associated with social movements. Although there were many movements before the emergence of Marcus Garvey (*e.g.*, Martin R. Delany in 1852 proclaimed "Africa for Africans" and Daniel Coker, the first bishop of the African Methodist Episcopal Church, sailed for the American Colonization Society with 90 free blacks in 1820), he was instrumental in raising the consciousness of black Americans about the continent of Africa. Although some of his many publications had the word Negro in their titles (*Negro History Bulletin, The New Negro Voice, The New Negro World*), some also stressed the importance of blackness (*The Black May* and *The Black Violet*). Throughout these publications the identification with Africa is stressed and the term African-American is used consistently. More importantly, the Garvey movement incorporated a strong ideology of race pride and praise of African physical characteristics, which were viewed as superior to those of Europeans. He and his followers praised black skin, black hair texture, the shapely image of men and women (e.g., protruding buttocks), and the alleged slow ag-

ing process of the race. His organization, the United Negro Improvement Association, was geared towards developing the group along spiritual, economic, and social lines. During the Garvey years, for those who followed him, there was a convergence of behavior, acceptance of black physical characteristics, and the ideology of identification with the African homeland. Although Garvey's movement used a variety of terms to identify blacks (Negro, Black, African, African-American), it is clear that the emphasis was on blacks as African-Americans. Despite the many criticisms and the outcome of this movement, Garvey was successful in getting blacks to like themselves and above all, to like their physical characteristics.

Unlike during the Garvey years, the term Negro was used throughout the modern civil rights movement. This is reflected in the papers of the period, including those of the NAACP and Southern Christian Leadership Association. This much-needed movement did not stress the importance of African characteristics, nor did it emphasize identification with the continent of Africa. It took the activities of the SNCC (Student Non-Violent Coordinating Committee), the student arm of the NAACP, to reinstate the importance of the African heritage for name identification. In *Black Power: The Politics of Liberation*, Stokely Carmichael and Charles Hamilton noted that an identification change was necessary for black Americans. Unlike Jesse Jackson's comments, which insist on the term African-American, Carmichael and Hamilton equated the terms African-Americans and Afro-Americans with the term black. They also reintroduced the theme of an appreciation of African characteristics that had been

so much a part of the Garvey movement:

> There is a growing resentment of the
> word "negro" ... because this term is
> the invention of our oppressor. Many
> blacks are now calling themselves Afro-
> Americans or black people because that
> is our image of ourselves.... From now
> on we shall view ourselves as African-
> Americans and as black people who are
> in fact energetic, determined, intelligent,
> beautiful, and peace-loving.

There was also a behavioral component
to this movement. Throughout the land
blacks began to show an appreciation
for their African characteristics as natural hairstyles and an appreciation for the
black skin became commonplace among
all age groups. There also developed a
sense of "color and hair texture democracy." This is a group that ranges in physical characteristics from fair European
to the blackest of African ebony. Black
publications proudly displayed men and
women of all the different colors of the
group, with perhaps those displaying
the most African characteristics enjoying
the most prestige. It was not culturally
acceptable within the group to use concepts such as "good hair" and "bad hair"
or "black but pretty." Like the Garvey
movement at the turn of the century,
and indeed like the movements during
earlier times when race consciousness
was raised, the behavior of the group reflected an identification with Africa (or
blackness) not only through name but
also through an appreciation of the biological characteristics that they share
with Africans. It is important to understand also that the emphasis was on the
appreciation of biological characteristics
rather than on the type of dress. Although
African dress styles played a part in both

the Garvey movement and the movement
of the 1960s, they never really became the
dominant mode of dress.

JACKSON'S CALL:
AN ANACHRONISM

The call by Jesse Jackson for blacks to refer to themselves as African-Americans
during this historical juncture is not at all
associated with any kind of systematic
movement, especially one that stresses
the importance of racial consciousness of
Africans and black Americans. More importantly, it comes at a time when there
is a general rejection of African biological characteristics and the decline of any
kind of consciousness about color democracy. This is reflected in the everyday
styles of black Americans and in major
publications where blacks with European
characteristics (hair, facial features, etc.)
are significantly more likely to be featured. If it is true that the generation of
the 1960s reintroduced the importance
of presenting oneself in a natural style
(natural hairstyles, an appreciation for
African art and music), it is also true that
the present generation shows no appreciation for African characteristics. Even
the people who grew up in the 1960s
have rejected natural presentations of self
and have reverted to European aesthetics.
Perhaps Abram Harris was correct when
he observed, in 1927, that blacks in America were simply too acculturated aesthetically to ever accept, even during periods
of race-conscious movements, their own
physical characteristics over long periods
of time:

> [The] cultural accommodation and above
> all, the physical contact which preceded
> and paralleled it, could have but one
> effect upon the Negro, the annihilation

of a Negro national physiognomy—and, in consequence, the Negro's repudiation of African aesthetic standards. The ready market which sellers of bleaching and hair straightening compounds find among Negroes indicates the extent of this repudiation. But a surging race consciousness among Negroes which has expressed itself in art and other forms may seem to belie the repudiation of African aesthetic standards, or it may be mistaken as the Negro's attempt to establish a Negro culture within the United States. Considerable controversy has centered about the question of Negro culture as a product distinct from United States culture. But close examination of the social facts underlying the Negro's position in the United States shows his race consciousness to be merely a device which he has contrived in order to compensate his thwarted ambition for full participation in American society.

Harris' observations are interesting and point to the obvious effect of European aesthetic standards on black Americans, and his observations about the 1920s can be applied to the group today. It is interesting to listen to and watch blacks argue for the use of the term African-American rather than other terms to identify the group. At a recent gathering, as the debate grew hot, all of the females had relaxed hair, high-powered faces, and some even had on blue contact lenses. Many of the males were "sporting" curls in their hair and other forms of "processed" hair. If some native Africans were to have shown up at such a gathering, they may have wondered in amusement and asked, "What race are these people?" Put simply, this is a strange time in black Americans' aesthetic history to issue a message asking people to call themselves African-Americans.

The behavior vis-à-vis aesthetics of black Americans today are in direct contrast to Jesse Jackson's comments when he called for the name African-American. He said, "To be called black is baseless... To be called African-American has cultural integrity." While it may be true that people want to identify themselves as descendants of Africa, it is also true presently that it is chic to look as European as possible. This fact gives new meaning to W.E.B. DuBois' concept of "two-ness," wherein he stressed the psychological state of living in two American worlds, one white and one black. In this case the emphasis would be placed on aesthetic identification rather than psychological identification. One would certainly think that pride in Africa would be accomplished by at least the acceptance of physical characteristics of Africans in America. Yet the cultural renaissance in America for blackness at this time is dead and shows no sign of reviving itself. It should be stressed that this is an issue that goes well beyond changes in fashion since we are speaking of the actual change of biological characteristics to fit those of Europeans. Those black Americans who have naturally European characteristics do not have to work as hard on changing their biological characteristics as their more African sisters and brothers. Like white Americans who seem to worship and praise those of the group with fair skin and blond hair, black Americans show a gravitation toward those in the group who possess European characteristics. While one cannot change the reality of skin color and hair color variation within black America, a call for the term African-American to identify the group should at least have a behavioral component that shows an aesthetic appreciation for the entire rainbow of the group. While there is certainly nothing wrong with being black and possessing European characteristics (which is also a natural biological state), it is problematic when African biological characteristics are not appreciated in the same manner. Throughout history, black Americans have had to work very hard in order to get their African characteristics accepted (even by themselves) as being "beautiful" on the human landscape of aesthetics.

IDENTIFICATION WITH A HOMELAND

There are, of course, other reasons given as to why black Americans should identify themselves as African-Americans, even if for the most part members of the group reject African aesthetics. One of the major reasons is that it allows the group to identify with a homeland, much like other ethnic groups. This reason is expressed in the following comment published in *Ebony* last year:

> Using African-American is of value in that it has some authenticity. The idea of saying "African-American" links us to a foundation.... We don't originally come from Georgia or South Carolina or Mississippi. African-American takes people back to the motherland, a place of origin. It gives us what the Jews have, a homeland. This designation gives us some credibility. We can now claim a land because a landless people are people without clout and without substance. Inasmuch as there is an Africa and that is our ultimate homeland, then to authenticate it we should identify with the homeland itself.

Contained in this quotation are the oldest and most convincing arguments as to why black Americans should call themselves African-Americans, for they are indeed of African descent. It gives the group a continent to identify with, and like other groups in America, this identification is important; this is true even if blacks in America cannot identify with a specific country in Africa. This is also important from an historical point of view, since, as noted earlier, there is no place called Negro, Afro, or blackland in the world.

But how do different ethnic groups relate to their homeland? Is there a difference between how black Americans relate to Africa as compared to their ethnic hyphenated counterparts?

One way that ethnic groups relate to their original homeland is through a celebration of their roots during festivals and other kinds of festive activities. On St. Patrick's Day, Irish-Americans wear green, have parades, and make everyone else Irish for a day. German-Americans celebrate Wurstfest, inviting everyone to enjoy the food and customs of Germany for a day. Throughout America celebrations of this type occur for different ethnic groups.

Ethnic groups in America also identify with their homeland by giving military support so that people in the old country can hold on to, capture, or recapture important historical territory from foreign invaders. Because of the richness of the economic stability of ethnic members in the United States, and the strong military presence that this country has in the world, groups occupying what Americans call "the Old Country" look for military help from their American counterparts. A growing literature reveals the fact that ethnic groups in America are giving military support to their counterparts in other parts of the world. This can be seen in the activities of some Greek American organizations that support arms for Greece so that it can maintain a degree of independence in its historical conflict with the Turks; Irish-Americans supply funds so that the Irish of Southern Ireland can continue their liberation efforts from the British. In a work entitled *The Lobby*, Edward Tivnan examines the importance of Jewish-Americans' lobbying efforts and their commitment to Israel. In an article entitled "The Arab Lobby: Problems and Prospects," Nabeel A. Khoury shows how Arab-Americans are trying to organize in order to influence important aspects of U.S. foreign policy in the Middle East. One can be assured that the purchase of weapons for Arab states will be of great importance to that developing lobby.

Although black Americans celebrate holidays, there is not a single established national holiday which brings out the connection between themselves and the African continent. Instead, important holidays are grounded more in the American experience and some have lost their significance over the years. Emancipation Day, celebrated on January 1, is traditionally a national holiday for black Americans but is not celebrated nationally as it was some 30 years ago (in Texas this is called Juneteenth and is celebrated in June because news of the emancipation of the slaves was late in arriving in the state of Texas). Martin Luther King's Birthday and Negro History Week are also American-specific. Unlike some ethnic groups, there is not a specific national day of celebration that ties the African continent and its food and traditions, to the black American experience of continent identification.

Like other ethnic groups, there has been a concentrated effort by black Americans to support Africans on the continent. Although black Americans have not lobbied Congress to sell weapons to black South Africans so that they can fight for their freedom, they have shown their concern by supporting international boycotts against the South African Government. This stands in sharp contrast to other ethnic groups in America who support the selling of arms to members of their "Old Country" so that they can maintain themselves and their traditions. It remains to be seen if black South Africans can pray and boycott their way to national independence or full political participation in South African society. Certainly they do not have the military clout to recapture their historical homeland from foreign invaders. Black Americans have also shown an interest in other problems on the African continent, such as hunger and education. Since the 1800s, for example, the African Methodist Episcopal Church has supported education in Africa. Black Americans do have a history of supporting, albeit in different ways from other ethnic groups, people of African descent who are on the African continent.

Another important issue is whether or not there is a relationship between what black Americans call themselves and their economic and social progress in the United States. After all, Jesse Jackson declared that to be called black is baseless. Historical evidence suggests that black Americans made the most progress in changing legal codes of discrimination when they referred to themselves as Negroes and that they also made significant economic progress when they called themselves blacks or Negroes. There is no evidence to suggest that calling oneself exclusively African-American translates into economic or any other kind of progress, whether it be spiritual or educational. There is no ethnic data to suggest that there is a relationship between ethnic identification (at the level of what a group called itself vis-à-vis the Old Country) and economic progress.

The issue of what blacks call themselves will continue, as it has in the past, to emerge as an issue during certain historical periods. What makes this period so different is that the call to refer to oneself as African-American by Jesse Jackson was not grounded in any kind of consciousness-raising movement. It comes at a time when, aesthetically, black Americans are as far from Africa as they have ever been. But there is no doubt that black Americans know who they are and that they are descendants of Africans. If one were to do a national survey, it is plausible that the data would show that what group members prefer to call themselves (black Americans, African-Americans, Afro-Americans, people of African descent) will be related to variables such as age, participation in community organizations, and economic status. And although members of this group may argue over what they want to be called, *they certainly know what they do not want to be called.* One can rest assured that African-American, as a name-identification label, will be placed on the census and other questionnaires developed by social scientists as they try to collect data on the diversity of the American experience. Although the issue of name identification will evolve during certain periods in the future, it should not overshadow the continued effort of the group to gain economic stability and political participation in America.

NO

Walter E. Williams

MYTH MAKING AND
REALITY TESTING

Whether blacks should now call themselves African-American surfaces as a result of Reverend Jesse Jackson's declaration: "To be called Black is baseless... To be called African-American has cultural integrity." Little that is meaningful, in the way of agreement or disagreement, can be said about the proposal of a new name. After all, people can call themselves anything they wish and blacks have exercised this option having called themselves: colored, Negro, black, and Afro-American.

But suppose we concede there is a benefit to a name change that has "cultural integrity." It is not clear that African-American is the correct choice. Africa(n) refers neither to a civilization, a culture, or even a specific country. Instead, Africa is a continent consisting of many countries, cultures, ethnic groups, and races. Referring to Africa as a culture reflects near inexcusable ignorance. Africa is a continent with significant cultural distinctions. These distinctions often manifest themselves in unspeakable slaughter such as that between the Tutsi and Hutu in Burundi where 200,000 Hutus lost their lives in the space of two months in 1972 and at least 20,000 in August in 1988. Between 600,000 and a million Lango and Acholi tribesmen perished at the hands of Idi Amin and Milton Obote in Uganda. Similar strife raged between the Ibos and Hausa in Nigeria during the late 1960s, as well as between the Shona and Ndebele in Zimbabwe. The horrors of ethnic conflict continue to this day in many African countries.

Many people who trace their roots to the African continent are not even black. Americans of Egyptian, Libyan, or Algerian descent find their ancestral home on the African continent. Would it be appropriate to call these Americans African-Americans? Would we call a person African-American who is an American citizen of Afrikaner descent, who traces his ancestry back to 1620 when the Dutch settled Cape Town? If one says that these people do not qualify as African-Americans, what meaning can we make from Jesse Jackson's "cultural integrity" argument? In other words, what cultural characteristics do black Americans, Egyptians, Libyans, Algerians, and Afrikaners share in common even though each can trace his roots to Africa?

From Walter E. Williams, "Myth Making and Reality Testing," *Society*, vol. 27, no. 4 (May/June 1990). Copyright © 1990 by Transaction Publishers. Reprinted by permission. All rights reserved.

America's ethnic mosaic consists of many hyphenated groups like Polish-Americans, Chinese-Americans, Italian-Americans, Japanese-Americans, and West-Indian Americans. In most cases, the prefix to the hyphenation refers to people of a particular country who may or may not share the same continent. Spanish-Americans, German-Americans, and Italian-Americans designate particular countries. Their ethnic identity would be lost if someone would consolidate them into European-Americans. It would be similar to calling anyone who can trace his or her ancestry to Africa, African-Americans.

If those who seek "cultural integrity" are to be more serious in their efforts, we would expect the new name(s) for blacks to have a country affiliation like: Nigerian-Americans, Ugandan-Americans, Ivory-Coast Americans, or at least south-of-the-Sahara-African-Americans—the latter since, to give a meaningful affiliation for blacks is nearly a hopeless task because of the extensive cross mixture, among blacks, which has occurred over the past 400 years in America.

FOCUS ON NON-ISSUES

American blacks share little or no cultural tie, which is not to deny an ancestral tie, with any of the many black ethnic groups in Africa. There is no shared language, religion, or culture. There are no holidays, ceremonies, or other outward linkages associated with the "motherland." In this sense, blacks are probably culturally more distinctly American than any of the other groups in America.

There is room for considerable legitimate disagreement and debate over what blacks should call themselves, and how much of a cultural tie exists with the

many black groups in Africa. But given the deteriorating state of affairs faced by large and increasing numbers within the black community, what blacks should now begin to call themselves is a non-issue and can only serve to divert attention from larger issues without contributing anything to their solution.

Assertions about the benefits of changing the name of blacks to African-Americans puts one in mind of the alleged benefits of "role model" argument fashionable during the 1960s and thereafter. According to this theory, blacks were deficient in role models and thus increasing the number of blacks in responsible positions such as teachers, school superintendents, police chiefs, politicians, and professors would contribute to upward mobility.

Enough time and changes have been made to allow us to tentatively evaluate the benefits of the role model theory. In many urban cities such as Detroit, Philadelphia, Chicago, Los Angeles, Washington, DC, Newark, East St. Louis, and others, blacks have risen to the ranks of mayors, chiefs of police, and firemen, superintendent of schools, school principals, and have wide representation among city councilmen. Yet, in these very cities, blacks are the least safe, live in some of the worst slums, receive the poorest education, and face the greatest breakdown of institutions and living conditions most of the country takes for granted.

Some blacks are now pushing for statehood for the District of Columbia. Whether DC statehood is desirable or not need not concern us here. Whether DC statehood and the promise of two black senators as role models, will mean any more to poor blacks than what black political strength has come to mean at the state and local levels of government seems highly unlikely. That being the case means that black political and economic resources devoted to DC statehood will have been expended, once again, for the benefit of the few.

The point is not to question the dramatic political gains made over the last two decades. They are spectacular and praiseworthy. The point is that the role model theory has not delivered on its promise to provide the kind of incentives envisioned by its advocates. Those who advocate the role model theory of socio-economic progress have never bothered to explain how they made their own achievements without role models.

THE REAL PROBLEMS

In many black communities, the rate of day-to-day murder, rape, robbery, assault, and property destruction stand at unprecedented levels. Criminal activity is not only a threat to life, limb, and property, it is a heavy tax and, as such, a near guarantee that there will be little or no economic development.

Crime is a tax in the sense that it raises all costs and lowers all values. Crime is a regressive tax borne mostly by society's poorest. High crime means people must bear the expense of heavy doors and window bars. Crime drives away businesses that would otherwise flourish. Poor people must bear higher transportation costs in order to do routine shopping in downtown areas and distant suburban malls, or else pay the high prices at Mom & Pop stores. The wanton destruction and vandalism of public facilities like pay telephones, swimming pools, and parks imposes additional costs on people not likely to have access to private phones, private swimming facilities, and national parks.

To the extent that crime drives out businesses, it means residents have fewer local employment opportunities. Crime lowers the value of all property held by the residents. Often property that could not fetch as much as $20,000 all of a sudden sells for multiples of $100,000 when "gentrification" occurs in former slum areas.

EDUCATION

By every measure, black education is in shambles. High school dropout rates in some cities exceed fifty percent. Even those who do graduate are often ill-equipped for the demands of jobs or higher education. Evidence of poor education is seen in black performance on standardized achievement tests.

In 1983, across the nation, 66 out of 71,137 black college-bound seniors (less than a tenth of 1 percent) achieved 699, out of a possible 800, on the verbal portion of the SAT (Scholastic Achievement Test), and fewer than 1,000 scored over 600. On the mathematics portion of the SAT, only 205 blacks scored over 699 and fewer than 1,700 scored 600 or higher.

By comparison, of the roughly 35,200 Asians taking the test, 496 scored over 699 (1.4 percent) on the verbal portion, and 3,015 scored over 699 on the mathematics. Of the roughly 963,000 whites taking the test, 9,028 scored over 699 on the mathematics. In 1983, there were 570 blacks who had a combined score on the verbal and mathematics portions of the test above 1,200 (less than one tenth of 1 percent) compared to 60,400 whites who did so (6 percent).

While there is considerable contro-versy over what academic achievement tests measure and how reliably they do so, the undebatable conclusion is that black students have not achieved the necessary background for the standard college curriculum. This in turn has led to high numbers of black students dropping out of college. Added to the lack of preparedness for colleges, the fact that companies and government agencies must lower entry level position requirements to meet affirmative action hiring guidelines is further testament to poor academic preparation.

There is little that is surprising about these academic outcomes. Given the conditions in many predominantly black schools, where assault, property destruction, high absenteeism rates (of students and teachers), and low academic standards (again, of students and teachers) are a part of the daily routine, one would be surprised by any other outcome.

The standard excuses for poor black academic performance are segregated schools and insufficient financial resources. Yet there are an increasing number of black independent schools whose student performance seems to challenge these standard excuses. Philadelphia's Ivy Leaf School has an entirely black population, in which students come from families earning low and moderate incomes. The cost per student is $1,750, yet 85 percent of the student body tests at, or above, grade level. By contrast, Philadelphia's public school per-student cost of education is nearly $5,000 a year, and less than 35 percent of the student population tests at, or above, grade level.

Other examples of black academic achievement can be found at Chicago's Westside Preparatory School, Los Angeles' Marcus Garvey School, and New York's A. Philip Randolph School. In each of these cases, and others including parochial and black Muslim schools, a higher quality education is achieved at fraction of public school cost and without racial integration.

IMPORTANCE OF FAMILY AND OTHER INSTITUTIONS

In the face of these facts, we can draw several conclusions: racial integration is not a necessary condition for black educational excellence and massive per-pupil expenditures are not a necessary condition either. What seems to be more important are caring and responsible parents, dedicated and qualified teachers, behaving students, and above all, the freedom of the school administrator from micro-management, regulatory burdens of politically motivated central authorities, and the freedom of parents to make choices. To promote academic excellence among black youth, what is needed is turning our focus away from black educational pathology to educational successes and finding out ways of duplicating it.

Very few people who "make it" can attribute their success solely as a result of their own efforts. Most of us need others. The most significant others for most people are parents and family members. Over the past several decades, there has been a virtual collapse of the black family. In 1950, 88 percent of white families and 78 percent of black families consisted of two-parent households. By the end of 1980, black two-parent families had slipped to 59 percent while white family structure remained virtually unchanged. In 1950, the black illegitimacy rate was 17 percent; today it is 55 percent, and black teenagers are a large part of the illegitimacy crisis.

Aside from whatever moral issues are involved in the high rate of illegitimacy, there are several others that spell disaster. There are always problems associated with female-headed households, but they are exacerbated when the female head is herself a child lacking the maturity and resources to assume the responsibility of another individual. High illegitimacy means high rates of dependency and the high probability that the process will be duplicated in the next generation. High rates of illegitimacy also mean that there is not so much a breakdown in the black family as much as the black family not forming in the first place.

In addition to changes in the black family, institutions like black churches and social and civic organizations no longer have the influence on the community that they once did in the past. Part of the answer for this is that government welfare programs have poorly replaced their functions. This has been very harmful in the sense that community-based and related organizations are far better at assessing the need and monitoring the provision of services—be they assisting a family fallen on hard times or the provision of scholarship assistance. Now this assistance is rendered by remote bureaucracies with little knowledge about individual need and perhaps little interest in the overall effects of welfare programs.

With generalized availability of public welfare, along with an erosion in values, behaviors once held as irresponsible and reprehensible have been made less costly for the individual and have become the behavioral norm rather than the exception. Any black over the age of 50 remembers there was once a time when pregnancy without the benefit of marriage was a disgrace to both the young lady and her family. Often she was shipped to live with a relative out of town. Today, there is no such social stigma; and with some high schools setting up day-care centers to accommodate infants of students, the appearance of sanction is given to teen sex and illegitimacy. There is a lower cost attached to behavior which risks pregnancy out of wedlock. Basic economic theory and empirical evidence suggest that whenever the cost of something decreases, one can expect more people to be engaged in that activity.

There is considerable room for debate as to the specific causal connections between crime, poor education, and institutional breakdown, on the one hand, and poverty, dependency, and discrimination, on the other. But the bottom line is that despite the gains made by most blacks, there is a large segment of the black community for whom there appears to be little hope. What we have been doing, as a part of the Great Society welfare programs, appears to have little effect in making a dent in the situation.

Part of the solution to the problems of the black underclass will come from reflection of yesteryear when there was far greater poverty among blacks and much more discrimination. During that period, businesses thrived in black communities, people felt far safer, children did not assault teachers or use foul language in front of adults, adults did not fear children, and there was not the level of property destruction we see today. The black community was one with far more civility than today.

When people ask what are we going to do about helping those for whom there appears to be little hope, a good question to ask first is how did the situation get this way in the first place? Why are some black communities far less civil today than in the past? This important question is swept under the carpet when people blame the problems of the black underclass on poverty and discrimination, failing to recognize that poverty and discrimination existed in the 1920s, 1930s, and 1940s, but they did not generate the level of pathology that we witness today. Answers to this question will go a long way toward generating meaningful solutions.

Advocates of changing the name of blacks to African-Americans bear the burden of showing how resources placed in this effort will do anything to make upward mobility a reality for blacks stuck in the daily nightmare of our major urban areas. It would seem that pride, self-respect, and cultural identity—which the name-change advocates seek—are more likely to come from accomplishment rather than title.

POSTSCRIPT

Should We Call Ourselves African Americans?

"I do not think my people should be ashamed of their history, nor of any name that people choose in good faith to give them."

—Booker T. Washington (1906)

The issue as debated by Butler and Williams and others boils down to these questions: What term is free of negative connotations? will generate pride among those so named? does not necessarily do violence to historical realities? does not deflect from real social problems? is a term that the majority of Black Americans will use and feel comfortable with? does not offend the sensitivities of others? and can and will be used consistently?

This debate goes back for generations and appears to be ongoing. It is now fashionable, for example, to use the term *people of color*. This term can be inclusive of African Americans or all nonwhite peoples. For a sophisticated approach to how labels are used to imprison minorities, see T. A. Van Dijk, *Elite Discourse and Racism* (Sage Publications, 1993). For a continuation of the Williams-Butler debate, see Doris Wilkinson, "Americans of African Identity," *Society* (May/June 1990). Ezola Foster attacks the current labeling fashion, which she equates with efforts to generate hate, in *What's Right for All Americans* (WRS Publishing, 1995); see especially the chapter entitled "Hyphenated Americans." For an interesting study of the negative effects of labeling on Black youths, see "Racial Differences in Informal Labeling Effects," by M. Adams et al., *Deviant Behavior* (April/June 1998).

Among the more recent polls it appears that for most Blacks it does not matter if the label "African American" or "Black" is used (60 percent). However, there are fissures within the community. Younger respondents and males are more likely to prefer "African American," while females tend to prefer "Black." See the *Gallup Poll Monthly* articles "African-American or 'Black'" (September 1994) and "Black or African-American?" (August 1995).

An interesting discussion of this issue from a Hispanic perspective is "State of the Art: Latino Writers," by F. Goldman, *Washington Post Book World* (February 28, 1999). Efforts among cultures outside the United States to minimize harms resulting from racial labels are examined in G. Lewthwaite, "South Africa's Hated K-Word," *The Baltimore Sun* (January 20, 1998). Among the classic statements are W. E. B. Du Bois's "The Name 'Negro,'" *The Thought and Writings of W. E. B. Du Bois, vol. 2* (Random House, 1971) and "Proper Name for Black Men in America," by Gilbert T. Stephenson, in his book *Race Distinctions in American Law* (Negro Universities Press, 1910).

ISSUE 9

Are Hispanics Making Significant Progress?

YES: Linda Chavez, from *Out of the Barrio: Toward a New Politics of Hispanic Assimilation* (Basic Books, 1991)

NO: Robert Aponte, from "Urban Hispanic Poverty: Disaggregations and Explanations," *Social Problems* (November 1991)

ISSUE SUMMARY

YES: Scholar, business consultant, and former political candidate Linda Chavez documents the accomplishments of Hispanics and asserts that they are making it in America.

NO: Social scientist Robert Aponte suggests that social scientists, following an agenda driven by government policy, have concentrated on Black poverty, which has resulted in a lack of accurate data and information on the economic status of Hispanics. Aponte argues that disaggregation of demographic data shows that Hispanics are increasingly poor.

For years, almost all minority relations scholars reflected a social psychological approach to the study of ethnic and racial minority relations. That is, they were interested in explaining attitudes and values and lifestyles of minorities. Sociologists were also interested in patterns of interaction, especially stages of assimilation of immigrants.

Scholarly interest in the dominant group was concentrated on dominant group attitudes toward, stereotypes of, and prejudices and discrimination against minorities. The distinction between prejudice (an attitude) and discrimination (behavior) was developed. Looking at institutional power arrangements, including systematic racism in the marketplace, government, education, religion, and so on, was largely nonexistent until the 1960s. Most scholarly works on racial and ethnic relations concentrated on the values, beliefs, and attitudes among the white majority that were inconsistent with American ideals of equality.

But since the 1960s, race and ethnicity has come to be seen as not just the working out of individual attitudes and lifestyles but as a fundamental dimension of social stratification. Minority conflict was reconceptualized as not simply a clash of cultures and myths but as conflict that results when one group attempts to obtain greater equality and another group acts to maintain its advantageous position.

Understanding poverty came to be seen as important to understanding the effects of inequality, and data on poverty was needed as a basis for policy formulation. Unemployment rates, degree of residential segregation, percentage receiving welfare assistance, percentage in managerial positions, and so on came to characterize the questions asked by sociologists, economists, and politicians about minorities. The very idea of "poverty" found its way back into mainstream sociology and public discourse. The benchmark for this shift was probably in the early 1960s with the publication of Michael Harrington's *The Other America.*

In the following selections, both Linda Chavez and Robert Aponte acknowledge methodological and definitional problems inherent in researching poverty. And neither one assumes a zero-sum model of minority-majority economic relations. That is, economic gains of ethnic minorities, including Hispanics, are not viewed as "taking something away from" the majority. As minorities obtain economic success, all of society gains.

In almost every other respect, however, Chavez and Aponte disagree. They clearly have a different definition of poverty. Chavez sees many Hispanic leaders dishonestly inflating the extent of poverty in order to create political capital for themselves and their group. She feels that government research and programs encourage some minority groups to jockey for entitlements by exaggerating the types and extent of Hispanic poverty.

Aponte also feels that significant, nonscientific factors have structured poverty research and policies. However, his interpretation is quite different. He feels that governmental policies based on identifying, and partially correcting, Black poverty, as commendable as they may be, have sometimes functioned to neglect the equally serious problem of Hispanic poverty. He is also incensed that researchers who ought to know better have generally collapsed Hispanics into one homogeneous ethnic group. He suggests that analytically and empirically there are huge differences in life chances and quality of life among various Hispanic groups.

As you review the following selections, note that the authors sometimes draw from the same data sets but reach very different conclusions. How can that be? Drawing from both Chavez and Aponte, identify an ethnic or racial group in which there are large variations among those you know personally. According to Aponte, how might thinking about and viewing every member of an ethnic group as the same be misleading?

YES

Linda Chavez

OUT OF THE BARRIO

IN THE BEGINNING

Before the affirmative action age, there were no *Hispanics,* only Mexicans, Puerto Ricans, Cubans, and so on. Indeed, few efforts were made to forge an alliance among the various Hispanic subgroups until the 1970s, when competition with blacks for college admissions, jobs, and other rewards of affirmative action made it advantageous for Hispanics to join forces in order to demand a larger share of the pie. In addition to having no common history, these groups were more or less geographically isolated from one another. Mexican Americans lived in the Southwest, Puerto Ricans in the Northeast, mostly in New York, and Cubans in Florida; . . .

The Second World War marked a turning point for Hispanic activism. Hispanics served with great distinction in the war, earning more Congressional Medals of Honor per capita than any other group. Moreover, unlike blacks, Hispanics served in integrated military units, which brought them into contact with other Americans and introduced them, for the first time, to Americans who lived outside the Southwest. More than 100,000 Puerto Ricans served in the military during the war; later, many of these men and their families decided to migrate from the island in search of greater economic opportunity in the United States. Hispanics returned from the war expecting better treatment than was the standard fare for Mexican Americans and Puerto Ricans in most places. Hispanics wanted to increase their earnings and social standing, live where they wanted, and send their children to better schools. Indeed, there was significant upward mobility for Mexican Americans in the period, especially in California and other areas outside Texas, and for the Puerto Ricans who migrated to New York City. . . .

* * *

"Each decade offered us hope, but our hopes evaporated into smoke. We became the poorest of the poor, the most segregated minority in schools, the lowest paid group in America and the least educated minority in this nation." This view of Hispanics' progress by the president of the National Council of La Raza, one of the country's leading Hispanic civil rights groups, is the prevalent one among Hispanic leaders and is shared by many outside the Hispanic community as well. By and large, Hispanics are perceived to be a disadvantaged minority—poorly educated, concentrated in barrios, economically impoverished; with little hope of participating in the American Dream. This perception has not changed substantially in twenty-five years. And it is wrong.

Hispanics have been called the invisible minority, and indeed they were for many years, largely because most Hispanics lived in the Southwest and the Northeast, away from the most blatant discrimination of the Deep South. But the most invisible Hispanics today are those who have been absorbed into the mainstream. The success of middle-class Hispanics is an untold—and misunderstood—story perhaps least appreciated by Hispanic advocates whose interest is in promoting the view that Latinos cannot make it in this society. The Hispanic poor, who constitute only about one-fourth of the Hispanic population, are visible to all. These are the Hispanics most likely to be studied, analyzed, and reported on and certainly the ones most likely to be read about. A recent computer search of stories about Hispanics in major newspapers and magazines over a twelve-month period turned up more than eighteen hundred stories in which the word *Hispanic* or *Latino* occurred within a hundred words of the word *poverty*. In most people's minds,

the expression *poor Hispanic* is almost redundant.

HAS HISPANICS' PROGRESS STALLED?

Most Hispanics, rather than being poor, lead solidly lower-middle- or middle-class lives, but finding evidence to support this thesis is sometimes difficult. Of course, Hispanic groups vary one from another, as do individuals within any group. Most analysts acknowledge, for example, that Cubans are highly successful. Within one generation, they have virtually closed the earnings and education gap with other Americans. (For a broad range of social and economic indicators for each of the major Hispanic groups, see table 1.) Although some analysts claim that the success of Cubans is due exclusively to their high socioeconomic status when they arrived, many Cuban refugees—especially those who came after the first wave in the 1960s—were in fact skilled or semiskilled workers with relatively little education. Their accomplishments in the United States are attributable in large measure to diligence and hard work. They established enclave economies, in the traditional immigrant mode, opening restaurants, stores, and other émigré-oriented services.... But Cubans are as a rule dismissed as the exception among Hispanics. What about other Hispanic groups? Why has there been no "progress" among them?

The largest and most important group is the Mexican American population.... [I]ts leaders have driven much of the policy agenda affecting all Hispanics, but the importance of Mexican Americans also stems from their having a longer history in the United States than does any other Hispanic group. If Mexican

Table 1

Characteristics of Hispanic Subgroups and Non-Hispanics

	Mexican-Origin*	Puerto Rican	Cuban	South/Central American	Other Hispanic	Non-Hispanic
Total population (in millions)	13.3	2.2	1.0	2.8	1.4	246.2
Median age	24.1	27.0	39.1	28.0	31.1	33.5
Median years of schooling (1988)	10.8	12.0	12.4	12.4	12.7	12.7
Percentage in labor force						
Male	81.2%	69.2%	74.9%	83.7%	75.3%	74.2%
Female	52.9%	41.4%	57.8%	61.0%	57.0%	57.4%
Percentage of unemployed	9.0%	8.6%	5.8%	6.6%	6.2%	5.3%
Median earnings (1989)						
Male	$12,527	$18,222	$19,336	$15,067	$17,486	$22,081
Female	$8,874	$12,812	$12,880	$10,083	$11,564	$11,885
Percentage of married-couple families	72.5%	57.2%	77.4%	68.7%	69.8%	79.9%
Percentage of female-headed families	19.6%	38.9%	18.9%	25.0%	24.5%	16.0%
Percentage of out-of-wedlock births	28.9%	53.0%	16.1%	37.1%	34.2%	23.9%**
Percentage of families in poverty	25.7%	30.4%	12.5%	16.8%	15.8%	9.2%

*Mexican-origin population includes both native- and foreign-born persons.
**Includes black out-of-wedlock births, 63.1% and white births, 13.9%.
Source: Bureau of the Census, *The Hispanic Population in the United States: March 1990,* Current Population Reports, ser. P-20, no. 449; median years of schooling are from *The Hispanic Population of the United States: March 1988,* Current Population Reports, ser. P-20, no. 438; out-of-wedlock births are from National Center for Health Statistics, *Advance Report of Final Natality Statistics, 1987.*

Americans whose families have lived in the United States for generations are not yet making it in this society, they may have a legitimate claim to consider themselves a more or less permanently disadvantaged group, like blacks. That is precisely what Mexican American leaders suggest is happening. Their proof is that statistical measures of Mexican American achievement in education, earnings, poverty rates, and other social and economic indicators have remained largely unchanged for decades. In 1959 the median income of Mexican-origin males in the Southwest was 57 percent that of non-Hispanics. In 1989 it was still 57 percent of non-Hispanic income. If Mexican Americans had made progress, it would show up in improved education attainment and earnings and in lower poverty rates, so the argument goes. Since it doesn't, progress must be stalled.

In the post–civil rights era, the failure of a minority to close the social and economic gap with whites is assumed to be the result of persistent discrimination. Progress is perceived not in absolute but in relative terms. The poor may become less poor over time, but so long as those on the upper rungs of the economic ladder are climbing even faster, the poor are believed to have suffered some harm, even if they have made absolute gains and their lives are much improved. However, in order for Hispanics (or any group on the lower rungs) to close the gap, they must progress at an even greater rate than non-Hispanic whites; their apparent failure to do so in recent years causes Hispanic leaders and the public to conclude that Hispanics are falling behind. Is this a fair way to judge Hispanics' progress? In fact, it makes almost no sense to apply this test today (if it ever did), because the Hispanic population itself is changing so rapidly. This is most true of the Mexican-origin population.

In 1959 the overwhelming majority of persons of Mexican origin living in the United States were native-born, 85 percent. Today only about two-thirds of the people of Mexican origin were born in the United States, and among adults barely one in two was born here. Increasingly, the Hispanic population, including that of Mexican origin, is made up of new immigrants, who, like immigrants of every era, start off at the bottom of the economic ladder. This infusion of new immigrants is bound to distort our image of progress in the Hispanic population, if each time we measure the group we include people who have just arrived and have yet to make their way in this society.

... In 1980 there were about 14.6 million Hispanics living in the United States; in 1990, nearly 21 million, an increase of about 44 percent in one decade. At least one-half of this increase was the result of immigration, legal and illegal.... [T]his influx consists mostly of poorly educated persons, with minimal skills, who cannot speak English. Not surprisingly, when these Hispanics are added to the pool being measured, the achievement levels of the whole group fall. It is almost inconceivable that the addition of two or three million new immigrants to the Hispanic pool would not seriously distort evidence of Hispanics' progress during the decade. Yet no major Hispanic organization will acknowledge the validity of this reasonable assumption. Instead, Hispanic leaders complain, "Hispanics are the population that has benefitted least from the economic recovery." "The Myth of Hispanic Progress" is the title of a study by a Mexican American professor, purporting to show that "it is simply wrong to assume that Hispanics are making gradual progress toward parity with Anglos." "Hispanic poverty is now comparable to that of blacks and is expected to exceed it by the end of this decade," warns another group.

Hispanics wear disadvantage almost like a badge of distinction, as if groups were competing with each other for the title "most disadvantaged." Sadly, the most frequently heard complaint among Hispanic leaders is not that the public ignores evidence of Hispanics' achievement but that it underestimates their disadvantage. "More than any group in American political history, Hispanic Americans have turned to the national statistical system as an instrument for advancing their political and economic interests, by making visible the magnitude of social and economic problems they face," says a Rockefeller Foundation official. But gathering all Hispanics together under one umbrella obscures as much information as it illuminates, and may make Hispanics—especially the native-born—appear to suffer greater social and economic problems than they actually do.

In fact, a careful examination of the voluminous data on the Hispanic population gathered by the Census Bureau and other federal agencies shows that, as a group, Hispanics have made progress in this society and that most of them have moved into the social and economic mainstream. In most respects, Hispanics—particularly those born here —are very much like other Americans; they work hard, support their own families without outside assistance, have more education and higher earnings than their parents, and own their own home. In short, they are pursuing the American Dream—with increasing success.

WORK

Hispanic men are more likely to be members of the labor force—that is, working or looking for work—than non-Hispanic whites. Among all Mexican-origin men sixteen years old or older in 1990, for example, participation in the labor force was substantially higher than it was for non-Hispanic males overall—81 percent compared with 74 percent. This fact bodes well for the future and is in marked contrast to the experience of black men, whose labor force participation has been steadily declining for more than twenty years. Most analysts believe that low attachment to the labor force and its correlate, high dependence on welfare, are prime components of underclass behavior. As the political scientist Lawrence

Mead writes in this book *Beyond Entitlement: The Social Obligations of Citizenship,* for many persons who are in the underclass, "the problem is not that jobs are *unavailable* but that they are frequently *unacceptable,* in pay or condition, given that some income is usually available from families or benefit programs." In other words, persons in the underclass frequently choose not to work rather than to take jobs they deem beneath them.... The willingness of Hispanic men to work, even at low-wage jobs if their skills qualify them for nothing better, suggests that Hispanics are in no immediate danger of forming a large underclass.

... During the 1980s, 3.3 million new Hispanic workers were added to the work force, giving Hispanics a disproportionate share of the new jobs. Hispanics benefited more than any other group in terms of employment growth in the last decade. By the year 2000, they are expected to account for 10 percent of the nation's work force.

EARNINGS

... Hispanic leaders charge that Hispanics' wages have failed to keep pace with those of non-Hispanics. Statistics on average Hispanic earnings during the decade appear to bear this out, but they should be viewed with caution. The changing composition of the Hispanic population, from a predominantly native-born to an increasingly immigrant one, makes an enormous difference in how we interpret the data on Hispanic earnings. Since nearly half of all Hispanic workers are foreign-born and since many of these have immigrated within the last ten years, we should not be surprised that the average earnings of Hispanics appear low. After all, most Hispanic immigrants are semi-skilled workers who do not speak English, and their wages reflect these deficiencies. When huge numbers of such workers are added to the pool on which we base average-earnings figures, they will lower the mean....

When earnings of native-born Mexican American men are analyzed separately from those of Mexican immigrants, a very different picture emerges. On the average, the weekly earnings of Mexican American men are about 83 percent those of non-Hispanic white men—a figure that cuts in half the apparent gap between their earnings and those of non-Hispanics. Even this gap can be explained at least in part. Schooling, experience, hours worked, and geographical region of residence are among several factors that can affect earnings. When we compensate for these variables, we find that Mexican American men earn about 93 percent of the weekly earnings of comparable non-Hispanic white men. English-language proficiency also plays an important role in the earnings of Hispanics; some economists assert that those who are proficient in English experience "no important earnings differences from native-born Anglos." ...

EDUCATION

Contrary to popular opinion, most Mexican American young adults have completed high school, being nearly as likely to do so as other Americans. But the popular press, the federal government, and Hispanic organizations cite statistics that indicate otherwise. They claim that about 60 percent of all Mexican-origin persons do not complete high school. The confusion stems, as it does with earnings data, from lumping native-born Hispanics with immigrants to get statistical averages for the entire group....

Traditionally, Hispanics, like blacks, were more likely to concentrate in fields such as education and the social sciences, which are less remunerative than the physical sciences, business, engineering, and other technical and professional fields. Recently this trend has been reversed; in 1987 (the last year for which such statistics are available), Hispanics were almost as likely as non-Hispanic whites to receive baccalaureate degrees in the natural sciences and were more likely than they to major in computer sciences and engineering.

OCCUPATIONAL STATUS

Fewer Hispanic college graduates will mean fewer Hispanics in the professions and in higher-paying occupations, but this does not translate into the doomsday predictions about their achievement that advocacy organizations commonly voice. It does not mean, for example, that there will be a "a permanent Hispanic underclass" of persons "stuck in poverty because of low wages and deprived of upward mobility," as one Hispanic leader suggested in a *New York Times* article. It may mean, however, that Hispanics will be more likely to hold jobs as clerks in stores and banks, as secretaries and other office support personnel, as skilled workers, and as laborers.... Only in the managerial and professional and the service categories are there very large differences along ethnic lines: 11 percent of all Hispanic males are employed in managerial or professional jobs compared with 27 percent of all non-Hispanics; conversely, 16 percent of the Hispanic males compared with only 9 percent of the non-Hispanic males are employed in service jobs. But these figures include large numbers of immigrants in the Hispanic population, who are disproportionately represented in the service industry and among laborers.

An increasing number of Hispanics are self-employed, many in owner-operated businesses. According to the economist Timothy Bates, who has done a comprehensive study of minority small businesses, those owned by Hispanics are more successful than those owned by blacks. Yet Mexican business owners, a majority of whom are immigrants, are less well educated than any other group; one-third have completed less than twelve years of schooling. One reason why Hispanics may be more successful than blacks in operating small businesses, according to Bates, is that they cater to a nonminority clientele, whereas blacks operate businesses in black neighborhoods, catering to black clients. Hispanic-owned businesses are concentrated in the retail field; about one-quarter of both Mexican and non-Mexican Hispanic firms are retail businesses. About 10 percent of the Mexican-owned firms are in construction.

POVERTY

Despite generally encouraging economic indicators for Hispanics, poverty rates are quite high; 26 percent of all Hispanics live below the poverty line. Hispanics are more than twice as likely to be living in poverty than are persons in the general population. Two factors, however, distort the poverty data: the inclusion of Puerto Ricans, who make up about 10 percent of Hispanics, one-third of whom live in poverty; and the low earnings of new immigrants. The persistence of poverty among Puerto Ricans is one of the most troubling features of the Hispanic population....

An exhaustive study of the 1980 census by Frank Bean and Marta Tienda, however, suggests that nativity plays an important role in poverty data, as it does in earnings data generally. Bean and Tienda estimate that the poverty rate among U.S.-born Mexican Americans was nearly 20 percent lower than that among Mexican immigrants in 1980. Their analysis of data from the 1970 census, by contrast, shows almost no difference in poverty rates between Mexican Americans and Mexican immigrants, with both groups suffering significantly greater poverty in 1970 than in 1980. This implies that while poverty was declining among immigrants and the native-born alike between 1970 and 1980, the decline was greater for Mexican Americans.

THE PUBLIC POLICY IMPLICATIONS OF SUCH FINDINGS

For most Hispanics, especially those born in the United States, the last few decades have brought greater economic opportunity and social mobility. They are building solid lower-middle- and middle-class lives that include two-parent households, with a male head who works full-time and earns a wage commensurate with his education and training. Their educational level has been steadily rising, their earnings no longer reflect wide disparities with those of non-Hispanics, and their occupational distribution is coming to resemble more closely that of the general population. They are buying homes—42 percent of all Hispanics owned or were purchasing their home in 1989, including 47 percent of all Mexican Americans—and moving away from inner cities....

* * *

There is much reason for optimism about the progress of Hispanics in the United States.... Mexican Americans, the oldest and largest Hispanic group, are moving steadily into the middle class, with the majority having established solid, working- and middle-class lives. Even Mexican immigrants and those from other Latin American countries, many of whom have very little formal education, appear to be largely self-sufficient. The vast majority of such immigrants—two-thirds—live above the poverty line, having achieved a standard of living far above that attainable by them in their countries of origin.

There is no indication that any of these groups is in danger of becoming a permanent underclass. If Hispanics choose to (and most *are* choosing to), they will quickly join the mainstream of this society.... [T]he evidence suggests that Hispanics, by and large, are behaving much as other ethnic groups did in the past. One group of Hispanics, however, appears not to be following this pattern. Puerto Ricans occupy the lowest rung of the social and economic ladder among Hispanics, and a disturbing number of them show little hope of climbing higher. ... Puerto Ricans are not simply the poorest of all Hispanic groups; they experience the highest degree of social dysfunction of any Hispanic group and exceed that of blacks on some indicators. Thirty-nine percent of all Puerto Rican families are headed by single women; 53 percent of all Puerto Rican children are born out of wedlock; the proportion of men in the labor force is lower among Puerto Ricans than any other group,

including blacks; Puerto Ricans have the highest welfare participation rate of any group in New York, where nearly half of all Puerto Ricans in the United States live. Yet, on the average, Puerto Ricans are better educated than Mexicans and nearly as well educated as Cubans, with a median education of twelve years....

SOME HOPEFUL SIGNS

Despite the overall poor performance of Puerto Ricans, there are some bright spots in their achievement—which make their poverty seem all the more stark. While the median family earnings of Puerto Ricans are the lowest of any Hispanic groups, *individual* earnings of both male and female Puerto Ricans are actually higher than those of any other Hispanic subgroup except Cubans. In 1989 Puerto Rican men had median earnings that were 82 percent of those of non-Hispanics; Puerto Rican women's median earnings were actually higher than those of non-Hispanic women. Moreover, the occupational distribution of Puerto Ricans shows that substantial numbers work in white-collar jobs: nearly one-third of the Puerto Rican males who are employed work in managerial, professional, technical, sales, or administrative support jobs and more than two-thirds of the Puerto Rican females who work hold such jobs.

Moreover, Puerto Ricans are not doing uniformly poorly in all parts of the country. Those in Florida, Texas, and California, for example, perform far better than those in New York....

In fact, as their earnings attest, Puerto Ricans who hold jobs are not doing appreciably worse than other Hispanics, or non-Hispanics, once their lower educational attainment is taken into account.

The low overall achievement of Puerto Ricans is simply not attributable to the characteristics of those who work but is a factor of the large number of those—male and female—who are neither working nor looking for work....

WHERE DO PUERTO RICANS GO FROM HERE?

Many Puerto Ricans are making it in the United States. There is a thriving middle class of well-educated professionals, managers, and white-collar workers, whose individual earnings are among the highest of all Hispanic groups' and most of whom live in married-couple families. These Puerto Ricans have done what other Hispanics and, indeed, most members of other ethnic groups have: they have moved up the economic ladder and into the social mainstream within one or two generations of their arrival in the United States....

The crisis facing the Puerto Rican community is not simply one of poverty and neglect. If anything, Puerto Ricans have been showered with too much government attention.... The fact that Puerto Ricans outside New York succeed proves there is nothing inevitable about Puerto Rican failure. Nor does the existence of prejudice and discrimination explain why so many Puerto Ricans fail when so many other Hispanics, including those from racially mixed backgrounds, are succeeding.

So long as significant numbers of young Puerto Rican men remain alienated from the work force, living by means of crime or charity, fathering children toward whom they feel no responsibility, the prospects of Puerto Ricans in the United States will dim. So long as so many Puerto Rican women allow the men who father their babies to avoid the duties of marriage and parenthood, they will deny their children the promise of a better life, which has been the patrimony of generations of poor immigrants' children. The solution to these problems will not be found in more government programs. Indeed, government has been an accomplice in enabling fathers to abandon their responsibility. Only the Puerto Rican community can save itself, but the healing cannot begin until the community recognizes that many of its deadliest wounds are self-inflicted.

... Hispanics have not always had an easy time of it in the United States. Even though discrimination against Mexican Americans and Puerto Ricans was not as severe as it was against blacks, acceptance has come only with struggle, and some prejudices still exist. Discrimination against Hispanics, or any other group, should be fought, and there are laws and a massive administrative apparatus to do so. But the way to eliminate such discrimination is not to classify all Hispanics as victims and treat them as if they could not succeed by their own efforts. Hispanics can and will prosper in the United States by following the example of the millions before them.

NO

Robert Aponte

URBAN HISPANIC POVERTY: DISAGGREGATIONS AND EXPLANATIONS

Nearly a quarter century since the passage of the Civil Rights Act and the initiation of the massive War on Poverty effort, substantial proportions of inner city minorities appear more hopelessly mired in poverty than at any time since these efforts were undertaken (Tienda 1989, Wacquant and Wilson 1989b, Wilson 1987). The poverty rate among central city blacks, for example, stood at about one person in three in 1989, having risen from a rate of one in four two decades earlier (U.S. Bureau of the Census 1980, 1990). Equally ominous is the poverty rate of central city Latinos (Hispanics), some three in ten, which exceeds that of central city whites by a factor of nearly two and one half (U.S. Bureau of the Census 1990). Associated with these indicators of deprivation among urban minorities have been other signs of potential distress. Available evidence indicates that minorities are experiencing rates of joblessness, welfare receipt, and female headship substantially in excess of the rates prevailing among whites (Tienda 1989, Tienda and Jensen 1988, Wacquant and Wilson 1989b, Wilson and Neckerman 1986).

These important issues have not escaped research attention, but until the 1980s, this research focused almost exclusively on blacks among the minority groups and how they compared to whites (Wilson and Aponte 1985). Indeed, prior to the 1980s, empirical research on the poverty of Hispanics in the United States beyond small scale studies was difficult to perform for lack of data. Hence, as we enter the 1990s, far too little is known about the complex configuration of factors underlying Latino poverty. In addition, while the various reports from the Current Population Survey began producing detailed information on "Hispanics" in the 1970s, often presenting the trends alongside those of blacks and whites, it was not until the mid 1980s that we began to consistently receive detailed, individualized data on the major

From Robert Aponte, "Urban Hispanic Poverty: Disaggregations and Explanations," *Social Problems*, vol. 38, no. 4 (November 1991), pp. 516–528. Copyright © 1991 by The Society for the Study of Social Problems. Reprinted by permission of University of California Press. Notes and references omitted.

ethnic groups within the hybrid category of "Hispanic." What little systematic research has been done on the topic has far too often treated the hybrid category as a single group.

Any reliance on the aggregate category "Hispanic" is fraught with a high potential to mislead. For analytic purposes beyond the most superficial generalizations, it is crucial that social and economic trends among Hispanics studied be as fully disaggregated as possible if an inquiry is to reveal rather than obscure the dynamics underlying the statistical indicators.* The major current streams of research on minority poverty have produced precious few paradigms with relevance to the Latino population, in part because of the lack of research directed toward the group as a whole, but also because of the failure to consider the individual national groupings separately. Even those analyses incorporating disaggregated indicators need to be interpreted with careful attention paid to the appropriate historic and contemporary circumstances surrounding the various Hispanic groups' incorporation into the mainland United States society.

In the relatively short period that the detailed data have been available, much of significance has been revealed that is consistent with the perspective advanced here. It has been shown, for example, that poverty among Puerto Ricans, the most urban and second largest Latino group, has hovered at a rate averaging over 40 percent in the last several years—a rate second to none among the major ethnic or racial groups for which there is data, and one substantially higher than that of the

*[Disaggregation is the process of breaking data down into smaller, more meaningful parts to better understand the information.—Ed.]

other Hispanic groups (cf. U.S. Bureau of the Census 1985a, 1986, 1987b, 1988, 1989b). In addition, the rate of poverty for all Hispanics has grown far more rapidly in recent years than that of whites or blacks, as dramatically shown in an important recent report by the Center on Budget and Policy Priorities (Greenstein et al. 1988).

The report notes that the 1987 Hispanic poverty rate of slightly greater than 28 percent is less than 5 percentage points lower than that of blacks, traditionally the poorest group, and nearly three times that of whites, despite the fact that the labor force participation rate of Hispanics is somewhat higher than that of these other groups. Moreover, the increase in Hispanic poverty over the 1980s shown in the Policy Center Report has been fueled largely by increases in poverty among two parent families. Thus, it cannot be blamed on the relatively modest rise in Hispanic single parent families over this particular period, nor can it easily be pinned on sagging work efforts, given the higher than average participation in the workforce of the group.

Importantly, the patterns outlined above appear to defy common sense interpretations. For example, the idea that discrimination can account for the patterning of such indicators falls short of explaining why Puerto Ricans are poorer than blacks even though they almost certainly experience far less discrimination (Massey and Bitterman 1985). Likewise, a human capital perspective by itself cannot explain why Mexicans, who speak poorer English than Puerto Ricans and are less educated than whites and blacks as well as Puerto Ricans, are more often employed than persons of the other three groups (U.S. Bureau of Labor Statistics 1990)....

DISAGGREGATIONS AND CONTEXT

To speak of Hispanic poverty in urban America at present is to speak of the two largest groups, those of Mexican and those of Puerto Rican extraction, who together account for roughly three-fourths of all U.S. Hispanics. Together these two groups accounted for over 80 percent of all 1987 Hispanic poor within metropolitan areas, their central cities taken separately, or the continental United States as a whole (U.S. Bureau of the Census 1989a). Cubans, the next largest group, have accounted for only about five to six percent of all Hispanics during the 1980s and have significantly lower rates of poverty (U.S. Bureau of the Census 1987a, 1989b; see also U.S. Bureau of the Census 1989b). Hence, this article focuses on Latinos of Mexican or Puerto Rican extraction.

While the diverse groups that comprise the remainder of the Latino population have not yet been numerous enough to have a great impact on the indicators for all Hispanics, it does not follow that their experiences have been trouble free. As noted by the Policy Center Report (Greenstein et al. 1988), available data suggests that many of these other groups are experiencing substantial poverty....

Contrasting sharply with the Cuban experience, the processes whereby Mexicans and Puerto Ricans entered the mainstream urban economy entailed a number of common features. Characteristics shared by these incoming groups include mother tongue, economic or labor migrant status, relatively low levels of skill, inadequate command of English, and little formal education. In addition to their relatively modest social status upon entry, these groups generally received no

special government assistance, and each sustained a fair amount of discrimination.

Though the urban settlement of Puerto Ricans on the mainland occurred rapidly, was highly concentrated in a major northern city, and began largely after the Second World War, among Mexicans the process transpired throughout much of the 20th century, was far more gradual and diffuse, and was contained largely within the southwest section of the country. Indeed, in only a few midwestern cities—notably Chicago—where small proportions of each group have settled, do Mexicans and Puerto Ricans maintain any substantial co-residence. In addition, the Puerto Ricans entered as citizens and were thereby entitled to certain rights that were available to only some Mexicans.

From less than 100,000 at the end of the Second World War, the Puerto Rican population on the mainland grew to well over 1 million by 1970, at which time a solid majority were residents of New York City (Moore and Pachon 1985). Although by 1980 the city no longer contained a majority of the nearly two million members of the group, most of those living elsewhere still resided in large metropolitan cities, and mainly in the Northeast....

While rapid immigration by Puerto Ricans is no longer evident, Mexican immigration into both urban and rural areas has continued in recent years. The estimated population of nearly 12 million Mexican-origin Hispanics in 1988 accounted for nearly 63 percent of all mainland Latinos and was about five times the size of the estimated 2.3 million Puerto Ricans (U.S. Bureau of the Census 1989b). If present trends continue, the gap in population size separating these groups will further widen.

These settlement differences may affect social mobility in several ways. First, the economic well-being of Puerto Ricans can be expected to hinge heavily on economic conditions *inside* the major cities of the eastern end of the snowbelt, especially New York, and be particularly dependent on the opportunity structure confronting the less skilled in those areas. Such conditions have not been favorable in recent decades due to the widely documented decline in manufacturing, trade, and other forms of low skilled employment that was most evident in northern *inner cities* beginning with the 1950s and accelerating during the 1970s (Kasarda 1985, Wacquant and Wilson 1989b). Moreover, such jobs have not returned to these places, even where sagging economies have sharply rebounded (as in New York and Boston), since the newer mix of jobs in such areas still tend to require more skills or credentials than previously (Kasarda 1983, 1988).

By contrast, Mexican Hispanics are more dependent upon the opportunity structures confronting less skilled labor in southwestern cities and their suburbs but without heavy reliance on only one or two such areas or on *central city* employment. These areas are believed to have better job prospects for the less skilled than northern cities because of the continued employment growth in low skilled jobs throughout the entire postwar period (Kasarda 1985, Wacquant and Wilson 1989b).

A second important distinction concerns social welfare provisions. Specifically, Puerto Ricans have settled into the *relatively* more generous states of the North, while their counterparts popu-late a band of states with traditionally low levels of assistance. A notable exception to this is California—the state with the largest number of Mexican Hispanics. However, many among the group in that state are ineligible for assistance due to lack of citizenship. At the same time, many eligible recipients likely co-reside with undocumented immigrants subject to deportation if caught. No doubt many of the impoverished among both such groups will not apply for assistance for fear of triggering discovery of the undocumented in their families or households.

As of 1987, *no state* in the continental U.S. provided enough AFDC [Aid to Families with Dependent Children] benefits to bring families up to the poverty line.... Recent research by Jencks and Edin (1990) demonstrates conclusively that very few AFDC families can survive in major cities on just the legally prescribed income; most are forced to cheat, many turn to petty crimes for supplementary income, and some even slip into homelessness (cf. Ellison 1990, Rossi and Wright 1989).

However, this was not always so (Tobier 1984, National Social Science and Law Center 1987). For example, in New York city during the late 1960s, the maximum AFDC benefit package for a family of three, discounting food stamps, could raise the family's income to 97 *percent* of the poverty line (Tobier 1984). The payment levels declined gradually during the first part of the 1970s....

The statistical indicators on these groups are consistent with such expectations. For example, among men aged 20 years and over, Puerto Ricans had a labor force participation rate 10 percentage points lower than that of Mexican origin men in 1987 (U.S. Bureau of Labor Statistics 1988), representing a widening of the respective 1977 gap of only five percentage points. The employment-to-population ratios exhibited a similar gap, but they remained unchanged over the ten year period, with the Puerto Rican ratio trailing that of the Mexican origin group by 10 percentage points (Newman 1978), suggesting that the Mexican unemployment rate is catching up to the Puerto Rican rate (Greenstein et al. 1988). Although these are national level trends, they should reflect urban conditions since both groups have become highly urbanized. As expected, Puerto Ricans are also poorer than Mexicans. The central city poverty rate for Puerto Ricans in 1987 was 46 percent, with the corresponding rate for Mexicans 30 percent. The metropolitan area rates were similarly distributed. Likewise, the proportion of families headed by women among central city Puerto Ricans was 49 percent, while only about 21 percent of the Mexican origin families were so headed (U.S. Bureau of the Census 1989a).

Finally, the Current Population Survey reveals that employed Puerto Ricans, on average, earn more than employed Mexicans (U.S. Bureau of the Census 1989b). The survey also reveals that many more Mexican families in poverty have members in the work force than do poor Puerto Rican families, while a substantially higher proportion of the latter group receive government assistance. For example, in 1987, 72 percent of all Mexican origin families in poverty had at least one member in the work force compared to only 24 percent of the Puerto Rican families. Conversely, 72 percent of Puerto Rican families in poverty that year received all of their income from some form of assistance or transfer compared to 25 percent of the Mexican families (U.S.

Bureau of the Census 1989a). In spite of the "assistance," not one of these needy families was brought over the poverty line, and many were left with incomes well below the designated level!

It seems likely that the kind of approach urged here, one that maximizes sensitivity to the varying conditions of the individual Latino groups' plights, can help in interpreting trends among data that are largely aggregated. For example, the Policy Center Report reached a number of findings that can be pushed further. The report concluded that recent increases in Hispanic poverty are associated only weakly, if at all, with recent increases in female headship or joblessness within the group. Rather, the poverty increases were strongly associated with declining real wages. The report also noted that the increase in poverty occurred mainly among Mexicans and in the Sunbelt and Midwest. However, the report did *not* make a connection between these factors.

Attending to Latino subgroup differences provides an explanation. We would expect declining real wages to bring more Mexicans into poverty than Puerto Ricans because proportionately more Mexicans hold very low wage jobs. In turn, Mexican dominance in the three regions outside of the Northeast helps explain why those regions, but *not* the Northeast, were more affected by the rise in poverty traceable to real wage declines, even as the Puerto Rican dominated northeastern region maintained the highest level of poverty.

Finally, consideration of the continuation of Mexican immigration leads to a second hypothesis about their vulnerability to falling real wages: Mexicans are employed in regions plagued by labor market crowding resulting from continued immigration, especially since much of it consists of "undocumenteds," a group that clearly constitutes cheaper labor. This especially hurts those with lower levels of education, since they are most likely to compete directly with the latest newcomers. Indeed, the Report singles out the lesser educated Hispanics as the group sustaining the most increased hardship....

Explanations of Urban Poverty

Most current popular theories about urban poverty fall short of fully accounting for the plight of the Hispanic poor because of a narrow focus on blacks. In spite of the apparent deficit, disaggregating the Hispanic figures allows us to apply some of this work to at least one of the two major groups under study.

The culture of poverty. The idea of a "culture of poverty" generally traces back to the work of Oscar Lewis (1959, 1966) who coined the phrase, although others have advanced similar notions. Lewis developed the core ideas of the argument while studying Mexican and Puerto Rican families. The work suggests that culturally-based attitudes or predispositions such as "present mindedness" and "obsessive consumption" are the major barriers to economic mobility for many of the poor, implying that providing opportunities to the poor will not be enough: some will need "cultural uplifting" as well. The major strength of the idea for my purposes is that it can apply equally well to the poor of any of the Latino groups.

However, the theory is largely discredited within academic circles.... In fact, numerous subsequent studies of poor people's values and attitudes have found little support for the theory (Corcoran et al. 1985, Goodwin 1972, Irelan et al. 1969)....

The welfare-as-cause argument. In his book *Losing Ground*, Charles Murray (1984) argues that the liberalization of welfare during the late 1960s and early 1970s made work less beneficial than welfare and encouraged low-income people to avoid work and marriage, in order to reap the benefits of welfare, and that this is a primary source of the rise in female headship and, indirectly, poverty itself....

We might ask if welfare payments were so lucrative, why did the poor fail to escape poverty, at least while "on the dole," but Murray does not address this issue.... Moreover, studies on the effects of welfare availability to changes in family structure have produced few results supporting a connection, the overall consensus being that such effects as they exist are relatively weak (Wilson and Neckerman 1986. U.S. General Accounting Office 1987).... Thus, welfare appears unlikely to be a major cause of female headship or joblessness among Hispanics, as among blacks. However, it may properly be seen as a major cause of Latino poverty insofar as so many of the Hispanic impoverished who are legally entitled to assistance are left destitute by miserly benefit levels while many other equally needy Hispanics are denied benefits altogether.

The mismatch thesis. This explanation... focuses mainly on older, northern, industrial towns. It finds recent urban poverty rooted in the movement of manufacturing and other blue-collar employment away from snowbelt central cities where blacks and Hispanics make up increasingly larger proportions of the population. As blue-collar industry moved from the cities to the suburbs and from the Snow Belt to the Sun Belt, central city job growth occurred primarily in white-collar jobs for which the black and Hispanic central city residents often did not qualify for lack of skills or credentials.

... While studies based on data for 1970 or earlier have tended to disconfirm the hypothesis, work on more recent periods has largely produced supporting results (Holzer 1991). Hence, the argument remains a viable hypothesis about joblessness in northern central cities. Once again, however, the idea offers no explanation for the poverty of Mexicans since relatively few live in those areas....

Labor market segmentation theories (dual labor market theory). According to early versions of labor market segmentation theories, racial and ethnic minorities were intentionally relegated to the "secondary" sector of the labor market characterized by highly unstable work with low pay and little room for advancement (Cain 1976). More recent versions often suggest that disadvantaged native workers all but openly shun such jobs because of their undesirable characteristics and that immigrants are therefore "imported" to fill the positions (Piore 1979)....

Though clearly of important explanatory potential, the segmentation theory falls short of providing a complete explanation for the patterns in question.... Thus, the argument would appear to operate better in cities such as New York which have received large numbers of immigrants in recent years than in places such as Buffalo, Cleveland, Philadelphia, or Rochester with proportionately fewer such persons. (Waldinger 1989). Yet, Puerto Ricans in these cities appear as plagued by poverty and joblessness as those in New York (U.S. Bureau of the Census 1985b)....

The underclass hypothesis. The underclass argument, proposed by William Julius Wilson (1987, 1988), begins with the observation that declining housing discrimination and rising incomes among some blacks have enabled many to leave the older central city ghettos. Their departure from the highly segregated and traditionally underserviced areas, characterized by higher than average rates of physical deterioration, exacerbates the purely economic problems confronted by the remaining population....

Ghetto residents subjected to the described conditions constitute Wilson's underclass. The combined material and environmental deprivation confronted by the group anchors them firmly to prolonged poverty, welfare dependence, and assorted illicit enterprises.... Once again, among Hispanics, only the Puerto Rican poor are as geographically isolated as poor blacks and, therefore, appear to be the only Hispanic population for which this explanation can hold.

CONCLUSION

... The data and discussions presented here, while far from providing a definitive analysis of Hispanic poverty, provide support to a number of generalizations about the problems and potential solutions. Decreased employment opportunities for the less skilled and educated, severely depressed wages among the employed, and restricted or nonexistent welfare benefits comprise the major causes of urban Hispanic poverty. Expanding employment, increasing wages, providing a better living to those unable to work, and promoting higher levels of human capital attainment are major public policy imperatives if these problems are ever to be adequately addressed.

POSTSCRIPT

Are Hispanics Making Significant Progress?

Early in the twenty-first century Hispanic/Latino Americans will be the largest minority in the United States, according to demographers. As Aponte shows, a major problem in understanding Hispanic poverty, which for some is so intense that they are considered an underclass, is the large variations in income, education, and status among groups of Spanish-speaking Americans.

As Chavez shows, many Hispanics have paralleled other ethnic and racial minority "success stories" of "making it" in the United States. Yet her data ignore significant pockets of poverty.

Are Hispanics making significant progress? Or is it an illusion, already crumbling in the face of America's recent economic downturns? Do all racial minorities require the same government programs?

For cutting-edge research and policy recommendations on the very real problem of continuing Latino poverty, see *Latinos in a Changing U.S. Economy* edited by Rebecca Morales and F. Bonilla (Sage Publications, 1993). An excellent article that looks at the effects of residential segregation and Hispanic poverty is Anne M. Santiago and M. G. Wilder, "Residential Segregation and Links to Minority Poverty: The Case of Latinos in the United States," *Social Problems* (November 1991).

An excellent delineation of the current Hispanic situation in the United States is *The Hispanic Condition: Reflections on Culture and Identity in America* by Ilan Stavans (HarperCollins, 1995). For a look at progress within universities, see *The Leaning Ivory Tower: Latino Professors in American Universities* edited by Raymond V. Padilla and Rudolfo C. Chavez (State University of New York Press, 1995). A helpful article on females in business is "Hispanic Women Small Business Owners," by Y. Sarason and C. Koberg, *Hispanic Journal of Behavioral Science* (August 1994). A discussion of health progress is in *Race, Gender, and Health* edited by Marcia Bayne-Smith, especially chapter 5, "Latino Women," by A. Giachello (Sage Publications, 1995). Public education achievements are discussed in "Educational Experiences of Hispanics in the U.S.," by W. Velez, in Alfredo Jimenez, ed., *Handbook of Hispanic Cultures in the United States* (Arte Publico Press, 1994).

Comparisons of Hispanics with other groups include Reynolds Farley, "Blacks, Hispanics, and White Ethnic Groups: Are Blacks Uniquely Disadvantaged?" *American Economic Review* (May 1990); "Blacks Holding Ground, Hispanics Losing in Desegregaton," *Phi Delta Kappan* (January 1987); and Robert M. Jiobu, *Ethnicity and Inequality* (State University of New York Press, 1993).

A look at ethnic identity, including that of Latinos, is found in *Ethnic Identity: Formation and Transmission Among Hispanics and Other Minorities* edited by Martha E. Bernal and George P. Knight (State University of New York Press, 1993). Ethnographic accounts of the experiences of ethnics include *Inside Separate Worlds: Life Stories of Young Blacks, Jews, and Latinos* edited by David Schoem (University of Michigan Press, 1991). For an excellent overview of progress being made by a small sample of Hispanic writers, see the special issue of *Washington Post's Book World* "I, Too, Sing American" (May 14, 1995).

ISSUE 10

Do Cultural Differences Between Home and School Explain the High Dropout Rates for American Indian Students?

YES: Jon Reyhner, from "American Indians Out of School: A Review of School-Based Causes and Solutions," *Journal of American Indian Education* (May 1992)

NO: Susan Ledlow, from "Is Cultural Discontinuity an Adequate Explanation for Dropping Out?" *Journal of American Indian Education* (May 1992)

ISSUE SUMMARY

YES: Professor of curriculum and instruction Jon Reyhner argues that the school dropout rate for Native Americans is 35 percent, almost double that of other groups. He blames this on schools, teachers, and curricula that ignore the needs and potentials of American Indian students.

NO: Educator Susan Ledlow argues that data on dropout rates for American Indians, especially at the national level, is sparse. She questions the meaning and measurement of "cultural discontinuity," and she faults this perspective for ignoring important structural factors, such as employment, in accounting for why Native American students drop out of school.

One of the things that is striking about the following arguments of Jon Reyhner and Susan Ledlow is the immense difference in what might be called the skeptical factor. Reyhner without doubt or hesitation embraces and cites the highest available statistic on American Indian school dropout rates: 35 percent. Ledlow, by contrast, begins by stating that reliable statistics simply do not exist.

Reyhner is highly skeptical of most schools and teachers. He doubts if many, if not most, really have Native American students' interests at heart. He blames the problem on the discontinuity between the backgrounds of the students and those of their white teachers. He seriously doubts that non-Indians, especially those whose training has been primarily or exclusively in subject content and not in Indian ways, can be effective teachers of Native Americans.

Formal education for Native American children has long been problematic and controversial, in part because much of it has been directed by the federal government as part of the management of reservation life. There have been many efforts in the past to replace Native American children's heritage with the skills and attitudes of the larger, white society, and the earliest formal schooling efforts placed great emphasis on Anglo conformity. Reyhner takes a detailed look at the schools today and the ways in which they are run, and he argues that the discontinuity between the life experiences of Native American schoolchildren and the schools and the curricula they teach explains the high dropout rates.

While admitting that some schools and some teachers may be inadequate, Ledlow seriously doubts if the cultural discontinuity theory is sound. She contends that we must look elsewhere for a more plausible and empirically correct explanation of high dropout rates. She even questions if the rates are indeed as high as the accepted wisdom says they are. She asks, Are those high rates derived from misinformation or misinterpretation of the data, repeated by the mass media and Native American lobbying groups? She suggests that, in some cases, the rates may be greatly inflated and/or statistical anomalies. As you consider this debate, compare other instances in which data has been misused to support political agendas. Examples might be the assertions that domestic abuse increases significantly on Super Bowl Sunday, that gay teenagers are more likely to commit suicide, and that there is a new law that will disenfranchise Black citizens, ending their right to vote.

Ledlow is also concerned with the assumption of Reyhner and others that a "culturally relevant" curriculum is superior to alternative ones. What is such a curriculum to begin with, she wonders? Even more important, where is the research that demonstrates that it is superior?

After providing a critique of cultural discontinuity theorists, Ledlow advances an alternative theory. Her explanation is largely derived from the neglected (at least within sociology circles) Marxist anthropologist J. U. Ogbu. Hers is basically a structural explanation. She emphasizes the importance of political and economic structures, especially the latter, in accounting for Native American dropout rates.

As you read these two selections, think back to when you were in high school. Were your "best" teachers necessarily warm and supportive? Were good teachers ever from radically different backgrounds than your own? Was your education geared to any specific minority group's needs? Would it have been more effective if it had been?

Extrapolate from Ogbu's typology as presented by Ledlow. Which minorities that you have studied so far, that you are familiar with, would fit into which part of his classification? Does it appear to be a sound one?

YES

Jon Reyhner

AMERICAN INDIANS OUT OF SCHOOL: A REVIEW OF SCHOOL-BASED CAUSES AND SOLUTIONS

During the summer of 1991, I taught a dropout prevention seminar at Eastern Montana College. In initial class discussions, the students, mostly members of Montana Indian tribes, blamed dysfunctional families and alcohol abuse for the high dropout rate among Indian students. If this allegation is correct, and Indian families and the abuse of alcohol are to be held responsible, then the implication exists that teachers and schools are satisfactory and not in need of change. However, the testimony given at the Indian Nations at Risk (INAR) Task Force hearings, held throughout the United States in 1990 and 1991, and other research reviewed, indicate that, both on and off the reservation, schools and teachers are to be held accountable as well. Academically capable American Indian students often drop out of school because their needs are not being met. Others are pushed out because they protest, in a variety of ways, how they are being treated. This article examines various explanations for the high dropout rate which oppose the dysfunctional Indian family and alcohol abuse resolution so popularly accepted.

American schools are not providing an appropriate education for Indian students who are put in large, factory-like schools. Indian students are denied teachers with special training in Indian education, denied a curriculum that includes their heritage, and denied culturally appropriate assessment. Their parents are also denied a voice in the education of their children....

EXTENT AND BACKGROUND OF THE PROBLEM

The National Center for Education Statistics (1989) reported that American Indian and Alaska Native students have a dropout rate of 35.5%, about twice the national average and the highest dropout rate of any United States ethnic or racial group [cited].... Regional and local studies gave similar rates (see for example Deyhle, 1989; Eberhard, 1989; Platero, Brandt, Witherspoon, & Wong, 1986; Ward & Wilson, 1989). This overall Indian dropout rate (35%) is not much higher than the 27.1% of Indians between the ages of 16 and 19 living on reservations who were found by the 1980 Census to be neither enrolled in

From Jon Reyhner, "American Indians Out of School: A Review of School-Based Causes and Solutions," *Journal of American Indian Education*, vol. 1, no. 3 (May 1992). Copyright © 1992 by The Center for Indian Education, College of Education, Arizona State University, Tempe, AZ 85287-1311. Reprinted by permission. Notes and references omitted.

school nor high school graduates. However, the Census figures also showed wide variation among reservations as to how many Indian teenagers between 16 and 19 were not in school. One New Mexico Pueblo had only 5.2% of those teenagers not getting a high school education whereas several small Nevada, Arizona, Washington, and California sites had no students completing a high school education (Bureau, 1985).

A recent compelling explanation as to why Indian students do poorly in school in the United States involves the cultural differences between Indian cultures and the dominant Euro-American culture [see Jacob and Jordan (1987) for an interesting discussion of explanations for the school performance of minority students]. As Estelle Fuchs and Robert J. Havighurst reported from the National Study of American Indian Education in the late 1960s, "many Indian children live in homes and communities where the cultural expectations are different and discontinuous from the expectations held by school teachers and school authorities" (1972, p. 299). In the INAR Task Force hearings several educators and community members testified on the need for Indian teachers and Indian curriculum to reduce the cultural conflict between home and school (Indian Nations at Risk Task Force, 1991).

Positive identity formation, as the psychiatrist Erik Erikson (1963) pointed out, is an ongoing, cumulative process that starts in the home with a trusting relationship established between mother and child and develops through the child's interaction with other children and adults. To build a strong positive identity, educators that the child interacts with in school need to reinforce and build on the cultural training and messages

that the child has previously received. If educators give Indian children messages that conflict with what Indian parents and communities show and tell their children, the conflicting messages can confuse the children and create resistance to school (Bowers & Flinders, 1990; Jacob & Jordan, 1987; Spindler, 1987). In the words of John Goodlad, ethnic minority children are "caught and often savaged between the language and expectations of the school and those of the home" (1990, pp. 6–7).

Too often, well-meaning remedial programs focus on finding the reason for failure in students and their homes thus, "blaming the victims." The idea that Indian students are "culturally disadvantaged" or "culturally deprived" reflects ethnocentrism rather than the results of educational research. When schools do not recognize, value, and build on what Indian students learn at home, the students are given a watered-down curriculum (meant to guarantee student learning) which often results in a tedious education, and their being "bored out" of school....

Students do not have to assimilate into the dominant Euro-American culture to succeed in school. Two studies (Deyhle, 1989; Platero et al., 1986) of Indian dropouts found that a traditional Indian orientation is not a handicap in regard to school success. The Navajo Students at Risk study reported that "the most successful students were for the most part fluent Navajo/English bilinguals" (Platero, 1986, p. 6). Lin (1990) found that Indian college students with traditional orientations outperformed students with modern orientations. Tradition oriented students are able to learn in school, in spite of negative characteristics of the schools, because of the strong sense of personal and group identity their native cultures give them.

WHY STUDENTS LEAVE SCHOOL

Research indicates a number of factors associated with higher student dropout rates. Particularly critical factors for Indian students include large schools, uncaring and untrained teachers, passive teaching methods, inappropriate curriculum, inappropriate testing/student retention, tracked classes, and lack of parent involvement....

1. LARGE SCHOOLS

The increasing size of American schools, especially the large comprehensive high schools with more than one thousand students, creates conditions conducive to dropping out. Goodlad (1984) criticized large schools for creating factory-like environments that prevent educators from forming personal relationships with students. He recommended that high schools maintain no more than 600 students....

Smaller schools can allow a greater percentage of students to participate in extra-curricular activities. Students participating in these activities, especially sports when excessive travel is not required, drop out less frequently (Platero, et al., 1986). However, many reservation schools do not have drama clubs, debate teams, and other non-sport extra-curricular activities which would help develop Indian student leadership and language skills.

The Navajo Students at Risk study (Platero, et al., 1986) reported that students who travel long distances to get to school are more likely to drop out. Large consolidated high schools in rural areas, in contrast to smaller more dispersed high schools, increase the distance some students must travel, and thus increase their risk of dropping out. Students who miss the school bus often cannot find alternative transportation, and many high schools today maintain strict attendance policies causing students who miss 10 days of school or more to lose their credit for the semester.

2. UNCARING AND UNTRAINED TEACHERS AND COUNSELORS

In an ethnographic study of Navajo and Ute dropouts that included both interviews with students and classroom observations, Deyhle (1989) reported that students "complained bitterly that their teachers did not care about them or help them in school" (1989, p. 39). Students who "experienced minimal individual attention or personal contact with their teachers" interpreted this neglect as "teacher dislike and rejection" (p. 39).

In comparison to other racial or ethnic groups, few Indian students report that "discipline is fair," that "the teaching is good," that "teachers are interested in students," and that "teachers really listen to me" (National, 1990, p. 43)....

It can be argued that in an attempt to improve the quality of teaching in the United States, changes have been made in teacher preparation programs and certification standards that aggravate rather than solve the problem of recruiting well-qualified caring teachers for Indian children. Increased certification standards are preventing Indian students from entering the teaching profession because [of] the National Teachers Examination (NTE) and similar tests that neither measure teacher commitment to educating Indian children nor their knowledge of

Indian cultures, languages, and teaching practices.

Indian students can successfully complete four or more years of college and receive a Bachelors Degree in education at an accredited college or university and be denied a license to teach Indian students on the basis of one timed standardized examination, usually the NTE, that does not reflect Indian education at all. At the same time, a non-Native who has never seen an Indian student, never studied native history, language, or culture, and whose three credit class in multicultural education emphasized Blacks and Hispanics, can legally teach the Indian students that the Indian graduate cannot.

The Winter 1989 issue of the *Fair Test Examiner* reported how teacher competency tests barred nearly 38,000 Black, Latino, Indian, and other minority teacher candidates from the classroom. In addition, teacher preparation and certification programs are culturally and linguistically "one size fits all," and the size that is measured is a middle-class, Western-European cultural orientation. Recent research (see for example, Reyhner, 1992) identifies a wide body of knowledge about bilingual education, Indian learning styles, and English-as-a-Second-Language (ESL) teaching techniques that teachers of Indian students need to know. In addition, teachers of Indian students should have an Indian cultural literacy specific to the tribal background of their students. But teachers often get just one generic multicultural course in accredited teacher education programs.

This lack of job-specific training is a factor in the high turnover rates among teachers of Indian children. Bureau of Indian Affairs (BIA) professional staff have a 50% turnover rate every two years (Office, 1988). When teaching, those instructors who are not trained to educate Indian children, as most teachers are not with our present teacher training system, tend to experience failure from the beginning. As these teachers often become discouraged and find other jobs, the students are left to suffer from continued educational malpractice.

Proper training and screening of teachers could solve this problem, especially the training of Indian teachers. However, today's commonly used screening devices of test scores and grade point averages do not measure teacher personality. The Kenney Report (Special, 1969) found that one-fourth of the elementary and secondary teachers of Indian children admitted not wanting to teach them.

These teachers also need to use interactive teaching strategies . . . to develop positive relationships with their students, because related to the high turnover is the fact that Indian students think worse of their teachers than any other group (Office, 1988). Studies (Coburn & Nelson, 1989; Deyhle, 1989; Kleinfeld, 1979; Platero et al., 1986) clearly show the Indian student's need for warm, supportive teachers. . . .

3. PASSIVE TEACHING METHODS

Too often educators of Indian students use passive teaching methods to instruct Indian children. Cummins (1989) argued that most teachers in the United States use a passive "transmission" method of instruction in which knowledge is given to students in the form of facts and concepts. These teachers, according to Bowers and Flinders (1990), view language simplistically as a conduit for the transmitting of information rather than as a metaphorical medium through which the teacher and students mutually build meaning through shared experiences and understandings. They expect students to sit passively, to listen to lectures, or to read and memorize the information they receive so that they can answer worksheet, chapter, or test questions (Deyhle, 1989). Students who refuse to sit quietly for long periods of time are considered discipline problems who, over time, are gradually encouraged in a variety of ways to drop out of school.

Although it is popularly assumed that students who drop out are academic failures, the Navajo Students at Risk study (Platero et al., 1986) showed that the academic performance of dropouts is not that different from students who remain in school. Forty-five percent of the Navajo dropouts are B or better students (Platero et al., 1986). Navajo students most frequently give boredom with school, not academic failure or problems with drugs and alcohol, as their reason for dropping out or planning to drop out.

Indian and other minority students are most likely to be the recipients of passive teaching strategies, and they are commonly placed in low track classes.... In a study of Alaskan education (Senate, 1989), seniors included the following reasons for their classmates dropping out of school: not being good at memorizing facts, boredom, larger class sizes, and unsupportive teachers.

4. INAPPROPRIATE CURRICULUM

In addition to inappropriate teaching methods, Indian schools are characterized by an inappropriate curriculum that does not reflect the Indian child's unique cultural background (Coladarci, 1983; Reyhner, 1992). Textbooks are not writ-

ten for Indian students, and thus they enlarge the cultural gap between home and school. In the INAR Task Force hearings, many Indian educators pointed out the need for teaching materials specially designed for Indian students. Despite vast improvement in the past two decades, there are still reports that "too many textbooks are demeaning to minorities" (Senate, 1989, p. 28)....

Related to the lack of Indian-specific curriculum and multicultural curriculum, which increases the cultural distance between the Indian student and school, is the use of standardized tests to measure how well students learn that inappropriate curriculum. The use of these tests, which do not reflect either Indian subject matter or ways of learning, is discussed below.

5. INAPPROPRIATE TESTING/ STUDENT RETENTION

The way tests are designed in this country, with an emphasis on standardized testing, a built-in failure is produced (Oakes, 1985; Bloom, 1981). In addition to the built-in sorting function of standardized tests, they have a cultural bias that has yet to be overcome (Rhodes, 1989). Some of the changes made to improve education in American schools recommended in *A Nation at Risk* (National, 1983) and other studies have hurt rather than helped Indian students.

The use of standardized tests to measure school success leads to more Indian students being retained in a grade, and retention leads to over-age students who drop out of high school. The National Education Longitudinal Study of 1988 (NELS:88) reported that 28.8% of Indian students have repeated at least one grade, the highest percentage of any racial or ethnic group reported (National, 1990, p. 9). The research on failing students (retaining them in grade for another year) indicates that it only creates more failure and more dropouts (Weis, et al., 1989). Even retention in kindergarten does not help students who are having academic problems (Shepard & Smith, 1989). With current practices, schools can make themselves look better by pushing out Indian students since they are evaluated on their average test scores. The more "at risk" students educators push out, the higher the schools' average test scores (Bearden, Spencer, & Moracco, 1989).

Without realizing they are comparing bilingual students' test scores with monolingual English student norms, school administrators and teachers use the California Test of Basic Skills (CTBS) and other standardized test scores to show that their present curriculum is not working. It is also common sense that achievement tests given to Indian students be aligned with what they are being taught in their schools. Testimony given at the INAR/NACIE joint issue sessions in San Diego gave instances of the inappropriate use of tests in schools. For example, tests designed for state mandated curricula were used on students who were not taught using those curricula in BIA schools....

The result of this misuse of tests is that educators keep changing the curriculum in a futile attempt to get Native language speaking students in the early grades to have English language test scores that match the test scores of students of the same age who have spoken English all their lives. Research indicates that it takes about five to seven years for non-English speaking students to acquire an academic proficiency in English which will give them a chance to match the English language test scores of students whose native language is English (Collier, 1989; Cummins, 1989).

6. TRACKED CLASSES

Teachers often have low expectations for Indian students and put them in a non-college-bound vocationally-oriented curriculum. This "tracking" of students is a common practice in secondary schools. The study body is divided into high achievers, average achievers, and low achievers, and each group is put in separate classes. Oakes (1985) described the negative effects of tracking in our nation's high schools and how ethnic minority students are disproportionately represented in the lower tracks where they receive a substandard education. She documented how, in tracked classrooms, "lower-class students are expected to assume lower-class jobs and social positions as adults" (p. 117) and that "students, especially lower-class students, often actively resist what schools try to teach them" (p. 120). Data from the NEL:88 show that less than 10% of Indian students are in the upper quartile of achievement test scores in history, mathematics, reading, and science whereas over 40% are in the lowest quartile (National, 1989). The low expectations of teachers for low track students, already unsuccessful in school, make a serious problem worse....

7. LACK OF PARENT INVOLVEMENT

The last factor to discuss is parent involvement. Greater Indian parent involvement can reduce the cultural distance between home and school. Often school staff say they want parent involvement, but what they really want is parents to get after their children to attend school and study....

Although getting parents to get their children to school is important, parent involvement also means educating parents about the function of the school and allowing parents real decision making power about what and how their children learn. Cummins (1989) noted that "although lip service is paid to community participation through Parent Advisory Committees (PAC) in many school programs, these committees are frequently manipulated through misinformation and intimidation" (p. 62). He goes on to list a number of studies supporting the need for minority parent involvement in schools.

PROMISING REMEDIES

Both educational literature and testimony at INAR hearings recommend solutions to the problems that result in Indian student failure. The following suggestions for improving Indian schools are targeted at the seven factors described above and involve restructuring schools, promoting caring teachers, using active teaching strategies, having culturally-relevant curriculum, testing to help students rather than to fail them, having high expectations of all students, and promoting community involvement....

Time and again in the INAR Task Force hearings Indian parents testified about the need for more Indian teachers who will stand as role models for their children. These instructors would offer students a unique cultural knowledge and would maintain the ability to identify with the problems their students face.

ACTIVE TEACHING METHODS

Obviously, just caring is not enough. Teachers also need to learn culturally appropriate teaching strategies in their teacher training and inservice programs and use these instructional methodologies in their classrooms.... Other studies of Indian students show the need for teachers to know more about the home culture of their students....

* * *

Beyond using active and culturally-appropriate teaching strategies, research (see for example Reyhner, 1992) showed the need for a culturally-appropriate curriculum. Extensive material exists to produce elementary and secondary culturally appropriate curriculum for Indian students, however, there is little incentive for publishers to produce material for the relatively small market that Indian education represents. Books such as Jack Weatherford's (1988) *Indian givers: How the Indians of the Americas transformed the world* indicate the wealth of information that could positively affect Indian students' understanding and self-concept. This information, however, does not seem to be reaching Indian students at the elementary and secondary level....

The best way to get schools to reflect parent and community values and to reduce cultural discontinuity between home and school is to have real parent involvement in Indian education. At many successful Indian schools, the school board, administrators, and teachers are Indian people. The extensive parent involvement at Rock Point Community School in Arizona is one example of how parents can come to feel ownership in their children's school and to translate that feeling into supporting their children's attendance and academic performance. Parent involvement at Rock Point includes quarterly parent-teacher conferences, a yearly general public meeting, and an eight-member elected parent advisory committee that formally observes the school several times a year (Reyhner, 1990). In addition, the Indian school board conducts its meetings in the Navajo language and each classroom has special chairs reserved for parents.

Parents need to have effective input as to how and what their children are taught. This is best achieved through Indian control of schools. However, curriculum restrictions placed by states on public schools, and even the BIA on BIA-funded schools, limit the effectiveness of Indian parent involvement. State and BIA regulations force Indian schools to use curriculum and textbooks not specifically designed for Indian children and to employ teachers who, though certified, have no special training in Indian education.

CONCLUSIONS

Supplemental, add-on programs such as Indian Education Act, Johnson-O'Malley (JOM), Bilingual Education, Special Education, and other federal programs have had limited success in improving the education of Indian children. However, add-on programs are only a first step in making schooling appropriate for Indian children....

If educators continue to get inadequate or inappropriate training in colleges of education, then local teacher-training programs need to provide school staff with information on what works in Indian education and information about the language, history, and culture of the Indian students. Tribal colleges are beginning to develop teacher training pro-

grams to fill this need. Parents and local school boards also need on-going training about what works in Indian education and what schools can accomplish. Head Start, elementary, and secondary schools need the support of tribal education departments and tribal colleges to design and implement effective educational programs that support rather than ignore Indian cultures.

Much testimony was given in the INAR Task Force hearings on the importance of self-esteem for Indian students. It is sometimes unclear that self-esteem is not an independent variable but is a reflection of how competent an Indian child feels. Having students memorize material to show success on standardized tests, a common element of the transmission model of teaching previously described, is a poor way to develop self-esteem. However, if students interact with caring, supportive adults, if students are allowed to explore and learn about the world they live in, including learning about their rich Indian heritage, if they are allowed to develop problem solving skills, if they are given frequent opportunities to read and write and to do mathematics and science in meaningful situations, and if they are encouraged to help improve the world they live in through community service, it is likely that Indian students will feel good about themselves and will be successful in life....

Teachers of Indian students need to have special training in instructional methodologies that have proven effective with Indian students and in using curriculum materials that reflect American Indian history and cultures. They also need to build on the cultural values that Indian parents give their children if teachers want to produce a strong positive sense of identity in their students.

Attempts to replace Indian identity with a dominant cultural identity can confuse and repel Indian students and force them to make a choice between their Indian values or their school's values. Neither choice is desirable or necessary. Students can be academically successful and learn about the larger non-Native world while at the same time retaining and developing their Indian identity. Indian students need to attend schools that reinforce rather than ignore or depreciate Indian cultural values.

NO
Susan Ledlow

IS CULTURAL DISCONTINUITY AN ADEQUATE EXPLANATION FOR DROPPING OUT?

AMERICAN INDIAN DROPOUT RESEARCH

On the national level, there is little information about overall rates for American Indian dropouts. Most national level educational research does not differentiate American Indian students as a separate cohort as with Blacks, Whites, or Hispanics....

There are a number of sources in the educational literature which discuss the issue of American Indian dropouts either directly or indirectly. A comprehensive review of the educational literature regarding American Indian dropout rates disclosed, literally, hundreds of reports; evaluation or annual reports; local, state, or national government reports; senate hearings; task force proceedings; or descriptions of dropout intervention programs. Some reports provided actual dropout rates for local areas or states. These reports suffer from the same weaknesses as many national studies: they define and count dropouts variously and, often, inaccurately (see Rumberger 1987 for a discussion of the problems with dropout research). What is most noteworthy is that there is very little research which specifically address the causes of American Indian students dropping out.

In spite of this dearth of knowledge about the causes for so many Indian students' decision to leave school, many of the reports commonly cite the need for making the school curriculum more "culturally relevant" or adding some type of Indian studies component to the regular curriculum in order to solve the problem. Cultural relevance is rarely defined and almost always assumed to be significant. With no evidence to support the claim and no definition of what a culturally relevant curriculum is, many of the school district and special program reports recommend that a culturally relevant curriculum will ameliorate Indian students' difficulties in school. How and why a relevant curriculum will solve the problems is rarely addressed;

From Susan Ledlow, "Is Cultural Discontinuity an Adequate Explanation for Dropping Out?" *Journal of American Indian Education*, vol. 1, no. 3 (May 1992). Copyright © 1992 by The Center for Indian Education, College of Education, Arizona State University, Tempe, AZ 85287-1311. Reprinted by permission. Notes and references omitted.

one assumes that the proponents of such solutions believe them to be based on some body of empirical knowledge, most probably the cultural discontinuity hypothesis, which originated in the ideas of anthropologists such as Dell Hymes (1974).

THE CULTURAL DISCONTINUITY HYPOTHESIS

The cultural discontinuity hypothesis assumes that culturally based differences in the communication styles of the minority students' home and the Anglo culture of the school lead to conflicts, misunderstandings, and, ultimately, failure for those students. The research focuses on the process, rather than the structure of education and concludes that making the classroom more culturally appropriate will mean a higher rate of achievement. Erickson offered three reasons for this. He stated that cultural adaptation may reduce culture shock for students, it may make them feel that the school and teacher hold a positive regard for them, and it simplifies learning tasks, in that students do not have to master a culturally unfamiliar way of behavior at the same time that they are expected to master academic content.

Susan Philips' research on children at the Warm Springs Reservation in Oregon is the premier example of this type of research. She focused on the differences in communication and interaction patterns in the school and in the Warm Springs community. Her argument is that

the children of the Warm Springs Indian Reservation are enculturated in their preschool years into modes of organizing the transmission of verbal messages that are culturally different from those of Anglo middle-class children. I argue that

this difference makes it more difficult for them to then comprehend verbal messages conveyed through the school's Anglo middle-class modes of organizing classroom interaction. (1982, p. 4).

Philips indicated that the hierarchical structure of the classroom, with the teacher as the focus of all communication is fundamentally at odds with the Warm Springs children's understanding of appropriate communication patterns. For example, teachers often assumed that Indian children were not paying attention because they did not look directly at the teacher or provide behavioral feedback that indicated they were listening (p. 101). These behaviors, however, are appropriate in their own community. She also noted that of four possible participant structures—whole class, small group, individual work, and one-to-one with the teacher—Indian students, when allowed to control their own interaction, most actively participated in one-to-one with the teacher and in small group work. Warm Springs students showed little enthusiasm for teacher-directed whole class or small group encounters or for individual desk work, which are the most commonly employed participant structures. The implication of her research is that more Indian teachers, culturally relevant materials, and teaching methods which emphasize appropriate participant structures will allow Indian students to experience greater success and achievement in school.

The Kamehameha Elementary Education Project (KEEP) is another well known example of research supporting the cultural discontinuity hypothesis. KEEP originated in response to the relative lack of success experienced by Native Hawaiian children compared with

Japanese, Chinese, and haole (of northern European ancestry) children. The project used research on socialization practices in Hawaiian homes, and how these differed from the patterns of interaction in the school, to develop a "K-3 language arts program that is culturally compatible for Hawaiian children, and that, both in the lab school and public schools, produced significant gains in reading achievement levels for educationally at-risk Hawaiian children" (Vogt, Jordan, and Tharp, 1987, p. 278).

Anticipating that the gains experienced by KEEP children might be interpreted as the result of better teaching methods, rather than culturally specific methods, the Rough Rock Community School on the Navajo reservation in Arizona replicated the KEEP project. Many of the strategies developed for use with Hawaiian children were found to be ineffective or actually counterproductive with Navajo students (Vogt, Jordan, and Tharp, 1987, pp. 282–285). Vogt, Jordan, and Tharp concluded that the KEEP research strongly supports the argument that cultural compatibility between home and school can enhance the likelihood of students' success, and conversely, cultural discontinuity is a valid explanation for school failure (1987, p. 286).

These two research projects are often cited in the field of Indian education and do seem to provide strong evidence that cultural discontinuity plays a role in some minority students' lack of success in school. Unfortunately, however, this hypothesis is now accepted as fact by many researchers and has become an underlying assumption rather than a research question in Indian education. I argue that the unquestioning acceptance of the cultural discontinuity hypothesis by many

educators, as a cause for dropping out of school, is misguided for two reasons. First, the body of research on the causes of American Indian students' dropping out does not specifically support the hypothesis, and, second, the focus on cultural discontinuity precludes examination of macrostructural variables which may, in fact, be far more significant.

WHY AMERICAN INDIAN STUDENTS DROP OUT

There are relatively few specific research studies which seek to identify the reasons why American Indian students drop out (Giles, 1985; Coladarci, 1983; Eberhard, 1989; Chan and Osthimer, 1983; Platero, Brandt, Witherspoon, and Wong, 1986; Milone, 1983; Deyhle, 1989), and those few certainly do not explicitly support the cultural discontinuity hypothesis. In fact, few directly address the issue as a research question, although they do contain both explicit and implicit assumptions about the importance of cultural relevance in curriculum.

Giles' (1985) study of urban Indian dropouts in Milwaukee is the only study which explicitly employed (but did not critically examine) the cultural discontinuity hypothesis. She stated that,

Considering the disproportionately high Native American dropout rate, one can reasonably assume that certain culturally-based Indian characteristics exist that clash with the urban public school environment (p. 2).

Based upon this assumption, Giles assigned the eight students she interviewed a place on a continuum between a "Native American value orientation" and an "American middle class value orientation." She reported that "it was evident that the more assimilated an Indian student is into the American middle class value orientation, the more likely that person is to complete high school" (p. 14). She goes on to discuss the implications of this finding with extensive reference to Susan Philips' (1982) work in a Warm Springs, Oregon reservation elementary school. She concluded by recommending that school counselors target those "traditional" students for dropout prevention programs, that Indian cultural values (such as a preference for cooperation) be incorporated into curricula, that Indian cultural activities be provided at the schools, and that teachers be trained to more effectively serve Indian students (pp. 26–27).

Giles' research, although undoubtedly inspired by the best of intentions, typifies the problem with assuming that cultural discontinuity between Indian students' culture and the culture of the school causes their academic difficulties (in this case dropping out), and that creating a congruence between the two cultures will solve the problems. There is no critical examination of this premise; the report attempted to show how this is true, rather than if this is true. In addition, Giles assumed that there is such a thing as a "Native American value orientation" and an "American middle class value orientation." She further assumed that the findings of Philips' ethnographic research into the communication styles of elementary school students on the Warm Springs reservation in Oregon is directly applicable to the situation of urban high school students in Wisconsin.

Several studies reported interviews with students specifically about the importance of cultural relevance or sensitivity. Coladarci (1983) supervised interviews of American Indian students who

dropped out of a Montana school district. Student interviews indicated five factors which significantly influenced their leaving school: 1) the lack of relevance of the school curriculum both in terms of future employment and native culture; 2) the perceived insensitivity of teachers; 3) the peer pressure to leave school; 4) having to remain in school for the full senior year when needing only a few classes to graduate; and 5) the problems at home (pp. 18–19). Coladarci recommended that the district critically examine the curriculum in terms of its relevance to both future job opportunities and sensitivity to American Indian culture (pp. 19–21). There is no independent verification of the student self reports, and Coladarci noted that the results should be considered cautiously and should be supported by ethnographic research.

Eberhard (1989) followed and interviewed four cohorts of urban American Indian students. Low test scores and GPAs were found to be significant to students' dropping out. Family constellation was not statistically significant, but more stay-ins came from two parent homes. Little gender difference was found, but family mobility was very significant (p. 37). Interviews indicated that both parents and students found the schools "culturally insensitive" (p. 38). Students also reported that they need more support from their parents. Again, there is no explicit research into cultural relevance and no supporting evidence which defines culturally insensitive.

Some researchers also related students' participation in or ties to traditional culture to their propensity to drop out. In a case study of Navajo students from public schools, Chan and Osthimer (1983) hired Navajo community researchers to interview nine college bound students, nine graduates with no immediate plans for continuing their education, and six dropouts. In addition, the project used school and community documents, interviews with "experts" on Navajo students, and student records.

Chan and Osthimer found that the student's first language was not as important a determinant to their success in school as the successful transition into English. Students who were English dominant or bilingual were less likely to drop out, regardless of their first language. Bilinguals were most likely to be college bound (pp. 24–27). Of particular interest is their finding that students from less traditional homes dropped out at higher rates. Students who reported their families as "moderate," meaning they observed Navajo traditions while having adopted certain Anglo conveniences, were most likely to be college bound (pp. 27–30). Achievement and attendance were not clear critical markers (perhaps due to the fact that these data were often incomplete), whereas high absenteeism was significant in predicting dropping out (pp. 30–36). Students who travelled long distances to school dropped out more (pp. 36–40), and students who had specific career goals/ambitions tended to persist (p. 42).

In a study commissioned by the Navajo tribal government, Platero, Brandt, Witherspoon, and Wong (1986) calculated the Navajo Nation's dropout rate to be 31%. They used a combination of school records and student questionnaires. They examined student demographic variables, socioeconomic variables, cultural variables, home support for education, transportation factors, academic expectations and performance, future orientation, extracurricular activities, school support programs, and behavioral problems (pp. 23–43). In addition, they included dropouts' own reports of why they left school. One of their most significant findings was that many students who were assumed to have dropped out had transferred to other schools (p. 63). There was little difference in grades or retention rates between dropouts and persisters (p. 66). Living a long distance from school was a significant factor in dropping out but "absenteeism was likely to be more of a symptom of dropping out, rather than a cause" (pp. 70–72). Having reliable backup transportation was important to students who missed the bus. Stayers were more likely to live within walking distance of their schools or to be driven to school (p. 81). Students themselves reported boredom, social problems, retention, and pregnancy or marriage as the most significant factors in their dropping out (p. 73). Although many of the problems experienced by the students in Platero et al. (1986) seemed to be economic or social, the authors nonetheless noted that,

> There is ample evidence from the student and dropout survey that dropouts have not acquired the cultural drives and behavioral molds the school systems wish to develop in their students.... This is obviously in part due to the variance these cultural values and social codes have with those of traditional Navajo culture and society (p. 74)....

The report makes a number of recommendations to the Navajo tribal government (pp. 182–186) including the development of a system for tracking dropouts in a more systematic manner, the development of prevention programs, and an improvement in transportation systems for students in remote areas. They also recommended that schools incorporate more Navajo cultural values into the school curriculum and daily operations....

Deyhle's 1989 study of Navajo and Ute school leavers represents a welcome departure from the current state of the art in educational research.... [S]ignificant numbers of students she interviewed mentioned the economic necessity of finding a job, long distance commutes to school, pregnancy, and academic problems as contributing to their decisions to leave school.

Particularly interesting in Deyhle's work is her discussion of the curricular issues which dominate other studies. She found that those students who came from the most traditional Navajo homes, spoke their native language, and participated in traditional religious and social activities (who, according to the prevailing assumptions, would experience the greatest cultural discontinuity) did not feel that the school curriculum was inappropriate to them as Indians (p. 42). Ute students who came from the least traditional homes felt that the curriculum was not important to them as Indians. These students experienced the highest dropout rates and most problems academically and socially in school. Deyhle concluded, "A culturally non-responsive curriculum is a greater threat to those whose own cultural 'identity' is insecure." (p. 42).

Deyhle noted, however, that the relevance of the school curriculum to the economic reality of the community is an important issue. There are few jobs in the community and fewer that require a high school diploma. There is no tangible economic benefit to students to remain in school.

Deyhle also reported specifically the issues of racism and cultural maintenance as important factors influencing students to leave school. She noted that there is considerable conflict between a number of factions in the school: between Anglos and Indians, Utes and Navajos, traditional Navajos and more acculturated Navajos, and Mormons and non-Mormons. These conflicts create an atmosphere of social unease in the school which, when coupled with academic difficulties, leave students with few positive experiences to encourage them to stay in school. In addition, many Indian students who were successful were berated by their peers for trying to act like Whites or for being perceived as looking down on their friends and families (pp. 48–49). Deyhle noted that there is some basis for this attitude; given the lack of jobs on the reservation, those who get more education and training frequently must move away to find jobs for which their training prepares them.

DISCUSSION OF DATA

It is difficult to draw any firm conclusions from the data available on American Indian dropouts. Dropping out **is** a serious problem for American Indian students, but there is little consensus as to the cause. Virtually all research indicate that Indian students drop out of school at very high rates—invariably at higher rates than Anglos and Asians, and often at higher rates than all other minorities. These rates vary from school to school, year to year, tribe to tribe, male to female, BIA to public school or, in other words, from study to study.

I argue that there is simply not enough evidence to conclude that cultural discontinuity plays a significant role, but there is overwhelming evidence that economic and social issues which are not culturally specific to being Indian (although they may be specific to being a minority) are very significant in causing students to drop out of school. Milone (9183) noted that

> many of the reasons given by Indian students for dropping out of school—such as pregnancy, drugs, wanting to be with friends, and boredom in school—are the same as those of non-Indians (p. 56).

Long commuting distances and the lack of relevance of school to reservation students' economic future may be the only differences between Indian and non-Indian students' reasons for dropping out. In the case of urban Indian students, are the problems they encounter which lead to their dropping out of school any different than the problems encountered by African-American or Hispanic students? Chances are, they are not. If there is a cultural discontinuity, it is not unique to their situation. If there is institutional racism, it is also not unique to them (although the lack of general awareness about American Indians is probably greater than for other groups). Poverty, discrimination, poor health care, and other problems may be more a result of the general status of being a minority in this country than the type of minority that you are. Reservation students may be in an economically and socially different situation. High unemployment rates and menial work opportunities in a community must certainly influence a student's perception of the value of school.

Most research has yet to look beyond the classroom and home to the wider influences of the economic and political environment of the community as a whole. How do the attitudes that teachers from the dominant culture have about Indian students' abilities contribute to their treatment of the students and the students' perceptions of their school experience? How does the curriculum prepare students for the political and economic opportunity structure that they experience when they graduate, especially on the reservation? Do some Indian students consciously avoid academic achievement because it means peer opposition for "acting White?" If so, how can schools hope to separate the two ideas? These questions have rarely been addressed and may point to more profitable areas of inquiry. A promising avenue of inquiry into the dropout problem among Indian students is the macrostructural or Marxist perspective.

MACROSTRUCTURAL EXPLANATIONS OF MINORITY SCHOOLING

Marxist anthropological theorists, principally John Ogbu (1974, 1978, 1981, 1982, 1983, 1985, 1987), found the "structured inequality" of American society to be the cause of minority student failure. Because of racism and discrimination, minority students have a lower "job ceiling" than do Anglo, middle-class students. The idea that hard work and achievement in school lead to economic success is contradicted by the circumstances of poverty in which the members of their communities live, leaving them with "disillusionment and lack of effort, optimism, and perseverance" (1982, p. 21). Ogbu believed that "children's school learning problems are ultimately caused by historical and structural forces beyond their control" (1985, p. 868).

Ogbu recognized that not all minority groups in the United States experience difficulty in school. He makes a distinction between autonomous, immigrant, and castelike (originally labeled subordinate) minorities (1974, 1978, 1982, 1983). Autonomous minorities are groups such as the Jews or the Amish in the United States who are "not totally subordinated by the dominant group politically or economically" (1983, p. 169), whereas immigrant minorities

> are people who have moved more or less voluntarily to their host societies.... As strangers they can operate psychologically outside established definitions of social status and relations. They may be subject to pillory and discrimination, but have not usually had time to internalize the effects of discrimination or have those effects become an ingrained part of their culture (1983, pp. 169–170).

The home country is the frame of reference for immigrant minorities who, although experiencing discrimination, may still feel themselves to be better off in the United States than in the political or economic situations they left behind. Ogbu noted that, as a group, autonomous and immigrant minorities do not experience failure in schools; his concern is the experience of the castelike minorities:

> Castelike minorities are distinguished from immigrant and other types of minorities in that (1) they have been incorporated into the society involuntarily and permanently, (2) they face a job and status ceiling, and (3) they tend to formulate their economic and social problems in terms of collective institutional discrimination, which they perceive as more than temporary. Examples of castelike minorities in the United States include blacks, Indians, Chicanos, and Puerto Ricans (1982, p. 299)....

Castelike minorities ... experience secondary cultural discontinuities which "develop *after* members of two populations have been in contact or *after* members of a given population have begun to participate in an institution, such as the school system, controlled by another group" (1982, p. 298). Castelike minority cultures may define themselves in opposition to Anglo culture and include "coping behaviors" which develop in response to systematic oppression. Coping behaviors, although effective in the social and economic context, may actually work against student achievement in school. In addition, defining oneself in opposition to Anglo culture may mean that the student will actively resist the attempts of the school to impart knowledge and values which are seen to be important to Anglo culture. In other words, to say that minority students experience failure merely due to cultural differences between their homes and the school is to deny the historical and structural context in which those differences are embedded.

Ogbu saw the shortcomings of the cultural discontinuity explanation as inherent to the microethnographic approach used so often to study minority student failure. He noted that many of these studies are poorly done in that they are not true ethnographies. The researcher may spend little time, if any, outside of the classroom, and the period of study is often inadequate. Ogbu also criticized the sociolinguistic bias in much of the research which sees schooling as a transmission of culture with little regard for the larger societal context in which it takes place....

CONCLUSIONS

Much more research is needed to understand the complex problem of American Indian dropouts. The cultural discontinuity hypothesis has played the strongest role in influencing the direction of research, or is, at least, used as an underlying assumption guiding the research questions, though it has not been convincingly demonstrated to be true. This exclusive focus on culture and curricular innovation draws attention from the very real possibility that economics and social structure may be more important. According to Ogbu, the castelike status of Indians and Mexican Americans are far more significant factors than their languages and cultures. He stated that

> This does not mean that cultural and language differences are not relevant; what it does mean is that their castelike status makes it more difficult for them to overcome any problems created by cultural and language differences than it is for immigrant minorities (1978, p. 237).

Although "culture" itself may truly be a significant factor in student success in school, it may be that the culture in the student's background, not in the school curriculum, is significant. There is some evidence from the research, especially in Deyhle (1989) but also in Chan and Osthimer (1983), that a strong sense of traditional cultural identity (as defined by speaking the native language fluently and engaging in traditional religious and social activities) provides a student with an advantage in school. The idea that traditional Indian students may have an academic advantage over more "acculturated" students is an important issue. This would seem to contradict the idea that the more different the culture of the home and school, the more problems students will experience. Traditional American Indian students might then be seen as more like Ogbu's immigrant minorities in that they have strongly developed identities and do not need to "resist" White culture to have an identity. They, therefore, do better in school. That traditional students do better in school does not necessarily mean that providing non-traditional students with traditional cultural information will make them achieve (even if it could be done). American Indian students from homes with little participation in traditional social or religious activities or little use of the native language may fit more closely into Ogbu's classification of castelike minorities. Those students' resistance to school seems to be a far more significant factor.

The assumption that schools have control over the critical variables affecting any student's success is yet unproven. This is not to say that many schools could not do a much better job, or that some schools are not now doing an excellent job in educating American Indian students. This is merely to note that the relationship between the microlevel and macrolevel variables in schooling remain largely unexplored. I would not argue that research into cultural discontinuities is inappropriate or irrelevant, but that it is surely insufficient to fully explain the problems that American Indian students experience in school. An understanding of minority school failure cannot be captured by focusing on children's "home environment," on their unique cultural background, or on their genetic makeup or idiosyncratic personal attributes (Ogbu, 1981, p. 23).... Further research into the problem of American Indian dropouts must test implicit notions about the importance of culture and devote equal attention to variables outside the boundaries of the school itself.

POSTSCRIPT

Do Cultural Differences Between Home and School Explain the High Dropout Rates for American Indian Students?

This debate deals with a relatively recent concern within minority studies, that of having sensitivity toward ethnic cultural needs, even if it means maintaining separation. Historically, both social scientists and the general public simply assumed that assimilation was the proper goal for everyone. And assimilation demanded that minorities not only conform to the dominant cultural values and practices but also subordinate their own ideas of desirable conduct. This was most pronounced in public schools, which were clearly supposed to function to socialize ethnic groups into the American mainstream.

In the past, the primary concerns for public schools were that a teacher should know his or her subject matter, know how to teach it—that is, be organized and present the concepts and assignments clearly in English—and be fair in grading. To many scholars socialized in the more recent generation of minority group theory—or those such as Reyhner, who have been teaching for several years and who have embraced the newer perspective—the above description of "good teaching" is barbaric. To them, the idea of a teacher's not worrying about students' cultural values but instead being concerned primarily or even exclusively about course content is outmoded.

A discussion of the teaching of history that emphasizes minorities is Eric Foner, "Teaching American History," *American Scholar* (October 1998). Two books that examine abuses of Native Americans are *The Earth Shall Weep: A History of Native America* by James Wilson (Grove/Atlantic, 1999) and *It Is a Good Day to Die* by Viola J. Herman (Random House, 1998), which presents recollections of the Battle of the Little Bighorn. A consideration of how scholars have treated American Indians is "Still Native," by D. Lewis, *Western Historical Quarterly* (May 1993). For a perspective dealing with different racial and ethnic learning styles, see A. Bishop, "Western Mathematics: The Secret Weapon of Cultural Imperialism," *Race and Class* (December 1990). An insightful account of cultural differences in economic behavior and styles is J. Moore's "How Giveaways and Pow-Wows Redistribute the Means of Subsistence," in Christopher G. Ellison and W. Allen Martin, eds., *Race and Ethnic Relations in the United States* (Roxbury, 1999).

Other helpful works are Rita Dunn and Shirley A. Griggs, *Multiculturalism and Learning Style* (Praeger, 1995) and Freddy A. Paniagua's *Assessing and Treating Culturally Diverse Clients: A Practical Guide* (Sage Publications, 1994), especially chapter 6, "American Indians." One of the best critiques of "white man's" science and learning and their distortions for Native Americans is Vine Deloria, Jr.'s *Red Earth, White Lies: Native Americans and the Myth of Scientific Fact* (Scribner, 1995).

ISSUE 11

Does Rap Music Contribute to Violent Crime?

YES: Dennis R. Martin, from "The Music of Murder," *ACJS Today* (November/December 1993)

NO: Mark S. Hamm and Jeff Ferrell, from "Rap, Cops, and Crime: Clarifying the 'Cop Killer' Controversy," *ACJS Today* (May/June 1994)

ISSUE SUMMARY

YES: Dennis R. Martin, president of the National Association of Chiefs of Police, theorizes that since "music has the power both to 'soothe the savage beast' and to stir violent emotions," then rising racial tensions and violence can be attributed to rock music's promotion of "vile, deviant, and sociopathic behaviors."

NO: Criminologists Mark S. Hamm and Jeff Ferrell reject Martin's analysis of the relationship between music and violence, charging that the theory is based on racism and ignorance of both music and broader cultural forces.

Traditionally, science has been about ascertaining causal relations between two or more variables. The producing, contributing, influencing, forcing, or cause variable is known as the *independent variable*, symbolized as X. The result, effect, outcome, produced, or caused variable is known as the *dependent variable*, or Y. In the social sciences, independent variables were generally traced to specific social factors (e.g., gender, wealth, education, neighborhood, family, race, religion, age, and so on). Such objective factors predicted or explained individuals' and groups' attitudes and behaviors.

Throughout the twentieth century, however, many philosophers of science have questioned the value and validity of causal analysis. This is especially true in the social sciences, including criminology. Drawing from the sixteenth-century philosopher David Hume, questions are asked about how we can ever "know" causes. Frequently, cause cannot be seen. In addition, in human behavior one must often take into account subjective attitudes, feelings, motivations, and such. There are no isomorphic relationships in criminology as there are in the physical sciences. That is, there are no one-to-one relationships, such as that at sea level, water will freeze at temperatures below 32 degrees or that what goes up on Earth must come down. Instead, there are only contingencies or probabilities, such as that living in an impoverished area and having a parent and several siblings in prison will probably result in a younger brother becoming a criminal as well. In such a situation there may be a *high probability*, but there is hardly a certain link between environment and behavior. Likewise, the child of a college professor will probably become a college student, but not necessarily.

Not only is there no inevitable relation between background factors and outcomes (such as crime), but usually the behavior of people has multiple causes: positive or negative parental role models, area of residency, types of and relations with peers, and so on. Sometimes influencing factors on subsequent behaviors lie dormant or gradually accumulate. Poverty, for instance, can demoralize individuals; coupled with racism, it can lead to low self-esteem and self-destructive behaviors such as alcoholism, partially resulting in medical problems, preventing working when jobs become available, which can lead to reinforcing prejudiced people's negative stereotyping that "poor people do not want to work anyway."

Due to these and other reasons, some social scientists eschew searching for causal relations. Instead, they search for correlations. For instance, when there is poverty, racism, declining jobs, and so on, there is usually more crime. All of the identified variables would be examined to determine if they correlate with crime and, if so, what type.

Ascertaining the causes of most things, especially human behavior, is remarkably difficult, and many view such a search as a waste of time. When there are widespread perceptions that serious problems are upon us and that things are "out of control" (such as the current views toward violent crime), people demand immediate solutions. Often the entire scientific process and even reason itself are short-circuited because powerful figures—or those wanting to become powerful—formulate "self-evident" explanations of the problem.

Although scholars trained in scientific methodology can see the fallacies and dangers of glib explanations (and concomitant glib solutions), for others it makes sense to blame some misunderstood phenomenon or even categories of people for societal problems. In its extreme version, this is scapegoating.

In the following selections, Dennis R. Martin provides many examples through history of how music has been linked with violence. He also discusses the marketing of some gangsta rap albums, which he maintains generate hostilities toward police officers and others because of their lyrics and strident sounds. Mark S. Hamm and Jeff Ferrell dismiss Martin's linking of rap music and violence as bad sociology, bad history, and worse criminology. They attack Martin's historical analysis of current music as being racist because he does not mention the positive contributions of Black musicians. They also maintain that rap musicians do little more than "tell it like it is" in inner cities.

What bearing do you think the murders of rappers Biggie Smalls (the Notorious B.I.G.) and Tupac Shakur will have on this debate? How do the April 1999 slayings at Columbine High School in Littleton, Colorado, affect this debate?

YES
Dennis R. Martin

THE MUSIC OF MURDER

In my career in law enforcement I have weathered the rough seas of society, first as a patrol officer, then as a director of police training, shift commander, police chief, and now as the President of the National Association of Chiefs of Police. As tumultuous as contemporary society is, it could not exist without the foundation of law. We Americans are fortunate to live under a government of laws, not of men.

The United States Constitution is a remarkable and unique compact between the government and its people. The First Amendment, in particular, states a once revolutionary concept with great power and simplicity: "Congress shall make no law ... abridging the freedom of speech". In our three-branched system of government, the will of the people is expressed through duly elected legislators in Congress and enforced by an elected executive; the Constitution finds its voice in the judicial branch. What are the people to do when the laws that are meant to ensure their freedom are abused in a manner that erodes the very foundation of law?

Early First Amendment cases sanctioned restrictions on speech where its free exercise created a clear, existing danger, or where a serious evil would result. In two centuries, First Amendment law has evolved to the point where practically the only prohibited speech involves the mention of God in public assemblies.

The misuse of the First Amendment is graphically illustrated in Time-Warner's attempt to insert into the mainstream culture the vile and dangerous lyrics of the Ice-T song entitled *Cop Killer*. The *Body Count* album containing *Cop Killer* was shipped throughout the United States in miniature body bags. Only days before distribution of the album was voluntarily suspended, Time-Warner flooded the record market with a half million copies. The *Cop Killer* song has been implicated in at least two shooting incidents and has inflamed racial tensions in cities across the country. Those who work closely with the families and friends of slain officers, as I do, volunteering for the American Police Hall of Fame and Museum, are outraged by the message of *Cop Killer*. It is an affront to the officers—144 in 1992 alone—who have been killed in

From Dennis R. Martin, "The Music of Murder," *ACJS Today* (November/December 1993). Copyright © 1993, 1996, 1999 by The National Association of Chiefs of Police, Inc. Reprinted by permission. All rights reserved.

the line of duty while upholding the laws of our society and protecting all its citizens.

Is it fair to blame a musical composition for the increase in racial tensions and the shooting incidents? Music has the power both to "soothe the savage beast" and to stir violent emotions in man. Music can create an ambiance for gentle romance, or unleash brutal sensuality. It can transcend the material world and make our hearts soar to a realm of spiritual beauty. Yet the trend in American rock music for the last decade has been to promote ever more vile, deviant, and sociopathic behaviors. Recognition, leading to fame and fortune far exceeding merit, propels performers and the industry to attack every shared value that has bound our society together for more than two centuries.

The power that music works on the human mind can be seen throughout history; it has existed in every known society. The Bible contains numerous references to music. Music is found in the ancient tales of China, as well as in the traditions of Native Americans. In the beginning of human history, music stood at the center of life, acting as an intermediary between the natural and supernatural. It was both handmaiden to religion and the cornerstone of education. While there may be music without culture, culture without music is unthinkable.

The earliest music consisted of a vocal melody with rhythmic, regular beats kept by the hands and feet. In time, the pattern of beats evolved into more complicated rhythms. Formal music found its roots in China, beginning around 2000 BC. Ritualistic music emerged around 1900 BC among the Israelites during the reign of the Canaanites. By setting stories and teachings to music, preliterate Hebrew leaders were able to memorize and recite long passages, and to entertain and instruct their audience with greater impact than words alone could convey. One generation handed down to the next Hebrew laws, traditions, and important historic events in song, often accompanied by a simple harp.

Folk music is the basis for formal music. The march, for example, dates from the Roman Empire. Its insistent rhythm, powerful major chords, and strong simple melody were designed to ignite courage in the hearts of those preparing for battle (and, possibly, fear in the enemies' camp).

Led by St. Benedict, the early Christian Church developed the art of choral singing. Over the centuries, sacred choral music has provided us with a view of the world to come. A branch of choral music evolved into opera, a form of music more than once credited with inciting riots. In 1830, the Brussels premiere of *La Muette de Portici* by Daniel Esprit Auber ignited the Belgian independence movement against the Dutch. In 1842, Giuseppe Verdi achieved overnight fame after the debut of his third opera, *Nabucca*, which inspired rioting in Milan. One of the choruses, *Va Pensilero*, so touched the Italian soldiers that it was adopted as the Italian anthem.

Perhaps the greatest composition combining choral and symphonic modes is the *Ninth Symphony* of Beethoven. An utterly revolutionary work, both musically and politically, it proclaims that all men will be brothers when the power of joy resides in their hearts, binding together the fabric of society torn asunder by different cultural mores. This was not a popular sentiment to express in Vienna, the seat of power of the reactionary Austrian Empire.

The twentieth century brought new sounds to America: atonal classical music, the big band era, jazz, and country and western, among others. History recorded two world wars in which Germanic leaders preyed upon human society; the American musical response, spearheaded by George M. Cohan, was proudly defiant, full of valor and resolve. Across the Atlantic, German composer Paul Hindemith was charged with a war crime because his compositions reflected spiritual ideas and themes of renewal. He was barred from performing music.

The 1950s and '60s ushered in a new era for music in which elements of jazz, bluegrass, and country music combined to create early rock and roll. Bill Haley, of Bill Haley and the Comets, holds the distinction of being the country's first composer of rock and roll, in 1955. With the rise of "the King of Rock and Roll," Elvis Presley, rock and roll forever changed the world. For the first time, contemporary music did not reflect the values of society but glamorized rebelliousness and adolescent sexuality.

Later, lyrics of the 1960s and '70s espoused drug abuse. Heavy metal bands of the '70s, '80s, and even into the '90s with bands such as Guns 'N' Roses, promote a panoply of anti-social behaviors and attitudes. The common denominator of their music is that self-gratification and self-expression excuse aggressively violent and sexual behavior inflicted on others.

The new kid on the popular music scene has stretched the fabric of our First Amendment like none before. Rap music is a culmination of the course charted by Elvis Presley. Put his rebellion, swagger, and sexuality into the pressurized cauldron of a black ghetto and the resulting music explodes with rage. It is primitive music—stripped of melodic line and original chord progressions. The beat alone propels the street smart rhyming verse lyrics through topics of deprivation, rebellion, poverty, sex, guns, drug abuse, and AIDS.

Since the Rodney King incident* and the subsequent riots in Los Angeles, the media has contributed to a climate wherein police bashing is socially and politically correct. Ignored is the role police play in safe-guarding the lives and liberties of all law-abiding citizens. The ingrained hatred of police authority, already prevalent in poor urban "hoods" is easily mobilized by the suggestive lyrics of rap.

The framers of the Constitution lived in a world far different from our own. Could they have imagined a day when music would become a tool to destabilize a democratic society by provoking civil unrest, violence, and murder? Yet, the lyrics of rapper Ice-T's *Cop Killer* do precisely that by describing steps to kill a cop. Time-Warner's recording company not only defended the "instructional" song, but marketed the album by shipping it in miniature body bags, complete with a three by four foot poster graphically depicting a cop killer. The company flooded the United States market with an additional half-million copies just prior to Ice-T's announcement that distribution would be suspended voluntarily.

While on patrol in July 1992, two Las Vegas police officers were ambushed

*[This refers to the severe beating of black motorist Rodney King by four white Los Angeles police officers in 1991, which was captured on videotape by a bystander and broadcast on national television. The later acquittal of the officers sparked public outrage and touched off the 1992 Los Angeles riots. —Ed.]

and shot by four juvenile delinquents who boasted that Ice-T's *Cop Killer* gave them a sense of duty and purpose, to get even with "a f—king pig". The juveniles continued to sing its lyrics when apprehended.

Notwithstanding the predictability of police being ambushed after such a rousing call-to-arms, Time-Warner continues to defend the song. In a letter addressed to Chief Gerald S. Arenberg, Executive Director of the National Association of Chiefs of Police, Time-Warner Vice Chairman Martin D. Payson gave his rationale for Warner Bros recording and mass-marketing *Cop Killer*:

> Ice-T is attempting to express the rage and frustration a young black person feels in the face of official brutality and systematic racism. Though the incidents of brutality may be perpetrated by a small number of police, the impact on the black community is intense and widespread. The anger that exists is neither an invention of Ice-T's nor a figment of the creative imagination. It is real and growing. Our job as a society is to address the causes of this anger, not suppress its articulation.

This last sentence is disingenuous at best. Is Time-Warner addressing the causes of black anger, or is it magnifying isolated instances of anger into a fashionable popular sentiment and reaping handsome profits in the process?

Would Thomas Jefferson have advocated using the First Amendment as a shield to publish a step-by-step guide on how to ambush and murder the police? The *Body Count* album also contains *Smoked Pork*, a song describing how Ice-T murders two police officers, with dialogue so graphic the lyrics were not printed with the album. Freedom of speech ought to end short of advocat-ing violent physical harm to fellow members of society. If Ice-T had, instead, produced a song describing how to sexually abuse and torture young children, perhaps there would be an appropriate public outcry. A full measure of consideration ought to be given to the lives and welfare of our nation's police officers and their families.

Safety and order in any community requires a partnership of a type that can exist only in a functioning democracy. Public attitudes toward the police may play a part in the frightening rise in crime rates. Disrespect for the law enforcement officer breeds disrespect for the law. A child who is raised to laugh at cops is not likely to grow up with any great respect for the laws that the police enforce. Youthful experimenters, confused by adolescent anxiety, look up to Ice-T as a powerful role model who supports hatred, racism, sexual abuse, and vile crimes that he depicts through dialogue in his lyrics.

Decades of misrepresentation and abuse of law enforcement in entertainment and education have left their mark. Society is now finding that it cannot ridicule the enforcers of the law on one hand and build respect for the law on the other. You cannot separate the two, any more than you can separate education from teachers, justice from judges, and religion from the ministry.

It is a sad irony that, in our society, scandal breeds financial gain. Sales of *Cop Killer*, and the *Body Count* album on which it appears, have soared since law enforcement officers from around the country rallied behind police organizations like the National Association of Chiefs of Police, CLEAT (Combined Law Enforcement Officers of Texas), and the American Federation of Police.

Ice-T is but one rapper encouraging violent reaction to the presence of law enforcement. Rap group Almighty RSO defiantly sings *One in the Chamber*, referring to the bullet they would use to kill a cop. Kool G-Rap and DJ Polo's song *Live and Let Die* describes how G-Rap brutally murders two undercover police officers as he tries to complete a drug deal.

Tragically, this violent message is too often followed by its young audience. On April 11, 1992, Trooper Bill Davidson, formerly with the Texas Department of Public Safety, was killed in cold blood as he approached the driver of a vehicle he had stopped for a defective headlight. The trooper's widow, Linda Davidson, described to me an account of the events surrounding the killing and the impact of this tragedy on the Davidson family. The teen-age killer, Ronald Howard, explained to law enforcement authorities that he felt hypnotized by the lyrics of six songs by the rap group 2 Pac, from their album *2 Pacalyypse Now,* which urge the killing of police officers. Howard claims that the lyrical instructions devoured him like an animal, taking control over his subconscious mind and compelling him to kill Trooper Davidson as he approached Howard's vehicle. The rap's influence, however, apparently continues to affect Howard's judgment. Two psy-chiatrists found that the music still affects his psycho-social behavior. In a meeting with Linda Davidson, Howard expressed his desire to completely carry out the rap's instruction by putting away a pig's wife and dusting his family. Howard's reaction has left Linda dumfounded, confused, bewildered, and most of all, angry.

The Davidsons' anger is aimed not solely at Howard, but has also expressed itself in a civil lawsuit against Time-Warner, the company that promotes 2 Pac. Again, Time-Warner claims the First Amendment protects its right to promote songs that advocate the killing of police. In preparation for trial, the corporation's lawyers are closely observing the criminal trial of Ron Howard. Given the current state of American law, one can only hope that Time-Warner will tire of the expense of defending state court actions prompted by such lyrics and attacks on police.

With growing lawlessness and violence in our society, every American is at risk of losing his property and his life to criminals. Police officers risk their lives daily to preserve peace and property rights for all Americans. The officers deserve protection from abusive speech when that abuse imperils not only their ability to protect citizens, but also their ability to protect their very lives.

NO

Mark S. Hamm and
Jeff Ferrell

RAP, COPS, AND CRIME: CLARIFYING THE "COP KILLER" CONTROVERSY

Perhaps the most enduring feature of the ACJS [Academy of Criminal Justice Sciences] is that it routinely brings practitioners and researchers together in a public forum where they can debate the current state of criminal justice. In this spirit, we offer a counterpoint to the attacks made by Dennis R. Martin, President of the National Association of Chiefs of Police, on rapper Ice-T's song "Cop Killer" and its alleged relationship to violent acts ("The Music of Murder," *ACJS Today*, Nov/Dec 1993).

"COP KILLER" IN CULTURAL CONTEXT

As a starting point, Martin offers a truncated and distorted description of rap's gestation that largely misses the music's social and cultural meanings. To suggest, as does Martin, that rap is "a culmination of the course charted by Elvis Presley" is to commit a double fallacy. First, Martin's characterization of Elvis Presley as the founder of rock 'n' roll, and Bill Haley as "the country's first composer of rock and roll," constitutes a racist and revisionist rock history which curiously excludes Louis Jordan, Chuck Berry, Bo Diddley, and a host of other black musicians and musical traditions which established the essentials of rock 'n' roll. (This sort of myopic ethnic insensitivity echoes in Martin's subsequent claim that rap is "primitive" (!) music.)

Second, Martin compounds these sorts of mistakes by tracing rap's lineage to rock 'n' roll—or, apparently, white Southern rockabilly. Rap artists have in fact explicitly denied this lineage. Early rappers, for example, sang "no more rock 'n' roll," and rappers Public Enemy have attacked Elvis Presley, and his racist attitudes, specifically. To draw a parallel between white Southern rockabilly of the mid-1950's and today's black urban rap is therefore analogous to comparing Joshua's trumpets at the battle of Jericho with the Wagnerian operas of Nazi storm troopers, or to equating the horn-calls which led Caesar's troops into England with the thrash metal of Slaughter and Megadeth

From Mark S. Hamm and Jeff Ferrell, "Rap, Cops, and Crime: Clarifying the 'Cop Killer' Controversy," *ACJS Today* (May/June 1994). Copyright © 1994 by Mark S. Hamm. Reprinted by permission. References omitted.

absorbed by US Air Force pilots prior to bombing raids during the Persian Gulf War. Other than to say that militaries have routinely used music to lead soldiers into battle, the analogies have little heuristic value. What Martin's analysis lacks is the crucial historical specificity and sociological contextualization, the framework of conceptual clarity and appreciation necessary to explain the complex relationship between particular forms of music, popular culture dynamics, and incidents of violence.

Most commentators, in fact, locate the beginnings of rap (or, more broadly, hip-hop) in the funkadelic period of the mid–late 1970s, a la George Clinton, Parliament, P-Funk, Kurtis Blow, and Grandmaster Flash and the Furious Five. Evolving from this musical base, rap gained its popular appeal in the grim ghettos of New York City—first in the Bronx, and then in Harlem and Brooklyn. Rap caught the sounds of the city, capturing the aggressive boasts and stylized threats of street-tough black males. By the mid-1980s, rap was injected into the American mainstream via Run-D.M.C.'s version of Aerosmith's "Walk this Way" and other cross-over hits. MC Hammer, Tone Loc, Public Enemy, Ice-T, NWA (Niggers with Attitude), De La Soul, and a legion of others soon followed, infusing rap with R and B, jazz, and other influences, and introducing rap to world-wide audiences of all ethnicities.

In ignoring this rich history, Martin misunderstands both the aesthetics and the politics of rap. Martin, for example, leaps to the extraordinary conclusion that rap is a "vile and dangerous" form of cultural expression, a "primitive music" that attacks "every shared value that has bound our society together for more than two-hundred years." From within this sort of uncritical, consensus model of contemporary society, Martin then locates this portentous social threat in a wider cultural crisis. "[T]he trend in American rock music for the last decade," he argues, "has been to promote ever more vile, deviant, and sociopathic behaviors." And if this trend is not reversed, Martin concludes, "every American is at risk of losing his [sic] property and his life to criminals." A careful analysis of rock's lyrical diversity and social effects would, of course, undermine these sorts of hysterical generalizations. A careful analysis of rap music's lyrical content and cultural context likewise reveals a very different social dynamic.

"Message Rap" (or "Gangster Rap," the focus of the remainder of this essay) deals head-on with universal themes of injustice and oppression—themes which have both bound and divided US society from its inception. But at the same time, gangster rap is proudly localized as "ghetto music," thematizing its commitment to the black urban experience. (This is also, by the way, part of what constitutes rap's appeal for millions of middle-class white kids who have never been inside a black ghetto.) In fact, rap focuses on aspects of ghetto life that most adult whites, middle-class blacks, and self-protective police officers and politicians would rather ignore. Rappers record the everyday experiences of pimping, prostitution, child abandonment, AIDS, and drugs (as in Ice-T's *anti*-drug song, "I'm Your Pusher"). Other rappers deal with deeper institutionalized problems such as poverty, racial conflict, revisionist history books, the demand for trivial consumer goods, the exploitation of disenfranchised blacks through military service, and black dislocation from Africa. And still other rap songs lay bare the desperate and often violent nature of ghetto life, as played out in individual and collective fear, sadly misogynistic and homophobic fantasies, street killings, and, significantly, oppressive harassment by police patrols.

These themes are packed in the aesthetic of black ghetto life, an aesthetic which features verbal virtuosity as a powerful symbol in the negotiation of social status. Rap is developed from US and Jamaican verbal street games like "signifying," "the dozens," and "toasting." Rap in turn encases this verbal jousting in the funky beat of rhythms reworked through the formal musical devices which give birth to the rap sound: "sampling," "scratch mixing," and "punch phrasing" (hardly the "primitive" or "stripped" music which Martin describes). The result of this complex artistic process is a sensual, bad-assed gangster who "won't be happy till the dancers are wet, out of control" and wildly "possessed" by the rapper's divine right to rhyme the ironies, ambiguities, and fears of urban ghetto life (Ice-T, "Hit the Deck"). Musically, rap certainly emerges more from studio funk and street poetry than the blues; but like Sonny Boy Williamson, Muddy Waters, Willie Dixon and a host of other great postwar US bluesmen, Ice-T and other rappers twist and shout from within a world of crippling adversity.

"COP KILLER" ON TRIAL

Because he misses this cultural context, it is no surprise that Martin attempts to "kill the messenger" by attacking rap music as itself a social problem. His choicest blows are saved for Ice-T, whose album *Body Count* integrates rap and "metal" styling, and includes a trilogy of protest sirens on police brutality written "for every pig who ever beat a brother down": "Smoked Pork," "Out in the Parking Lot," and "Cop Killer." Martin argues that one of these, "Cop Killer," is a "misuse of the First Amendment" because it has been "implicated in at least two shooting incidents and has inflamed racial tensions in cities across the country."

Here, though, is the available evidence on "Cop Killer": Since its release in early 1992, an unknown number of persons have heard the song. Martin claims that Time-Warner shipped 500,000 copies of *Body Count* upon its *initial* release. This number is important because subsequent pressings of *Body Count* did not contain "Cop Killer." It was pulled by Time-Warner after US Vice-President Dan Quayle, Parents' Music Resource Center spokeswoman and future Vice-Presidential associate Tipper Gore, and a host of influential media personalities and "moral entrepreneurs" leveled a highly organized and well-publicized campaign of "moral panic" against the song (see Becker, 1963; Cohen, 1972).

But our repeated inquiries to Time-Warner revealed that no such sales figures are available. We were told that Ice-T has since left Time-Warner and is now under contract with Profile records. Yet Profile cannot document sales figures for the first *Body Count* album either, claiming that these figures are known only to Ice-T himself—who, despite our attempts to reach him, remains unavailable for comment. We simply don't know—and neither does Martin—how many young Americans have heard "Cop Killer."

Setting all this aside, let's assume that the President of the National Association of Chiefs of Police is correct: some 500,000 persons have heard "Cop Killer" via the music recording industry. Because popular music is a highly contagious commodity (especially among the young), we may cautiously estimate that three times that number have listened to this song (each buyer sharing the song with just two others). From this very conservative estimate, then, it is not unreasonable to conclude that at least 1.5 million young Americans have heard "Cop Killer."

According to Martin, 144 US police officers were killed in the line of duty during 1992. This is indeed a tragic fact, the seriousness of which we do not wish in any way to diminish. But the fact also remains that there is no evidence to show that the perpetrators of these 144 homicides were influenced by "Cop Killer." Martin bases his argument on a brief review of four juveniles arrested in Las Vegas (NV) for wounding two police officers with firearms, allegedly behind the emotional impetus of "Cop Killer." Put another way, while some 1.5 million persons may have listened to this song, only four may have acted on its message. Thankfully, none were successful.

In summary, Martin claims that "Ice-T's *Cop Killer* [sic] gave [the Las Vegas youths] a sense of duty and purpose, to get even with a f—king pig." If so, we should expect this same "sense of duty and purpose" to influence the behavior of some of the other 1.5 million listeners. Martin, in fact, describes popular music as "a tool to destabilize a democratic society by provoking civil unrest, violence, and murder," and argues that "the lyrics of rapper Ice-T's 'Cop Killer' do precisely that…". He further notes the "predictability of police being ambushed after such a rousing call-to-arms…". But we cannot, in fact, find another "predictable" case. The relationship between listening to "Cop Killer"

and committing subsequent acts of violence appears to more closely resemble a statistical accident than a causal equation. (The probability of attacking a police officer with a loaded firearm after listening to "Cop Killer" is, according to Martin's count, less than 1 in 375,000). Treating this relationship as one of cause and effect therefore not only misrepresents the issues; it intentionally engineers self-serving moral panic around rap music, and obstructs solutions to the sorts of problems which rap portrays.

"COP KILLER," CULTURE, AND CRIME

Ice-T is not the first artist to embed a "cop killer" theme in United States popular culture. This theme has been the subject of countless cinematic and literary works, and has appeared many times before in popular music. During the Great Depression, for example, musicians celebrated Pretty Boy Floyd and his exploits, which included the murder of law enforcement personnel. Similarly, the highly respected fiddler Tommy Jarrell wrote and sang "Policeman," which begins, "Policeman come and I didn't want to go this morning, so I shot him in the head with my 44." But perhaps the best-known case is Eric Clapton's cover version of Bob Marley and the Wailers' "I Shot the Sheriff," which reached the top of the US music charts in the mid-1970s (a feat not approached by Ice-T). "I Shot the Sheriff," though, never suffered the sort of moral and political condemnation leveled at "Cop Killer." How do we account for this difference?

First, "I Shot the Sheriff" was released by a white artist, and in an era when the availability and allure of firearms and ammunition had not reached the saturation point we see to-day. Clapton's white bread portrayal of an armed and heroic Jamaican "rude-boy" was therefore comfortably abstract and romantic. In contrast, Ice-T's shotgun-toting black US gangster is all too concrete, stripped of romantic pretense and lodged uncomfortably in everyday life. Firearms and ammunition are now prevalent in the black community, and are the leading cause of death among young black males. Within the context of gangster rap, artists like Ice-T portray, with chilling clarity, this tragic obsession with lethal weapons.

Second, the social aesthetic of rap music creates a key cultural and political difference. Because rap constitutes a strident form of cultural combat and critique, it generates in response organized censorship, blacklisting, arrests, and the police-enforced cancellation of concerts. Rap's cultural roots and primary audience are among the impoverished, minority residents of US inner cities. While many of these citizens are unable or unwilling to speak out—for lack of access to cultural channels, for fear of reprisal—rappers invoke a militant black pride, and portray and confront social injustice in ways that threaten the complacent status quo of mainstream society. And as part of this critique, rappers lay bare the daily reality of police violence against minority populations, and remind us how many Rodney Kings haven't made it onto videotape.

For these reasons, Dennis Martin and other defenders of the status quo are loath to acknowledge or appreciate rap on any level—as innovative music, verbal virtuosity, or cultural critique. In fact, their discomfort with rap's politics intertwines with their displeasure over its style and sound. Gangster rap is frequently raunchy, sometimes violent, and often played loud, with a heavy emphasis on the staccato, thumping back beat. By artistic design, it is meant to be "in your face" and threatening. This, in combination with the evocative power of rap's imagery, generates loud and urgent condemnations of rap from those who benefit, directly and indirectly, from contemporary social arrangements. For them, personal offense becomes a measure of political superiority.

Finally, the remarkable attention given to "Cop Killer" reflects a growing concern, among both criminologists and the general public, over the intersections of popular culture and crime. Our own studies in this area have led us to conclude that contemporary music can in some cases be significantly linked to criminality—but only when particular forms of music take on meaning within the dynamics of specific subcultures like neo-Nazi skinheads (Hamm, 1993) or hip-hop graffiti artists (Ferrell, 1993). And in this regard, we end by commending Martin for an important discovery. The fact that four youths may have in fact used the cultural material of "Cop Killer" as an epistemic and aesthetic framework for attacking two police officers is cause for serious criminological concern. And to demonstrate *how* this song may have changed the social and political consciousness of these would-be cop killers, within the dynamics of their own subcultural arrangements, is of paramount importance for understanding the situated social meanings of gangster rap.

But this sort of research requires something more than Martin offers in his essay. It demands an attention to ethnographic particulars, in place of Martin's wide generalizations and blanket condemnations. It calls for a sort of criminological *verstehen*, a willingness to pay careful attention to the lyrics of gangster rap and to the lives of those who listen to it, in place of Martin's dismissive disregard. Ultimately, it requires that criminologists confront and critique the kinds of social injustices which rap exposes, rather than participating, as does Martin, in their perpetuation.

POSTSCRIPT

Does Rap Music Contribute to Violent Crime?

Neither Martin nor Hamm and Ferrell mention that in many ways the twentieth century is relatively unique in that much of the popular music sharply divides generations. In the past, it was rare to think about "old people's music," "teenagers' music," and so on. Today's popular music often functions to divide generations as well as regions, races, and ethnic groups.

Both sides of this issue are highly selective in their sensitivities. Martin is offended because police are treated with contempt on some rap albums. Hamm and Ferrell are indignant that racism and poverty are facts of life. Neither side of the controversy considers the fact that rates of violence and homicide committed by young Blacks against other Blacks is skyrocketing. Might teenagers in inner cities who listen to messages of violence turn heightened hostilities on each other instead of the police or whites? Note that the alleged criminal acts of performers such as Snoop Doggy Dogg, Dr. Dre, Marion "Suge" Knight (currently serving nine years for assault), and others involved Black, not white, victims.

Many Black religious and political leaders, writers, and columnists would be amused by criminologists' characterizing rappers as Robin Hoods, romantic messengers, voices of the oppressed, and such. Some Blacks resent what they see as whites' justifying rap lyrics because they allegedly speak for poor (or any) Blacks. Moreover, the April 1999 student slayings at Columbine High School in Littleton, Colorado, have fueled calls for a decrease in violence in music, movies, and television programs, as well as increased monitoring of the Internet. Some complain that people get worried about violence in the media only when rich, white kids get killed; when Black youths kill Black youths, violent lyrics are considered merely expressions of a way of life or defended as protected free speech.

Rap music has evolved significantly since Martin and Hamm/Ferrell wrote their articles. Consider whether or not the content of this music genre is as violent as it used to be.

For a follow-up to this debate, see the technical discussion *Spectacular Vernaculars: Hip-Hop and the Politics of Postmodernism* by Russell A. Potter (State University of New York Press, 1995). Recent discussions of the effects of rap music include "Rap Goes from Urban Streets to Main Street," by Cathy Scott, *Christian Science Monitor* (February 26, 1999) and *Hip Hop America* by Nelson George (Viking, 1998). For an alternative theory of violence, see "A Test of the Black Subculture of Violence Thesis: A Research Note," by L. Cao and A. Adams, *Criminology* (May 1997).

ISSUE 12

Are Arabs and Other Muslims Portrayed Unfairly in American Films?

YES: Jack G. Shaheen, from "We've Seen This Plot Too Many Times," *The Washington Post* (November 15, 1998)

NO: Lawrence Wright, from "Open Your Mind to the Movie We Made," *The Washington Post* (November 15, 1998)

ISSUE SUMMARY

YES: Author and *CBS News* consultant Jack G. Shaheen contends that Hollywood's long history of denigrating Arabs as villains and terrorists continues in the film *The Siege.* He maintains that portrayals of Arabs as thugs significantly increases attacks on Muslims in the United States.

NO: Lawrence Wright, a staff writer for the *New Yorker* and coauthor of *The Siege,* acknowledges that films in the past have portrayed minorities, including Arabs, unfairly. However, he asserts that the producers of *The Siege* were supportive of Arabs and that the movie's depiction of a heroic Muslim police officer as well as of dangerous, unfair treatment of Arabic Americans indicate that the movie was anything but denigrating.

The role of the mass media in creating misunderstandings, prejudice, and hate has long been noted by researchers. The epic 1915 film *Birth of a Nation,* which legitimized the emergence of the Ku Klux Klan as a necessary organization to control the "blood-thirsty" and "savage" former slaves in the South of the 1860s and 1870s is a notorious example. In the 1920s Hollywood films had an ambivalent relation with Arab stereotyping. For instance, the heartthrob of the silent film era, Rudolph Valentino, portrayed an Arab sheik waiting to snatch a blonde, white girl to carry her off to his tent to have his way with her. To some, such films were sexist, anti-Arab, and anti-foreigner. To others, they were great fun—just plain, old-fashioned make-believe entertainment.

Throughout the 1930s Hitler's minister of propaganda, Joseph Goebbels, raised films as avowed political propaganda to unprecedented levels. His productions effectively sold Germans the lies about *untermenschen* (inferior "races," such as Jews and Eastern Europeans). They also presented the Nazi leaders as God-like heroes whose only aim was to bring a pure German "race" to its rightful destiny. Many prominent individuals, both inside and outside of Germany, participated in this cinematic cultural carnage.

Critics argue that throughout its history, Hollywood has helped to maintain America's bigotry, if not to create it. Most minorities have been presented unfavorably as a group, and minority actors and actresses have been locked into demeaning roles, such as servants, half-wits, the "lovable oaf," and the butt of jokes. The early ritual of actors and actresses' being assigned new names was partly to eliminate foreign-sounding names that might offend theatergoers. Although some minority actors were allowed to maintain their original names, (e.g., the Cuban Cesar Romero), they were almost always locked into roles as tokens.

To be fair, many important films have aimed to create understanding and tolerance, such as *Gentlemen's Agreement* (1947), which addressed religious discrimination. However, it seems fair to say that, until recently, much of Hollywood's thrust was to maintain society's prejudices against minority groups in its hiring, casting, and story lines.

In the following selection, Jack G. Shaheen traces the celluloid depiction of Arabs since 1970 and finds that American movies, including the 1998 film *The Siege*, are full of anti-Muslim, anti-Arabic biases. In his rebuttal, Lawrence Wright contends that *The Siege* is quite different from traditional depictions of Arabic peoples for several reasons.

Much of Shaheen and Wright's disagreement reflects the difficulties of agreeing on what is meant by "negative portrayals." For example, some assert that the charges of racism that are currently being leveled against *Gone With the Wind* (1939) are highly chronocentric, or unfairly based on contemporary values. Some accuse the Black actresses and actors who starred in that film of selling out by playing roles that are demeaning to Blacks. Others counter that at least the film offered many jobs for Black actors. It is also argued that many of the Black characters in the film had dignity and decency, in contrast to the notorious white heroine, Scarlett O'Hara.

To many, then, the blanket dismissal of some films as racist or unfair can be based on misunderstanding or standards that distort reality instead of clarifying it. As you review the debate, relate the disagreements over *The Siege* and its treatment of the Arab characters—both terrorists (a few) and nonterrorists (the vast majority)—to other movies with which you are familiar. Are they unfair toward minorities? Are they unfairly criticized for their treatment of minorities?

YES

Jack G. Shaheen

WE'VE SEEN THIS PLOT
TOO MANY TIMES

After all these years, Hollywood still doesn't get it. Since 1970, more than 300 major films have vilified Arabs. They have featured Arab curs drawing sabers ("Paradise"), abducting blondes ("Sahara"), buying America ("Network"), siding with the Nazis against Israel ("Exodus") and tossing bombs—even nuclear ones—at the West ("True Lies").

Now we have "The Siege," in which Arab terrorists methodically lay waste to Manhattan. The movie not only reinforces historically damaging stereotypes, but promotes a dangerously generalized portrayal of Arabs as rabidly anti-American.

I don't mean to deny or diminish the horror of recent acts of Arab terrorism, nor even to suggest that movies should exclude Arab terrorists from their stories. But it troubles me that almost *all* Hollywood stories about Arabs are about bad ones. History teaches painful lessons about how bigoted images such as these can tarnish our judgments of another culture.

I became involved with "The Siege" [in] March [1998] after a group of Muslim-American extras alerted the Council on Arab-Islamic Relations (CAIR) of the movie's focus. Because my specialty is analyzing stereotypical images of racial and ethnic groups—notably Arabs and Muslims—CAIR asked me to comment on the screenplay, which I read immediately.

The scenario troubled me profoundly. Arab immigrants, assisted by Arab-American auto mechanics, university students and even a college teacher, kill more than 700 innocent New Yorkers. The extremists blow up the city's FBI building, murdering scores of government agents; they blast theatergoers, and detonate a bomb in a crowded bus.

So, on April 2, accompanied by two CAIR officials, I met with director Edward Zwick and producer Lynda Obst. Given how vulnerable Arab and Muslim Americans are to defamation in the wake of recent violence, we wanted to know: Why single them out as terrorists? "The Siege" lumped our country's 6 million to 8 million hard-working and law abiding doctors, construction workers, police women and artists together with the lunatic fringe. And it failed to reflect the world's 1.1 billion Arabs and Muslims accurately. We reminded Zwick and Obst of a 1995 Los Angeles Times report, stating that of 171 people indicted in the United States for terrorism and related activities that year, just "6 percent were connected to Arab groups."

Zwick pointed out that he and Obst were willing to make minor changes, which—to their credit—they did. Dozens of offensive words and gratuitous scenes (such as a segment showing an Arab cab driver refusing to pick up an African-American FBI agent, portrayed by Denzel Washington) ended up on the cutting room floor as a result of our meeting.

But we could never agree on a major issue. Zwick argued that, because some scenes in the movie show innocent Arab Americans being tossed indiscriminately into detention centers, the film would make American moviegoers examine their reactions to terrorism, that it would "provoke thought." I countered that it was more likely to provoke violence: After seeing Arab thugs murder hundreds of New Yorkers, some viewers may think that Arab Americans belong in those camps. The film may be fiction, but the terrorists' on-screen killings take place in a real city, the Arabs are rounded up in Brooklyn, where many peace-loving Arab Americans reside.

Zwick argued that he had created a balance in the film, that actor Tony Shalhoub plays a decent Arab-American FBI agent. The director's token good guy reminded me of how film producers of the past tried to justify their hostile depiction of American Indians by pointing to Tonto in movies that focused on savage Indians massacring settlers.

In my opinion, minor edits would not suffice. Unless the major plot line linking religion—Muslims and Islamic prayers—with violence was changed, the film

could advance hatreds, I felt. I offered possible alternatives, suggesting "The Siege" could work well if Arab-Muslim heavies were replaced with generic or multicultural terrorists. Why not making radical militia men or renegade military/government agents the villains?

Looking back now, I realize I was asking them to change the very essence of the film. It was a story about evil Arabs, and it was naive of me to think I might be able to get them to change that.

After our meeting, I reiterated my concerns to Obst and Zwick in three faxes. On April 30, Obst wrote CAIR, saying my story ideas were "impractical and frankly comical," and that my creative suggestions were "inappropriate," "border[ing] on sophistry." She pointed out that our viewpoints were at odds, saying "you [CAIR] are in the business of educating and enlightening, and we are in the business of storytelling." We do not have "a monolithic view of the Middle East," she wrote, nor do we have a "political agenda."

Obst may believe that, but not much has changed since movie mogul Darryl F. Zanuck declared in the 1940s that motion pictures are "the greatest political fact in the world today." The truth is that stereotypical images gain force by repetitive play. Film can be used as a powerful propaganda tool. Persisting in defiance of all evidence, movie images can affect the way people think and behave. You only have to look back to the way Jews were portrayed in Nazi-inspired German movies ("The Rothschilds' Shares in Waterloo" and "The Eternal Jew") to realize how effective the big screen can be in provoking hatred. Today, no other group is so flagrantly vilified by the film industry as Arabs. And, as Hollywood culture is the dominant culture, today's films are distributed in more than 100 countries worldwide.

Stereotypes do not exist in a vacuum. As Attorney General Janet Reno said to those attending an American-Arab anti-discrimination committee conference in Washington in June, "There is a direct link between false perceptions of the Arab American community and harassment." The most troubling examples of this followed the 1995 bombing of Oklahoma City's Alfred P. Murrah Federal Office Building, which killed 169 people. Speculative reporting encouraged, according to CAIR, more than 300 hate crimes against Arabs and Muslims in America. Several mosques were trashed around the country; community members received bomb threats; children were mocked at schools.

I am not suggesting that the cinema exclude portrayals of Arab terrorists. I am suggesting that Hollywood cease uniformly projecting Arabs and Muslims as having a monopoly on terrorism, that the industry being projecting them as they do other people—no better, no worse. The time is long overdue for Hollywood to end its undeclared war on Arabs and Muslims.

NO

OPEN YOUR MIND TO
THE MOVIE WE MADE

All over the country, Muslims have been leafleting and protesting the opening of "The Siege," a movie I co-wrote (with Menno Meyjes and director Edward Zwick). The protesters assert that it perpetuates Hollywood stereotypes of Arabs as terrorists. They even say they will hold the filmmakers responsible for hate crimes that may be committed against Arab Americans because of the reaction to this movie.

Well, the protesters must be seeing a different movie than the one I see. I see a movie that takes as its subject the danger of stereotyping and scapegoating groups for the crimes of individuals. On one level, "The Siege" is a thriller. On another, it is a story of what we might do to our constitutional liberties if we reacted to terrorist threats with the same hair-trigger mentality that was evident, for instance, in the Waco catastrophe.

I can understand why the plot—which depicts the imposition of martial law, the suspension of civil rights and house-to-house searches for people of Arab descent who are then interned in detention camps—would frighten some Arab and Muslim citizens. Many of them thought that a similar contingency plan was prepared by the Department of Defense during the Gulf War. The movie is intended as a cautionary tale about what might happen in this country if terrorism were to escalate to the point that has already been reached in Israel, France and Great Britain. In such a scenario there is little doubt that we would be debating our responses for real, just as the movie causes us to debate them now, hypothetically.

I also see a movie that has an Arab-American hero in the character of Frank Haddad, an FBI agent, who is played by the Lebanese-American actor Tony Shalhoub. In all the talk about how Arabs are portrayed in this film, little is said about the fact that this is the first fully rounded, positive role for an Arab American in modern Hollywood history—maybe ever. Yes, he drinks and cusses, but he's not meant to be a paragon of Islamic virtue—he's a copy. He's also the only character in the movie whose family life, and to some extent his religious life, is approvingly explored. The anxiety, the torn loyalties, the weight of prejudice that are part of the daily experience of life

From Lawrence Wright, "Open Your Mind to the Movie We Made," *The Washington Post* (November 15, 1998). Copyright © 1998 by Lawrence Wright. Reprinted by permission of The Wendy Weil Agency, Inc.

in Muslim and Arab-American communities are embodied in the character of Frank Haddad.

But the critics of the movie want to make it pay for the sins of Hollywood's past. Those sins are mighty, no doubt. Hollywood has stereotyped Arabs in cartoonish movies simply because they make easily accepted villains. The filmmakers of "The Siege" went out of their way to make a movie that is not simplistic, but one that is grounded in the frightening reality of modern terrorism. Some of the people who are now criticizing the movie acted as advisers during the making of it; indeed, they had an unprecedented degree of access to the director and the producer, and many of their suggestions about the script and the characters were heeded. But in the end they wanted one change that the filmmakers would not accommodate: that the terrorists be made "generic"—i.e., something other than Arabs.

Frankly, this demand still distresses me. After the bombing of the World Trade Center, the subsequent trials of Sheik Omar Abdul Rahman and Ramzi Ahmed Yousef and other Islamic extremists, the destruction of two American embassies in Africa and the retaliatory U.S. strikes in Afghanistan and Sudan, it would be disingenuous to say that the United States is not engaged in a worldwide struggle against Arab terrorism. There are certainly other sources of terrorism within our own country, and it would be absurd to suggest that all Arabs are terrorists. Indeed, the whole point of the movie is to demonstrate that in overreacting to the crimes of a few, we may punish an innocent but vulnerable minority. This point is made so explicitly in the movie that the misreading of "The Siege" by its critics seems entirely willful.

Moreover, there is also a connection between terrorism and fundamentalist religious beliefs. I've explored this connection in religions other than Islam—most recently, in a New Yorker article ("Forcing the End," July 20) about evangelical American Christians, and Israeli ultra-Orthodox Jews who would like to blow up the mosques on top of the Haram al-Sharif, or Temple Mount, in Jerusalem. Islam has no monopoly on violence. The enemy is not Islam. It is fanaticism—in whatever religious guise it chooses to hide behind.

The critics have charged that "The Siege" is too real and too sophisticated for audiences to take on the level that it is intended. I admit that I, too, have been jarred by the coincidence of events in real life that seem shockingly similar to elements in the film. For instance, the opening sequence depicts the U.S. abduction of a sheik who is accused of sponsoring terrorism. Now we learn that the CIA had a similar plan to capture alleged terrorist godfather Osama bin Laden. Such eerie parallels are bound to resonate with anyone who reads the news.

The subject of terrorism is frightening precisely because we know how vulnerable we are. Terrorists have already changed our lives. We see the barricades around our monuments and public buildings. We read about the establishment of counterterrorist task forces in our major cities. The question is whether any serious movie can be made about this vital subject that does not invite the kind of campaign of vilification to which this movie has been subjected. The reason most Hollywood movies are so bland or cartoonish is that they steer away from controversy. And yet movies that draw deep from the well of reality can do us the favor of approximating actual experience. They allow us as a society to address questions about ourselves that we hope we don't ever have to face in real life.

The very act of posing these questions in a genuine and hard-edged drama is one of the highest callings of art. Even the critics would have to admit that this movie has opened a debate—more than one, in fact—about how Arabs are treated in America, about the danger terrorism poses to our civil liberties, about the connection between violence and fundamentalism, and finally about what kind of country we might become in the post-Cold War world. The question that the movie asks is: How do we avoid becoming the enemy we are fighting against?

POSTSCRIPT

Are Arabs and Other Muslims Portrayed Unfairly in American Films?

As both authors indicate, the United States had been extremely lucky until recently in that it had been relatively free of the pains of terrorism, unlike many other nations. Prior to the 1993 bombing of the World Trade Center, Americans could only imagine what terrorists on a large scale looked like when operating in the United States. For many Americans, political cartoon depictions of Palestine Liberation Organization chairman Yasser Arafat before he was redefined as an acceptable Arabic statesman provided their only perception of Arab or terrorist leaders. The fact that such mental baggage was inaccurate mattered little.

Because of the World Trade Center bombing and the destruction of a federal office building in Oklahoma City in 1995, massive effects of terrorism are no longer a Hollywood fiction. The World Trade Center bombing was apparently done by Arabs, which resulted in many members of this minority being attacked throughout the United States. Immediately after the Oklahoma City bombing, Muslims were again attacked. As Attorney General Janet Reno warned, "There is a direct link between false perceptions of the Arab American community and harrassment."

It might be expected that anti-Arab sentiments in Hollywood films would expand even more after the bombings. However, it was quickly discovered that the bombers of the federal building were working-class, right-wing Americans. Wright maintains that he and others' purpose in making *The Siege* was to warn Americans of the dangers of overreacting to anti-Arab sentiments. He points out that the Arab American FBI agent is depicted as a hero, and he cites the moving account of Arab citizens' being confined to concentration camps. Shaheen insists that the overall thrust of this and other movies is to depict Arabs unfairly and inaccurately.

Neither protagonist seems to consider the broader issue that even if a film is grossly unfair in its treatment of minorities, should it be censored? Does expanding the definition of and laws against hate crimes to include one-sided treatments of minorities in films risk preventing potentially important ideas from being shown? Should the artistic merits of *The Siege* and other controversial films be completely neglected in favor of debating its ideological position?

Shaheen argues that films dealing with terrorism should portray the terrorists as a multicultural, ethnically, racially, and gender diversified sort of UN. Does such a recommendation have merit? Is the fact that a scene showing an Arab taxicab driver refusing to pick up a Black man was cut from *The Siege*

ostensibly because it might inflame Black-Arab relations be a cause to celebrate? Or should this act be condemned as racist because it denies the fact that
many Black males are ignored by taxi drivers of many different nationalities?

Does *The Siege* fairly present many different aspects of modern life, including some of the great strengths of Muslims? If, as Shaheen insists, it hurts
innocent Arabs and other Muslims, what, if anything, should be done to punish the film's producers? How could Hollywood minimize the chances of this
happening again? Would the advantages of keeping all material that might
be offensive to minorities out of films equal the potential disadvantages?

For additional reading on this controversy, see Shaheen's *Arab and Muslim Stereotyping in American Popular Culture* (Georgetown University Press,
1997). A thoughtful essay on the backgrounds of Arab Americans and their
unfair stereotyping is H. Noor Al-Deen's "Understanding Arab Americans:
A Matter of Diversities," in Alberto Gonzalez, Marsha Houston, and Vic-
toria Chen, eds., *Our Voices: Essays in Culture, Ethnicity, and Communication*
(Roxbury, 1994). A new book that is critical of some Muslim sociological scholarship is *Questions from Arab Societies* edited by A. Zghal and A. Ouaderni
(International Sociological Association, 1998). A useful discussion of Muslim
communities in the United States is Yvonne Yazbeck Haddad's "Belonging
in the West," *The World & I* (September 1997). A useful book on how to systematically research the electronic media is *Research Paradigms, Television, and
Social Behavior* edited by Joy Keiko Asamen and George L. Berry (Sage Publications, 1998). An outstanding reader on media stereotyping of minorities
is Coramae Richey Mann and Marjorie S. Zata, eds., *Images of Color, Images of
Crime* (Roxbury, 1998).

For a helpful discussion of emerging controversial issues pertaining to the
Koran, see "What Is the Koran?" by T. Lester, *The Atlantic Monthly* (January
1999). Among the many outstanding publications dealing with Muslim issues
is the monthly *Muslim Magazine*, published by the Islamic Supreme Council
of America. The most recent novel by Salman Rushdie, whose *Satanic Verses*
(Viking Penguin, 1988) resulted in a *fatwa* on his head (open contract for his
execution) and probably generated far more anti-Muslim sentiment than any
movie ever did, is *The Ground Beneath Her Feet* (Henry Holt, 1999). Finally,
V. S. Naipaul, a longtime bitter critic of the Arab world, recently published
Beyond Belief: Islamic Excursions Among the Converted Peoples (Random House,
1998).

On the Internet . . .

http://www.dushkin.com

Desegregating the University of Florida, 1950 to the Present

A collective product of undergraduate history majors at the University of Florida, this Web site offers a history of the integration of the university. According to the authors, the events that transpired on the Gainesville campus are, in many respects, a microcosm of the broader struggle by African Americans and their white allies to turn the purported national commitment to freedom and equality into reality.
http://www.clas.ufl.edu/users/brundage/website/draft.html

Center for Immigration Studies

The Center for Immigration Studies is a nonpartisan, non-profit organization founded in 1985. It is the United States' only think tank devoted exclusively to research and policy analysis of the economic, social, demographic, fiscal, and other impacts of immigration on the United States.
http://www.cis.org

American Immigration Lawyers Association (AILA)

Founded in 1946, the American Immigration Lawyers Association (AILA) is a national bar association of over 5,200 attorneys who practice and teach immigration law. At this site, you can access general background about immigration, descriptions of the services that immigration lawyers provide, and updates on the latest changes to immigration-related laws and regulations.
http://www.aila.org

PART 3

Immigration, Segregation, and Leadership

With the important exception of indigenous peoples, everyone on the North American continent, whether a minority or majority group member, is an immigrant or a descendant of an immigrant. What patterns are formed when so many different people come together? What unanticipated consequences result from these patterns? Are pluralism, assimilation, and integration so bad when compared with separation, balkanization, imperialism, and even genocide? How are vital myths—for example, the myth of the melting pot—formed, threatened, or altered when new demographic processes occur? Has the road toward integration become so bumpy that it should be abandoned? Has any other nation consistently and over time been more just to as many diverse peoples? Do many minority leaders, who are perhaps remarkably similar to majority leaders, live off their constituents instead of for them?

■ Is Racial Segregation Necessarily Bad?

■ Is Immigration a Problem in the United States?

■ Is There an Ethnic Revolt Against the Melting Pot?

■ Are Black Leaders Part of the Problem?

ISSUE 13

Is Racial Segregation Necessarily Bad?

YES: Paul Ruffins, from "Segregation Is a Sign of Failure," *Crisis* (December/January 1998)

NO: Glenn C. Loury, from "Integration Is Yesterday's Struggle," *Crisis* (December/January 1998)

ISSUE SUMMARY

YES: Paul Ruffins, executive editor of *Crisis*, identifies three arguments supporting school segregation in the 1990s: it is possible to make separate equal, court decisions make further integration impossible, and segregation does not really harm anyone. He rejects these arguments and asserts that efforts to achieve school integration should be increased.

NO: Glenn C. Loury, director of the Institute on Race and Social Division at Boston University, contends that school racial integration is an untenable goal because schools are more segregated now than they were 30 years ago, the courts and public sentiment no longer support school busing, and enforced integration implies Black inferiority. It is better, he says, to increase support services in the schools.

In *Plessey v. Ferguson* (1896) the Supreme Court upheld the right of states to create and maintain racial segregation in virtually all areas of public life, including restaurants, theaters, public transportation, parks and recreation facilities, jobs, and schools. The stipulation for the latter was that schools could be segregated if they were "separate but equal." In parts of the deep South, this served to legitimate all but a return to the pre–Civil War status of Blacks as slaves. It certainly allowed passage of the notorious Jim Crow laws in the 1870s and 1880s, which banned Blacks from almost all public interactions with whites.

For most Blacks the Jim Crow laws denied them constitutional rights as U.S. citizens. The forced separation was not only insulting, but it greatly hampered the newly freed slaves and their children from participating in American life and from gaining the knowledge and skills needed to compete in a rapidly developing industrial society. "Colored schools," as they came to be known, were almost never "equal" to white schools. When they had books and other supplies at all, they were dated hand-me-downs from white schools. Black teachers' salaries and standards were usually far less than those of white teachers. Later in the twentieth century, Black youngsters (and sometimes

whites as well) were bused—in some cases many miles away from home—
so they could attend segregated schools. Much later in the 1970s, defenders
of school busing to achieve integration pointed this out.

In 1910 the National Association for the Advancement of Colored People
(NAACP) was founded. It, along with other African American organizations,
was intent on overthrowing racial segregation. When this practice was in full
force, there was little doubt among most Black people that it was horrible.
Yet through phenomenal fortitude and perseverance, Blacks survived. Many
talented, creative, and prominent Americans were a product of segregated
schools: W. E. B. Du Bois, Paul Dunbar, Paul Robeson, Ralph Bunche, Martin
Luther King, Thurgood Marshall, and countless others. For Black professionals, one of the few avenues of vertical mobility was in becoming a teacher.
Although teachers' salaries were low, Blacks were able to achieve respect in
the Black community and sometimes among whites as well.

Throughout the 1930s and 1940s the NAACP—especially its legal defense
branch, which was headed by the young attorney Thurgood Marshall—
zealously pursued the goal of eliminating legal racial segregation, especially
in schools. Marshall's strategy was to whittle away at racial segregation.
At first, segregation in southern law schools and other professional schools
was overthrown through several brilliant court cases. Eventually, university
segregation was overturned, and in 1954 the "big one" was finally fought
out: *Brown v. Board of Education of Topeka, Kansas.* The justices ruled in that
case that enforced racial segregation was liable "to do irreparable harm" to
Black children. Although entrenched southern politicians and white racists
began a campaign of "massive resistance" and other strategies, both peaceful
and extremely violent, the writing was on the wall: victory had finally been
achieved.

School desegregation, however, was never really achieved in most of the
United States. Initially, after legal resistance had ended for the most part,
white children were sent to private schools. This was quickly supplemented
by massive "white flight" from America's cities. There is now far more racial
segregation than there was in 1970.

In the recent past, even a hint of abandoning the goal of racial integration
was anathama to traditional Black leaders. Indeed, the head of an NAACP
chapter in North Carolina was instantly terminated when he called for a
return to segregation. Naturally, there have always been Black leaders who
objected to the goal of integration as demeaning for Blacks. However, until
recently, most Blacks rejected segregation.

The current social, economic, political, and educational situations seem to
demand an abandonment of the former goal. Note the many reasons that
Paul Ruffins gives in the following selection for rejecting racial segregation.
Consider if his delineation of what he considers to be three myths is accurate.
Note the reasons why Glenn C. Loury defends segregation in the second
selection. Also think about whether Blacks and other minorities would be
better off or worse off with segregation.

YES

Paul Ruffins

SEGREGATION IS A SIGN OF FAILURE

In recent years, America's public schools have become more, rather than less segregated. This has painfully frustrated those who fought segregation in the belief that integrated schools were the basis of a tolerant, multi-cultural society. Because integration has not been easy, even some African Americans now argue that civil rights organizations should abandon desegregation cases, and no longer advocate busing black children to better schools in white neighborhoods, or support constructing magnet programs to draw white students back into public schools. Instead, they argue, we should focus on the "real issue" of getting black children more resources. This thinking is based on erroneous myths about how social and educational integration actually works.

Myth One: It is possible to make separate equal.

There is no contradiction between fighting to improve schools that are predominantly black or Latino, and also striving for social and racial integration. However, there are just some things that can not be learned in segregated environments. One can teach basic math in an all-black setting. However, you can't give black or Latino students confidence that they can learn calculus as fast as Asian or Jewish kids if they have never tested their skills against kids from other backgrounds.

   More importantly, it is naive to think that white, or even middle-class black citizens will be willing to provide a high level of resources to a school system where there are few if any white or middle class students. As Elaine Jones of the NAACP Legal Defense Fund Points out, "In Kansas City, Missouri, from almost the precise moment the school district became majority black, the majority white electorate consistently voted against bond issues and tax levies, precipitating a catastrophic decline in the capital and educational resources of the school district." This has happened again and again as conservatives move to reduce local property taxes.

   According to Gary Orfield, who ran the Harvard Project on School Segregation, separate is unlikely to ever be equal because the most important predictors of academic achievement are not school-related variables, such as class size, but family, parental and student variables.

In schools with large concentrations of poor students, it is virtually impossible to supply small enough classes or good enough teachers to make up for the lack of educated parents or stable families. If majority-black cities like Detroit, Washington D.C. or Newark could have provided high enough levels of resources to make segregated, high-poverty schools work, they would have done so. One of the reasons they can't is because they lost their tax bases as the middle class fled to the suburbs.

This is why busing is an economically efficient tool for increasing the academic achievement of black students. For example, for the price of a bus ride a student can receive the invaluable experience of attending a school where most kids plan to attend college.

Myth Two: After the Supreme Court's **Milliken vs Bradley** *decision preventing city suburban busing, further integration is virtually impossible.*

This myth is based on several false assumptions. One is that the Supreme Court will never reverse itself and require busing across city lines. The *Brown* decision itself was a reversal of earlier thinking. The court can change its mind.

Another assumption is that the boundaries between city and suburban school districts are unchangeable. In some parts of the country, such as North Carolina and Tennessee, the trend is toward merging smaller districts into county-wide school systems to increase efficiency. Nearly 20 states have court cases calling for statewide funding, creating the real

potential that city/suburban boundaries may be re-drawn.

The final false assumption is there can't be any meaningful progress on integration because white students are too small a percentage of the public school population. In Boston, white students may only be 18% of the public school students, but this does not mean they only make up 18% of the school-age children. If school reform succeeds, there are many non-racist parents who would prefer to bring their children and their energies back to public schools rather than pay to send their children to private schools.

Social integration is also not limited to black and white. The key may be to entice middle-class African-American, Asian and Hispanic parents to return to the public schools to restore family stability and cultural diversity.

Finally, there is value in holding on to federal desegregation orders, even in places like Prince George's County, Maryland, where the schools are now 75% African-American. Desegregation orders don't just mandate busing. They also help to prevent discrimination against black teachers and staff, and ensure equitable funding.

Myth Three: As long as it isn't forced, segregation doesn't really hurt anyone.

In virtually every case, increasing segregation has had a terrible effect on black students, leaving them more ghettoized and marginalized than ever before. However, recent ecological research is beginning to show that even "voluntary residential segregation" is having a terrible effect on white citizens and on the physical environment. Another word for white (and often black) flight out of the cities is suburban sprawl, which is paving over farms and woodlands as Americans try to run from, rather than solve, their urban and racial problems. Many families feel severe strain as a result of having to own, insure and maintain two or more cars, and drive several hours to work each day.

Segregation is a sign that Americans have failed to complete the hard work of creating a society where a diverse population can live comfortably side by side. If we don't face this problem soon, we'll run out of places to run to.

NO

Glenn C. Loury

INTEGRATION IS YESTERDAY'S STRUGGLE

A report of the Harvard Project on School Desegregation issued [recently] found that racial segregation in the nation's public schools has increased steadily over the last 15 years to a level greater than at any time since the 1971 Supreme Court decision in *Swann v. Charlotte-Mecklenburg Board of Education*, which authorized "forced busing" to achieve racial balance. This development has alarmed many in the civil rights community who worry that this increasing racial isolation portends disaster for the black community. I believe those concerns are misplaced.

This is not to say that all is well with the education of African American youngsters. For example, the National Assessment of Educational Progress, a comprehensive effort to test the knowledge of a representative national sample of primary and secondary school students, has revealed a widening gap between the educational achievements of white and black students over the past decade. But while great disparities do exist in the quality of public education—black and Latino students in central cities are especially poorly served—a renewed emphasis on racial integration is the wrong response. Achieving true equality of opportunity for the poorest public school students means securing for them better teachers, smaller class sizes, longer school hours and greater support services in the schools they attend. If these things can be achieved, our youngsters will do well, whatever the racial composition of their schools.

In any event, both the Supreme Court and the American people have shown little enthusiasm for open-ended judicial intervention aimed at securing racial balance. The Court's opinion in the 1995 case *Missouri v. Jenkins*, for example, reversed a lower court's order that Kansas City undertake an expensive plan

From Glenn C. Loury, "Integration Is Yesterday's Struggle," *Crisis* (December/January 1998). Copyright © 1998 by *Crisis*. Reprinted by permission of Crisis Publishing Co., Inc., the publisher of the magazine of the National Association for the Advancement of Colored People.

to attract suburban whites to an increasingly black, inner-city district through specialized "magnet schools." Indeed, Federal courts around the country—especially in the South—have relaxed earlier decrees ordering school districts to promote integration, even though those districts have been moving toward resegregation.

I am not arguing that these cases were rightly decided in every instance. What is clear, however, is that it would be unwise to expect a revival of 1970s-style judicial activism on behalf of the cause of integration. Moreover, the flight of white middle-class families from urban districts subject to desegregation decrees has made it all but impossible to achieve anything beyond token integration in many places.

Thus, in 1972, before court-ordered busing began, 60 percent of Boston's public school students were white. Although the courts have been more flexible about integration efforts in recent years, only 18 percent of the students in this struggling school system now are white. Denver, Norfolk, Va., and Savannah, Ga., which were subject to mandatory busing, have also seen white enrollment decline, reflecting the decisions of white parents to live in suburban communities or to send their children to private schools. Such decisions are a stubborn reality, restricting the prospects that judicial mandates can much increase the extent of racial mixing in the schools. The Supreme Court's decision some twenty years ago in *Milliken v. Bradley*, put sharp limits on the ability of federal courts to use metropolitan-wide, cross-district busing plans to promote integration.

Of course, no public school district should discriminate on the basis of race, or actively promote racial segregation.

But in the many districts where most students are non-white, it has long made more sense to address those students' educational needs directly, rather than to spend scarce resources trying to get white families to send their children to the same schools as minorities.

Many non-white parents are more concerned about the quality of their children's schools than about racial balance for its own sake. All parents want basically the same things from public schools: safety, order, and the teaching of solid academic skills. Regardless of racial composition, schools that deliver these things will be judged successful.

Also, a compulsive focus on racial integration can involve condescension (no doubt unintended) toward non-white students and their families. Justice Clarence Thomas put it well in his concurring opinion in *Missouri v. Jenkins*: "It never ceases to amaze me that the courts are so willing to assume that anything that is predominantly black must be inferior." The belief that "black students suffer an unspecified psychological harm from segregation that retards their mental and educational development," Justice Thomas said, rests on an assumption of black inferiority. This echoes something W.E.B. DuBois once wrote in the pages of *The Crisis* over a half-century ago: "Never in the world should our fight be against association with ourselves because by that very token we give up the whole argument that we are worth associating with."

To presume that blacks must have a sufficient quota of whites in the classroom in order to learn, is to presume that there is something inherently wrong with blacks. But while black kids may not need to have whites sitting nearby in order to master arithmetic, the most disadvantaged children do need better schools, with resources sufficient to compensate for the influences of poverty they bring to the classroom. Integrationists assume that the presence of whites is the only sure way to draw attention to this need. But that was yesterday's struggle.

Advocates of the interests of African-American youngsters should focus on achieving equal educational opportunity, but not by forced racial mixing. Instead, we must demand that students isolated in hard-pressed, big-city school districts receive the attention and resources which, as Americans, they so richly deserve.

POSTSCRIPT

Is Racial Segregation Necessarily Bad?

Ruffins contends that separate but equal is impossible because, among other reasons, whites will somehow shortchange Black schools as they have in the past. If economic equity could be rigorously maintained (equal budgets), would school segregation be desirable? Neither Ruffins nor Loury discuss schools that are both racially and gender-segregated, such as programs in which young Black males are taught only by Black male teachers. Are such programs a good idea? Do females, either Black or white, necessarily do a less effective job teaching Black males?

Ruffins bases much of his argument around school busing, which he feels is effective and should be resumed. He also argues for elimination of school boundaries between cities and counties. What objections might parents, either Black or white, have to these proposals? Both Loury and Ruffins seem critical of parents who flee the inner cities or place their children in private schools. However, should any society ever be expected to gamble with its children's lives in order to benefit one group or even future generations?

How might broader issues, such as the AIDS epidemic among Black Americans, the high rate of female-headed households, high rates of violent crime, high dropout rates, and high unemployment rates, be tied into the issue of school segregation? Do these and other conditions say more about American society than people may be willing to face? Could the school segregation issue be dismissed as a dangerous smoke screen to deflect public concerns away from the continued pervasiveness of racism and inequality?

Neither Ruffins nor Loury considers the widely discussed partial solution of school privatization or school vouchers. Both embrace the idea that pumping more dollars into needy schools will alleviate the problem. Is this accurate? More and more Black parents are calling for a voucher system that would allow them to send their children to the schools of their choice. Is this a better idea than abandoning integration?

Among the many stimulating readings on the topic of segregation are NAACP head Kweisi Mfume's "We Demand a Fully Integrated Society," *Crisis* (October 1997); *Dismantling Desegregation: The Quiet Reversal of Brown v. Board of Education* by Gary Orfield, Susan E. Eaton, and the Harvard Project on School Desegregation (New Press, 1997); and C. Canady, "America's Struggle for Racial Equality," *Public Policy* (January/February 1999). An interesting case study of a specific school system's efforts to reverse the resegregation trend is "Remedies to De Facto School Segregation: The Case of Hartford," by Monte Piliawsky, *Black Scholar* (Summer 1998). Conservative M. Lind takes a liberal position in "Race and Reason: Moving Beyond Demagogues Toward a Color-Blind Society," *The Washington Monthly* (May 1998).

For a broad discussion of racial segregation, see former U.S. secretary of education Lamar Alexander's "Created Equal: The Principles of Racial Reconciliation," *Policy Review* (November/December 1998). Among the growing number of books written by and about successful Black families whose education enabled them to partially transcend racism is *Our Kind of People: Inside America's Black Upper Class* by Lawrence Graham (HarperCollins, 1999). For a discussion of continued segregation in colleges, see "Segregation Continues in Southern Colleges," *Society* (November/December 1998). A moving account of the courageous efforts to end segregation by Black leaders is *Walking With the Wind: A Memoir of the Movement* by John Lewis and Michael D'Orso (Simon & Schuster, 1998). An account of efforts to maintain segregation is Grace Elizabeth Hale's *Making Whiteness: The Culture of Segregation in the South, 1890–1940* (Pantheon, 1998).

School chaos in countries outside the United States is described in "Japan's Once-Orderly Schools Face 'Classroom Collapse,'" *Christian Science Monitor* (March 8, 1999). An interesting view is Robin Kelley's *Yo' Mama's Disfunktional: Fighting the Culture Wars in Urban America* (Beacon Press, 1997). Also helpful is "The 50 Best Colleges for African Americans," by T. LaVeist and M. Desir, *Features* (January 1999).

ISSUE 14

Is Immigration a Problem in the United States?

YES: Peter Brimelow, from *Alien Nation: Common Sense About America's Immigration Disaster* (Random House, 1995)

NO: David Cole, from "The New Know-Nothingism: Five Myths About Immigration," *The Nation* (October 17, 1994)

ISSUE SUMMARY

YES: Peter Brimelow, senior editor of *Forbes* and *National Review*, links the recent increase in immigration to many of America's major problems, including crises in health care, education, and pollution, and the potential loss of American identity.

NO: David Cole, a professor at the Georgetown University Law Center, maintains that, throughout history, immigrants to the United States have been poor, culturally different, and perceived as a threat by U.S. citizens and that these perceptions obscure reason and fairness. He refutes what he considers to be myths about immigrants to show that these people are beneficial to America.

It remains a paradox that both statistically and culturally, the United States is almost exclusively dominated by descendants of immigrants (most within the past 100 years) but that the country has always had significant problems accepting "outsiders." In the mid-1800s, for example, the Know-Nothing party, which was composed of Americans who felt that the influx of Germans and Irish was ruining the country's stock, emerged to fight for rigid restrictions on U.S. immigration laws. Established Americans despised these immigrants not only because they were foreign but also because their loyalty to Catholicism threatened the country's mostly Protestant ways. Prejudice toward these people was evident well into the twentieth century, as many factories announced that "Irish need not apply" in their help wanted advertisements and some rooming houses and restaurants refused service to Irish people.

Starting in the 1840s much of the worry was focused on the Chinese, whose opium dens, alleged low regard for human life, and general "mental and moral inferiority" were perceived as a threat to the United States. Many Asian immigrants in California and parts of the Southwest were beaten and lynched, often for no other reason than that they were different.

In spite of such ignorance and bigotry, many sociologists observe that during these times of immigration, *in general* America was a melting pot.

Most ethnic groups eventually assimilated into the "American" way of life. Historically, this has been the avowed aim of most immigrants to the United States. Indeed, at least in terms of the Irish, the election of John F. Kennedy to the presidency in 1960 represented full inclusion into American society. By the 1960s scholars were predicting that it was just a matter of time before most, if not all, minorities would be accepted, at least symbolically.

The civil rights movement in the 1960s, through affirmative action, often emphasized group entitlements as much as individual rights. This, coupled with the dramatic drop in immigrants from Europe, led many commentators to conclude that pluralism, not assimilation, reflected changing immigration realities. Ideologically, these attitudes were reinforced by multiculturalists, who insisted that expecting others to "melt" into the majority culture was elitist and racist. These critics argued that all groups should maintain their own cultural identities and reside as "equals with differences." Current debates over bilingual education reflect the strength of this aspect of the controversy.

The complexion of U.S. immigrants is clearly changing. Between 1900 and 1920 Europeans constituted 85 percent of all newcomers. According to the U.S. Immigration and Naturalization Service, in the past 15 years 84 percent of new immigrants were Hispanics and Asians. The composition is changing in other ways too. In 1996, for example, more than 140,000 of the approximately 915,000 immigrants to the United States were political and humanitarian refugees. Recent court cases have allowed women from African and Muslim countries who were fleeing ritual female genital mutilation to obtain asylum. The current events in Kosovo will increase this category of immigrants (political refugees) as well.

In the following selections, Peter Brimelow argues that trends in immigration pose a problem to the United States. He suggests that most Americans disagree with liberal immigration policies and that these policies must be radically revised to reduce the number of annual immigrants and to retain a distinctly American culture. David Cole asserts that the current negativity toward immigration is an instance of history repeating itself. He maintains that not only are liberal U.S. immigration policies just but they actually help the economy and reduce other problems.

As you compare these two points of view, consider what statistics both authors cite and what interpretations they make. What practical impacts would Brimelow's concept of a new, anti-immigration society have on the United States? Are the five myths of immigration that Cole repudiates relevant to the overall issue? Is immigration a problem in the United States? In what ways might it be hurting or helping America? In debating this issue, should all immigrants be considered the same? Or are some more helpful or harmful than others? Last, consider the drastically different emigration patterns that are rapidly unfolding in Kosovo and other parts of central Europe: some 400,000 people are leaving their homes as a consequence of ethnic conflict or genocide. Are these problems similar to those addressed in this issue?

YES

Peter Brimelow

IMMIGRATION: DISSOLVING THE PEOPLE

There is a sense in which current immigration policy is Adolf Hitler's posthumous revenge on America. The U.S. political elite emerged from the war passionately concerned to cleanse itself from all taints of racism or xenophobia. Eventually, it enacted the epochal Immigration Act (technically, the Immigration and Nationality Act Amendments) of 1965.

And this, quite accidentally, triggered a renewed mass immigration, so huge and so systematically different from anything that had gone before as to transform—and ultimately, perhaps, even to destroy—the one unquestioned victor of World War II: the American nation, as it had evolved by the middle of the 20th century.

Today, U.S. government policy is literally dissolving the people and electing a new one. You can be for this or you can be against it. But the fact is undeniable.

"Still," *Time* magazine wrote in its fall 1993 "Special Issue on Multiculturalism," "for the first time in its history, the U.S. has an immigration policy that, for better or worse, is truly democratic."

As an immigrant, albeit one who came here rather earlier than yesterday and is now an American citizen, I find myself asking with fascination: What can this possibly mean? American immigration policy has always been democratic, of course, in the sense that it has been made through democratic procedures. Right now, as a matter of fact, it's unusually undemocratic, in the sense that Americans have told pollsters long and loudly that they don't want any more immigration; but the politicians ignore them.

The mass immigration so thoughtlessly triggered in 1965 risks making America an alien nation—not merely in the sense that the numbers of aliens in the nation are rising to levels last seen in the 19th century; not merely in the sense that America will become a freak among the world's nations because of the unprecedented demographic mutation it is inflicting on itself; not merely in the sense that Americans themselves will become alien to each other,

From Peter Brimelow, *Alien Nation: Common Sense About America's Immigration Disaster* (Random House, 1995). Copyright © 1995 by Peter Brimelow. Reprinted by permission of Random House, Inc.

requiring an increasingly strained government to arbitrate between them; but, ultimately, in the sense that Americans will no longer share in common what Abraham Lincoln called in his first inaugural address "the mystic chords of memory, stretching from every battlefield and patriotic grave, to every living heart and hearth stone, all over this broad land."

Alexander James Frank Brimelow is an American, although I was still a British subject and his mother a Canadian when he shot into the New York delivery room, yelling indignantly, one summer dawn in 1991. This is because of the 14th Amendment to the U.S. Constitution. It states in part:

"All persons born or naturalized in the United States, and subject to the jurisdiction thereof, are citizens of the United States and of the State wherein they reside."

The 14th Amendment was passed after the Civil War in an attempt to stop Southern states denying their newly freed slaves the full rights of citizens. But the wording is general. So it has been interpreted to mean that any child born in the United States is automatically a citizen. Even if its mother is a foreigner. Even if she's just passing through.

I am delighted that Alexander is an American. However, I do feel slightly, well, guilty that his fellow Americans had so little choice in the matter.

But at least Maggy and I had applied for and been granted legal permission to live in the United States. There are currently an estimated 3.5 million to 4 million foreigners who have just arrived and settled here in defiance of American law. When these illegal immigrants have children in the United States, why, those children are automatically American citizens too.

And right now, two-thirds of births in Los Angeles County hospitals are to illegal-immigrant mothers.

All of which is just another example of one of my central themes:

The United States has lost control of its borders—in every sense. A series of institutional accidents, of which birthright citizenship is just one, has essentially robbed Americans of the power to determine who, and how many, can enter their national family, make claims on it—and exert power over it.

In 1991, the year of Alexander's birth, the Immigration and Naturalization Service reported a total of over 1.8 million legal immigrants. That was easily a record. It exceeded by almost a third the previous peak of almost 1.3 million, reached 84 years earlier at the height of the first great wave of immigration, which peaked just after the turn of the century.

The United States has been engulfed by what seems likely to be the greatest wave of immigration it has ever faced. The INS [Immigration and Naturalization Service] estimates that 12 million to 13 million legal and illegal immigrants will enter the United States during the 1990s. The Washington, D.C.-based Federation for American Immigration Reform (FAIR), among the most prominent of the groups critical of immigration policy, thinks the total will range between 10 million and 15 million.

It's not just illegal immigration that is out of control. So is legal immigration. U.S. law in effect treats immigration as a sort of imitation civil right, extended to an indefinite group of foreigners who have been selected arbitrarily and with no regard to American interests.

The American immigration debate has been a one-way street. Criticism of immigration, and news that might support it, just tends not to get through.

For example, the United States is in the midst of a serious crime epidemic. Yet almost no Americans are aware that aliens make up one-quarter of the prisoners in federal penitentiaries—almost three times their proportion in the population at large.

Indeed, many problems that currently preoccupy Americans have an unspoken immigration dimension.

Two further instances:

- The health care crisis. Americans have been told repeatedly that some 30 million to 40 million people in the country have no health insurance at any one point in time. Typically, nobody seems to know how many are immigrants. But immigrants certainly make up a disproportionate share—particularly of the real problem: the much smaller hard core, perhaps 6 million, that remains uninsured after two years.
- The education crisis. Americans are used to hearing that their schools don't seem to be providing the quality of education that foreigners get. Fewer of them know that the U.S. education system is also very expensive by international standards. Virtually none of them know anything about the impact of immigration on that education system.

Yet the impact of immigration is clearly serious. For example, in 1990 almost one child in every 20 enrolled in American public schools either could not speak English or spoke it so poorly as to need language-assistance programs. This number is increasing with striking speed: Only six years earlier, it had been one child in 31.

Current law is generally interpreted as requiring schools to educate such children in their native language. To do so, according to one California estimate, requires spending some 65 percent more per child than on an English-speaking child. And not merely money but, more importantly, teacher time and energy are inevitably being diverted from America's children.

My thesis is that the immigration resulting from current public policy:

- Is dramatically larger, less skilled and more divergent from the American majority than anything that was anticipated or desired.
- Is probably not beneficial economically —and is certainly not necessary.
- Is attended by a wide and increasing range of negative consequences, from the physical environment to the political
- Is bringing about an ethnic and racial transformation in America without precedent in the history of the world —an astonishing social experiment launched with no particular reason to expect success.

Some of my American readers will be stirring uneasily at this point. They have been trained to recoil from any explicit discussion of race.

Because the term "racist" is now so debased, I usually shrug off such smears by pointing to its new definition: anyone who is winning an argument with a liberal. Or, too often, a libertarian. And, on the immigration issue, even some confused conservatives.

This may sound facetious. But the double standards are irritating. Anyone who has got into an immigration debate with, for example, Hispanic activists must be instantly aware that some of them really are consumed by the most intense racial animosity—directed against whites. How come what's sauce for the goose is not sauce for the gander?

I have indeed duly examined my own motives. And I am happy to report that they are pure. I sincerely believe I am not prejudiced—in the sense of committing and stubbornly persisting in error about people, regardless of evidence—which appears to be to be the only rational definition of "racism." I am also, however, not blind.

Race and ethnicity are destiny in American politics. And, because of the rise of affirmative action quotas, for American individuals too.

My son, Alexander, is a white male with blue eyes and blond hair. He has never discriminated against anyone in his little life (except possibly young women visitors whom he suspects of being baby-sitters). The sheer size of the so-called "protected classes" that are now politically favored, such as Hispanics, will be a matter of vital importance as long as he lives. And their size is basically determined by immigration.

For Americans even to think about their immigration policy, given the political climate that has prevailed since the 1960s, involves a sort of psychological liberation movement. In Eugene McCarthy's terms, America would have to stop being a colony of the world. The implications are shocking, even frightening: that Americans, without feeling guilty, can and should seize control of their country's destiny.

If they did, what would a decolonized American immigration policy look like? The first step is absolutely clear:

The 1965 Immigration Act, and its amplifications in 1986 and 1990, have been a disaster and must be repealed.

It may be time for the United States to consider moving to a conception of itself more like that of Switzerland: tolerating a fairly large foreign presence that comes and goes, but rarely if ever naturalizes. It may be time to consider reviving a version of the bracero program, the agricultural guest-worker program that operated from the 1940s to the 1960s, allowing foreign workers to move in and out of the country in a controlled way, without permanently altering its demography and politics.

This new conception may be a shock to American sensibilities. Many Americans, like my students at the University of Cincinnati Law School, are under the charming impression that foreigners don't really exist. But they also tend to think that, if foreigners really do exist, they ought to become Americans as quickly as possible.

However, the fact is that we—foreigners—are, in some sense, all Americans now, just as Jefferson said everyone had two countries, his own and France, in the 18th century. That is why we are here, just as the entire world flocked to Imperial Rome. The trick the Americans face now is to be an empire in fact, while remaining a democratic republic in spirit. Avoiding the Romans' mistake of diluting their citizenship into insignificance may be the key.

NO

David Cole

THE NEW KNOW-NOTHINGISM: FIVE MYTHS ABOUT IMMIGRATION

For a brief period in the mid-nineteenth century, a new political movement captured the passions of the American public. Fittingly labeled the "Know-Nothings," their unifying theme was nativism. They liked to call themselves "Native Americans," although they had no sympathy for people we call Native Americans today. And they pinned every problem in American society on immigrants. As one Know-Nothing wrote in 1856: "Four-fifths of the beggary and three-fifths of the crime spring from our foreign population; more than half the public charities, more than half the prisons and almshouses, more than half the police and the cost of administering criminal justice are for foreigners."

At the time, the greatest influx of immigrants was from Ireland, where the potato famine had struck, and Germany which was in political and economic turmoil. Anti-alien and anti-Catholic sentiments were the order of the day, especially in New York and Massachusetts, which received the brunt of the wave of immigrants, many of whom were dirt-poor and uneducated. Politicians were quick to exploit the sentiment: There's nothing like a scapegoat to forge an alliance.

I am especially sensitive to this history: My forebears were among those dirt-poor Irish Catholics who arrived in the 1860s. Fortunately for them, and me, the Know-Nothing movement fizzled within fifteen years. But its pilot light kept burning, and is turned up whenever the American public begins to feel vulnerable and in need of an enemy.

Although they go by different names today, the Know-Nothings have returned. As in the 1850s, the movement is strongest where immigrants are most concentrated: California and Florida. The objects of prejudice are of course no longer Irish Catholics and Germans; 140 years later, "they" have become "us." The new "they"—because it seems "we" must always have a "they"— are Latin Americans (most recently, Cubans), Haitians and Arab-Americans, among others.

But just as in the 1850s, passion, misinformation and shortsighted fear often substitute for reason, fairness and human dignity in today's immigration debates. In the interest of advancing beyond know-nothingism, let's look at five current myths that distort public debate and government policy relating to immigrants.

America is being overrun with immigrants.

In one sense, of course, this is true, but in that sense it has been true since Christopher Columbus arrived. Except for the real Native Americans, we are a nation of immigrants.

It is not true, however, that the first-generation immigrant share of our population is growing. As of 1990, foreign-born people made up only 8 percent of the population, as compared with a figure of about 15 percent from 1870 to 1920. Between 70 and 80 percent of those who immigrate every year are refugees or immediate relatives of U.S. citizens.

Much of the anti-immigrant fervor is directed against the undocumented, but they make up only 13 percent of all immigrants residing in the United States, and only 1 percent of the American population. Contrary to popular belief, most such aliens do not cross the border illegally but enter legally and remain after their student or visitor visa expires. Thus, building a wall at the border, no matter how high, will not solve the problem.

Immigrants take jobs from U.S. citizens.

There is virtually no evidence to support this view, probably the most widespread misunderstanding about immigrants. As documented by a 1994 A.C.L.U. Immigrants' Rights Project report, numerous studies have found that immigrants actually *create* more jobs than they fill. The

jobs immigrants take are of course easier to see, but immigrants are often highly productive, run their own businesses and employ both immigrants and citizens. One study found that Mexican immigration to Los Angeles County between 1970 and 1980 was responsible for 78,000 new jobs. Governor Mario Cuomo reports that immigrants own more than 40,000 companies in New York, which provide thousands of jobs and $3.5 billion to the state's economy every year.

Immigrants are a drain on society's resources.

This claim fuels many of the recent efforts to cut off government benefits to immigrants. However, most studies have found that immigrants are a net benefit to the economy because, as a 1994 Urban Institute report concludes, "immigrants generate significantly more in taxes paid than they cost in services received." The Council of Economic Advisers similarly found in 1986 that "immigrants have a favorable effect on the overall standard of living."

Anti-immigrant advocates often cite studies purportedly showing the contrary, but these generally focus only on taxes and services at the local or state level. What they fail to explain is that because most taxes go to the federal government, such studies would also show a net loss when applied to U.S. citizens. At most, such figures suggest that some redistribution of federal and state monies may be appropriate; they say nothing unique about the costs of immigrants.

Some subgroups of immigrants plainly impose a net cost in the short run, principally those who have most recently arrived and have not yet "made it." California, for example, bears substantial costs for its disproportionately large undocumented population, largely because it has on average the poorest and least educated immigrants. But that has been true of every wave of immigrants that has ever reached our shores; it was as true of the Irish in the 1850s, for example, as it is of Salvadorans today. From a long-term perspective, the economic advantages of immigration are undeniable.

Some have suggested that we might save money and diminish incentives to immigrate illegally if we denied undocumented aliens public services. In fact, undocumented immigrants are already ineligible for most social programs, with the exception of education for schoolchildren, which is constitutionally required, and benefits directly related to health and safety, such as emergency medical care and nutritional assistance to poor women, infants and children. To deny such basic care to people in need, apart from being inhumanly callous, would probably cost us more in the long run by exacerbating health problems that we would eventually have to address.

Aliens refuse to assimilate, and are depriving us of our cultural and political unity.

This claim has been made about every new group of immigrants to arrive on U.S. shores. Supreme Court Justice Stephen Field wrote in 1884 that the Chinese "have remained among us as a separate people, retaining their original peculiarities of dress, manners, habits, and modes of living, which are as marked as their complexion and language." Five years later, he upheld the racially based exclusion of Chinese immigrants. Similar claims have been made over different periods of our history about Catholics, Jews, Italians, Eastern Europeans and Latin Americans.

In most instances, such claims are simply not true; "American culture" has been created, defined and revised by persons who for the most part are descended from immigrants once seen as anti-assimilationist. Descendants of the Irish Catholics, for example, a group once decried as separatist and alien, have become Presidents, senators and representatives (and all of these in one family, in the case of the Kennedys). Our society exerts tremendous pressure to conform, and cultural separatism rarely survives a generation. But more important, even if this claim were true, is this a legitimate rationale for limiting immigration in a society built on the values of pluralism and tolerance?

Noncitizen immigrants are not entitled to constitutional rights.

Our government has long declined to treat immigrants as full human beings, and nowhere is that more clear than in the realm of constitutional rights. Although the Constitution literally extends the fundamental protections in the Bill of Rights to all people, limiting to citizens only the right to vote and run for federal office, the federal government acts as if this were not the case.

In 1893 the executive branch successfully defended a statute that required Chinese laborers to establish their prior residence here by the testimony of "at least one credible white witness." The Supreme Court ruled that this law was constitutional because it was reasonable for Congress to presume that nonwhite witnesses could not be trusted.

The federal government is not much more enlightened today. In a pending case I'm handling in the Court of Appeals for the Ninth Circuit, the Clinton Administration has argued that permanent resident aliens lawfully living here should be extended no more First

Amendment rights than aliens applying for first-time admission from abroad—that is, none. Under this view, students at a public university who are citizens may express themselves freely, but students who are not citizens can be deported for saying exactly what their classmates are constitutionally entitled to say.

Growing up, I was always taught that we will be judged by how we treat others. If we are collectively judged by how we have treated immigrants—those who appear today to be "other" but will in a generation be "us"—we are not in very good shape.

POSTSCRIPT

Is Immigration a Problem
in the United States?

Are immigrants to the United States a problem? National legislation since 1965 has clearly provided immigrants with group entitlements that were unheard of in the past. Is this necessarily bad? Should the fact that one out of every five school-aged children is foreign-born be viewed as a source of concern or as a healthy challenge to Americans to live up to their ideals?

Until recently, the population problem for most other countries, especially European ones, has been emigration; too many people were leaving. The main problem was the depletion of skilled laborers and other needed workers. Now, according to the U.N. Population Fund, there are over 100 million international migrants, most of which migrate from poorer nations to wealthier ones. Many countries have mocked the perceived xenophobia (fear of foreigners) in the United States and prided themselves on their tolerant immigration policies and lack of ethnic and racial conflict. However, the United States has always contained far greater numbers of immigrants reflecting a far greater diversity than any other country in the world. Moreover, in the 1990s many nations that traditionally welcomed immigrants, especially those from former colonies, have passed laws sharply restricting immigration. Many have also experienced bitter ethnic conflicts.

Brimelow states that there are now more immigrants entering the United States than there were during the highest point of immigration between 1900 and 1910. Yet he does not mention that the *proportion* of immigrants either entering or currently residing in America is much lower than it was in the past. On the other hand, Cole does not seem to take into account that the origins of current immigrants to the United States are radically different than they were in the past or that other changes might impede comparing immigration today with immigration in the past. These changes include legislative changes that provide ethnic group entitlements (including education and social services), an increasingly militant faction of racial and ethnic leaders demanding preservation of immigrants' national identities and preferences, and the public denunciation by many intellectuals of American values and institutions.

Should major immigration policy changes be put into effect? Should the United States refuse to automatically grant citizenship to children born inside its borders? Should there be clearer demarcations between political refugees, temporary workers, permanent immigrants, and single immigrants versus those with families, as well as stricter enforcement against and more severe punishment for illegal immigrants? Should the United States simply shut down its borders and refuse to accept immigrants whose cultures, values, and appearances are vastly different from Americans'?

In addition to the rapidly changing international situation, relations with Mexico and other nations that are vital to U.S. interests are influenced by U.S. immigration policies. The federal government's actions since 1996 have been to give the Immigration and Naturalization Service increasing powers to deport immigrants or to block their entry. At the state level California's Proposition 187, which denies public support for illegal immigrants and which is currently being challenged in the courts, has wide public support. Meanwhile, debates rage over how immigrants do or do not contribute to the economy, whether or not they take jobs away from U.S. citizens, how much they add to the crime problem, and so on.

Articles supporting Brimelow's thinking include Norman Matloff, "How Immigration Harms Minorities," *The Public Interest* (Summer 1996); Mark Krikorian, "Will Americanization Work in America?" *Current* (October 1998); and "The Politics of Permanent Immigration," by John J. Miller, *Reason* (October 1998). Linda Chavez, a conservative and the daughter of immigrants, shares her views in "Rising to Overcome Criticism," *The Washington Times* (March 19, 1999). A spirited attack on Chavez's ideas by several critics and her response can be found in "Immigration and Multiculturalism," *Commentary* (September 1998).

Support for Cole's position can be found in "International Migration: Dangerous Myths," by Demetrios G. Papademetriou, *Current* (May 1998); "Back into the Melting Pot: The Welcome Effects of Latino Immigration," by M. Barone, *The Weekly Standard* (July 6/13, 1998); *The Other Americans* by J. Millman (Viking, 1997); *In Defense of the Alien, vol. 20,* edited by L. Tomast (Center for Migration Studies, 1999); and "Land of Opportunity," by R. Brenner, *Forbes* (October 12, 1998). The "mend it, don't end it" position is reflected in M. Lind's "Hiring from Within," *Mother Jones* (July/August 1998).

Two useful reports on legal changes are "In California, a Softer Stance on Immigrants?" by D. Wood, *Christian Science Monitor* (April 1, 1999) and M. Valburn's "Clamor for U.S. Citizenship Spurs Debate on Its Cause," *The Wall Street Journal* (February 25, 1999). A work that systematically looks at Mexican immigration is *Crossings: Mexican Immigration in Interdisciplinary Perspectives* edited by Marcelo M. Suárez-Orozco (Harvard University Press, 1998). Among the many heartbreaking accounts of forced immigration is M. Fritz's *Lost on Earth: Nomads of the New World* (Little, Brown, 1998). A helpful article that looks at the extreme backlash in Europe is "Thunder from the Racist Right," by M. Drohan, *World Press Review* (June 1998).

Among the proliferating literature on crime and immigrants is Tony Waters, *Crime and Immigrant Youth* (Sage Publications, 1999) and *The Russian Mafia in America: Immigration, Culture, and Crime* by James Finckenauer and Elin Waring (Northeastern University Press, 1998). A seminal study of female immigrants is Donna Gabaccia, ed., *Seeking Common Ground* (Praeger, 1992).

ISSUE 15

Is There an Ethnic Revolt Against the Melting Pot?

YES: Editors of *Social Justice*, from "Five Hundred Years of Genocide, Repression, and Resistance," *Social Justice* (Summer 1992)

NO: Arthur M. Schlesinger, Jr., from *The Disuniting of America: Reflections on a Multicultural Society* (W. W. Norton, 1992)

ISSUE SUMMARY

YES: The editors of *Social Justice* reject almost all previous formulations of ethnicity and assimilation in the United States. Their aim is to "reclaim the true history" of the continent, which, they say, is one of enslavement, torture, and repression of people of color, who are now in revolt against lies and exploitation.

NO: Historian Arthur M. Schlesinger, Jr., argues that the genius of the United States lies in its unity—the ability of its citizens to embrace basic, common values while accepting cultural diversity. He bitterly attacks "ethnic ideologues" who are bent on disuniting America, not on bringing about positive changes.

> *The dawn of the twentieth century found white Europe master of the world.... Never before in the history of civilization had self-worship of a people's accomplishment attained the heights that the worship of white Europe by Europeans reached.... Was there no other way for the advance of mankind? Were there no other cultural patterns, ways of action, goals of progress, which might and may lead man to something finer and higher?*
>
> —W. E. B. Du Bois

"It may be too bad that dead white European males have played so large a role in shaping our culture. But that's the way it is. One cannot erase history." So argues Arthur M. Schlesinger, Jr., in the following selection. "Not so," argue the editors of *Social Justice* in the second selection. First, the perpetuation of the myth that only Western cultural productions are worthy of being taught is in itself a continuation of the dominance of dead white European males. Until the past few years, the editors say, ethnic and racial minorities were treated as if they had no history, no customs, and no culture worthy of being taught.

Schlesinger contends that that is what multicultural education is: the teaching about other peoples. He says that descendants of Europeans number 80 percent in the United States and that they should be able to learn about their own history. He points out that in 78 percent of all American colleges it is possible to graduate without taking a single Western history course. To him this is a consequence of the work of opponents of the United States and Western culture.

The *Social Justice* editors contend that sexism, racism, and bigotry are so strong in the United States and that the oppressions of the past are so real and pervasive that the old culture must be torn up by its roots. That is, a new society needs to be created.

Schlesinger and many other traditional minority relations scholars feel that this type of analysis reveals people who are locked into the insights of their own times and who unfairly and inaccurately superimpose them on patterns of conduct of the past. Schlesinger also charges those who share the views of the editors of *Social Justice* with being unfair and selective in their historical analysis.

Social critics of America argue that people like Schlesinger are caught up in the iron shackles of the myths that they grew up with and simply cannot shake them off. They want to believe the myths that they have taught their students and have written about for years.

The problem is simply one of sharply competing frames of reference. What a new, badly needed minority theory will look like and what kind of research agenda it will contain is a question that many American sociologists and historians would contend remains unanswerable. As *Social Justice* editorial board member Anthony Platt puts it, "We need the kind of interdisciplinary and comparative theory that not only gives us a better grasp of the dynamics of racism and ethnicity, but also enables us to construct a political vision of equality that resonates in the public imagination. There is much to both rethink and unthink."

Schlesinger's argument is that the genius of the American experience is its ability to maintain religious, ethnic, and racial diversities in a stable fashion. The whole society is held together by the common value of *e pluribus unum*, all for one and one for all. Schlesinger argues that the common goal of fitting in, working together, and assimilating enables diverse people to remain in the same society without civil war.

As you read these two diametrically opposed selections, try to decide what elements in both discussions provide helpful information on minority relations. Which do you feel is more historically accurate? Why? Which perspective have you been taught in American history? What might be the policy implications for the *Social Justice* editors' analysis in terms of programs for minorities? Those of Schlesinger's position? Which position is more "politically correct"? Why?

YES

Editors of Social Justice

FIVE HUNDRED YEARS OF GENOCIDE, REPRESSION, AND RESISTANCE

With this issue of *Social Justice* the editors wish to add our voices to the millions that are reclaiming the true history of this continent over the last five centuries and celebrating its indigenous people as part of "500 years of Resistance." We do this not only out of revulsion at the crimes of genocide that began with Columbus' arrival in 1492, but also because both the genocide and native resistance to it continue today. We do this not only in tribute to the indigenous peoples, but also because their cultures and values represent a planet-saving alternative to contemporary capitalist society. We do this because understanding the global meaning of 1492 is a crucial step in making the next 500 years better than the last.

Columbus and subsequent invaders set in motion a world-historic process of European colonization, by which a nascent capitalist system expanded monumentally across the earth—in the Americas, Africa, and Asia. It was a process based on human and environmental exploitation, the legacies of which continue to this day. The merciless assault on indigenous peoples served as the bedrock upon which Western culture and the capitalist economy were built in the Americas. Indeed, Europe also semi-enslaved its own for gain, beginning with the indentured servants who came to the Americas early on.

Human society had seen racism before, but nothing could approach the forms it took on this continent as the capitalist process unfolded. The destruction of indigenous societies, the enslavement of Africans, and the theft of the mestizo homeland in today's Southwest were logical steps. All served primitive accumulation, as did the later importation of Asian labor.

We can also say that the planet had been mistreated before, but nothing could approach its post–1492 fate. Whether we think of global warming, deterioration of the ozone layer, destruction of the rain forests, or all the effects of environmental abuse on human communities, especially those of color, we know that disaster now faces life on this earth. Simply put, today's environmental crisis results from 500 years of unbridled capitalist exploitation. "Progress" has not come without a staggering price, if it can be called progress at all.

The full meaning of the European invasion of the Americas would have been unimaginable to Bartolomé de Las Casas, our best-known eyewitness. Nonetheless, he described with devastating clarity what was to become a model for such imperialist expansion. Originally a soldier with the invaders and later a priest, de Las Casas left us an account of events, *The Devastation of the Indies*, published in 1552, describing the atrocities and suffering that attended the Spanish invasion as it proceeded province by province. He apologizes repeatedly for not including every incident of horror, stating: "Were I to describe all this, no amount of time and paper could encompass this task."

What is there is enough. One hesitates to turn the page for fear of discovering another way that one human destroyed another: stabbing, dismembering, burning, beating, throwing against rocks, feeding to dogs, torturing, starving, raping, enslaving, and working to death. As described by de Las Casas, the invaders behaved like wild animals in a frenzy of blood lust—and the Spaniards were not alone among Europe's colonial assassins.

Never in history has there been such systematic destruction of an entire continent, and in so short a time. The genocide against the native peoples of Latin America was accomplished in less than 50 years. De Las Casas reports that in New Spain (Mexico), "the Spaniards have killed more Indians here in 12 years... than anywhere else in the Indies... some four million souls." Regarding the islands of San Juan (Puerto Rico) and Jamaica, he said, "I believe there were more than one million inhabitants, and now, in each of the two islands, there are no more than two hundred persons." A total of 25 million victims across the continent does not

seem exaggerated and, in the opinion of some scholars, would be too low a figure.

De Las Casas' appeal to Spain's King Charles I to end the massacres produced royal edicts that went ignored by the invading soldiers and officials. Yet de Las Casas' "Brief Account" stands as an example of speaking out against injustice. It stands as a call for people today, 500 years later, to tell the truth about the history of this continent and to redress the legacy of racist violence that continues against both land and people.

Hans Koning takes up the call... by exposing the myth of Columbus as navigator, hero, discoverer. "We find ourselves in a fight," he declares, "to establish the truth about our past, *finally;* a fight about how we teach our history to our children.... It is high time *to overcome* the Columbus legacy." Ward Churchill takes on "Deconstructing the Columbus Myth" with penetrating observations about Columbus as proto-Nazi and the resemblance of "New World" settlements to Nazi rule. In another article, Bill Bigelow offers an insightful exposé of Columbus as he is presented to children, describing how an entire worldview is developed from the assumptions and historical inaccuracies of the Columbus legend.

In answering that call from de Las Casas, we must look at certain underlying issues raised by the invaders' devastation. We must ask ourselves if a profound immorality was fundamental to all Western/non-Western relations from the beginning. One answer is unavoidable: the ideological foundation of genocide is dehumanization, as the story of physical and cultural genocide in the Americas demonstrates. The native peoples were not "Christians," therefore not human. With industrialization, the denial of humanity intensified as more and more people became objects to generate profit. In their book on Brazil, *Fate of the Forest*, Susanne Hecht and Alexander Cockburn comment that because of massive destruction in the Amazon, "the extinction is not only of nature but of socialized nature."

Today we see an intensification of racism in the United States and around the world based on this same process of defining people as "the Other." African Americans, Chicanos, and other Latinos, Asian Americans, immigrants in general, and, of course, today's Native Americans —all people of color—are feeling the brunt of contemporary dehumanization. This is one reason why the fight for multiculturalism... is important. Poet-essayist Luis Rodriguez offers a vision of culture with room for both people of color and European strengths, while reminding us that we had "better be prepared to remake our continent with the full and equal participation of all." Such perspectives suggest the aggressive campaign to demand social justice that is so needed today. For both physical and cultural genocide continue; we cannot file them away as distant history, a lamentable white man's burden.

RESISTANCE ALSO CONTINUES

As Rigoberta Menchú states... "we are a people who refuse to be annihilated.... We know our struggle is just—it's the only reason we still exist." Resistance by indigenous peoples, as de Las Casas confirms, goes back 500 years and it continues today in many arenas: treaty and land rights, education, culture, language and traditional ways, repression and harassment of activists, drugs and alcohol in Native American communities, racism

and exploitation.... The longstanding campaign to free Leonard Peltier, described... by Roxanne Dunbar Ortiz, offers an especially powerful symbol of the Native American resistance movement and its efforts to free political prisoners.

Native Americans are not the only people fighting the ravages of 500 post-Columbus years. Puerto Rico, whose indigenous peoples were wiped off the face of the earth within a few years, remains a full-fledged colony today.... Suzie Dod and Piri Thomas remind us of the healthy, thriving, cooperative, ecosystemic Taino people, who typify the Caribbean societies that Spain destroyed, and the very different life facing today's Puerto Rican people. There and elsewhere, respect for what we call the environment is crucial to people of color for reasons of human as well as planet survival. A movement against environmental racism has begun in the United States to combat the disproportionate presence of toxic wastes in poor and minority communities....

TOWARD A DIFFERENT 500 YEARS

No condemnation of the European invasion and colonization of the Americas can be too strong, as even the smallest study of indigenous history confirms. Yet along with righteous anger and an insistence on listening to silenced histories, the quincentennial year offers a unique chance to put forth radical alternatives to the Western expansionist model.

In her groundbreaking essay, Annette Jaimes makes a strong case for "revisioning native America," which she begins by challenging claims that indigenous peoples were "backward" in areas ranging from agriculture to medicine. She also questions the concept of all indigenous life as unending drudgery to achieve minimum survival by pointing to societies where many have subsisted adequately or better on a few hours of work per week. What does that say about how we assess quality-of-life in relation to labor process?

Jaimes affirms that "the conceptual key to liberation of native societies is . . . also the key to liberating Eurocentrism from itself, unchaining it from the twin fetishes of materialism and production. . . ." She believes that "the reemergence of a vibrant and functioning Native North America in the 21st century would offer a vital prefiguration of what humanity as a whole might accomplish." Only by recognizing the wisdom and values retained by "Stone Agers" of the modern indigenous world, she argues, "will we be able to forge a multifaceted but collectively held worldview that places materialism and spirituality in sustainable balance with one another."

With this hope of liberating modern capitalist society from itself, and thus transforming the world as shaped by European expansion 500 years ago, we can dream of a new and different 500 years to come. Nor can it be merely a dream. As María Elena Ramírez says in her "Resistance Rap" the issue is "insistence on our very existence—on our planet's existence."

NO

Arthur M. Schlesinger, Jr.

THE DISUNITING OF AMERICA

Is Europe really the root of all evil? The crimes of Europe against lesser breeds without the law (not to mention even worse crimes—Hitlerism and Stalinism—against other Europeans) are famous. But these crimes do not alter other facts of history: that Europe was the birthplace of the United States of America, that European ideas and culture formed the republic, that the United States is an extension of European civilization, and that nearly 80 percent of Americans are of European descent.

... It may be too bad that dead white European males have played so large a role in shaping our culture. But that's the way it is. One cannot erase history.

These humdrum historical facts, and not some dastardly imperialist conspiracy, explain the Eurocentric slant in American schools. Would anyone seriously argue that teachers should conceal the European origins of American civilization? or that schools should cater to the 20 percent and ignore the 80 percent? Of course the 20 percent and their contributions should be integrated into the curriculum too, which is the point of cultural pluralism.

But self-styled "multiculturalists" are very often ethnocentric separatists who see little in the Western heritage beyond Western crimes. The Western tradition, in this view, is inherently racist, sexist, "classist," hegemonic; irredeemably repressive, irredeemably oppressive. The spread of Western culture is due not to any innate quality but simply to the spread of Western power. Thus the popularity of European classical music around the world—and, one supposes, of American jazz and rock too—is evidence not of wide appeal but of "the pattern of imperialism, in which the conquered culture adopts that of the conqueror."

Such animus toward Europe lay behind the well-known crusade against the Western-civilization course at Stanford ("Hey-hey, ho-ho, Western culture's got to go!"). According to the National Endowment for the Humanities, students can graduate from 78 percent of American colleges and universities without taking a course in the history of Western civilization. A number of institutions... require courses in third-world or ethnic studies but not in Western civilization. The mood is one of divesting Americans of the sinful

NO Arthur M. Schlesinger, Jr. / 249

European inheritance and seeking re-demptive infusions from non-Western cultures.

* * *

One of the oddities of the situation is that the assault on the Western tradition is conducted very largely with analytical weapons forged in the West. What are the names invoked by the coalition of latter-day Marxists, deconstructionists, poststructuralists, radical feminists, Afrocentrists? Marx, Nietzsche, Gramsci, Derrida, Foucault, Lacan, Sartre, De Beauvoir, Habermas, the Frankfurt "critical theory" school—Europeans all. The "unmasking," "demythologizing," "decanonizing," "dehegemonizing" blitz against Western culture depends on methods of critical analysis unique to the West—which surely testifies to the internally redemptive potentialities of the Western tradition.

Even Afrocentrists seem to accept subliminally the very Eurocentric standards they think they are rejecting. "Black intellectuals condemn Western civilization," Professor Pearce Williams says, "yet ardently wish to prove it was founded by their ancestors."...

Radical academics denounce the "canon" as an instrument of European oppression enforcing the hegemony of the white race, the male sex, and the capitalist class....

* * *

Is the Western tradition a bar to progress and a curse on humanity? Would it really do America and the world good to get rid of the European legacy?

No doubt Europe has done terrible things, not least to itself. But what culture has not? History, said Edward Gibbon, is little more than the register of the crimes, follies, and misfortunes of mankind. The sins of the West are no worse than the sins of Asia or the Middle East or of Africa.

There remains, however, a crucial difference between the Western tradition and the others. The crimes of the West have produced their own antidotes. They have provoked great movements to end slavery, to raise the status of women, to abolish torture, to combat racism, to defend freedom of inquiry and expression, to advance personal liberty and human rights.

Whatever the particular crimes of Europe, that continent is also the source —the *unique* source—of those liberating ideas of individual liberty, political democracy, the rule of law, human rights, and cultural freedom that constitute our most precious legacy and to which most of the world today aspires. These are *European* ideas, not Asian, nor African, nor Middle Eastern ideas, except by adoption....

There is surely no reason for Western civilization to have guilt trips laid on it by champions of cultures based on despotism, superstition, tribalism, and fanaticism. In this regard the Afrocentrists are especially absurd. The West needs no lectures on the superior virtue of those "sun people" who sustained slavery until Western imperialism abolished it (and, it is reported, sustain it to this day in Mauritania and the Sudan), who still keep women in subjection and cut off their clitorises, who carry out racial persecutions not only against Indians and other Asians but against fellow Africans from the wrong tribes, who show themselves either incapable of operating a democracy or ideologically hostile to the democratic idea, and who in their tyrannies and massacres, their Idi

Amins and Boukasas, have stamped with utmost brutality on human rights.

... What the West would call corruption is regarded through much of Africa as no more than the prerogative of power. Competitive political parties, an independent judiciary, a free press, the rule of law are alien to African traditions.

It was the French, not the Algerians, who freed Algerian women from the veil...; as in India it was the British, not the Indians, who ended (or did their best to end) the horrible custom of *suttee*—widows burning themselves alive on their husbands' funeral pyres. And it was the West, not the non-Western cultures, that launched the crusade to abolish slavery—and in doing so encountered mighty resistance, especially in the Islamic world (where Moslems, with fine impartiality, enslaved whites as well as blacks). Those many brave and humane Africans who are struggling these days for decent societies are animated by Western, not by African, ideals. White guilt can be pushed too far.

The Western commitment to human rights has unquestionably been intermittent and imperfect. Yet the ideal remains —and movement toward it has been real, if sporadic. Today it is the *Western* democratic tradition that attracts and empowers people of all continents, creeds, and colors....

* * *

... History is littered with the wreck of states that tried to combine diverse ethnic or linguistic or religious groups within a single sovereignty. Today's headlines tell of imminent crisis or impending dissolution in one or another multiethnic polity—the Soviet Union, India, Yugoslavia, Czechoslovakia, Ireland, Belgium, Canada, Lebanon, Cyprus, Israel, Ceylon, Spain, Nigeria, Kenya, Angola, Trinidad, Guyana.... The list is almost endless. The luck so far of the American experiment has been due in large part to the vision of the melting pot. "No other nation," Margaret Thatcher has said, "has so successfully combined people of different races and nations within a single culture."

But even in the United States, ethnic ideologues have not been without effect. They have set themselves against the old American ideal of assimilation. They call on the republic to think in terms not of individual but of group identity and to move the polity from individual rights to group rights. They have made a certain progress in transforming the United States into a more segregated society. They have done their best to turn a college generation against Europe and the Western tradition. They have imposed ethnocentric, Afrocentric, and bilingual curricula on public schools, well designed to hold minority children out of American society. They have told young people from minority groups that the Western democratic tradition is not for them. They have encouraged minorities to see themselves as victims and to live by alibis rather than to claim the opportunities opened for them by the potent combination of black protest and white guilt. They have filled the air with recrimination and rancor and have remarkably advanced the fragmentation of American life.

... [F]or all the damage it has done, the upsurge of ethnicity is a superficial enthusiasm stirred by romantic ideologues and unscrupulous hucksters whose claim to speak for their minorities is thoughtlessly accepted by the media.... They have thus far done better in intimidating the white majority than in converting their own constituencies.

"No nation in history," writes Lawrence Fuchs, the political scientist and immigration expert in his fine book *The American Kaleidoscope*, "had proved as successful as the United States in managing ethnic diversity. No nation before had ever made diversity itself a source of national identity and unity." ...

Americanization has not lost its charms. Many sons and daughters of ethnic neighborhoods still want to shed their ethnicity and move to suburbs as fast as they can....

The ethnic identification often tends toward superficiality. The sociologist Richard Alba's study of children and grandchildren of immigrants in the Albany, New York, area shows the most popular "ethnic experience" to be sampling the ancestral cuisine.... "It is hard to avoid the conclusion," Alba writes, "that ethnic experience is shallow for the great majority of whites."

Most blacks prefer "black" to "African-Americans," fight bravely and patriotically for their country, and would move to the suburbs too if income and racism would permit.

As for Hispanic-Americans, first-generation Hispanics born in the United States speak English fluently, according to a Rand Corporation study; more than half of second-generation Hispanics give up Spanish altogether....

Nor, despite the effort of ethnic ideologues are minority groups all that hermetically sealed off from each other, except in special situations, like colleges, where ideologues are authority figures.... Around half of Asian-American marriages are with non-Orientals, and

the Census Bureau estimates one million interracial—mostly black-white—marriages in 1990 as against 310,000 in 1970.

* * *

When we talk of the American democratic faith, we must understand it in its true dimensions. It is not an impervious, final, and complacent orthodoxy, intolerant of deviation and dissent, fulfilled in flag salutes, oaths of allegiance, and hands over the heart. It is an ever-evolving philosophy, fulfilling its ideals through debate, self-criticism, protest, disrespect, and irreverence; a tradition in which all have rights of heterodoxy and opportunities for self-assertion. The Creed has been the means by which Americans have haltingly but persistently narrowed the gap between performance and principle. It is what all Americans should learn, because it is what binds all Americans together.

... If we now repudiate the quite marvelous inheritance that history bestows on us, we invite the fragmentation of the national community into a quarrelsome spatter of enclaves, ghettos, tribes....

Our task is to combine due appreciation of the splendid diversity of the nation with due emphasis on the great unifying Western ideas of individual freedom, political democracy, and human rights. These are the ideas that define the American nationality—and that today empower people of all continents, races, and creeds.

"What then is the American, this new man? ... Here individuals of all nations are melted into a new race of men." Still a good answer—still the best hope.

POSTSCRIPT

Is There an Ethnic Revolt
Against the Melting Pot?

This issue brings together many clashing views. The debate is part of the broader "cultural war" being bitterly waged over many other issues, including whose interpretation of Western history is correct, whether the canon of humanistic knowledge should be scrapped as racist and sexist, whether American history standards are valid, whether the social system in America is completely racist, whether Western science is valid, and so on. As minorities, including racial, ethnic, religious, and gender minorities, are busy redefining themselves, intellectuals, too, are playing the search-for-self game. The family, the economy, the polity, and religion are all being reexamined, and America's past is being dramatically reinterpreted. Moreover, intellectuals themselves seem to be desperately trying to understand what their role should be: bitter social critics of all that has ever existed in the United States or valiant defenders of the "genius" of America.

Ironically, with the crumbling of the former Soviet Union and the seemingly obvious failure of Marxian politics and economics, many Western radical scholars seem to be increasingly contemptuous of the United States and its institutions, values, and history. On the other hand, as the pervasiveness of racism, prejudice, exploitation, and sexism are routinely documented, members of the public, politicians, and some scholars are becoming more conservative and are apparently searching for a mythical past in which whites and Blacks, male and female, young and old, "got along" and conflict was nonexistent.

Meanwhile, most people, even those who are painfully aware of the continuing inequities experienced by many members of minority groups, shudder to think of the United States becoming as disunited as Serbia, Ireland, and Rwanda or facing the Canadian spectacle of separation. Conservatives predict that what they see as hysterical criticisms of America by extremists, including intellectuals and radical minority members, will lead directly to such bloodletting. They insist, as does Schlesinger, that minorities, including racial, ethnic, religious, and gender ones, have it far better in America than their counterparts do in virtually every other country in the world. Indeed, some argue that many minorities in the United States, even those who are having the most difficult time achieving equality, are far better off than they would be if they were "back home" in their tribe or nation of origin.

Is there a revolt against the melting pot? What would the end product of such a revolt consist of? New nations? Separate states for Hispanics, Indians (who some feel are already in enforced isolation), Blacks, and Asians? Should members of the majority be barred from holding elective offices, corporate leaderships, and large amounts of wealth? Since there is no other country that has the degree of ethnic and racial heterogeneity as the United States, there is no comparable model for how we should treat minorities. Indeed, some point out that even nations who are seemingly color-blind still have subtle racial discrimination. How then can we construct a hypothetical ideal society? What would it look like? Where would it be located? Who would be its leaders? the most discriminated against? the weakest? the intellectuals? Some would ask, When have minorities, especially those with markedly different backgrounds, customs, and characteristics, ever been treated fairly over time?

There have been a spate of books and articles addressing this issue. Many of them side with Schlesinger. They seem to be saying that America, while it has minority problems, remains a good society or could be if its critics would give it a chance. See, for example, Michael Lind, *The Next American Nation: The New Nationalism and the Fourth American Revolution* (Free Press, 1995). There are also many articles on this topic, including Gordon S. Wood and Sean Wilentz, "America's Unending Revolution," *Wilson Quarterly* (Spring 1999) and Linda Chavez, "Our Hispanic Predicament," *Commentary* (June 1998). A recent interview with Schlesinger can be found in the Summer 1998 issue of *Tikkun*. For a bitter attack on radicals who rewrite history, see Jorge Amselle's "Misremember the Alamo!" *The Weekly Standard* (October 20, 1997). Additional articles that partially deal with the changing views of American history expressed by Schlesinger can be found in the January/February 1999 issue of *Society*. See also "Teaching American History," by William Cronon et al., *American Scholar* (Winter 1998) and Peter Berger, ed., *The Limits of Social Cohesion* (Westview Press, 1998).

Current articles that agree with the views of the *Social Justice* editors include Angie Y. Chung and Edward Taehan Chang, "From Third World Liberation to Multiple Oppression Politics: A Contemporary Approach to Interethnic Coalitions," *Social Justice* (Fall 1998); Marc Pizarro, "Contesting Dehumanization: Chicana/o Spiritualization, Revolutionary Possibility and the Curriculum," *Aztlán* (Spring 1998); and Alastair Bonnett, "Who Was White? The Disappearance of Non-European White Identities and the Formation of European Racial Whiteness," *Ethnic and Racial Studies* (November 1998). A helpful study that partially reflects Schlesinger's thinking is Alan Wolfe's *One Nation, After All* (Penguin Books, 1998).

One of the many excellent studies that point out the irony of better educated, wealthier, and more intellectual Americans being the most critical is Jennifer L. Hochschild's *Facing Up to the American Dream: Race, Class, and the Soul of the Nation* (Princeton University Press, 1995). Ronald Takaki's critical perspective parallels that of the editors of *Social Justice*. See, for instance, his widely acclaimed *From Different Shores: Perspectives on Race and Ethnicity in America*, 2d ed. (Oxford University Press, 1994) and *A Different Mirror: A History of Multicultural America* (Little, Brown, 1994).

ISSUE 16

Are Black Leaders Part of the Problem?

YES: Eugene F. Rivers III, from "Beyond the Nationalism of Fools: Toward an Agenda for Black Intellectuals," *Boston Review* (Summer 1995)

NO: Edmund W. Gordon and Maitrayee Bhattacharyya, from "Have African Americans Failed to Take Responsibility for Their Own Advancement?" *Long Term View* (Fall 1994)

ISSUE SUMMARY

YES: Eugene F. Rivers III, founder and pastor of the Azusa Christian Community, notes the many social and economic problems of Black youth in the United States and argues that three types of Black leaders—celebrity intellectuals, detached scholars, and rabble-rousers—have contributed to the problems rather than the solutions.

NO: Emeritus professor of psychology Edmund W. Gordon and researcher Maitrayee Bhattacharyya maintain that neither Blacks nor their leaders are responsible for the poor state of Black development. The problem, they argue, is intentional neglect and racism by all of society.

It has been said that among any great people, there are often bitter controversies reflecting profound disagreements. Indeed, some attribute greatness, as well as survival, to a group's *not* walking in lockstep to the beat of a single drummer.

Blacks in the United States have never been a unified, homogeneous entity or of a single mind. For generations there have been rifts, controversies, and conflicts of a stimulating yet divisive nature. One of the most noteworthy schisms crystallized at the start of the twentieth century: the profound disagreement between Booker T. Washington (1856–1915), the conservative Black leader and founder of the Tuskegee Institute, and prominent Black intellectual W. E. B. Du Bois (1868–1963). Du Bois, a Harvard Ph.D., spent many years debating Washington's call for Black self-help. Du Bois demanded that Blacks organize and fight for equal rights, and he rejected the idea that Blacks, through hard work, thrift, and good habits, had to first demonstrate that they "deserved" the rights that whites already enjoyed as citizens.

The role of leaders among any group of people is always problematic at best. Among marginalized, exploited, subjugated people, it is even more difficult. In the past, the only way leaders of acutely oppressed minorities could obtain benefits from the dominant group was by being servile or at least by seeming to pose no threat. After the 1960s, however, Black leaders who worked this way were openly disdained as "Uncle Toms." Washington's policy of self-help was either ridiculed or forgotten by the Black community. By the 1970s even Dr. Martin Luther King, Jr's dream of men and women being judged not "by the color of their skin, but by the content of their character" was ignored as unrealistic. The feeling was that Blacks had been and continued to be so overcome and victimized by racism that it was impossible and unfair to judge them by their character.

In the following selections, Eugene F. Rivers III states that a new breed of Black leader—ranging from intellectuals and politicians to talk-show celebrities—is promoting the image of Blacks as helpless victims who are not responsible for their own actions or destinies. He argues that these leaders must stand up and lead their communities in finding solutions to the Black problem. Edmund W. Gordon and Maitrayee Bhattacharyya contend that Black leaders cannot be blamed for the problems of Black people. The blame, they argue, resides with all of society and the forces within that prevent Blacks and other minorities from successfully developing.

As you read this debate, consider each selection's emphasis on individual actions or group actions. How does Rivers classify Black leaders? What heuristic value does this classification have? From Gordon and Bhattacharyya's point of view, what should white capitalists do or stop doing to help Blacks? Which modern Black leaders would you say are contributing to the problems of the inner city? Which ones are contributing to the solutions?

YES
Eugene F. Rivers III

BEYOND THE NATIONALISM OF FOOLS: TOWARD AN AGENDA FOR BLACK INTELLECTUALS

Each day 1,118 Black teenagers are victims of violent crime, 1,451 Black children are arrested, and 907 Black teenage girls get pregnant. A generation of Black males is drowning in its own blood in the prison camps that we euphemistically call "inner cities." And things are likely to get much worse. Some 40 years after the beginning of the Civil Rights movement, younger Black Americans are now growing up unqualified even for slavery. The result is a state of civil war, with children in violent revolt against the failed secular and religious leadership of the Black community.

Consider the dimensions of this failure. A Black boy has a 1-in-3,700 chance of getting a PhD in mathematics, engineering, or the physical sciences; a 1-in-766 chance of becoming a lawyer; a 1-in-395 chance of becoming a physician; a 1-in-195 chance of becoming a teacher. But his chances are 1-in-2 of never attending college, even if he graduates high school; 1-in-9 of using cocaine; 1-in-12 of having gonorrhea; and 1-in-20 of being imprisoned while in his 20s. Only the details are different for his sister.

What is the responsibility of Black intellectuals in the face of this nightmare? I raised this question three years ago in an open letter to the *Boston Review* (September/October, 1992). My point of departure was the stunning disparity between the grim state of Black America and the recent successes of the Black intelligentsia. My aim was to encourage Black intellectuals to use their now-considerable prestige and resources to improve the lives of Black Americans. The letter provoked wide-ranging discussion—forums at Harvard and MIT, attended by 1,500 people, with participation by bell hooks, Margaret Burnham, Henry Louis Gates, Jr., Cornel West, Glenn Loury, Regina Austin, Selwyn Cudjoe, K. Anthony Appiah, and Randall Kennedy; a series of letters and short essays in *Boston Review* by, among others, Eugene Genovese, Eric Foner, Farah Griffin, and john powell; debates on NPR and public television. Although the discussion did not have clear practical consequences, much of it was constructive.

Recently, a number of less constructive articles on Black intellectuals have appeared in the *New Yorker, Atlantic, New Republic, Village Voice, Los Angeles Times,* and *New York Times Book Review.* Those articles fall into two categories. First, there are what Northwestern University political scientist Adolph Reed rightly described as "press releases." Articles by Michael Bérubé in the *New Yorker* (January 9, 1995) and Robert Boynton in the *Atlantic* (March, 1995), for example, applauded the achievements of a celebrity intelligentsia, but failed to ask any hard questions: for example, what have we learned from the recent work of leading Black intellectuals?

Then we have the more provocative, "you dumb and yo-mamma's ugly" perspective. This second approach was pioneered by Leon Wieseltier in a *New Republic* attack on Cornel West (March 6, 1995), and perfected by Adolph Reed in his *Village Voice* "I-hate-you-because-you're-famous-and-I'm-not" attack on West, Michael Dyson, bell hooks, Robin Kelley, and Skip Gates for being little more than the academic wing of the entertainment industry—a collection of mutual back-slapping, verbally adept "minstrels" (April 11, 1995).

Reed did score some important points. For many Black intellectuals, fame and fortune appear to be ends in themselves. Displays of erudition and post-modern fashion masquerade as intellectual contribution: no new ideas, just expensive theater. But Professor Reed is hardly the one to be leveling these charges. He has devoted himself to criticizing Jesse Jackson and Cornel West, and presenting himself as the only smart native in the jungle, not to advancing an alternative political, theoretical, or policy project.

The debate about responsibility has degenerated into star-worship and name-calling, the stuff of television talk shows. The issues are too serious for that. It is time to get back on track. The Black community is in a state of emergency; Black intellectuals have acquired unprecedented power and prestige. So let's quit the topic of salaries and lecture fees, leave the fine points about Gramsci on hegemony to the journals, and have a serious discussion of how intellectuals can better mobilize their resources to meet the emergency.

* * *

An historical model provides useful instruction. W.E.B. Du Bois was asked by Atlanta University President Horace Bumstead to head an annual conference series to produce "the first . . . thoroughly scientific study of the conditions of Negro life, covering all its most important phases, . . . resulting in a score of annual Atlanta University publications." The studies, Bumstead hoped, would result in an authoritative statement about the lives of Black Americans. According to Du Bois, the work at Atlanta University from 1897 to 1910 developed "a program of study on the problems affecting American Negroes, covering a progressively widening and deepening effort, designed to stretch over the span of a century."

The first Atlanta Conference, held in 1896, focused principally on the health problems of the Black community. "For 13 years," Du Bois wrote in his autobiography, "we poured fourth a series of studies; limited, incomplete, only partially conclusive, and yet so much better done than any other attempt of the sort." The studies were published as Proceedings of the Annual Conferences on the Negro Problem, and included: *Social and*

Physical Condition in Cities (1897); *The Negro in Business* (1899); *the Negro Common School* (1901); *The Negro Artisan* (1902); *The Negro Church* (1903); *Some Notes on Negro Crime* (1904); *The Health and Physique of the Negro American* (1906); *Negro American Family* (1908); *Efforts for Social Betterment Among Negro Americans* (1910); and *Morals and Manners Among Negro Americans* (1915).

So nearly 100 years ago, a Black intelligentsia—endowed with few resources, facing every imaginable form of racial disenfranchisement, living in a world of routine racist lynchings—conducted an intellectually serious program of cooperative and engaged research, focused on the basic life conditions of Black Americans.

Concerns about these conditions remain as urgent today as they were then. And with the maturation of African-American studies as an academic field, vastly greater resources are now available for pursuing an Atlanta-type project that would explore the life conditions of Black Americans, and evaluate strategies for improving those conditions. But no comparable project is now in evidence.

In Greater New England, we have Harvard's Du Bois Institute and the University of Massachusetts' William Monroe Trotter Institute, and at least 25 academic departments, committees, subcommittees, or museums devoted to African or African-American Studies. Consider the distinguished roster of African-American intellectuals in the region: Henry Louis Gates, Jr., Cornel West, Evelyn Brooks-Higginbotham, Orlando Patterson, James Jennings, Hubert Jones, K. Anthony Appiah, James Blackwell, Willard Johnson, Theresa Perry, Marilyn Richardson, John Bracey, Michael Thelwell, Constance Williams, Stephen Carter, Charles Ogletree. How have these institutions and scholars failed—despite their incomparably superior information, financial and institutional support, and comparative wealth, freedom, and safety—to produce a coherent and coordinated research agenda addressing the contemporary devastation of the Black community? Why has this generation's peculiar collective genius been to product to little from so much?

* * *

This question is of interest in its own right, and will make a good research topic for some future historian. Of more immediate concern is how we might start to change directions. In a constructive spirit, I will make some suggestions about two sorts of challenges we need to address.

The first challenges are conceptual—matters of political philosophy. Developing a rational vision of and for the Black community will require ridding ourselves of obsolete and malign intellectual categories. That means a new, anti-antisemitic Black intellectual movement, aimed at resurrecting a vision of hope and faith in the face of the spiritual nihilism and material decay in our inner cities. More specifically, we need to reassess our understanding of social and political equality; reconsider the meaning of freedom in a post–Civil Rights era; examine the implications of secularization for Black culture, politics, and social thought; come to terms with the intimate connections between rights and responsibilities; and show the central role of theological ideas in moral doctrine and ethical life.

These are all large issues, and I cannot develop any of them in detail here. But I will offer two illustrations of the kind of philosophical discussion that we need.

Consider first the issue of equality. After the Supreme Court announced its 1954 decision in *Brown v. Board of Education*, Thurgood Marshall told the *New York Times* that, as a result of the decision, school segregation would be stamped out within five years, and all segregation within seven. Marshall's views were utopian, but not unrepresentative of the middle-class leadership of the period. That leadership assumed—despite much counter-evidence—that the US political system was racially inclusionary and politically capable of fully integrating the Black Americans into national life. The assumption reflected and reinforced an *integrationist* conception of racial equality. The integrationist idea was that the American racial caste system would be replaced with civil and political equality only through racial integration of schools, neighborhoods, and businesses, rather than—as a competing *nationalist* conception argued—through a strategy focused at least initially on building strong, autonomous Black institutions.

For more than 40 years, the integrationist conception of racial equality has dominated the nationalist alternative. But skin color determines life-chances; millions of Blacks continue to be excluded from American life: segregated residentially, educationally, and politically. Moreover, racial barriers show no signs of falling, and affirmative action is all but dead. Committed to racial equality, but faced with a segregated existence, we need to rethink our identification of racial equality with integration, and reopen debate about a sensible nationalist conception of racial equality. As historian Eugene Genovese said in his reply to my open letter: "The Black experience in this country has been a phenomenon without analog." Blacks constitute a "nation-within-a-nation, no matter how anti-separatist their rhetoric or pro-integrationist their genuine aspirations" (*Boston Review*, October/November 1993). What are the political implications of this distinctive history?

Before addressing this question, I need to eliminate a common confusion about Black nationalism. Leonard Jeffries and Louis Farrakhan are widely regarded, even by such experts as Cornel West, as representatives of the Black nationalist perspective. This is a serious misconception. Jeffries and Farrakhan, along with Tony Martin, Khalid Muhammad, and Frances Cress Welsing, represent the *nationalism of fools*. They are cynically antisemitic, mean-spirited, and simply incompetent. Their trains, unlike Mussolini's, do not run on time; in fact, they do not run at all. They are all demagoguery, uniforms, bow ties, and theater. Because they lack programmatic and policy substance, Jeffries and company are not really Black nationalists at all, but ambitious competitors on the game-show circuit posing in nationalist red, black, and green. Their public prominence reflects the leadership vacuum created by a cosmopolitan intelligentsia lacking any pedagogical relationship to poor, inner-city Blacks—the natural outcome of a bankrupt integrationist project.

This nationalism of fools should not be confused with the serious Black nationalist tradition, which has claimed among its adherents such extraordinary 19th century figures as Robert Alexander Young, Henry Highland Garnet, Martin R. Delaney, Henry McNeill Turner, Henry Bibb, and Mary Ann Shadd, and in the 20th century W.E.B. Du Bois, Paul Robeson, Albert Cleage, Harold Cruse,

Sterling Stuckey, Joyce Ladner, Nathan Hare, and John H. Bracey, Jr. (Along with such international allies as Frantz Fanon, Aimé Césaire, Walter Rodney, C.I.R. James, and George Beckford).

Endorsing this serious nationalist project does not mean adopting an essentialist or biological conception of racial difference; Black nationalism is rooted in politics, culture, and history, not biology. Nor does it mean, as Genovese puts it, "a separatist repudiation of the American nationality;" Black Americans are part of the American nation, and should start being treated as such. Nor certainly does it mean that we should return to forced racial segregation, which violates basic human rights.

A sensible nationalist strategy, while taking individual rights seriously, is principally about advancing the interests of a community—a "nation-within-a-nation." Its account of that nation starts from the central role of slavery in the formation of Black identity, emphasizes the subsequent experience of racial subordination, and highlights the special importance of religion in the evolution of the Black nation. As Genovese has argued: "[b]lack religion [was] more than slave religion . . . because many of its most articulate and sophisticated spokesmen were Southern free Negroes and Northerners who lived outside slave society, but because of the racial basis of slavery laid the foundation for a black identity that crossed class lines and demanded protonational identification. The horror of American racism . . . forced them out of themselves—forced them to glimpse the possibilities of nationality rather than class." Drawing on this distinctive experience, and its religio-cultural expression, the nationalist project aims to improve the lives of Black Americans by concentrating the scarce resources of time, money, and political will on addressing the grave deficiencies of, for example, Black churches, Black schools, Black neighborhoods—on reconstructing the institutions of Black civil society. Moreover, this project of improvement and reconstruction—unlike the nationalism of fools—has a deeply universalistic core. Once more, Genovese has formulated the point with particular power: "the black variant of Christianity laid the foundations of protonational consciousness and a the same time stretched a universalist offer of forgiveness and ultimate reconciliation to white America."

Despite their universalism, nationalists always rejected the integrationist project as impractical. The integrationist idea, as Richard Cloward and Frances Fox Piven described it in 1967, was that Blacks and Whites "ought to reside in the same neighborhoods, go to the same schools, work together and play together without regard to race and, for that matter, without regard to religion, ethnicity, or class." To the Black middle class, this dream has had a measure of reality. For the Black poor in northern cities, integration was always hopelessly irrelevant. Nationalist critics understood that irrelevance; they predicted that the project would fail because of intense White resistance. They turned out to be right.

But even if it could have worked at the time, its time has passed. The Civil Rights movement assumed the health of Black communities and churches, and he integrationist approach to racial equality built upon them (and upon a widespread commitment to an activist national government). But we can no longer make that assumption (nor is there the commitment to activist national government).

Given current conditions in inner cities, a strategy for ending a racial caste system in which color fixes life-chances now needs to focus on rebuilding Black institutions: this should be acknowledged by all, whatever their ultimate ideals. Such rebuilding may, of course, involve strategic alliances with other organizations and communities—joining, for example, with largely White unions and environmental groups in efforts to rebuild metropolitan economies. But those alliances will deliver benefits to the inner-city core of those economies only if we also build our own organizational capacities.

Consider next the issue of freedom. What does freedom mean when, 30 years after the passage of the Voting Rights Act, Black Americans lock themselves in their homes and apartments to avoid being caught in urban cross-fire? What does freedom mean for a people psychologically debased by its own internalized racism? What does freedom mean for a people enslaved by the spiritual and political blindness of its own leadership? What does freedom mean for a generation of young people who buy what they want and beg for what they need?

For the Civil Rights movement, freedom was principally a matter of rights. That idea contains a truth of fundamental importance: in our relations with other citizens and the state, rights are essential. They express our standing as moral equals, and as equal citizens.

But a new vision of freedom cannot simply address relations of Black citizens to the broader political community and the state. As American politics devolves and inner-city life degenerates, our vision must also be about the relations within our communities: about Black families and the importance of parental responsibilities to the health of those families, the

evil of Black-on-Black violence, the stupidity of defining Black culture around antisemitism of other forms of racial and ethnic hatred, the value of education and intellectual achievement, the importance of mutual commitment and cooperative effort, and the essential role of personal morality and of religious conviction in defining that morality.

*   *   *

The second set of challenges is more programmatic. Suppose we agree to stop the name-calling and back-slapping long enough to have a serious discussion about a common research agenda to improve the current state of Black America. What might such a discussion look like? What follows is a sketch of an answer. In essence, my proposal is that we follow the Atlanta project model, and convene a multi-year *Conference on Black America:* a coordinated research effort, based in current African American studies programs, focused on basic life conditions of Black Americans, issuing in a series of publications backed by the authority of the convening institutions, and developing new strategies to address the state of emergency in Black communities.

• **Convene Annual Meetings:** Major institutes of African American studies —for example, the Du Bois and Trotter Institutes—should jointly commit to convening a series of annual meetings, each of which would be thematically defined, and devoted to examining some fundamental aspect of Black American life.
• **Begin with Economics and Politics:** Early meetings should explore two themes:

  Urban Economies: The economic fate of Black Americans continues to be tied to inner cities, which are economic basket cases. Are there promising strategies of economic development—for example, metropolitan strategies—that would deliver new employment opportunities in inner cities?

Blacks and Democrats: Black support for the Democratic Party is rooted in the post–New Deal nationalization of American politics, the role of the Democrats as the party of national government, and the importance of national government in ensuring civil rights. What are the implications of the denationalization of American politics and a post–civil rights Black political agenda for this political alliance?

- **Stay With Fundamentals:** Topics for subsequent meetings might include: Black-on-Black violence; the state of Black families; equalizing employment opportunities for Black women; the narcotics industry and its role in Black communities; and the current state of mathematical, computer, and scientific literacy among Black youth.
- **Publish the Results:** Each meeting would result in a published volume. These volumes should not simply collect the separate contributions of participants, but provide—where possible—a consensus statement of problems, diagnoses, and directions of potential response.

- **Focus on Policy:** Above all, the Conference should produce practical policy recommendations. And those recommendations will need to be addressed to different actors: the Black community, faith communities, state and federal government, the private sector, and foundations.

- **Measure the Effects:** How will we know if we are doing anything to address the current crisis in Black America? We should measure the health of a community by the conditions of its least advantaged members. So part of the work of the Conference on Black America should be to monitor those conditions, and to assess the effects of its own work on improving them.

* * *

No series of analyses, papers, discussions, and books will stop the slaughter in our streets, or children from having children, or men from beating up women. The role of intellectuals is limited; excessive expectations will only produce disappointment. But that limited role is crucial, and fears of disappointment should not serve as an excuse for continuing along the current course. The fate of Black America is in the balance: or, if that description of the stakes seems too collective, then think of the fates of the millions of Black Americans whose lives are now at risk.

NO

Edmund W. Gordon and Maitrayee Bhattacharyya

HAVE AFRICAN AMERICANS FAILED TO TAKE RESPONSIBILITY FOR THEIR OWN ADVANCEMENT?

The question is not whether African Americans have failed to take responsibility for their own development. Rather, the more correct question is whether the forces that have frustrated the development of African Americans and other minority groups in the United States have been sufficiently identified and addressed.... All of us must become more aware that the problems of poor people and low status minorities in this country are the result of intentional neglect and systemic design which serve the surplus profit-making motives of a few.

The assertion that Black people fail to work toward their own self-development is obviously fallacious and may be a deliberate misrepresentation or obfuscation, advanced by the forces in our society which stand to benefit from such distortion and fiction. Subordinated minorities, such as African Americans in the United States, who have been pushed into surplus labor pools, disenfranchised groups, and dysfunctional underclasses, have extremely limited opportunities to determine their own development. To speak of the relative absence of a minority group's assumption of responsibility for its own development in a heterogenous capitalist society like ours, where one group has achieved hegemony at the cost of the subjugation of others, is ludicrous and borders on being immoral.

This does not mean that we wish to assert that marginalized people have no responsibility for participating in their own development. In fact, these are the very people who must assume responsibility, since oppressors cannot be expected to support the liberation of the oppressed. It is remarkable that persons of African descent have wrested as much as they have from systems of political-economic relations that have been designed to enslave, exploit, and contain Blacks rather than enable them and facilitate their development.

From Edmund W. Gordon and Maitrayee Bhattacharyya, "Have African Americans Failed to Take Responsibility for Their Own Advancement?" *Long Term View* (Fall 1994). Copyright © 1994 by *Long Term View*. Reprinted by permission.

The initiative of Black folks throughout the history of the African diaspora in the United States is evidence enough that this lesson was learned. Despite enormous odds against success, Blacks resisted their enslavement; some fled from their masters, others learned to read and write, and most importantly, Blacks created a unique culture that retained elements of their African heritage and gave them a measure of independence even during the worst days of slavery.

In the period of the Reconstruction, and even after its betrayal, Blacks joined with disenfranchised Whites to assert political power, to advance public responsibility for education, to develop the economic infrastructures of African American communities, and to establish stable families.

The reactions of the dominant social forces interrupted these developments. Nevertheless, at a later period, when Blacks relocated en masse to the urban and industrial centers of the nation, strong Black cultural and economic networks again developed. Black families restabilized. Religious, economic, cultural and social groups flourished. Black people sought education and many became as well educated as they could in schools that were not meant to educate them well or equally. And let us not forget the leadership role that Blacks took more recently during the Civil Rights movement, a movement that benefited Blacks and non-Blacks alike.

Despite these achievements, African American progress has been challenged, frustrated, and disrupted repeatedly. The African American community has never gained nor been able to even initiate invulnerable or sustained development. Time and time again, advancement has been brought to a screeching halt by the forces of external circumstances.

Today, the issues of African American self-determination and responsibility for advancement are complicated by the declining economic health of this country. At the very time that African Americans had developed enough social capital to support accelerated group development, the United States entered a period of economic stagnation and dislocation. In this advanced stage of capitalism, the United States has experienced the exportation of its industrial capacity and its job opportunities. Businesses have searched elsewhere for a cheaper and more docile labor force than the one that has developed in the United States, where employees have organized to demand proper benefits, work conditions, and wages. These economic conditions have thrown all of society into a state of social disorder, political turmoil, and economic chaos. As significant members of the surplus labor pool, many African Americans now face some of the most imposing obstacles to success as a result of the current societal decay.

There is no question that in comparison with other minority groups in the United States, with the exception of ethnically identifiable Native Americans, fewer African Americans have attained economic, academic, and professional successes and stability. African Americans even appear to have developed less productive self-help groups, and many communities that are primarily African American appear self-destructive. "Black-on-Black" violence has been increasingly featured in the media, prompting greater worry about the psychosocial development of African Americans, especially adolescent males. As we focus on the unfortunate fact that many African Americans live in communities where violence, drugs, and crime abound, there are those who reason that African Americans have brought this condition upon themselves.

But the question is not whether African Americans have failed to take responsibility for their own development. Rather, the more correct question is whether the forces that have frustrated the development of African Americans and other minority groups in the United States have been sufficiently identified and addressed. Scholars who have sought to explain these differences in group development call attention to the ubiquitous problem of racism, the caste status of Blacks in the United States, the absence of Blacks' access to capital, and the changes in the political economy that miserably coincided with the very time that Blacks had developed enough social capital to support accelerated group development. But none of these explanations seem to quiet the pervasive and widespread impression that Blacks are inherently incapable of taking full advantage of the opportunities available in the latter 20th century U.S.A.

* * *

Questions concerning Blacks' failures to take responsibility for their own development have possibly arisen because of the disproportionate number of African Americans who are poverty stricken, who are characterized as socially dysfunctional, and who must depend on the nation's welfare system for support. While poverty, dysfunctionality, and dependency reduce the capacity for autonomous behavior, for a segment of the African American community these ailments are due to the devastating breakdown in the economic infrastructure and social networks which are necessary for group development. In James Wel-

don Johnson's words, "hope unborn had died" in too many instances. Thus, we do see evidence in many of our people of learned helplessness and resignation —in part as a function of an inept system of welfare support, in part also as a result of a tradition of alienation and exclusion from the society, and in part as a function of a degree of depression and lethargy that leaves no energy for self-development. The society which has created this social pathology is doubly culpable when it then blames the victims for their failure to correct their oppression and underdevelopment.

We can not end on this point, however. As pessimistic as we may be in light of the current state of the Black community and the country, it should be obvious that Black people have and will continue to try to overcome the barriers to opportunity and advancement that they face. Perhaps an unprecedentedly large part of the community has given up hope, but it is too soon to dismiss the possibility that the community will stabilize once again and gather momentum as a whole. While members of the Black community face uncertain, precarious development, there are persons who have made it against the odds and even more who are trying. Effective Black families *do* exist, and in countless small communities across this country tiny groups of Black people struggle daily to make better lives for themselves and their children. Individuals and groups from the Black community *have* made important contributions to society at large, and they are usually the products of Black communities which provided the only support for their development. Nor can we can ignore the several national organizations which year after year advocate, organize, demonstrate, provide services, and raise money in support of the development of Black people.

These successful Blacks and their life strategies should not be forgotten, but neither should their example be held against those who have not made it as proof of a culpability that lies with those who are underachieving or less fortunate. It is a mistake to view the problem of Black underdevelopment through the narrow lens of our least developed members. The success of a handful must not blind us to the problems of racism that face all African Americans.

* * *

Could it be that we ask whether the victims are responsible for their misery so we will worry more about responsibility for the self and less about society's collective responsibility for all? National values which favor collective responsibility just might require radical redistribution of our nation's resources and access to power for all people. As long as we believe that poor people are responsible for their poverty, that African Americans and other low status peoples are caught up in abusive, drug related, and violent behaviors of their own choosing, and that African Americans do not want to end their marginalization, the privileged and those who are simply more fortunate can look the other way and do nothing.

All of us must become more aware that the problems of poor people and low status minorities in this country are the result of intentional neglect and systemic design which serve the surplus profit-making motives of a few. The present challenge is not so much the determination of responsibility as it is the creation of a greater sense of national community, which would enable all segments of society to assume responsibility and engage in corrective action. The nation can not survive the current economic, political, and social problems without eliminating the tremendous gap between the "haves" and the "have nots." A sense of national community demands collective action to facilitate the development of both the self and others. Those who continue to enjoy privilege must realize that while it is "them" who are marginalized today, it may be "us" tomorrow.

POSTSCRIPT

Are Black Leaders Part of the Problem?

Many people in America today are fed up with affirmative action and criminal rehabilitation programs that do not seem to be effective. In light of this, will Gordon and Bhattacharyya's demand for even more inner-city support likely be heeded? What (if anything) do you think prominent Black leaders of the past, such as W. E. B. Du Bois, Martin Luther King, Jr., Booker T. Washington, Ella Baker, and Fannie Mae Coppin, would be able to do to solve the problem of Black poverty, crime, drugs, and demoralization today? Which modern leaders, both Black and white, seem to be working for Blacks? Which ones seem to be taking advantage of the Black situation?

Several articles that debate this issue can be found in the Fall 1994 edition of *Long Term View*, from which the selection by Gordon and Bhattacharyya was taken. John Leland, in "Savior of the Streets," *Newsweek* (June 1, 1998), provides an update on Gene Rivers, who, unlike many leaders, white or Black, is living what he preaches in that he resides in an impoverished, drug-infested ghetto in Boston, Massachusetts.

For attacks on white and Black liberals who allegedly work to prevent self-sufficiency, see Shelby Steele's "How Liberals Debase Black Achievements," *Policy Review* (November/December 1998) and his book *A Dream Deferred: The Second Betrayal of Black Freedom in America* (HarperCollins, 1998). For a review of Steele's thinking, see "Beneath the Skin," by Alan Wolfe, *The New Republic* (November 23, 1998). Among the many direct attacks on Black leadership are *Member of the Club: Reflections on Life in a Racially Polarized World* by Lawrence O. Graham (HarperCollins, 1995); *We Have No Leaders: African Americans in the Post–Civil Rights Era* by Robert C. Smith and Ronald W. Waters (State University of New York Press, 1996); and *Masters of the Dream: The Strength and Betrayal of Black America* by Alan L. Keyes (William Morrow, 1995). For an attack on Keyes, see "Alan Keyes and Other False Prophets," by C. Lusane, *The Baltimore Sun* (May 12, 1995). A witty attack on leaders and Black males can be found in *What's Going On? Personal Essays* by Nathan McCall (Random House, 1998).

For a collection of essays by top Black journalists, see Dewayne Wickham, ed., *Thinking Black: Some of the Nation's Most Thoughtful and Provocative Black Columnists Speak Their Minds* (Crown, 1996). Herb Boyd and Robert Allen's *Brotherman: The Odyssey of Black Men in America* (Ballantine Books, 1996) provides positive information for young Blacks. Finally, a witty dissection of this and other race-related issues is Stanley Crouch's *The All-American Skin Game, or, the Decoy of Race: The Long and the Short of It, 1990–1994* (Pantheon Books, 1995).

On the Internet . . .

American Indian Research and Policy Institute (AIRPI)

The American Indian Research and Policy Institute (AIRPI), founded in 1992, is a nonprofit center for research, policy development, and education on critical Indian issues. The AIRPI's mission is to provide government leaders, policymakers, and the general public with accurate information about the legal and political history of American Indian nations and the contemporary situation for American Indians.
http://www.quest-dynamics.com/airpi/aboutus.html

Citizens Jury Project Home Page

The Citizens Jury Project was created in January 1995 by the Vera Institute of Justice—a nonprofit organization dedicated to enhancing justice in institutions of government—with grants from the Commonwealth Fund and the New York Community Trust. Click on "Articles of Interest" to see, among others, a couple of articles on race-based jury nullification.
http://broadway.vera.org/jury/

Race Issues in the Criminal Justice System

This page offers a selective list of resources—including journal articles, books, government documents, and Web resources—on race issues in the criminal justice system.
http://www.lib.cmich.edu/departments/reference/diversity/justice.htm

Race and Racism in American Law

Race and Racism in American Law considers how race and racism intersect with American law, racism and racial distinctions in the law, and the role of the law in promoting or alleviating racism. It includes statutes, cases, excerpts of law review articles, annotated bibliographies, and other documents related to racism and race.
http://www.udayton.edu/~race/

PART 4

Affirmative Action, Legal Issues, and New Policies

Why is it that in all societies some people are "more equal" than others? What forms do these inequalities and their consequences take? For years sociologists have pointed out the importance of ethnicity and race for creating and maintaining systems of stratification (i.e., the distribution of society's power, wealth, and opportunities). As we enter the twenty-first century, most Americans reject inequalities based on ethnicity and race as unfair. Yet many, while expecting individuals to try to be successful, still seem to think that an individual's lack of success and even criminal conduct can be separated from his or her ethnicity or race. What policies are needed to ensure that all citizens are competing on a level playing field? Has affirmative action helped to bring about fairness in college admissions? Does federal support of increasing autonomy for some minorities make matters better or worse? Are recent legal policies to control crime merely old racism in new bottles?

■ Should Race Be a Consideration in College Admissions?

■ Should Sovereignty for American Indians Be Increased?

■ Should Jury Nullification Be Used to Reduce Ethnic and Racial Inequities?

■ Is Systemic Racism in Criminal Justice a Myth?

■ Is the Drug War Harming Blacks?

ISSUE 17

Should Race Be a Consideration in College Admissions?

YES: William G. Bowen and Derek Bok, from "Get In, Get Ahead: Here's Why," *The Washington Post* (September 20, 1998)

NO: Dinesh D'Souza, from "A World Without Racial Preferences," *The Weekly Standard* (November 30/December 7, 1998)

ISSUE SUMMARY

YES: William G. Bowen, president of the Andrew W. Mellon Foundation, and Derek Bok, former president of Harvard University, contend that the high rate of success of the Black college graduates that they studied would not have happened if they had attended lesser schools. Because admission to the elite schools for many of these students resulted from affirmative action, Bowen and Bok argue that the policy of considering race should be continued.

NO: Dinesh D'Souza, the John M. Olin Scholar at the American Enterprise Institute, dismisses the conclusions of Bowen and Bok and asserts that admission to any organization should always be based on merit, not preferential treatment. He maintains that judging people by the color of their skin, which he sees affirmative action as doing, is an insult to the memory of Dr. Martin Luther King, Jr., and may be largely a strategy used by white and Black elites to advance their own agendas at the expense of common sense and morality.

Benjamin Disraeli (1804–1881), a writer who later became England's prime minister, wrote in his acclaimed novel *Sybil* in the 1840s that England had become two countries consisting of the rich and the poor. Following riots in the 1960s, the Kerner Report concluded that the United States consisted of two societies that were drifting apart. More recently, writers on race relations have lamented the "two nations, separate and unequal" theme.

Paradoxically, many African Americans' lives have improved significantly within the past 30 years. There is a rapidly expanding Black middle class; several thousand elected officials, including mayors of many cities, are Black; Black females, especially professionals, are reflecting gains well above those of both male and female whites; and almost 8 percent of all lawyers and doctors in the United States are Black, compared with less than 2 percent in the 1960s. However, many aspects of Black culture and their problems pervade the mass media: Black illegitimacy, Black leadership, Black artistic accomplishments, Black illnesses, Black language, Blacks in sports, Blacks and AIDS, Afrocentrism in schools and universities, continued racism, Black entertainers, and Black criminals are frequent topics of America's news stories. The Black racial minority arguably dominates America more than all other ethnic, religious, and racial minorities combined. Judging from the media accounts, the political debates, and the educational and social agendas, both white and Black Americans are fascinated with Blacks.

Yet America remains for many (at least) two nations. There are now more Blacks under the umbrella of America's justice system (i.e., in prison, on parole or probation, or in jail awaiting trial) than at any other time in U.S. history. A young Black male, reports say, has a greater chance of being killed in the streets by other Blacks or being arrested than of going to college. The sheer despair and ugliness of America's inner cities, which are now spreading to small towns and suburbs as "mini-ghettoes," provide ample evidence that while many Blacks are succeeding, for a significant number of Blacks something is terribly wrong. Or, as William G. Bowen and Derek Bok imply in the following selection, the continued wretchedness of the existence of many Black Americans shows that something is not right with U.S. society.

In addition to hard work and perseverance, the traditional road to success in the United States has been education. Yet it has always been known that life's opportunities are stacked clearly in favor of wealthy children, males, whites, and Protestants, as well as those born in affluent urban areas. More recently, many Americans have come to the conclusion that an oppressive, exploitive, racist system has handicapped Blacks in the United States. For years some had assumed that since discrimination in hiring practices had been legally prohibited, Black nuclear physicists, for example, could apply for a good job and be hired. Quickly it became apparent that due to years of discrimination, very few Blacks were trained in nuclear physics (or many other professions). Logically, an easy remedy would be to monitor all schools —especially the elite colleges—to ensure that qualified Blacks could get in. However, as Bowen and Bok point out, unless race is taken into account along with other standard criteria, many Blacks simply would not be admitted to elite colleges. This, in turn, would deny the Black community of vital civic leadership and of Black doctors, lawyers, and businesspeople.

In the second selection, Dinesh D'Souza argues that even if Bowen and Bok's contention were true, both Blacks and the nation as a whole would be better off living up to the original dream of achieving a color-free society.

Should race be a consideration in college admission? What are the possible negative and positive consequences thus far of this policy?

YES   William G. Bowen and Derek Bok

GET IN, GET AHEAD: HERE'S WHY

In his classic 1969 study of Wall Street lawyers, Erwin Smigel reported that: "I only heard of three Negroes who had been hired by large law firms. Two of these were women who did not meet the client." Smigel's statement should not surprise us. In the 1960s, barely 2 percent of America's doctors and lawyers were black, and only 280 blacks held elected office of any kind. At that time, few leading professional schools and nationally prominent colleges and universities enrolled more than a handful of blacks. Late in the decade, however, selective institutions set about to change these statistics, not by establishing quotas, but by considering race, along with many other factors, in deciding whom to admit.

This policy was adopted because of a widely shared conviction that it was simply wrong for overwhelming numbers of blacks to continue to hold routine jobs while the more influential positions were almost always held by whites. In a nation becoming more racially and ethnically diverse, these educators also considered it vital to create a learning environment that would prepare students of all races to live and work together effectively.

In recent years, the use of race in college admissions has been vigorously contested in several states and in the courts. In 1996, a federal appeals court in New Orleans, deciding the Hopwood case, declared such a race-sensitive policy unconstitutional when its primary aim is not to remedy some specific wrong from the past. Californians have voted to ban all consideration of race in admitting students to public universities. Surprisingly, however, amid much passionate debate, there has been little hard evidence of how these policies work and what their consequences have been.

To remedy this deficiency, we examined the college and later-life experiences of more than 35,000 students—almost 3,000 of whom were black—who had entered 28 selective colleges and universities in the fall of 1976 and the fall of 1989. This massive database, built jointly by the schools and the Andrew W. Mellon Foundation, for the first time links information such as SAT scores and college majors to experiences after college, including graduate and professional degrees, earnings and civic involvement. Most of our study focused on African Americans and whites, because the Latino population at these schools was too small to permit the same sort of analysis. What did we discover?

Compared with their extremely high-achieving white classmates, black students in general received somewhat lower college grades and graduated at moderately lower rates. The reasons for these disparities are not fully understood, and selective institutions need to be more creative in helping improve black performance, as a few universities already have succeeded in doing. Still, 75 percent graduated within six years, a figure well above the 40 percent of blacks and 59 percent of whites who graduated nationwide from the 305 universities tracked by the National Collegiate Athletic Association. Moreover, blacks did not earn degrees from these selective schools by majoring in easy subjects. They chose substantially the same concentrations as whites and were just as likely to have difficult majors, such as those in the sciences.

* * *

Although over half of the black students attending these schools would have been rejected under a race-neutral admissions regime—that is, if only high school grades and test scores had been counted—they have done exceedingly well after college. Fifty-six percent of the black graduates who had entered these selective schools in 1976 went on to earn advanced degrees. A remarkable 40 percent received either PhDs or professional degrees in the most sought-after fields of law, business and medicine, a figure slightly higher than that for their white classmates and five times higher than that for blacks with bachelor's degrees nationwide. (As a measure of change, it is worth noting that by 1995, 7.5 percent of all law students in the United States were black,

up from barely 1 percent in 1960; and 8.1 percent of medical school students were black, compared with 2.2 percent in the mid-1960s. Black elected officials now number more than 8,600.)

By the time of our survey, black male graduates who had entered selective schools in 1976 were earning an average of $85,000 a year, 82 percent more than other black male college graduates nationwide. Their black female classmates earned 73 percent more than all black women with bachelor's degrees. Not only has the marketplace valued the work of these graduates highly, but the premium associated with attending one of these selective institutions was substantial. Overall, we found that among blacks with similar test scores, the more selective the college they attended, the more likely they were to graduate, earn advanced degrees and receive high salaries. This was generally true for whites as well.

Despite their high salaries, the blacks in our study were not just concerned with their own advancement. In virtually every type of civic activity, from social service organizations to parent-teacher associations, black men were more likely than their white classmates to hold leadership positions. Much the same pattern holds for women. These findings should reassure black intellectuals who have worried that blacks—especially black men—would ignore their social responsibilities once they achieved financial success.

* * *

Were black students demoralized by having to compete with whites with higher high school grades and test scores? Is it true, as Dinesh D'Souza asserts in his book "Illiberal Education," that "American universities are quite willing to sacrifice the future happiness of many young blacks and Hispanics to achieve diversity, proportional representation, and what they consider to be multicultural progress"? The facts are very clear on this point. Far from being demoralized, blacks from the most competitive schools are the most satisfied with their college experience. More than 90 percent of both blacks and whites in our survey said they were satisfied or very satisfied with their college experience, and blacks were even more inclined than whites to credit their undergraduate experience with helping them learn crucial skills. We found no evidence that significant numbers of blacks felt stigmatized by race-sensitive policies. Only 7 percent of black graduates said they would not attend the same selective college if they had to choose again.

Former students of all races reported feeling that learning to live and work effectively with members of other races is important. Large majorities also believed that their college experience contributed a lot in this respect. Consequently, almost 80 percent of the white graduates favored either retaining the current emphasis on enrolling a diverse class or emphasizing it more. Their minority classmates supported these policies even more strongly.

Some critics allege that race-sensitive admissions policies aggravate racial tensions by creating resentment among white and Asian students rejected by colleges they hoped to attend. Although we could not test this possibility definitively, we did examine the feelings of white students in our sample who had been rejected by their first-choice school. Significantly, they said they supported an emphasis on diversity just as strongly as students who got into their first-choice schools.

Our findings also clarify the much misunderstood concept of merit in college admission. Many people suppose that all students with especially high grades and test scores "deserve" to be admitted and that it is unfair to reject them in favor of minority applicants with lower grades and test scores. But selective colleges do not automatically offer admission as a reward for past performance to anyone. Nor should they. For any institution, choosing fairly, "on the merits," means selecting applicants by criteria that are reasonably related to the purposes of the organization. For colleges and universities, this means choosing academically qualified applicants who not only give promise of earning high grades but who also can enlarge the understanding of other students and contribute after graduation to their professions and communities. Though clearly relevant, grades and test scores are by no means all that matter.

Because other factors are important —including hard-to-quantify attributes such as determination, motivation, creativity and character—many talented students, white and black, are rejected even though they finished in the top 5 percent of their high school class. The applicants selected are students who were also above a high academic threshold but who seemed to have a greater chance of enhancing the education of their classmates and making a substantial contribution to their professions and society. Seen from the perspective of how well they served the missions of these educational institutions, the students admitted were surely "meritorious."

Could the values of diversity be achieved equally well without considering race explicitly? The Texas legislature has tried to do so by guaranteeing admission to the state's public universities for all students who finish in the top 10 percent of their high school class. Others have suggested using income rather than race to achieve diversity. Our analysis indicates that neither alternative is likely to be as effective as race-sensitive admissions in enrolling an academically well prepared and diverse student body. The Texas approach would admit some students from weaker high schools while turning down better-prepared applicants who happen not to finish in the top tenth of their class in academically stronger schools. Income-based strategies are unlikely to be good substitutes for race-sensitive admissions policies because there are simply too few blacks and Latinos from poor families who have strong enough academic records to qualify for admission to highly selective institutions.

What would happen if universities were flatly prohibited from considering race in admissions? Our findings suggest that over half of the black students in selective colleges today would have been rejected. We can estimate what would be lost as a result:

• Of the more than 700 black students who would have been rejected in 1976 under a race-neutral standard, more than 225 went on to earn doctorates or degrees in law, medicine or business. Approximately 70 are now doctors and roughly 60 are lawyers. Almost 125 are business executives. The average earnings of all 700 exceeds $71,000, and well over 300 are leaders of civic organizations.

• The impact of race-neutral admissions would be especially drastic in admission to professional schools. The proportion of black students in the Top Ten law, business and medical schools would probably decline to less than 1 percent. These are the main professional schools from which most leading hospitals, law firms and corporations recruit. The result of race-neutral admissions, therefore, would be to damage severely the prospects for developing a larger minority presence in the corporate and professional leadership of America.

The ultimate issue in considering race-sensitive admissions policies is how the country can best prepare itself for a society in which one-third of the population will be black and Latino by the time today's college students are at the height of their careers. With that in mind, would it be wise to reduce substantially the number of well-prepared blacks and Latinos graduating from many of our leading colleges and professional schools? Considering students' own views about what they have gained from living and learning with classmates from different backgrounds and races, and the demonstrated success of black graduates in the workplace and the community, we do not think so.

NO
Dinesh D'Souza

A WORLD WITHOUT RACIAL PREFERENCES

"If color-blind admissions policies are put into effect," I was warned at a recent debate on the topic, "the number of black students at the most selective colleges and universities would plummet to around 2 percent. Should we as a society be willing to live with such an outcome?"

I hesitated, and in that moment of hesitation, my interlocutor saw his opportunity. "Well, should we?" he pressed.

The answer, it turns out, is yes. But it is an answer that supporters of the current system consider outrageous. They take for granted that the only possible response is "Of course not." So, for example, two pillars of the education establishment, former Princeton president William Bowen and former Harvard president Derek Bok, have just published a widely reviewed defense of affirmative action, *The Shape of the River: Long-Term Consequences of Considering Race in College and University Admissions.* They insist that some form of preferential recruitment is inevitable to avoid the unthinkable outcome of very few African Americans at top-ranked universities. "The adoption of a strict race-neutral standard would reduce black enrollment at ... academically selective colleges and universities by between 50 and 70 percent," Bowen and Bok observe. "The most selective colleges would experience the largest drops in black enrollment."

These numbers are more or less correct. But what they actually illustrate is not the unacceptable future but the unconscionable present: the magnitude of racial preferences currently in effect. Affirmative action in practice does not mean—as its supporters claim—considering two equally qualified applicants and giving the minority candidate the nod. It has instead come to mean admitting Hispanic and African-American students with grade-point averages of 3.2 and SAT scores of 1100, while turning away white and Asian-American applicants with GPAs of 4.0 and SAT scores of 1300. Far from waging a war against discrimination, advocates such as Bowen and Bok find themselves waging a war against merit. And far from vindicating idealism and promoting social justice, they find themselves cynically subverting the principle of equal rights under the law to the detriment of society as a whole.

* * *

Before we can decide whether it is simply too embarrassing to permit elite institutions to enroll a very small percentage of blacks or other minorities, we must first ask the question of what produces the racial disparities that so unsettle us and that seem to require affirmative action to counteract. Consider the example of the National Basketball Association. It is no secret that the NBA does not "look like America": African Americans, who are 12 percent of the population, make up 79 percent of the players, while Jews and Asian Americans are conspicuously scarce.

Of course, one never hears demands that the NBA establish a preferential recruitment program for Jews or Asians. But before the notion is dismissed as simply silly, it is instructive to ask why. The answer is presumably that it is merit and not discrimination that produces the racial imbalance on the basketball court. If the coaches hire the best passers and shooters, we tend to think, it shouldn't matter if some ethnic groups dominate and others are hardly represented.

The lesson to be drawn from this example is that inequalities in racial outcomes that are produced by merit are far more defensible than inequalities produced by favoritism or discrimination. And when we turn from the NBA to America's elite colleges and universities, we discover a similar result: Ethnic inequalities are the result not of biased selection procedures but of unequal performance on the part of different groups.

Affirmative action has traditionally been defended as necessary to fight discrimination. But has anyone demonstrated that the blacks and Hispanics preferentially admitted to the best universities were in fact victims of discrimination? Has anyone uncovered at Berkeley or Princeton bigoted admissions officers seeking to exclude minorities? And is there any evidence that the white and Asian-American students refused admission were discriminating against anyone? The answer to these questions is no, no, and no. No one has even alleged unfairness of this sort.

There was, at one time, an attempt by advocates of affirmative action to argue for racial and cultural bias in the SAT and other standardized tests that most elite universities require their applicants to take. This argument, however, has collapsed in recent years, and even Bowen and Bok admit that it is no longer possible to claim that the SAT discriminates against blacks or other minorities. In *The Shape of the River*, they try to confuse the issue by insisting on the obvious point that standardized-test scores "do not predict who will be a civic leader or how satisfied individuals will be with their college experience or with life." But they are at last forced to the chagrined confession: "Almost all colleges have found that when they compare black and white undergraduates who enter with the same SAT scores, blacks earn *lower* grades than whites, not just in their first year but throughout their college careers.... Tests like the SAT do not suffer from prediction bias."

This is not to say that the test describes genetic or biological ability. It merely measures differences in academic preparation, and Bowen and Bok acknowledge that the low black enrollments at elite universities that affirmative-action policies seek to remedy are primarily produced by "continuing disparities in pre-collegiate academic achievements of black and white students." On those measures of merit that selective colleges use to decide who gets in, not all groups perform equally.

For the civil-rights leadership, these results have come as a nasty surprise. The movement led by Martin Luther King Jr. originally placed itself on the side of merit in opposition to racial nepotism. If laws and public policies were allowed to judge solely on the basis of individual merit, King repeatedly promised, we would see social rewards in America widely dispersed among groups.

In the generation since King's death, it is this premise—that equality of rights for individuals would invariably produce equality of results for groups—that has proved false. The dismaying truth is that even merit sometimes produces ethnic inequality. Consequently it is hardly surprising that some who manned the barricades alongside King now insist that merit is the new guise in which the old racism manifests itself. It is now fashionable for advocates of affirmative action to place the term "merit" in quotation marks or to speak sarcastically of "so-called merit." Their main objection is that merit selection is not producing the outcomes they desire, and their enthusiasm for affirmative action can be attributed to their rediscovery of the blessings of nepotism.

* * *

Meanwhile, behind the scenes, there has been underway a fascinating debate about why merit produces such ethnic inequality. Two views have dominated the debate. The first is the "bell-curve" position, put forward most publicly in recent years by Charles Murray and Richard Herrnstein, which implies that there may be natural or biological differences between groups that would account for their unequal performance on indices of merit. The second is the traditionally liberal position, which insists that when group differences in academic achievement and economic performance exist, they have been artificially created by social deprivation and racism.

* * *

These two views have functioned like a see-saw: When one goes up, the other goes down. In the early part of this century, most people took for granted that there were natural differences between the races and that these accounted for why some groups were advanced and others relatively backward. This view was fiercely attacked in the middle of this century by liberals who argued that it was unreasonable and unconscionable to contend that natural deficiencies were the cause of blacks' doing poorly when blacks were subjected to so much legal and systematic discrimination, especially in the South.

The liberal view was entirely plausible, which is why the biological explanation was largely discarded. But the liberal view has begun to collapse in recent years, precisely as it proved unable to explain the world that resulted from its triumph. Consider a single statistic: Data from the college board show that, year after year, whites and Asian Americans who come from families earning less than $15,000 a year score higher on both the verbal and math sections of the SAT than African Americans from families earning more than $60,000 a year.

This stunning statistic, whose accuracy is unquestioned by anyone in this debate, is sufficient by itself to destroy the argument of those who have repeated for years that the SAT is a mere calibration of socioeconomic privilege. But it is equally devastating to the liberal attribution of black disadvantage to racial discrimination. Even if discrimination were widespread, how could it operate in such a way as to make poor whites and Asians perform better on math tests than upper-middle-class blacks?

On this question, most advocates of affirmative action do not know how to react. Some simply refuse to discuss the implications of the evidence. Others, like Nathan Glazer, seem to adopt a private conviction of the veracity of the bell-curve explanation. A few years ago, in a review of Murray and Herrnstein in the *New Republic*, Glazer seemed to accept the existence of intrinsic differences in intelligence between the races—while objecting to any mention of the fact in public.

In more recent articles, Glazer has reversed his longtime criticism of affirmative action and said he is now willing to bend admissions standards to avoid the distressing outcome of very few blacks in the best universities. Glazer's second thoughts about affirmative action point to something often missed in such debates, for if the bell-curve thesis is correct, then it in fact constitutes the strongest possible argument *in favor* of affirmative action.

If there are natural differences in ability between ethnic groups that cannot easily be eradicated, then it makes sense for those of us who do not want America to be a racial caste society to support preferential programs that would prevent the consolidation of enduring group hierarchies. Forced, by the collapse of the liberal view, to accept natural inequality, Glazer unsurprisingly now treats blacks as a handicapped population that cannot be expected to compete against other groups.

* * *

But there is, in fact, a third possible view of racial inequality—a view advanced by Thomas Sowell and me and others who find profoundly condescending and degrading the notion that blacks require a "special Olympics" of their own. Basically, we contend that there are cultural or behavioral differences between groups. These differences can be observed in everyday life, measured by the techniques of social science, and directly correlated with academic achievement and economic performance. Even *The Black-White Test Score Gap*, a recent study by two noted liberal scholars, Christopher Jencks and Meredith Phillips, proves upon careful reading to implicitly endorse this cultural view. Jencks and Phillips make all the appropriate genuflections to racial pieties, but they are courageously seeking to make the cultural argument more palatable to liberals.

A few years ago, a Stanford sociologist named Sanford Dornbusch was puzzled at claims that Asian Americans do especially well in math because of some presumed genetic advantage in visual and spatial ability. Dornbusch did a comparative study of white, black, Hispanic, and Asian-American students in San Francisco and concluded that there was a far more obvious reason for the superior performance of Asian Americans: They study harder. Asian Americans simply spend a lot more time doing homework than their peers.

* * *

Of course, this sort of finding leaves unanswered the question of why they study harder. The causes are no doubt complex, but one important factor seems to be family structure. It is obvious that a two-parent family has more time and resources to invest in disciplining children and supervising their study than does a single-parent family. For Asian Americans, the illegitimacy rate in this country is approximately 2 percent. For African Americans, it's nearly 70 percent.

Such a huge difference cannot easily be corrected. Indeed, in a free society, public policy is limited in its ability to transform behavior in the private sphere. Still, while not reverting to the discredited liberal position, the cultural view of racial inequality is at least more hopeful than the bell-curve acceptance of ineradicable difference: We cannot change our genes, but we can change our behavior.

One thing is clear: Racism is no longer the main problem facing blacks or any other group in America today. Even if racism were to disappear overnight, this would do nothing to improve black test scores, increase black entrepreneurship, strengthen black families, or reduce black-on-black crime. These problems have taken on a cultural existence of their own and need to be confronted in their own terms.

The difficult task is rebuilding the cultural capital of the black community, and the role of black scholars, black teachers, black parents, and black entrepreneurs is crucial. The rest of us cannot be leaders, but we can be cheerleaders. Rather than try to rig the numbers to make everyone feel better, we are better off focusing our collective attention on developing the skills of young African Americans at an early age so that they can compete effectively with others in later life.

* * *

So why doesn't this obvious solution win broad support? In his new book, *A Dream Deferred: The Second Betrayal of Black Free-dom in America*, Shelby Steele argues that affirmative action is popular with black and white elites because it serves the purposes of both groups. White elites get to feel morally superior, thus recovering the ethical high ground lost by the sins of the past, and black elites enjoy unearned privileges that they understandably convince themselves they fully deserve. (In *The Shape of the River*, Bowen and Bok devote several chapters to proving the obvious point that blacks who go to Ivy League schools derive financial benefits in later life as a result and are generally satisfied with attending Yale instead of a community college.)

Steele's book bristles with the psychological insights that are his distinctive contribution to the race debate. White liberals, Steele argues (and he might as well be speaking directly of Bowen and Bok), are quite willing to assume general blame for a racist society causing black failures—so long as it's the careers of other people, all the qualified Asian-American and white students rejected from Harvard and Princeton, that are sacrificed in order to confer benefits on blacks and win for liberals recognition as the white saviors of the black race.

* * *

What Steele is doing—and it has drawn considerable criticism from reviewers—is something that advocates of affirmative action have always done: questioning the motives of the other side. For years, conservatives have treated liberals as well meaning in their goals though mistaken in their means. And during that same period, liberals have treated conservatives as greedy, uncaring racists. By asking advocates of preferences what's in it for them, Steele unmasks the self-interest that frequently hides behind the banners of equality, diversity, and social uplift.

Steele's main objective is to show that neither the black nor the white elites have an interest in asking fundamental questions: Isn't color-blindness the only principle that is consistent with the fundamental principles of American society? Isn't equality of rights under the law the only workable basis for a multiracial society? Is the black community well served in the long term by a public policy that treats them as an inferior people incapable of competing with others?

Advocates of racial preferences "offer whites moral absolution for their sins and blacks concrete benefits that are hard to turn down," Steele observed to me a few weeks before the recent electoral victory of a referendum abolishing affirmative action in Washington state. "I think we are going to lose because our side has only one thing to offer, and that is moral principle." I ruefully agreed that the scales were tipped in precisely that way. But the astonishing triumph of the referendum in Washington by a comfortable majority—like the triumph of a similar measure two years ago in California—shows that we should not underestimate the power of moral principle in American politics.

When the issue is posed in the basic vocabulary of right and wrong—a lexicon that is utterly incomprehensible to Bowen and Bok—the tortured rationalizations of affirmative-action advocates collapse and the common-sense moral instinct of the American people tends to prevail. There is no cause for conservatives to lose their nerve. The election in 2000 could be the moment when color-blindness is at last the issue on the ballot in many states and at the center of the Republican party's agenda.

POSTSCRIPT

Should Race Be a Consideration in College Admissions?

In several states over the past four years, voters and courts have decided to reject preferences based on race for college admissions (as well as other areas involving recruitment). While Americans are supportive of "fair play" and of compensating victims of past injustice, they have consistently opposed a quota system based on race in hiring or college admissions. For some ethnic and religious minorities, opposition is partially based on their groups' members sometimes being denied college admission because of preferential treatment programs for Blacks and partially on the fact that in the past, quotas were used to keep many of them *out* of elite universities. For instance, Harvard University and other colleges apparently limited the number of Jews they would allow to attend any given class.

Yet there has always been some form of a preferential quota system in operation. The children of alumni, star athletes, wealthy donors, and others have traditionally been favorites for admission. There have also been subtle biases in favor of wealthy, male, Protestant students for generations, as well as prohibitions against the admission of Blacks and others (e.g., females in law or medical schools). Has the system ever been fair in this matter?

Neither Bowen and Bok nor D'Souza address the issue that research seems to show that the best predictor of college success is high school curriculum quality. The more academic and better the curriculum is, the greater likelihood of college success. One question that has been asked is, would the 28 elite schools studied by Bowen and Bok be willing to send their faculties on a grand scale into inner-city schools to strengthen the schools' curricula? Also, would they be willing to triple or even just double their class sizes in order to admit two or three times more academically needy racial minority students?

Another concern that applies to many related ethnic-racial minority debates is that of class. Some ask, shouldn't preferences, if they are to exist at all, be based on wealth and income, not race? On many university campuses there is a high number of poor whites and poor Asians, both in terms of percentages and gross numbers. Indeed, critics such as D'Souza maintain that many preferentially admitted Black students are of solid middle-class or higher backgrounds. Should the Blacks be given special consideration? Doesn't this put middle-class whites and others in direct conflict over scarce educational resources with the Black middle class?

Another related issue is, what good have the impressive accomplishments of many of the Black alumni from the elite schools been for the majority of Blacks who are poor? How much of these Black physicians' and lawyers' time is spent, professionally or socially, with needy Blacks and other poor people? Does Bowen and Bok's research necessarily show anything other than that graduates of elite schools, white or Black, are successful and generally do all the ritualistic things that are expected of them (including earning huge salaries) while leaving the system intact?

At another level, are D'Souza's insinuations that liberals who support affirmative action are self-serving hypocrites fair? If nothing else, haven't preferences demonstrated at least symbolically that many Americans, including members of the judicial system, are making a good-faith effort to better minorities' social status? Finally, although initial studies showed immediate sharp declines in minority enrollments in top universities in states banning admission based on race, subsequent research reveals that less prestigious but otherwise excellent schools are "catching" many of these students. Doesn't it make more sense for racial minorities to attend colleges for which, based on traditional standards, they technically qualify?

For their original research, see Bowen and Bok's *The Shape of the River: Long-Term Consequences of Considering Race in College and University Admissions* (Princeton University Press, 1998). A good overview of the debate arising out of California's ban of race consideration for public university applicants is "What Has Happened to Faculty Diversity in California?" by A. Schneider, *Chronicle of Higher Education* (November 20, 1998). Reflecting America's confusion over the issue is "Racial Preferences Are Outdated," by W. Terry, *Parade Magazine* (May 31, 1998) and "Affirmative Action Debate Rages On," *Parade Magazine* (April 4, 1999). A look at the defense of using preferences to maintain campus diversity is "Back to Square One," by Adam Cohen, *Time* (April 20, 1998). For an interesting reversal of himself, see Nathan Glazer's "In Defense of Preference," *The New Republic* (April 6, 1998). Glazer's sometimes rival has a different argument in "How to Mend Affirmative Action," by Glenn Loury, *The Public Interest* (Spring 1997). A different perspective is "Beyond Quotas," by Roger Clegg, *Policy Review* (May/June 1998).

Among those who partially defend D'Souza's position are M. Rees, "Still Counting by Race," *The Weekly Standard* (April 27, 1998); R. Worth, "Beyond Racial Preferences," *The Washington Monthly* (March 1998); and Stephan Thernstrom and Abigail Thernstrom, *America in Black and White: One Nation, Indivisible* (Simon & Schuster, 1997). For a broader, more liberal view, see Farai Chideya's *The Color of Our Future* (William Morrow, 1999). Raymond W. Mack gives a succinct overview in "Whose Affirmative Action?" *Society* (March/April 1996). A discussion of what many feel is an unfortunate effort to censure ideas is "Black Conservatives Shunned as Heretics," *The Washington Post* (August 1, 1998). The January–February 1997 issue of *Academe* debates the controversy in several articles. Finally, a sad discussion of a Black lawyer who thought he had it all only to be dashed in midcareer by racism is *The Good Black* by Paul M. Barrett (Dutton, 1999).

ISSUE 18

Should Sovereignty for American Indians Be Increased?

YES: Joseph P. Kalt and Jonathan B. Taylor, from "Means-Testing Indian Governments: Taxing What Works," *Indian Country Today* (September 22–29, 1997)

NO: Hendrik Mills, from "A Deadly Mix," *The American Enterprise* (November/December 1998)

ISSUE SUMMARY

YES: Joseph P. Kalt, codirector of the Harvard Project on American Indian Economic Development, and Jonathan B. Taylor, director of Indian Projects at the Economics Resource Group, Inc., in Cambridge, Massachusetts, argue that increasing sovereignty (freedom from external control) will give Native Americans the ability to help themselves.

NO: Hendrik Mills, a writer and teacher, maintains that since the 1960s, Indian militants and their allies have received increased federal monies to fight poverty and recognition of their increasing sovereignty but that mismanagement botched these opportunities while legitimizing absurd victim excuses based on a mythical heroic past.

Traditionally, members of dominant groups often disdained those who were different because of a lack of communication or understanding, which often led to fear and even hate. Others disdained those who had different language, appearance, religion, customs, and other distinguishing characteristics for more pragmatic reasons: members of other groups could be paid lower salaries, locked into physically difficult labor, cheated in business deals without legal recourse, or even enslaved. Throughout history (especially in the United States) some people have made large amounts of money by creating and maintaining the disadvantaged status of gender, racial, and ethnic minorities.

As relatively powerless people started challenging the status quo by protesting, filing legal briefs, and working harder than others, societal responses were mixed. Often responses were extremely harsh. Many minority group members were arrested or killed, forced into segregated areas, or, in the case of Native Americans, placed on reservations, after which treaties were continuously broken and the conditions in which they had to live grew increasingly worse.

Since the 1960s ethnic, racial, and gender minorities have experienced more social, economic, media, political, and especially legal recognition and support than at any other time in U.S. history. Predictably, those in majority positions have reacted (and continue to react in many cases) quite angrily. Some majority members protested and resisted however they could, including engaging in violence. However, because of generally enforced civil rights laws, the changing mood of the country, and the growing power and self-confidence of minority groups, openly hostile resistence is now far more difficult. Others objected to these changes simply because they were novel or perceived as moving too fast. Still others who opposed minority enhancements operated from purely self-serving agendas. Some benefited economically from the subordination of minorities. Many political leaders feared increased minority power would put them into competition for minority votes or against minority candidates.

The reasons for supporting increased minority rights are probably equally variable. Minorities themselves, once they understood the issues, generally supported the changes, often vigorously. Many members of the majority group supported the changes simply because they were felt to be right and deserving. Formally educated citizens, college professors, and students, especially in the social sciences, reflecting an image of themselves as "sensitive" or "decent," would usually support such changes, at times with fervor.

Many other supporters' motivations were considerably more complex. According to conservative critics, opportunists saw that there was money to be made in helping minorities and that elections could be won by playing the ethnic or racial minority card. Many formerly oppressed opportunists saw the chance and grabbed it—clearly living *off* other Blacks, Hispanics, or Native Americans, not *for* them—by huckstering their group's claimed needs to enrich themselves. Apparently, intellectuals and even entire academic programs are not immune to such temptations. Some critics, for instance, contend that formerly moribund disciplines within the social sciences and humanities are now achieving a renaissance by catering to minority-centered demands, justifiable or not, for ethnic, racial, religious, and gender-related programs and curricula.

As you review the following selections, consider some of the broader issues. Bear in mind that Joseph P. Kalt and Jonathan B. Taylor see sovereignty as a good that is threatened not only by the means test (required justification for awarding federal monies to tribal governments, with the potential for denying needed funds to councils that are doing well) but by general encroachments of the federal government in violation of agreements. Also decide if Hendrik Mills's attacks on sovereignty and most other aspects of Native American reservation life are fair.

YES

Joseph P. Kalt and
Jonathan B. Taylor

MEANS-TESTING INDIAN GOVERNMENTS: TAXING WHAT WORKS

Led by Sen. Slade Gorton (R.-Washington), Chair of the Senate Interior appropriations subcommittee, a push is on in Congress that would strike a major blow at the only policy that has produced progress in this century on the perennial problem of poverty in Indian Country: tribal self-governance and the accompanying government-to-government relationship between tribes and the Federal Government. Fueled by the publicity that surrounds the success with gaming of a handful of the country's 500+ tribes, Gorton's proposal would means-test federal funding of tribal governmental functions.

The Federal Government does not have a record to be proud of when it comes to the problems of economic and social despair on American Indian reservations. For almost two centuries, federal policy essentially treated Indians on reservations as dependents, with the federal authorities and bureaucracies calling the shots on everything from where kids went to school to when and where a tree could be harvested.

The results? By 1990, American Indians on reservations were the poorest minority in America. Unemployment across all reservations averaged close to 50%, pushing to 85% in some places. On most reservations, what little employment did exist was only in the public service sector of schools, law enforcement, health care, and the like. Under these conditions, it is not surprising that almost every indicator of social distress—poverty rates, suicide rates, death by disease and accident, teenage pregnancy, and so on—placed reservation Indians practically off the charts when compared to other American citizens. The advent of gaming on reservations has not appreciably altered this scene. The number of tribes hitting big-time success in gaming is in single digits.

The sorry history of U.S. Indian policy is well enough known that it has become a folklore founded in fact. The folklore is used by non-Indian Americans who are into guilt to justify paternalistic policies that haven't worked. What is not widely understood is that, beginning with first steps in the Nixon and Ford Administrations, federal policy started a slow turn toward a new direction: self-governance.

Over the last two decades, Indians on reservations have fought to re-establish long-lost powers of self-rule. Governed by constitutions, tribes now have powers akin to those of the U.S. states, including powers to make rules and regulations, to wield law enforcement and judicial authority, to tax, and—like states—to run gaming operations.

Even prior to the gaming that has attracted so much attention in the 1990s, the evidence became clear that self-rule is the indispensable first ingredient needed to turn reservation economies around. Indeed, it was under the federal policy of self-determination that took hold in the 1970s and 80s that certain tribes began to break out of the pack of impoverishment. They did this by escaping the stranglehold of federal development planning and creating the investment environment needed to develop export-based economies.

The Mississippi Choctaw, for example, built the Hong Kong of Indian Country on the strength of manufacturing industries—from auto parts to greeting cards —that now make the Tribe among the very largest employers in Mississippi. Not only are tribal members working, but more than 6,000 white and black workers commute to work at the Tribe's businesses. The Mississippi Choctaw run their own affairs—their own schools, their own laws, their own courts, their own business policies. The result is an environment that the capital markets trust.

The Salish and Kootenai Tribes of the Flathead Reservation in Montana have also competed successfully in the market to attract investors. They've done it by creating a rule of law, including an intertribal supreme court, that should be the envy of every emerging democracy in the world. The result is a thriving private sector economy based in agriculture, recreation, and tourism. The Flathead reservation was off and running years prior to the arrival of gaming as an option.

At the Fort Apache reservation in Arizona, the White Mountain Apaches' first-class ski resort, multi-million dollar saw mill, and premier outdoor recreation businesses are the economic anchors for thousands of Apache and non-Indian jobs. When these were threatened by federal intrusion on endangered species grounds, the never-retreat Apaches built their own environmental management systems. Under a model government-to-government agreement, these have enabled the Tribe to displace federal managers.

The stories of economic success in Indian Country share at least one common ingredient. In case after case, the defining trait of the successful tribes is their aggressive assertion of their rights to govern themselves. In particular, they are marked by de jure and de facto replacement of outside federal decision makers with their own governmental capacity. There is not a single case of sustained economic development in Indian Country where the tribe is not in the decision-making driver's seat. As the world has learned from Central and Eastern Europe, outside authorities are really lousy at planning and developing an economy of people who want to govern themselves.

How ironic it is that federal policy may now be directed at handicapping effective and stable tribal governments. If one cannot distinguish between individual American Indians and American Indian tribal governments, or if one likes to imagine that all American Indians are junior Donald Trumps rolling in income from gaming operations, the Gorton means-testing proposal might sound sensible. In fact, however, it amounts to nothing more than a tax on tribal governments which are successful in pursuing the interests of their citizens.

As a matter of federal policy, a state government that enters the gambling industry with a high-stakes lottery is not means-tested when it comes to allocating basic federal funding for governmental services. To date, tribal governments have been similarly treated. In both cases, policy has recognized that, to the extent that a state or tribe is carrying out basic governmental functions such as law enforcement or environmental protection, federal policy ought to encourage these governments to be effective. This has been a key component of the government-to-government essence of U.S. federalism.

Consider the illustration provided by one state's lottery—California. Through its gaming enterprise, the government of California takes in net income on the order of three-quarters of a billion dollars per year. All of the net proceeds are earmarked for education, yet federal dollars allocated to the State Government are not means-tested, even for the relatively rich and lottery-rich State of California. Instead, if California's investment in education pays off in a healthier economy and higher incomes, the Federal Government stands ready with its income taxes to catch its share of the returns.

American Indians stand in the same relationship to the Federal Government. To the extent that monies from tribal governments' gaming or other operations show up as income to individuals and businesses, such income is subject to federal income taxes. Moreover, individual Indian citizens are subject to means testing, just as are other Americans, when it comes to food stamps, housing subsidies, and other nationwide welfare programs.

Means-testing tribal governments makes no sense at all if one is concerned about the well-being of American Indian people. In and of itself, a tribal government's (or a state government's) revenues from gaming, natural resource leases, or any other set of operations provide no assurances as to how well its citizens are living. High revenues in a jurisdiction with a very low standard of living may help, but can't be said to cure, centuries of social and economic deprivation. In fact, it is not surprising that, even on reservations with relatively strong economies, the social legacy of deprivation is proving hard to erase.

To date, the government-to-government basis for federal funding of tribal (and state) governmental functions has provided positive incentives for reinvestment of tribal government income, since passing earnings out as cash subjects them to taxation. The Gorton proposal would replace this with disincentives to effective and efficient governmental operations. A tribe might as well go easy on holding down costs since higher net incomes would subject the tribe to Gorton's success tax. Of course, this is precisely the kind of effect of federal Indian policy that tribes have been bucking in the era of self-governance. By penalizing successful and effective tribal government, the Gorton proposal would be a sad step backward for the only thing that has worked in Indian Country—letting people govern themselves.

NO

Hendrik Mills

A DEADLY MIX

An article of faith among Indian activists and their liberal allies today is that any problems experienced by Native Americans are caused by their unjust, rapacious treatment at the hands of whites, including a continuing "cultural genocide." This victimology is reinforced by many romantic beliefs about Indians, including the conviction that they are less materialistic, more spiritual, more in tune with the earth and inclined to care for the environment than other Americans. These sorts of beliefs, widespread in areas distant from Indian country, have served to justify a great web of public programs for Native Americans.

Unfortunately, these seemingly generous programs have resulted, to a shocking degree, in social disintegration on the nation's reservations. That's because they are based on a false understanding of what the real obstacles to Indian progress and happiness are today.

Never mind "cultural genocide." A much more straightforward picture of the kinds of problems plaguing Native Americans today can be seen in a recent, sadly typical story from the Great Falls, Montana *Tribune*. It reported that a four-year-old Indian girl had been struck and killed by an auto at the intersection of Cheyenne Avenue and Dull Knife Drive in the town of Lame Deer. Speed was not a factor, and the 49-year-old woman driving the car was not to blame.

The first problem was that the four-year-old was not being escorted by any parent or other adult. She crossed the street alone while returning from a Boys & Girls Club she had visited with her brother and sister.

The second problem was that three broken street lights blackened the intersection. "It was dark," Highway Patrol officer Tim Lytle said. "Had the lights been working, it would have made a big difference." Area residents told Lytle that vandalism to street lights in the area was a recurring problem. The culprits? Indian juveniles.

The simple elements of this tragic story—crime, and a lack of parental supervision and involvement with children, resulting in premature death— crisply capture conditions in many Native American communities today. I know because my family and I have lived for five years on and near the

From Hendrik Mills, "A Deadly Mix," *The American Enterprise* (November/December 1998). Copyright © 1998 by *The American Enterprise*. Reprinted by permission of *The American Enterprise*, a Washington-based magazine of politics, business, and culture.

Fort Belknap Indian Reservation in north central Montana. I haven't always been skeptical of the "Indian-pride" point of view. In October 1991, I was one of those protesting against Columbus Day at a rally in downtown Denver sponsored by the American Indian Movement. When my wife and I initially decided to move to, and work in, Indian country, it was because we sympathized with Native American claims.

Initially, it was the goings-on in the schools here in Harlem, Montana, that forced me to re-examine my beliefs. Until the 1970s, white and Indian children had peaceably attended these schools together and had received solid educations. But in recent years, the local schools have been plagued by indiscipline, violence, and drastically lowered academic standards. Only a few local white parents still have their children in Harlem public schools. Instead they drive them daily to neighboring towns where they attend public schools in which discipline and the work ethic are still intact. As I began to investigate, I met former teachers who told horror stories of Indian parents coming into the school to curse at teachers because their child had been assigned "too much homework" or had been disciplined for fighting in school. Parents told me of racially motivated playground and street violence against their children.

How could this have happened? It was in answering that question that my radical-leftist illusions began to die. I queried many residents of our area, both old-timers and young, Indian and non-Indian, on and off the reservation. I read widely, including *Indian Country Today*, a national Indian newspaper, and other writings by Indians, as well as many other books and journals. And I discovered it was my own generation that, in the 1960s, set in motion the processes of racial separatism and social and economic change that ultimately resulted in the chaotic schools and other social failures in Indian country.

The main demands of Indian militants and their political allies since the 1960s have been: (1) enlargement of the reservations; (2) federal dollars to remedy unemployment and poverty on the reservations; (3) recognition of Native American sovereignty (the idea that each reservation is a self-determining nation); and (4) official support for an Indian culture separate from the rest of America. Only the first demand has been largely denied.

The request for federal funds has been granted in spades. It is widely believed that Native Americans have been forgotten and impoverished by the actions—or inaction—of mainstream America. In fact, present-day Indians are surrounded by a cradle-to-grave system of benefits enjoyed by no other racial group in America. The U.S. Indian Health Service provides free health care with no co-payment whatever to all Indians living on or near reservations —everything from filling cavities, to intensive care after a heart attack, to reconstructing facial contours injured in a barroom brawl. Through the Department of Education's "impact aid" program, school districts with a large number of Indians receive millions of dollars of extra annual aid, to cover everything from routine operating expenses to the running of bilingual Indian-language programs. The "impact aid" program doesn't just fill the coffers of the school district, it also mandates that the local tribal council must agree to the school district's budget in order for the federal money to be granted.

Tribal colleges, set up on almost every reservation, provide two-year community college curricula right where the students are. Scholarships and living stipends are the rule, not the exception, for Indian students attending tribal colleges.

"Treaty money"—a lump sum often exceeding $10,000—is given to Indian youngsters of many tribes when they reach the age of majority. This is justified as a settlement of various historic claims that activists, beginning in the 1960s, asserted against the U.S. government.

Indians who live and work on reservations here in Montana are also exempt from many kinds of taxes: new-vehicle licensing taxes, county taxes, state income tax, and in some cases federal income tax. Gambling laws that ban or restrict casinos off-reservation often do not apply on the reservation, which is why there has been an explosive growth of Indian gambling casinos.

Head Start is a fixture on all reservations, providing federally funded child care for every Indian child, as well as an array of health care, feeding, and educational services. Welfare is freely available; the Montana state welfare authorities recently announced that all Indians on reservations in Montana would fall under the "hardship exemption" to the recent welfare reform law, thereby exempting them from the law's work requirements.

Many other programs likewise transfer cash, goods, and services to Native Americans. Back when many of the government Indian programs were begun in the 1970s, there was a great increase in the number of self-described Native Americans; so the U.S. government instituted the "$1/8$ rule" to determine who would be eligible for federal benefits. This rule states that a person who possesses at least "$1/8$ blood quantum" is an Indian, and Indians are issued wallet-sized cards specifying their blood quantum, e.g. "$3/16$ Assiniboin, $5/32$ Gros Ventre." Nowhere, therefore, is the linkage between race and government payoffs more mechanistic, strained, and ultimately harmful than it is for Indians.

Pitiful stories of Indian poverty are often told to support continued expansion of government programs. But lack of money is not the main component of Indian poverty today. The owner of a taxi service in Havre told me and my co-workers one day that he gets a lot of business from Indians on the first day of every month, when welfare checks arrive. Someone asked, "Are they going to the grocery store to buy food?" He replied, "No, most want rides to the casinos."

At the local dump, one can regularly see discarded food thrown away by people who are supposedly in dire need. Fruit juice, canned fruit, macaroni, soup, rice, and beans are sometimes thrown by the case into municipal dumpsters by Indians who are allegedly so poor their children must be given extra tax-subsidized meals at school. The source of these discarded groceries is a U.S. Department of Agriculture "surplus" food distribution program that operates on reservations. Improvidence of this sort makes it impossible to solve Indians' problems by transferring resources to them.

Since the 1960s, government has taken on many of the traditional functions of parents on the Indian reservations. Many mothers and fathers have willingly ceded responsibility for their offspring to this rich uncle. An Indian Health Service dentist I know tells of parents bringing in pre-school children with their entire set of teeth rotted at the gumline. When the dentist asks them whether they have followed the advice given in every clinic not to leave a baby alone in a crib with a bottle of milk or soda pop propped before him, the parents sometimes respond, "You fix his teeth; that's your job!" Books and even toys are scarce in most reservation homes, but junk food and television are omnipresent.

Thanks to the progressive disintegration of the Indian family, parental negligence makes some children *de facto* orphans. An elementary school principal who works in Indian country told me about a little girl who came to school on a Monday morning with a staple embedded in her hand and an infection already begun. He had the staple removed and the infection treated by the Indian Health Service. He found out it had been in her hand all weekend, and no caring adult had been present in her home.

In the worst homes, Indian children are growing up without ever being socialized to acceptable norms. These are the promiscuous teenagers who produce fetal-alcohol afflicted babies. These are the young men who steal insulin syringes from their grandparents... so they can shoot up the drug "crank." Crime, including murder and assault, is a serious problem in Indian country. While gang activity is growing, crime rates on reservations and nearby towns are typically two or three times as high as in non-Indian areas.

In many Indian extended families today, several serious older people are the only remaining source of cohesion. Grandmothers raising babies are now a common sight in Indian country, as fathers and mothers go to jail, wallow in crank or alcohol, and forget about their offspring.

Ironically, the many orphans and near-orphans in Indian country cannot be adopted by non-Indian families—due to a federal law intended to protect Indian children from cultural assimilation. This disastrous provision, the Indian Child Welfare Act, should be scrapped as soon as possible, so that the underage victims of rampant social decay can find stable and loving homes elsewhere.

There are bright spots. Responsible parenting seems to run in certain families on the Indian reservations. The Indians who operate working ranches or farms often seem to turn out successful children. In those households, children are given responsibilities and hard work from an early age, and they learn useful, satisfying skills. But the consensus in Indian country is that large numbers of Indian parents have abdicated their parenting responsibilities...

In 1996 our local tribal council flexed its sovereign muscles and imposed the so-called Tribal Employment Rights Organization Tax, a per-capita levy on every non-Indian working, even temporarily, on the reservation. A Montana road crew, repairing the main paved artery through the reservation at no cost to the reservation, was kept from working because they employed some non-Indians, and the state balked at paying for the privilege of repairing the reservation's road. The telephone company was held up in its attempt to install new phone lines to Indian residences because its linemen were non-Indian. Trucks delivering goods to Indian-owned stores on the reservation refused to pay the tax, and so delivery to these stores was delayed. I could tell many other similar stories of the accomplishments of the sovereign tribal governments.

Aside from matters of efficiency, there remains an important question of principle in the exercise of Indian sovereignty. Can any group be considered "sovereign" when most of its funding comes from an outside source? When sewers or schools or water plants are built in the rest of America, they are funded by local property tax levies. But there is relatively little economic production carried out by Indians on reservations, thus scarcely any local tax base. The main strategy for raising money followed by the tribal councils and the reservation school districts is simply to lobby the federal government. Many Indians have become quite adept at this, and the public opinion campaigns that go with it, skillfully wielding "victim" stories to maximize external public funding of their "sovereignty."

The proliferation of easy, make-work jobs reserved for tribal members has eroded the Indian work ethic. A young Indian man once came into the garage where I used to work as a mechanic.... Since he seemed bright and curious, I encouraged him to go to the vocational school.... His reply: "No man, that's too much work." I saw him a few months later driving a car with U.S. government plates, "working" for the federal Indian bureaucracy.

One elderly Montana businessman I know notes that many Indians now living on reservations in states of semi-unemployment once worked in skilled trades in places like Seattle's shipyards or Los Angeles's factories. It wasn't until the federal government began building subsidized housing and offering other benefits on reservations in the 1960s that many of these productive citizens came "home" to idle. The result has been the creation of a largely unproductive pop-ulation intensely dependent on government favors.

A number of Indian parents do not work at all. Many others hold jobs whose salary would be impossible to attain, given their level of education and productivity, in the competitive world away from the reservation. Both of these examples discourage schoolchildren from working hard in school. Combine these disincentives with the breakdown of Indian parenting and with the prevailing notion on reservations that "America owes us," and one begins to see that the misbehavior of so many Indian children is almost a logical outcome.

I want to note that many Indians have "made it" in America. They have jobs, or are employers themselves. In our area of northern Montana, the largest wholesale distributor of gasoline and diesel is owned by an Indian named Ezzie Ereaux. The area's main tourist resort is owned and operated by an Indian family. One of the biggest ranchers and businessmen in our county is an Indian; his son holds an M.D. Another Indian family includes two M.D.s, a retired hospital administrator, and a hospital nursing supervisor. A local Indian girl recently won a full scholarship (not specifically targeted to Indians) to Montana State University. I hear from a fellow teacher that the greatest math talent in the area is a teenaged Indian boy.

Off our local reservation, many Indians work at jobs just like any other American. Indians who show the requisite reliability, punctuality, and willingness to work have no trouble finding and keeping positions. Banks, groceries, convenience stores, and ranches often have Indian employees. Indian-run ranches and farms are common on the reservation, although much of the economic activity consists of white farmers growing crops or raising cattle on land leased from Indian landowners.

Many Indians are successful, for the same reasons other Americans succeed: They have a work ethic, literacy, frugality and business acumen, and a command of standard English that allows them to play in the same league as other Americans. The sad thing is that many more Indians could be succeeding with them, instead of drowning in pathology—if only they were treated more like other citizens, and less like a race apart.

POSTSCRIPT

Should Sovereignty for American Indians Be Increased?

There are many striking things about Native Americans as an ethnic minority. First, it is the only ethnic group in the United States that was subordinated to the rest by military conquest. Second, it is the only minority group that has been permanently placed on reservations. Third, Native Americans are unique in that they have been awarded sovereignty, ostensibly to encourage them to achieve self-help and autonomy. Fourth, in spite of the setbacks experienced by other minority groups, no group has the extensively documented lies, oppression, exploitation, and sheer robbery by the federal government itself that American Indians do. For example, their land holdings have been reduced from 138 million acres to about 48 million acres. Some 20 million acres of the remaining land (about 42 percent) is arid and agriculturally worthless. Moreover, when it was discovered that large amounts of oil, copper, and other natural resources were under the reservations, additional exploitation resulted; tribes now receive less than 20 percent of the profits from their resources. In addition to their poverty, disease, medical, and educational problems, Native Americans are subjected to several thousand more laws than the rest of the U.S. population.

The recent successes by a small number of tribes in obtaining gambling and betting rights clouds the issue even more. On one hand, such permission is evidence that a few tribes have achieved more sovereignty. On the other hand, this has generated tremendous divisiveness both among members of the same reservations and between tribes.

Many books and articles continue to be published about sovereignty and other pressing controversies related to American Indians. See, for instance, "Keeping Our Word to the Indians," by Ben Nighthorse Campbell and John McCain, *The Washington Post* (September 10, 1997). Also see M. James, "Federal Indian Identification Policy: A Usurpation of Indigenous Sovereignty in North America," in Christopher G. Ellison and W. Allen Martin, eds., *Race and Ethnic Relations in the United States* (Roxbury, 1999). One overview of this problem that reflects Kalt and Taylor's position is *The Earth Shall Weep: A History of Native America* by James Wilson (Grove/Atlantic, 1999). Works reflecting a historical perspective include John Sugden's *Tecumseh: A Life* (Henry Holt, 1999) and Viola J. Herman's *It Is a Good Day to Die* (Random House, 1998).

In addition to the many magazines and journals that deal exclusively with Native American affairs, articles in *American Archaeology* often address the problem of burial mounds, artifacts, and other aspects of the Native American past being destroyed.

ISSUE 19

Should Jury Nullification Be Used to Reduce Ethnic and Racial Inequities?

YES: Paul Butler, from "Racially Based Jury Nullification: Black Power in the Criminal Justice System," *Yale Law Journal* (December 1995)

NO: Randall Kennedy, from "After the Cheers," *The New Republic* (October 23, 1995)

ISSUE SUMMARY

YES: Paul Butler, an associate professor at the George Washington University Law School, notes that a vastly disproportionate number of Blacks in America are under the auspices of the criminal justice system. In order to balance the scales of justice, he argues, Black jurors should acquit Black defendants of certain crimes, regardless of whether or not they perceive the defendant to be guilty.

NO: Randall Kennedy, a professor at the Harvard University Law School, in examining the acquittal of O. J. Simpson, finds it tragic that Black jurors would pronounce a murderer "not guilty" just to send a message to white people. He maintains that, although racism among the police and others is deplorable, allowing Black criminals to go free does not help minorities, particularly since their victims are likely to be other Blacks.

> *The man that is not prejudiced against a horse thief is not fit to sit on a jury in this town.*
>
> —George Bernard Shaw (1856–1950)

The jury system of justice in the United States is considered by many to be sacred. Some 200,000 criminal and civil trials are decided by approximately 2 million jurors each year. Although the vast majority of cases do not go to trial, the symbolic importance of jury trials is great.

In theory, during a trial, the judge decides on correct legal procedures and matters of legal interpretation, while juries decide, based on the evidence, the guilt or innocence of the defendant. Generally, a person accused of a felony (a serious crime) or a misdemeanor in which a sentence of six months or more is possible, could request a jury trial. In all but six states and in the federal courts, juries consist of 12 jurors. In most states, a conviction must be by unanimous decision. Judges can sometimes set aside guilty verdicts that they feel are unfair, but verdicts of not guilty can never be changed.

The jury system is not without its critics. Many have expressed concern that juries do not always consist of the defendant's peers. In many states, for example, women were not allowed to serve on juries until relatively recently. Blacks and other minorities were either directly blocked from serving or were kept off juries by the jury selection process itself. Furthermore, in most states jurors were drawn from voter registrations, which meant that the poor—for whom political elections are frequently not of great concern—were disproportionately underrepresented. In many states, attorneys could exclude Blacks from serving on juries. But in *Batson v. Kentucky* (1986), the U.S. Supreme Court ruled that jurors could not be challenged solely on the basis of their race.

Jury nullification—in which a jury acquits a criminal defendant even though guilt has been proven—can be seen throughout U.S. history. Before the Revolutionary War, for example, some juries acquitted men who they felt were being treated unfairly by the British. Many northern juries refused to convict people accused of aiding runaway slaves. And juries have acquitted defendants because they felt that the police or prosecutors were bullying or unfairly treating them. Note that in these examples, the justification for nullification seems to be based on the juries' sense of justice, not on the guilt or innocence of the defendant.

However, not all historical instances of jury nullification are what would likely be considered noble reasons. For instance, until not long ago, very few whites accused of killing Blacks were ever found guilty in many parts of the United States. None until the 1960s were ever sentenced to death for killing a Black person. Few who participated in Black lynchings were even charged with a crime, and the few who were always got off.

In the following selections, Paul Butler—despite jury nullification's checkered past—encourages jurors to acquit Black defendants in many cases to remedy past and current discrimination in the criminal justice system. Randall Kennedy argues that the "need to convict a murderer" and the "need to protest the intolerability of official racism" must remain separate if either need is to be met. He maintains that promoting jury nullification as a legitimate way to right racial wrongs will only worsen the crime situation in Black communities. As you read this debate consider what unanticipated consequences, both positive and negative, might arise if jury nullification is widely accepted.

YES
Paul Butler

RACIALLY BASED JURY NULLIFICATION: BLACK POWER IN THE CRIMINAL JUSTICE SYSTEM

In 1990 I was a Special Assistant United States Attorney in the District of Columbia. I prosecuted people accused of misdemeanor crimes, mainly the drug and gun cases that overwhelm the local courts of most American cities. As a federal prosecutor, I represented the United States of America and used that power to put people, mainly African-American men, in prison. I am also an African-American man. During that time, I made two discoveries that profoundly changed the way I viewed my work as a prosecutor and my responsibilities as a black person.

The first discovery occurred during a training session for new assistants conducted by experienced prosecutors. We rookies were informed that we would lose many of our cases, despite having persuaded a jury beyond a reasonable doubt that the defendant was guilty. We would lose because some black jurors would refuse to convict black defendants who they knew were guilty.

The second discovery was related to the first but was even more unsettling. It occurred during the trial of Marion Barry, then the second-term mayor of the District of Columbia. Barry was being prosecuted by my office for drug possession and perjury. I learned, to my surprise, that some of my fellow African-American prosecutors hoped that the mayor would be acquitted, despite the fact that he was obviously guilty of at least one of the charges —an FBI videotape plainly showed him smoking crack cocaine. These black prosecutors wanted their office to lose its case because they believed that the prosecution of Barry was racist.

There is an increasing perception that some African-American jurors vote to acquit black defendants for racial reasons, sometimes explained as the juror's desire not to send another black man to jail. There is considerable disagreement over whether it is appropriate for a black juror to do so. I now believe that, for pragmatic and political reasons, the black community is better off when some non-violent lawbreakers remaining the community rather than

From Paul Butler, "Racially Based Jury Nullification: Black Power in the Criminal Justice System," *Yale Law Journal* (December 1995). Copyright © 1995 by The Yale Law Journal Company. Reprinted by permission of The Yale Law Journal Company and Fred B. Rothman & Company.

go to prison. The decision as to what kind of conduct by African Americans ought to be punished is better made by African Americans, based on their understanding of the costs and benefits to their community, than by the traditional criminal justice process, which is controlled by white lawmakers and white law enforcers. Legally, African-American jurors who sit in judgment of African-American accused persons have the power to make that decision. Considering the costs of law enforcement to the black community, and the failure of white lawmakers to come up with any solutions to black antisocial conduct other than incarceration, it is, in fact, the moral responsibility of black jurors to emancipate some guilty black outlaws.

* * *

Why would a black juror vote to let a guilty person go free? Assuming the juror is a rational, self-interested actor, she must believe that she is better off with the defendant out of prison than in prison. But how could any rational person believe that about a criminal?

Imagine a country in which a third of the young male citizens are under the supervision of the criminal justice system—either awaiting trial, in prison, or on probation or parole. Imagine a country in which two-thirds of the men can anticipate being arrested before they reach age thirty. Imagine a country in which there are more young men in prison than in college.

The country imagined above is a police state. When we think of a police state, we think of a society whose fundamental problem lies not with the citizens of the state but rather with the form of government, and with the powerful elites in whose interest the state

exists. Similarly, racial critics of American criminal justice locate the problem not with the black prisoners but with the state and its actors and beneficiaries.

The black community also bears very real costs by having so many African Americans, particularly males, incarcerated or otherwise involved in the criminal justice system. These costs are both social and economic, and they include the large percentage of black children who live in female-headed, single-parent households; a perceived dearth of men "eligible" for marriage; the lack of male role models for black children, especially boys; the absence of wealth in the black community; and the large unemployment rate among black men.

According to a recent *USA Today/CNN/Gallup* poll, 66 percent of blacks believe that the criminal justice system is racist and only 32 percent believe it is not racist. Interestingly, other polls suggest that blacks also tend to be more worried about crime than whites; this seems logical when one considers that blacks are more likely to be victims of crime. This enhanced concern, however, does not appear to translate to black support for tougher enforcement of criminal law. For example, substantially fewer blacks than whites support the death penalty, and many more blacks than whites were concerned with the potential racial consequences of the strict provisions of last year's crime bill. Along with significant evidence from popular culture, these polls suggest that a substantial portion of the African-American community sympathizes with racial critiques of the criminal justice system.

African-American jurors who endorse these critiques are in a unique position to act on their beliefs when they sit in judgment of a black defendant. As jurors, they have the power to convict the accused person or to set him free. May the responsible exercise of that power include voting to free a black defendant who the juror believes is guilty? The answer is "yes," based on the legal doctrine known as jury nullification.

Jury nullification occurs when a jury acquits a defendant who it believes is guilty of the crime with which he is charged. In finding the defendant not guilty, the jury ignores the facts of the case and/or the judge's instructions regarding the law. Instead, the jury votes its conscience.

The prerogative of juries to nullify has been part of English and American law for centuries. There are well-known cases from the Revolutionary War era when American patriots were charged with political crimes by the British crown and acquitted by American juries. Black slaves who escaped to the North and were prosecuted for violation of the Fugitive Slave Law were freed by Northern juries with abolitionist sentiments. Some Southern juries refused to punish white violence against African Americans, especially black men accused of crimes against white women.

The Supreme Court has officially disapproved of jury nullification but has conceded that it has no power to prohibit jurors from engaging in it; the Bill of Rights does not allow verdicts of acquittal to be reversed, regardless of the reason for the acquittal. Criticism of nullification has centered on its potential for abuse. The criticism suggests that when twelve members of a jury vote their conscience instead of the law, they corrupt the rule of law and undermine the democratic principles that made the law.

There is no question that jury nullification is subversive of the rule of law.

Nonetheless, most legal historians agree that it was morally appropriate in the cases of the white American revolutionaries and the runaway slaves. The issue, then, is whether African Americans today have the moral right to engage in this same subversion.

Most moral justifications of the obligation to obey the law are based on theories of "fair play." Citizens benefit from the rule of law; that is why it is just that they are burdened with the requirement to follow it. Yet most blacks are aware of countless historical examples in which African Americans were not afforded the benefit of the rule of law: think, for example, of the existence of slavery in a republic purportedly dedicated to the proposition that all men are created equal, or the law's support of state-sponsored segregation even after the Fourteenth Amendment guaranteed blacks equal protection. That the rule of law ultimately corrected some of the large holes in the American fabric is evidence more of its malleability than its goodness; the rule of law previously had justified the holes.

If the rule of law is a myth, or at least not valid for African Americans, the argument that jury nullification undermines it loses force. The black juror is simply another actor in the system, using her power to fashion a particular outcome. The juror's act of nullification —like the act of the citizen who dials 911 to report Ricky but not Bob, or the police officer who arrests Lisa but not Mary, or the prosecutor who charges Kwame but not Brad, or the judge who finds that Nancy was illegally entrapped but Verna was not—exposes the indeterminacy of law but does not in itself create it.

A similar argument can be made regarding the criticism that jury nullification is anti-democratic. This is precisely why many African Americans endorse it; it is perhaps the only legal power black people have to escape the tyranny of the majority. Black people have had to beg white decision makers for most of the rights they have: the right not to be slaves, the right to vote, the right to attend an integrated school. Now black people are begging white people to preserve programs that help black children to eat and black businesses to survive. Jury nullification affords African Americans the power to determine justice for themselves in individual cases, regardless of whether white people agree or even understand.

* * *

At this point, African Americans should ask themselves whether the operation of the criminal law system in the United States advances the interests of black people. If it does not, the doctrine of jury nullification affords African-American jurors the opportunity to exercise the authority of the law over some African-American criminal defendants. In essence, black people can "opt out" of American criminal law.

How far should they go—completely to anarchy, or is there someplace between here and there that is safer than both? I propose the following: African-American jurors should approach their work cognizant of its political nature and of their prerogative to exercise their power in the best interests of the black community. In every case, the juror should be guided by her view of what is "just." (Have more faith, I should add, in the average black juror's idea of justice than I do in the idea that is embodied in the "rule of law.")

In cases involving violent *malum in se* (inherently bad) crimes, such as murder, rape, and assault, jurors should consider the case strictly on the evidence presented, and if they believe the accused person is guilty, they should so vote. In cases involving non-violent, *malum prohibitum* (legally proscribed) offenses, including "victimless" crimes such as narcotics possession, there should be a presumption in favor of nullification. Finally, for non-violent, *malum in se* crimes, such as theft or perjury, there need be no presumption in favor of nullification, but it ought to be an option the juror considers. A juror might vote for acquittal, for example, when a poor woman steals from Tiffany's but not when the same woman steals from her next-door neighbor.

How would a juror decide individual cases under my proposal? Easy cases would include a defendant who has possessed crack cocaine and an abusive husband who kills his wife. The former should be acquitted and the latter should go to prison.

Difficult scenarios would include the drug dealer who operates in the ghetto and the thief who burglarizes the home of a rich white family. Under my proposal, nullification is presumed in the first case because drug distribution is a non-violent *malum prohibitum* offense. Is nullification morally justifiable here? It depends. There is no question that encouraging people to engage in self-destructive behavior is evil; the question the juror should ask herself is whether the remedy is less evil. (The juror should also remember that the criminal law does not punish those ghetto drug dealers who cause the most injury: liquor store owners.)

As for the burglar who steals from the rich white family, the case is troubling, first of all, because the conduct is so clearly "wrong." Since it is a non-violent *malum in se* crime, there is no presumption in favor of nullification, but it is an option for consideration. Here again, the facts of the case are relevant. For example, if the offense was committed to support a drug habit, I think there is a moral case to be made for nullification, at least until such time as access to drug-rehabilitation services are available to all.

* * *

Why would a juror be inclined to follow my proposal? There is no guarantee that she would. But when we perceive that black jurors are already nullifying on the basis of racial critiques (i.e., refusing to send another black man to jail), we recognize that these jurors are willing to use their power in a politically conscious manner. Further, it appears that some black jurors now excuse some conduct—like murder—that they should not excuse. My proposal provides a principled structure of the exercise of the black juror's vote. I am not encouraging anarchy; rather I am reminding black jurors of their privilege to serve a calling higher than law: justice.

I concede that the justice my proposal achieves is rough. It is as susceptible to human foibles as the jury system. But I am sufficiently optimistic that my proposal will be only an intermediate plan, a stopping point between the status quo and real justice. To get to that better, middle ground, I hope that this [selection] will encourage African Americans to use responsibly the power they already have.

NO

Randall Kennedy

AFTER THE CHEERS

The acquittal of O. J. Simpson brings to an end an extraordinary criminal trial that attracted, like a magnet, anxieties over crime, sex, race and the possibility of reach truth and dispensing justice in an American courtroom. The verdict is difficult to interpret since juries are not required to give reasons for the conclusions they reach and since, even if jurors do articulate their reasons, there remains the problem of deciphering them and distinguishing expressed views from real bases of decision.

My own view is that the verdict represents a combination of three beliefs. One is that the prosecution simply failed to prove that O. J. Simpson was guilty beyond a reasonable doubt. Reasonable people could come to this conclusion. After all, police investigators displayed remarkable incompetence, the prosecution erred mightily—remember the gloves that did not fit!—and, of course, there was the despicable [police officer] Mark Fuhrman. Even with help given by several questionable judicial rulings before the trial and near the end, the prosecution did permit a reasonable juror to vote to acquit on the basis of the evidence presented. I disagree with that conclusion. But I do concede that it could be reached reasonably and in good faith.

If this belief is what prompted the decision of all twelve of the jurors who acquitted Simpson, their decision has little broader cultural significance than that reasonable jurors sometimes come to different conclusions than those which many observers favor. I doubt, though, that this belief was the only or even the dominant predicate for the acquittal. I say this based on what I have heard many people say and write about the evidence presented at the trial and also on the remarkably short time that the jury deliberated. If the jury was at all representative of the American public, particularly that sector of the public which leaned toward acquittal, it was probably influenced considerably by two other beliefs.

The first is characterized by an unreasonable suspicion of law enforcement authorities. This is the thinking of people who would have voted to acquit O. J. Simpson even in the absence of Mark Fuhrman's racism and the L.A. police department's incompetence and even in the face of evidence that was more incriminating than that which was produced at trial. There is a paranoid,

From Randall Kennedy, "After the Cheers," *The New Republic* (October 23, 1995). Copyright © 1995 by The New Republic, Inc. Reprinted by permission.

conspiracy-minded sector of the population that would honestly though irrationally have rejected the state's argument virtually without regard to the evidence. One of the things that nourishes much of this community, particularly that part comprised of African Americans, is a vivid and bitter memory of wrongful convictions of innocent black men and wrongful acquittals of guilty white men. A key example of the former were the convictions of the Scottsboro Boys in the 1930s for allegedly raping two white women. Now it is widely believed that these young men were framed. A key example of the latter was the acquittal of the murderers of Emmett Till forty years ago. In the face of overwhelming evidence of guilt, an all-white jury in Sumner, Mississippi, took an hour and seven minutes to acquit two white men who later acknowledged that they had killed Till for having whistled at the wife of one of them. Asked why the jury had taken an hour to deliberate, one of the jurors declared that it would not have taken so long if they hadn't paused for a drink of soda pop. Some readers may find it hard to believe that these despicable events of sixty and forty years ago influence the way that people now evaluate people and events. But just as some in the Balkans remember battles fought 600 years ago as if they happened yesterday, so too do many blacks recall with pained disgust the racially motivated miscarriages of justice that they have helplessly witnessed or been told about. That recollection, refreshed occasionally by more recent outrages, prompts them to regard prosecutions against black men—especially black men accused of attacking white women—with such an intense level of skepticism that they demand more than that which should convince most reasonable people of guilt beyond a reasonable doubt.

A third belief is that to which [defense lawyer] Johnnie Cochran appealed directly in his summation when he pleaded with jurors to help "police the police." This belief animates jury nullification. By nullification, I mean the act of voting for acquittal even though you know that, in terms of the rules laid down by the judge, the evidence warrants conviction. A nullifier votes to acquit not because of dissatisfaction with the evidence but because, in the phrase of choice nowadays, he wants "to send a message." In many locales, black people in particular want to send a message that they are way past tolerating anti-black racism practiced by police and that they are willing to voice their protest in a wide variety of ways, including jury nullification. Frustrated, angry and politically self-aware, some black citizens have decided to take their protest against racism in the criminal justice system to the vital and vulnerable innards of that system: the jury box.

In a certain way, the specter of this sort of jury nullification represents an advance in American race relations. Not too long ago, blacks' dissatisfactions with the criminal justice system could often be largely ignored without significant immediate consequence because whites, on a racial basis, excluded them from decisionmaking. Invisible in courthouses, except as defendants, blacks could safely be permitted to stew in their own resentments. Now, however, because of salutary reforms, blacks are much more active in the administration of criminal justice and thus much more able to influence it.

* * *

Notwithstanding this advance, however, the current state of affairs as revealed by the Simpson case is marked by several large and tragic failures. The first and most important is the failure on the part of responsible officials to clearly, publicly and wholeheartedly abjure racism of the sort that Mark Fuhrman displayed during his hateful career as a police officer. Fuhrman's prejudice and his ability to act on it likely had much to do with O. J. Simpson's acquittal. His bigotry provided a vivid basis for the argument that the police framed Simpson. His bigotry also provided an emotionally satisfying basis upon which to follow Cochran's invitation to "send a message" by voting to acquit. In other words, the state inflicted upon itself a grievous wound when its representatives failed to establish a rigorous, anti-racist personnel policy that might have obviated the problem that ultimately crippled the prosecution most. Perhaps more headway on this front will now be made; practicality and morality dictate a more vigorous push against racism in law enforcement circles.

A second failure has occurred within the ranks of those who cheered the acquittal. I have no objection to cheers based on the assumption that the jury system worked properly, that is, cheers based on an honest and reasonable perception that the acquittal has freed a man against whom there existed too little evidence for a conviction. I get the impression, though, that there are other sentiments being voiced in the celebrations of some observers, including feelings of racial solidarity, yearnings to engage in racial muscle-flexing and a peculiar urge to protect the hero status of a man whose standing within the black community rose precipitously by dint of being charged with murder.

The failure of those moved by these sentiments is two-fold. First, such feelings can only predominate by minimizing the stark fact that two people were brutally murdered and by resisting the claim that *whoever* committed that dastardly deed ought to be legally punished, regardless of his color and regardless of the racism of Mark Fuhrman and company. To subordinate the need to convict a murderer to the need to protest the intolerability of official racism is a moral mistake. Both could have been done and should have been done. Contrary to the logic of Johnnie Cochran's summation, neither jurors nor onlookers were trapped in a situation in which they had to choose one imperative over the other. Second, as a practical matter, it cannot be emphasized too frequently the extent to which the black community in particular needs vigorous, efficient, enthusiastic law enforcement. As bad as racist police misconduct is, it pales in comparison to the misery that criminals (most of whom are black) inflict upon black communities. After all, blacks are four times as likely as whites to be raped, three times as likely to be robbed, twice as likely to be assaulted and seven times as likely to be murdered.

The problem of criminality perpetrated by blacks is the one that many black political leaders appear to have trouble discussing thoroughly. A good many prefer condemning white racist police to focusing on ways to render life in black communities more secure against ordinary criminals. That Simpson allegedly killed two white people makes him in some eyes far easier to rally around than had he allegedly killed two black people. This difference in sympathy based on the race of victims is itself a profoundly destructive racialist impulse, one deeply rooted in our political culture. But there is yet another difficulty with this particular racialist response. Like so much else about the Simpson case, the racial demographics of those who were killed was atypical. Because the more typical scenario features black victims of murder, those who claim to speak on behalf of blacks' interests should be extremely wary of supporting anything that further depresses law enforcement's ability to apprehend and convict those who prey upon their neighbors.

The O. J. Simpson trial is obviously a complicated event that will take years to understand more fully and place into proper perspective. At this point, however, the result, like so much of the trial itself, leaves me—normally an optimist—overcome by a sense of profound gloom.

POSTSCRIPT

Should Jury Nullification Be Used to Reduce Ethnic and Racial Inequities?

Should jury nullification be used to reduce inequities? Can a jury's decision to acquit a guilty person be considered a form of discretion, comparable to a person's decision to dial or not to dial 911 in an emergency or a police officer's deciding whether or not to arrest a potential suspect? Butler says, "Jury nullification affords African Americans the power to determine justice... regardless of whether white people agree or even understand." Is this statement blatantly racist? One critic has suggested that Butler's discussion is actually a satire. Could this be true?

An interesting concept that neither Butler nor Kennedy consider is the possibility of victim, community, or police "nullification." In other words, if many felt that criminals who were minority members would be allowed to go free by sympathetic juries, the probability would be high that even fewer cases would get to trial than currently do: the police, victims' families, or even vigilantes might be driven to administer "neighborhood justice" in order to ensure that criminals are punished.

The acquittal of murder suspect O. J. Simpson on October 3, 1995, revived debate on jury nullification. A thoughtful discussion is James Q. Wilson, "Reading Jurors' Minds," *Commentary* (February 1996). Support of nullification can be found in C. Page, "Overriding Law to Create Justice," *The Baltimore Sun* (November 16, 1995). For a balanced discussion of the Simpson trial process and outcome, see J. Abramson, "After the O. J. Trial: The Quest to Create a Color-Blind Jury," *Chronicle of Higher Education* (November 3, 1995). An interesting comparison of case dispositions is J. Leiber, "A Comparison of Juvenile Court Outcomes for Native Americans, African Americans and Whites," *Justice Quarterly* (June 1994). Also see *African Americans and the Criminal Justice System* by Marvin D. Free, Jr. (Garland Publishers, 1995). A useful comparison of early English juries with modern American ones is *The Law of the Other: The Mixed Jury and Changing Conceptions of Citizenship, Law, and Knowledge* by Marianne Constable (University of Chicago Press, 1994). Finally, the classic jury study remains H. Kalven, Jr., and Hans Zeisel's *The American Jury* (University of Chicago Press, 1960).

ISSUE 20

Is Systemic Racism in Criminal Justice a Myth?

YES: William Wilbanks, from "The Myth of a Racist Criminal Justice System," *Criminal Justice Research Bulletin* (vol. 3, no. 5, 1987)

NO: Coramae Richey Mann, from *Unequal Justice: A Question of Color* (Indiana University Press, 1993)

ISSUE SUMMARY

YES: Criminology professor William Wilbanks advances the thesis that the criminal justice system is not now racist, and he argues that claims that it is are myths.

NO: Criminologist Coramae Richey Mann argues that at almost every point in the criminal justice system—from arrest, to prosecution, to plea bargaining or jury trial—racism persists.

According to polls, the acquittal of murder suspect O. J. Simpson is "proof" for many whites that Blacks are now being treated fairly by the criminal justice system. Indeed, tragically, some whites even view it as an indicator that Blacks nowadays can "get away with murder." By sharp contrast, polls reveal that Blacks have diametrically opposed views of the trial and its outcome.

In spite of the fact that a vast majority of Blacks concurred with the jury decision, the rationales behind the support were mixed. For instance, some Blacks indicated it was simply a matter of a rich person getting off scot-free, the way it always happens, only this time the rich person was Black. A significantly larger number, although unsure of Simpson's guilt or innocence, felt that the police had clearly bungled the case. In addition, they cited the lack of credibility of the racist Los Angeles police officer Mark Fuhrman as planting a reasonable doubt in their minds (many whites were also disturbed at the incompetence of both police and forensic experts in that trial).

Others, citing defense attorney Johnnie Cochran's impassioned plea against racism in America, felt that the jury was sending a needed message to Americans. For the vast majority of Americans, both Black and white, the opposing perceptions of the trial and its outcome were simply a matter of men and women of reason and good will plainly disagreeing. How did this gap in perceptions come about? Who is right about the criminal justice system? Since his acquittal, Simpson has lost civil suits brought against him by the murdered victims' families, losses that cost Simpson millions of dollars and forced him to sell his home and football trophies. To many, this shows that there is still justice in the system.

Historically, within the field of minority group research, virtually no expression of racism was more blatant, widespread, and easy to document than the mistreatment of Blacks by the criminal justice system. In most states, Blacks were more likely to be arrested, obliged to stand trial, given longer prison sentences, or sentenced to death. The latter was especially true in the South.

Blacks were also much more likely to be intimidated by the police and subject to being rounded up when a crime needed to be solved immediately. Blacks were more likely to be held incommunicado and generally harassed as well as tortured.

Lynchings of Blacks (3,446 between 1882 and 1968) were at least implicitly sanctioned by local police, and they were brutal and gruesome affairs. Almost nothing was ever done to prosecute the murderers. Lynching and its sanctioning by officials was symbolically the most important image of criminal justice racism.

William Wilbanks, though not the first, is one of the few to challenge the perception that the system is still racist. Wilbanks does not deny that racism has existed in the system and he does not deny there are individuals in the system who are racists, from police officers to probation officers. But he insists that the criminal justice system is no longer plagued by institutional racism. To claim otherwise, he says, is to perpetuate a myth.

Coramae Richey Mann, almost anticipating the Simpson verdict and providing an explanation for Blacks' cynicism of the criminal justice system, rejects Wilbanks's and others' claims. She tries to show how and where in the justice process racism leaks in or could leak in, which begins with patrol officers on the beat. Who do they initially suspect, investigate, and arrest in many cases? What charges are they likely to bring against Blacks, as compared to charges leveled against whites (allegedly much lighter)? Who is likely to be able to post bail or, for that matter, to have lower bail assigned to begin with? These and other factors, she insists, increases the likelihood of poorer defendants being forced to accept a plea bargain (admission of guilt for a shorter sentence, including time already served). Meanwhile, she points out, members of grand juries, juries, lawyers, prosecutors, and judges are all likely to be white, at least in certain parts of the United States.

As you read this debate (which the two authors have been carrying on for years without coming close to resolution), think about the moral and policy implications of Wilbanks's thesis. Why does he seem so sure that the image of the criminal justice system as racist is a dangerous myth?

As you read Mann's selection, pay close attention to the dates of the articles that she cites. Could the times have changed (as Wilbanks maintains) enough to make those findings no longer relevant? Mann provides several underlying rationales for most of her arguments, but does she provide sufficient empirical support?

YES

William Wilbanks

THE MYTH OF A RACIST CRIMINAL JUSTICE SYSTEM

White and black Americans differ sharply over whether their criminal justice system is racist. The vast majority of blacks appear to believe that the police and courts do discriminate against blacks, whereas a majority of whites reject this charge. A sizable minority of whites even believe that the justice system actually discriminates **for** blacks in "leaning over backward" for them in reaction to charges of racism from the black community and the media.

The contrasting views of blacks and whites as to the fairness of the criminal justice system are of more than academic interest as research indicates that the higher level of offending by blacks may be due in part to the belief that "the system" is unfair. This belief produces a "justification for no obligation" or the attitude that "I don't respect a system that is racist, and so I don't feel obliged to abide by the laws of that system." This view in the collective has led to riots in Miami and other cities. Furthermore, the hostility to police generated by the belief has led to a mutual expectation of violence between police and blacks that has produced more violence as part of a self-fulfilling prophesy. Finally, the white backlash to affirmative action programs may be due in part to the perception that blacks complain about racism in a society that actually practices reverse discrimination (favoritism toward blacks).

THE THESIS

I take the position that the perception of the criminal justice system as racist is a myth. This overall thesis should not be misinterpreted. I do believe that there is racial prejudice and discrimination **within** the criminal justice system, in that there are individuals, both white and black, who make decisions, at least in part, on the basis of race. I do not believe that **the system** is characterized by racial prejudice or discrimination **against** blacks. At every point from arrest to parole there is little or no evidence of an overall racial effect, in that the percentage outcomes for blacks and whites are not very different. There is evidence, however, that some individual decision makers (e.g., police officers, judges) are more likely to give "breaks" to whites than to blacks. However,

From William Wilbanks, "The Myth of a Racist Criminal Justice System," *Criminal Justice Research Bulletin*, vol. 3, no. 5 (1987). Copyright © 1987 by William Wilbanks. Reprinted by permission.

there appears to be an **equal** tendency for other individual decision makers to favor blacks over whites. This "canceling-out effect" results in studies that find no **overall** racial effect.

The assertion that the criminal justice system is not racist does not address the reasons why blacks appear to offend at higher rates than whites before coming into contact with the criminal justice system. It may be that racial discrimination in American society has been responsible for conditions (e.g., discrimination in employment, housing and education) that lead to higher rates of offending by blacks, but that possibility does not bear on the question of whether the criminal justice system discriminates against blacks. Also, the thesis that racism is not systematic and pervasive in the criminal justice system does not deny that racial prejudice and discrimination have existed or even been the dominant force in the design and operation of the criminal justice system in the past.

DEFINING RACISM

One of the main barriers to the discussion and resolution of the issue of racism in the criminal justice system involves the multiple uses and meanings of the term "racism." Definitions of this term range from a conscious attitude by an individual to an unconscious act by an institution or even to the domination of society by white culture. I have suggested that the term "racism" be abandoned in favor of the terms "racial prejudice" (an attitude) and "racial discrimination" (an act).

Any discussion of the pervasiveness of racism in the justice system is clouded by the tendency of Accusers (e.g., those who claim the system is racist) to use a double standard in that the term is used only to apply to whites. For example, it is often pointed out that 50% of the victims of police killings are black and that this fact alone presents a prima facie case of racism. But it is seldom pointed out that 50% of the police officers who are killed are victimized by blacks. If the first fact indicates racism by white police officers why does not the second fact indicate racism by black killers of police?

At times the use of the term racism appears to constitute a "non-falsifiable thesis" in that any result is defined as racist. For example, in McCleskey v. Georgia (a case before the U.S. Supreme Court this term) the petitioner claims that he received the death penalty because he (a black) killed a white whereas those who kill blacks seldom receive the death penalty.* Thus lenient treatment given to black killers (or those who kill black victims) is defined as racism. But if black killers had been more likely to be sentenced to death that result would also be (and has been) viewed as racist. Thus the term is defined so that any result is indicative of racism (i.e., a non-falsifiable thesis). The double standard of racism is also seen in this case in that the death penalty statistics actually indicate harsher treatment of white than black killers but this result is not seen as racism (against whites).

In a similar fashion a lower percentage of blacks (than whites) being convicted has been interpreted by Accusers as racist in that this result indicates that charges against blacks were often without substance. On the other hand, if more blacks were convicted this result would also be viewed by Accusers as being in-

*[The U.S. Supreme Court supported Georgia, and McCleskey has since been executed.—Ed.]

dicative of racism since black defendants were treated more harshly.

THE DATA

The book [*The Myth of A Racist Criminal Justice System,* of which this article is a summary] was undertaken to explain why blacks in the U.S. are 8 times more likely, on a per capita basis, to be in prison than are whites. The major point of the book is that the approximate 8:1 per capita ratio of blacks to whites in prison is the result of an approximate 8:1 level in offending and not the result of racial selectivity by the police and the courts. In other words, the 8:1 black to white ratio at offending is not increased as offenders are brought into and processed by the criminal justice system.

Some original data are presented in an appendix to the book on the black vs. white gap from arrest to incarceration in prison for two states—California and Pennsylvania. In 1980 felony cases, blacks in California were arrested 5.1 times as often as whites. This black/white gap increased to 6.2 at incarceration. Thus the black/white "gap" increased by 20% from arrest to prison. However, the reverse occurred in Pennsylvania where the 8.1 gap at arrest decreased to 7.4 at incarceration (a decline of 9%). Overall, it would appear that the black/white gap does not increase from arrest to prison. Thus there is no evidence overall that black offenders processed by the criminal justice system fare worse than white offenders.

But perhaps the black/white gap at arrest is a product of racial bias by the police in that the police are more likely to select and arrest black than white offenders. The best evidence on this question comes from the National Crime Survey which interviews 130,000 Americans each year about crime victimization. Those who are victimized by violent crime are asked to describe the offenders (who were not necessarily caught by the police) as to age, sex and race. The percent of offenders described by victims as being black is generally consistent with the percent of offenders who are black according to arrest figures. For example, approximately 60% of (uncaught) robbers described by victims were black and approximately 60% of those arrested for robbery in the U.S. are black. This would not be the case if the police were "picking on" black robbers and ignoring white robbers.

Given the above figures, those who claim that racism is systematic and pervasive in the criminal justice system should explain why the black/white gap does not cumulatively increase from arrest to prison. Furthermore, those who claim racism is pervasive should be asked to specify the number of black offenders that are thought to receive harsher treatment (e.g., whether 10%, 50% or 100%) and the extent of that "extra" harshness in cases where "it" is given. For example, at sentencing do those mistreated black offenders receive on the average a 10%, 50% or 100% harsher sentence?

There is a large body of research on the alleged existence of racial discrimination at such points as arrest, conviction and sentencing. The bibliography of my books lists over 80 sentencing studies which examined the impact of race on outcome. A number of scholars have examined this large body of research and concluded that there is no evidence of systematic racial discrimination. James Q. Wilson, the most prominent American criminologist, asserts that the claim of discrimination is not supported by the evidence as did a three volume study of the sentencing literature by the National Academy of Sciences.

METHODOLOGICAL PROBLEMS

However, some studies do claim to have found evidence of racial discrimination. However, as Wilson and others have pointed out, most of these studies are marked by flaws in design or interpretation. One chapter of *The Myth of a Racist Criminal Justice System* is devoted to seven models of design and/or interpretation which have been utilized in studies of the possible existence of racial discrimination. Many of the studies claiming to have found racial discrimination utilized a model of analysis that ensured such a result.

But many readers will be thinking at this point that "one can prove anything with statistics" and thus that the validity of the claim for a racist criminal justice system should be determined by what one knows by personal experience or observation. However, the layperson's confidence in and reliance upon "commonsense" in rejecting the statistical approach to knowledge in favor of what one knows by personal experience and observation is misplaced. The layperson does not take into account the impact of bias (and in some cases racial prejudice) in personal experience and observation.

Let us take, for example, the question as to whether there is racial discrimination in the use of force by the police. Those who reject studies of large numbers of "use of force" incidents which do not show evidence of racial discrimination by race of victim suggest that "unbiased" observation will reveal racism. But suppose that several people see a white police officer hit a black youth. There are a mul-

titude of explanations (e.g., the youth hit the officer first, the youth resisted authority, the officer was the macho type who would hit any victim who was not properly deferential, the officer was a racist) for such an act. The tendency is for those with a particular bias to select that explanation which is consistent with their bias. For example, other police officers or white citizens might select the explanation that the youth resisted authority while black citizens might select the explanation that the officer was a racist. In either case the observer simply infers the explanation that is most consistent with his/her bias and thus knowledge via observation is anything but unbiased. Large scale statistical studies allow one to control for factors (other than race) which might impact on a decision or act. Without such studies those who disagree on the impact of racism will simply be trading anecdotes ("I know a case where...") to "prove" their case.

CONCLUSION

Racial prejudice, in my view, is the process by which people assign positive traits and motives to themselves and their race and negative traits and motives to "them" (the other race). Blacks tend to see the beating of a black youth by a white police officer as being indicative of racism (an evil motive or trait attributed to the "out-group") while whites (or police officers) tend to see the beating as being the result of some improper action by the black youth. The white view is also influenced by the assigning of evil motives or traits to the out-group (to the black youth). In both cases the observers, whether black or white, have been influenced by racial prejudice in their assigning of blame or cause for the incident.

My basic position is that both the black and white views on the extent of racism in the criminal justice system are "ignorant" in that personal knowledge is gained primarily via observation and experience—methods which are heavily influenced by bias and racial prejudice. In other words, racial prejudice keeps the races polarized on this issue since each race sees the "facts" which "prove" its thesis. Statistical studies of large numbers of blacks and whites subjected to a particular decision (e.g., the use of force) are a safeguard against personal bias and are far more valid as a means to "truth" than personal observation and experience. It is my view that an examination of those studies available at various points in the criminal justice system fails to support the view that racial discrimination is pervasive. It is in this sense that the belief in a racist criminal justice system is a myth.

The Myth of a Racist Criminal Justice System examines all the available studies that have examined the possible existence of racial discrimination from arrest to parole. For example, the chapter on the police examines the evidence for and against the charge that police deployment patterns, arrest statistics, the use of force ("brutality") and the use of deadly force reflect racism. The chapter on the prosecutor examines the evidence for and against the charge that the bail decision, the charge, plea bargaining, the provision of legal counsel, and jury selection are indicative of racism. The chapter on prison looks at evidence concerning the possibility of racism as reflected through imprisonment rates for blacks vs. whites, in racial segregation, in treatment programs, in prison discipline and in the parole decision. In general, this examination of the available evidence indicates that support for the "discrimination thesis" is sparse, inconsistent, and frequently contradictory.

NO

Coramae Richey Mann

UNEQUAL JUSTICE:
A QUESTION OF COLOR

Injustice anywhere is a threat to justice everywhere.

—Martin Luther King Jr. (1963)

THE PRETRIAL EXPERIENCES OF MINORITIES

A great deal of criminological attention and research has been devoted to final sentencing outcomes for minority offenders; however, there has been scant concentration on portentous actions and decisions occurring earlier on the route to court after an arrest has been effected. This oversight is particularly misleading, since it has been found that "when racial differences in processing occur, they are likely to occur at stages prior to final sentencing" (Farnworth and Horan, 1980: 381). The assignment of bail and preventive detention demonstrate that either minorities are denied the opportunity to make bond and thereby secure release from jail, or bond is frequently set at such an exorbitant amount that a minority defendant is unable to raise it and remains in detention until the case is heard. In both events the accused is deprived of precious freedom and simultaneously denied the right to assist in the adequate preparation of his/her case. The exclusion of minority group members from grand juries and trial juries has been and continues to be a central problem in the administration of justice. The need for minority legal representation and opinions of defense attorneys held by minority defendants are rarely discussed but are additional important pretrial issues.

The far-reaching influence and excessive discretion of the prosecutor frequently have detrimental effects on minorities at each step of the criminal justice process, ranging from charging and grand jury indictments to plea bargaining and final court dispositions. Poor and minority defendants are more likely to waive the constitutional right to a trial and thus tend to plea bargain in hopes of obtaining more lenient sentences, although there is some doubt that plea negotiations are really "bargains." Each of these stumbling blocks has its own deleterious effect, and by the time of the court date, collectively, they can be devastating for the minority defendant.

BAIL AND DETENTION

After a suspect has been taken into custody, one of the most important discretionary decisions is whether the accused will be held or released before trial (Levine, Musheno, and Palumbo, 1986: 342). The major factors involved in a bail decision center on (1) whether the suspect has to put up bail, (2) the amount of bail required, and (3) the consequences of detention if bail is not granted or cannot be met. . . .

Somehow the purpose of bail—to ensure the accused's appearance for trial —loses its significance when minorities are the defendants. The reliance on money bail was widely condemned in the 1960s because of apparent discrimination against the poor and minorities, specifically because those incarcerated before trial were frequently sentenced more severely than similarly charged defendants who were freed before their trials (Bynum, 1982: 68). In a study of trial courts in Chicago, Lizotte (1978: 572, 577) found that it was economically more difficult for nonwhites and defendants of lower occupational status to make bail, and an indirect effect of not making bail was "outright discrimination and longer prison sentences." . . .

The implications of the "repressive application of bail laws" are enormous for minority defendants. The National Minority Advisory Council on Criminal Justice, a national fact-finding body, found that minorities experienced the imposition of (1) legal maximum bail settings; (2) exorbitant bail for alleged major crimes

and conspiracies; (3) extremely high bails for minor offenses; (4) overcharges at arrest with concomitant high, impossible bail; and (5) the application of multiple charges, with bail imposed at the legal maximum for each separate charge (NMAC, 1980: 204).

Judges often use criteria such as crime prevention and retribution or punishment to assign bails that are unrelated to guaranteeing court appearances, "since they do not want to look bad in the public's eye when they have released people who commit new crimes while awaiting trial" (Levine, Musheno, and Palumbo, 1986: 346). . . .

The issue of the public perception of dangerousness and an insistence upon the protection of society often leads judges to set bail so high for some defendants that, in practice, it becomes a mechanism for preventive detention. . . . The stereotyping of African Americans and other minorities as dangerous puts them more at risk of this type of social and judicial bias. The injustice incumbent in such practices is frequently overlooked. . . .

Although the Eighth Amendment of the U.S. Constitution specifies that "excessive bail shall not be required," in reality, minority suspects, particularly in political protest or riot situations, have often been assigned impossibly high bails for both preventive and punishment purposes. . . . [T]he National Minority Advisory Council on Criminal Justice found that the bail bond system discriminates against minorities and poor people on a daily basis. . . .

Because of the way the money bail system operates, minority suspects who are poor are jailed for inordinately long periods of time, while whites go free: "Both are equally presumed innocent; money is the discriminating factor. As a result, the country's jails are packed to overflowing with the nation's poor—with red, brown, black, and yellow men and women showing up in disproportionate numbers" (Burns, 1973: 161). The consequences of such bail malpractice can be overwhelming for minorities. In addition to the possibility of being convicted and receiving a more severe sentence as a result of pretrial detention, other serious repercussions can result from incarceration pending trial. Pretrial detention prevents the accused from locating evidence and witnesses and having more complete access to counsel. It disrupts employment and family relations. If pretrial incarceration results in the loss of employment, the families of the detained accused may require public assistance for survival (Bynum, 1982: 68).

Detention subjects people to what are often ghastly jail conditions. Defendants awaiting trial are indiscriminately mixed with convicted felons, many of whom are violent offenders, and scores of detainees each year are beaten, raped, and murdered (Inciardi, 1984: 451–452). Pretrial detention also limits defendants' ability to help with their own defenses, and stigmatizes them if they indeed go to trial (Levine, Musheno, and Palumbo, 1986: 342). It coerces defendants who are detained in jail into plea negotiations in order to settle the matter more rapidly (Inciardi, 1984: 451). Finally, as previously noted, sentence severity is greatest for defendants who are detained prior to trial. Research has demonstrated repeatedly that detainees are more likely to be indicted, convicted, and sentenced more harshly than released defendants....

There are several ways an accused minority can be abused when at the financial mercy of a professional bondsman.

First, substantial capital is a necessary prerequisite for the occupation, the majority of bondsmen are Euro-Americans. Consequently, those who harbor racial prejudices will not accept minority defendants. Second, whether or not a defendant gains release depends on the discretion of the bonding agent, who may not select poor (or minority) defendants because of the low fees associated with low bails (Goldkamp, 1980: 182). A third possibility of refusal to assume the bonds of minorities may be that the bondsman adopts the stereotypical attitude that minorities are poor bail risks who will abscond and forfeit the bondsman's money. Fourth, some bondsmen, who are as crooked as the persons they represent, are reputed to gouge minorities by taking what few possessions they have as additional collateral and never returning them....

JURY SELECTION

The methods used in empaneling and composing a jury can result in unfair treatment of minorities during the jury selection process. Since grand juries have almost unlimited power to hand down criminal indictments, the lack of minority representation on grand juries, as well as on juries in trials where minorities are defendants, indicates an abrogation of the Sixth Amendment constitutional right to an impartial jury in criminal cases—that is, to be tried by one's peers.

A grand jury can arrive at its indictment decision on its own initiative through accusations based on its observations or knowledge; or, as is common practice, it can indict a person solely on evidence presented by the prosecutor (Inciardi, 1984: 459). In either case, an indictment is returned on the basis of a majority vote and arrived at privately and secretly without the accused or accused's defense counsel being present.... The implications of such an enormous amount of discretion and power in the hands of a simple majority is discomforting; for a minority suspect, the ramifications of the grand jury selection procedure can be petrifying.

Grand juries are generally composed using the "key man" method. Key men are prominent members of the community, usually white, propertied males whom the court chooses for the purpose of selecting jurors (NMAC, 1980: 206)....The subjective bias of such a system is obvious—key men select men like themselves, not persons of color or poor people.

Jury selections using other, more objective methods, such as lists of registered voters, automobile registrations, or property tax rolls, also have built-in biases that favor the middle class, specifically the white middle class.... Minorities who through a variety of methods have been kept from registering to vote can never serve on juries in areas that use voter status as a criterion. "Redlining" voting districts and other means of preventing minority voting reduce the numbers of African Americans, Hispanics, Native Americans, and Americans of Asian descent on the voter rolls. The National Minority Advisory Council on Criminal Justice (1980) points out that many minorities will try to avoid jury duty because, as lower-level, blue-collar employees, they cannot afford the loss of hourly wages that jury duty entails. The result of these and other barriers is that most empaneled juries consist of white, middle-class, middle-aged persons whose beliefs and cultural attitudes mirror those of the dominant (white) political and economic

structure, and ultimately prove potentially damaging to a minority defendant's right to an equitable trial....

Jury size has been found to be a discriminatory factor in felony cases of African Americans and other minorities in the half-dozen states that permit less than twelve-person juries.... If twelve-person juries rarely include African Americans and other minorities, selection of a jury of six from an already unrepresentative pool will be less likely to provide a cross-section of the community....

THE LEGAL ACTORS: DEFENSE AND PROSECUTING ATTORNEYS

The right to counsel is one of the most vital due process rights an individual in a criminal court proceeding is constitutionally assured. Such legal representation is necessary in an adversary system of justice such as ours....

[I]n 1986, almost $1 billion was spent on indigent defense services in the 4.4 million cases tried in local and state courts, an increase of 60 percent over the sum spent in 1982. These cases utilized one of three primary types of indigent defense systems—*assigned counsel systems, contract systems,* or *public defender programs....*

Under an assigned counsel system, it is often judges who have the immense authority and discretion to appoint attorneys, a situation that is conceivably more discomforting because the judges also ultimately hear the cases. Judges, like states attorneys, are also subject to ethnocentricity or to having personal racial prejudices. Even under the coordinated, administrative method of assigning counsel, a sole administrator has this authority. It should not be overlooked that the southern and midwestern regions more frequently use these methods and are renowned as the areas of the country most likely to face charges of racism in the administration of justice. Whether racially biased or not, there is still the danger of the "good old boy" system, where such appointments are rooted in favoritism or nepotism, thereby screening out minority attorneys or those nonminority lawyers who are inclined toward civil rights concerns and justice.

Contract attorney programs could also be accused of partisanship, particularly since this method of indigent defense selection is peculiar to small counties. Under this system, a single lawyer or firm, a bar association, or a nonprofit organization receives a fixed sum or "block grant" through direct negotiations with the county (Gaskins, 1984: 5–6; Spangenberg, Kapuscinski, and Smith, 1988: 3). This method is in contrast to both the use of public defenders who are salaried and the voucher systems used in assigned counsel programs. The enormous political autonomy in small counties is legendary. Every potential abuse of power identified in the other systems—local politics, bigotry, other-culture ignorance, favoritism, and nepotism—is likely to be exacerbated in smaller communities using the contract system. Although this type of program has been adopted in only 10.7 percent of the counties, its growth by nearly two-thirds from 1982 to 1986 attests to its increasing popularity, particularly in the West.

The implications for racial discrimination under public defender systems are most appropriately centered upon the political system in a community. A chief public defender is an appointed figure who, in turn, generally has license to hire the public defenders on his/her staff. The possible misapplication of such power and discretion is obvious: if the administrator has personal biases against, or ignorance of, indigent peoples of color, such attitudes and beliefs could be influential in the selection of attorneys and the climate of the public defender's office, and could eventually filter throughout the entire judicial system, that is, become institutionalized.

Under any of these systems, political or financial dishonesty is always possible in such appointments. The public generally likes to think of the legal profession as honorable; nonetheless it is conceivable (and media-exposed scandals often so indicate) that many attorneys who defend the indigent in criminal cases do it simply for the money, are appointed for political favors owed to them, or represent such cases for other types of monetary reasons (e.g., "kickbacks"). Too often the results of these unlawful liaisons are shoddy legal defenses of clients.

The Quality of Criminal Defense

The quality of service provided by assigned counsel systems is generally thought not to be as high as that of privately retained counsel....

Despite conflicting evidence about the effectiveness of public defenders and assigned counsel, minority defendants have a higher opinion of and more trust in privately obtained, or hired, counsel. Minority defendants criticize public defender attorneys because they are white, middle-class professionals who they feel have more in common culturally with the prosecutors (and judges) than they have with the majority of indigent defendants, who are minority, poor, and of a different social and economic class from that of the defense attorney (NMAC, 1980: 213).

The Prosecutor

The other legal actor in the adversarial court process is the prosecutor who indicts and tries a criminal defendant.... [H]e or she has "virtually unlimited authority" to decide who will be prosecuted and "sole discretion" to determine the prosecution charges, since after an arrest is made, prosecutorial discretion begins (Abadisky, 1987: 319–320). For minorities, the inequities ensuing from this absolute and unrestricted authority center on the increased likelihood of being charged, overcharged, and indicted.

... [A] California study of reasons for release on felony charges which did include race found that "if we combine the reasons for police and prosecutor release, we see that insufficient evidence accounted for *approximately 95 percent* of those released" (Petersilia, 1983: 25; emphasis added). The discriminatory practice originated with the arresting officers and was compounded further by the prosecutor. These data revealed racial disparity in both filing and release —of those arrested, only 21.1 percent of whites were not charged, compared to 31.5 percent of blacks and 28 percent of Hispanics, leading the researcher to conclude: "These data suggest that blacks and Hispanics in California are more likely than whites to be arrested under circumstances that provide insufficient evidence to support criminal charges" (ibid.: 26).

A more poignant example of the abuse of prosecutorial discretion was seen recently at the highest level of government when the United States attorney general used sex to entrap the African American mayor of the nation's capital. As one reporter observed..., while the U.S. attorney general zealously pursued the African American mayor's cocaine case,
he simultaneously neglected to investigate the alleged frequent cocaine use of one of his own close friends, who was also his special assistant. There was no sex trap, surveillance, or harassment in that case. This type of sensational incident pales in comparison to the thousands of such inconsistencies faced daily by African American, Asian American, Hispanic, and Native American citizens because of their skin color....

Plea "Bargaining"

Although outright dismissal—refusal, nolle prosequi, and dismissal by the prosecutor or judge—is the most common disposition of criminal arrests, the most common disposition once a case is accepted for prosecution is a plea of guilty; such pleas account for almost all convictions....

In contrast to the legal actors, the accused is rarely involved in direct negotiations and plays only a small role, limited to an acceptance or rejection of the prosecutor's offer.... The fear of a determination of guilt and a harsh sentence if they go to trial often convinces minorities to plead to a lesser charge (NMAC, 1980: 211), especially when it is known that more severe penalties are exacted as a result of jury trials (Uhlman and Walker, 1979: 231).

When a defendant makes bail, it seriously handicaps the prosecutor in conducting plea negotiations, since the defendant will experience less pressure to plead guilty (Lizotte, 1978: 572). Earlier, it was pointed out that minority arrestees are less able to make bail. Therefore, it follows that there is more pressure upon incarcerated minorities to plead guilty and thereby obtain release from deplorable county jails....

THE COURTROOM ACTORS

In addition to the sentencing practices of judges and juries, the courtroom milieu and its occupants contribute to a scenario that does not generally favor minorities.... The constant interaction between courtroom actors leads to the development of informal relationships that exist inside and outside the courtroom. Whether on the golf links, at the bridge club, or in the course of any other middle- to upper-class socializing, the key "players" in this scenario are socially intertwined at a socioeconomic level far beyond that of the average criminal court defendant, particularly the minority defendant.

The Judge

... The method of selecting judges practically ensures the introduction of class bias into the trial courtroom. Often the selection ignores such characteristics as "professional incompetence, laziness, or intemperance which should disqualify a lawyer from becoming a judge." ...

The problem of incompetence comes about because trial judges are usually either appointed or elected, and both methods are potentially contaminated by class and/or political influences....

The "merit selection" of judges, also known as the Missouri Plan because it was adopted there initially, offers no better justice than election or appointment, since the method resembles the "key man" method of jury selection. A "blue ribbon" committee (or commission), in this case composed of lawyers, submits a list of candidates for consideration by the governor for judicial appointment.

"Known as the ABA Plan or 'merit selection,' it calls for a gubernatorial appointment to be made from a list of nominees drafted by a commission of lawyers, members of the lay electorate, and an incumbent judge." ...

Unfortunately, most studies of the social backgrounds of judges do not assess how a judge's personal values are transposed into court decision-making, but instead are either simple compilations of background characteristics or hypothesized and tested relationships between such variables and decision-making patterns.... Closely enmeshed with a judge's social and political background, social values, and attitudes is the formulation of negative stereotypes of minorities that could impact upon court decisions....

RACE AND NONCAPITAL SENTENCING

There are substantial differences among the states in their laws and sentencing practices; however, more recent tendencies emphasize mandatory sentencing. Research efforts on this subject document positions which support the notion of differential sentencing because of race, as well as the contrary positions that there is no discrimination in sentencing because of racial status. Such mixed and controversial findings continue to make the question of racial discrimination in sentencing inconclusive. In a sense the issue is like being "a little bit pregnant"— one either is or is not—and the implications of the various sentencing practices, those in the past as well as those indicated by recent evidence, continue to suggest racial discrimination in sentencing.

POSTSCRIPT

Is Systemic Racism in Criminal Justice a Myth?

What did you decide? Mann almost challenges you to personally ride along with police; go to the courthouse; watch arrests, processing, and bail setting; and listen in on private snatches of conversations of white police officers, judges, and others.

Wilbanks, with equal feeling, maintains that the numbers tell the story. Blacks are not necessarily being arrested unfairly; they are not being denied their constitutional rights; they are not more likely to receive longer sentences upon conviction for the same crime; nor are they less likely to be denied parole. The conclusion, Wilbanks insists, is that it is a myth to label the system as still being racist.

Recent horrors in New York City—a Black immigrant was tortured by police, and another man, an unarmed Black, was shot dozens of times by police officers—seem to support Mann's position. Other critics cite the racial profiling that is often used by police to detain Blacks or the incident in Buffalo, New York, in which five police officers apologized and were suspended without pay for sending electronic mail messages that slurred Blacks and other minorities. In March 1999 white racist John King beat and dragged a Black man, James Byrd, Jr., to death with his pickup truck. King was sentenced to death. How might Wilbanks argue that each of these terrible incidents actually supports his position? How would Mann reply?

For outstanding current information on crime rates, criminal justice personnel, crime victims, and almost all matters related to crime, including race, you can order free bulletins from the Bureau of Justice Statistics, U.S. Department of Justice, Washington, DC 20531. For a more comprehensive delineation of his thesis, see Wilbanks's *Myth of a Racist Criminal Justice System* (Brooks/Cole, 1987). Also see his collection of articles assembled in *Wilbanks on Race, Crime, and Criminal Justice: A Sourcebook* (Florida International University, 1991). Works by Mann include *Unequal Justice: A Question of Color* (Indiana University Press, 1993) and *Images of Color, Images of Crime* coedited by Marjorie S. Zatz (Roxbury, 1997).

Among the many works that agree with Mann's position are David Cole's *No Equal Justice: Race and Class in the American Criminal Justice System* (New Press, 1999) and Kathryn K. Russell's *Color of Crime* (New York University Press, 1998). An outstanding discussion of turn-of-the-century efforts to link biology and crime is Nicole H. Rafter's *Creating Born Criminals: Biological Theories of Crime and Eugenics* (University of Illinois Press, 1997). Also see Samuel Walker, Cassia Spohn, and Miriam DeLone, *The Color of Justice: Race,*

Ethnicity and Crime in America (Wadsworth, 1996) and Marvin D. Free, Jr., *African Americans and the Criminal Justice System* (Garland, 1996).

An interesting and generally fair delineation of police work and related problems can be found in the *Law Enforcement News*. See, for example, the story on the Buffalo police incident, "Around the Nation," and the story on the alleged racism of police quotas, "Quotas Make Strange Bedfellows," in the January 15/31, 1999, issue. For a summary of the John King murder trial, see "Evil to the End," by Matt Bai and Vern E. Smith, *Newsweek* (March 8, 1999).

For two early discussions of the issue, see W. E. B. Du Bois's *Philadelphia Negro* (Benjamin Bloom, 1899) and *Some Notes on Negro Crime* (Atlanta University Press, 1904). Two works by S. Gabbidon that provide clarification of related terms and elements of racism within the criminal justice system and the discipline of criminal justice itself are "W. E. B. Du Bois on Crime: American Conflict Theorist," *The Criminologist* (January/February 1999) and "Blackaphobia: What Is It, and Who Are Its Victims?" in P. Ray Kedia, ed., *Black on Black Crime: Facing Facts—Challenging Fiction* (Wyndham Hall Press, 1994). See also L. Ross and H. McMurray, "Dual Realities and Structural Challenges of African-American Criminologists," *ACJS Today* (May/June 1996) and the special issue of *Journal of Contemporary Criminal Justice* entitled "Race, Crime and Criminal Justice" (May 1992). The works of Marc Mauer delineate the pervasiveness of racism. See, for example, "Americans Behind Bars," *Criminal Justice* (Winter 1992) and "Race and Class in Sentencing," *The Long Term View* (Summer 1997).

Works that challenge Mann include those of James Q. Wilson and John DiIulio, Jr. See, for instance, DiIulio's "The Question of Black Crime," *The Public Interest* (Fall 1994), which includes several responses. See also DiIulio's "A More Gated Union," *The Weekly Standard* (July 7, 1997).

S. Rothman and S. Powers deny that capital punishment is racist in "Execution by Quota," *The Public Interest* (Summer 1994), while the authors of "Should Capital Punishment Be Abolished?" *Jet* (February 13, 1995) insist that it is.

Carefully read the newspapers for several days. Are you able to identify reports on the criminal justice system that substantiate Wilbanks's thesis or the concerns of Mann?

A study that documents racism in capital crime sentencing is Adalberto Aguirre, Jr., and David V. Baker, "Empirical Research on Racial Discrimination in the Imposition of the Death Penalty," *Criminal Justice Abstracts* (March 1990). For a discussion of young Black males in the criminal justice system, see M. Mauer's *Young Black Men and the Criminal Justice System* (Sentencing Project, 1990).

ISSUE 21

Is the Drug War Harming Blacks?

YES: Thomas Szasz, from *Our Right to Drugs: The Case for a Free Market* (Praeger, 1992)

NO: James A. Inciardi, from "Against Legalization of Drugs," in Arnold S. Trebach and James A. Inciardi, *Legalize It? Debating American Drug Policy* (American University Press, 1993)

ISSUE SUMMARY

YES: Psychiatrist and psychoanalyst Thomas Szasz maintains that the current drug war harms almost all people, especially Blacks, and that its main function is to increase the power of the medical and criminal justice establishments.

NO: James A. Inciardi, director of the Center for Drug and Alcohol Studies at the University of Delaware, surveys several arguments supporting the legalization of drugs and rejects them all, insisting that Blacks and others would be hurt by legalization.

Throughout the twentieth century, America's problems have often been traced to dubious origins that have served primarily as scapegoats. The shifting nature of the American family; the changing behavioral patterns of the young; the broadening of opportunities for Blacks, women, and other minority groups; and increasing political disenchantment—which were all partially the result of increasing modernization, an unpopular war, and other specific structural precipitants—were variously blamed on the movie industry, comic books, bolshevism, gambling, alcohol, organized crime, and, now and then, the devil himself. Currently, the continued concern with the changing nature of the American family, the increasing fear of crime, and the widening generation gap are linked with drug use. If only we could get the dealers off the streets or at least get the kids to say no to drugs, then we could restore our family system. If only we could arrest everyone who takes drugs, then we could eliminate crime, since it is drugs that cause most people to commit crimes. If only the students in our junior high schools, high schools, and colleges were not taking drugs, then they would not only do better on their academic achievement tests but once again love and obey their parents.

The entire criminal justice system, it seems, has been marshalled to fight in the war on drugs. A 1998 report by the National Center on Addiction and Substance Abuse indicates that the tripling of the prison population from 500,000 in 1980 to 1.7 million in 1997 is largely attributable to drug dealing, drug abuse, and drug- and alcohol-related felonies. One of every 14 Black males is behind bars (compared with one of every 144 U.S. citizens). In some urban areas, one of every four Black males is under the auspices of the criminal justice system, many because of drug crimes. A young Black male has a higher chance of being incarcerated than being in college.

The costs of fighting the drug war are enormous, and greater expenditures for police, prisons, and drug control continue with no end in sight. The drug war is seen by critics as demoralizing entire communities, especially the poor. Paradoxically, far more whites use drugs than Blacks, but the war is clearly pitched at inner-city dwellers.

Opinions on this issue are divided. On the one hand, politicians frequently attack anyone who is seen as "soft" on drugs. On the other hand, many visible problems related to drug control grow. These include sharp criticisms by scholars that crime is not decreasing, minorities are becoming increasingly estranged from the police, and the costs are escalating. In addition, cases of police abuse are often uncovered, ranging from harassment of minorities to police themselves being arrested for trafficking in drugs (44 such arrests were made in early 1998 in Ohio).

Defenders of current drug policies counter that without the drug war (i.e., if drugs were decriminalized), crime, poverty, hopelessness, demoralization, and loss of direction, especially among the young and minorities, would be far worse than it is now. If we let up on fighting drugs, they assert, crime would skyrocket. For many, even the idea of providing clean needles to heroin addicts is offensive.

This debate is crucial for criminal justice and minority relations. Specifically, some feel that the handling of crimes that are largely blamed on minorities through the powerful legal system is a good measure of society's commitment to fairness and justice, as opposed to discrimination and racism. As you read the following selections, you will notice that it differs from most standard discussions of the issue: it puts up front the effects of the drug war on those who are most directly and frequently affected.

Thomas Szasz, emphasizing individual liberty, chides both the medical establishment, for usurping American's right to select drugs, and the criminal justice system, for defining drug use (and sales) as a crime. Szasz also ridicules many Black leaders for waging the drug war, claiming genocide and enslavement, and bootlegging victimhood as rational talk. James A. Inciardi, in response, itemizes specific types of drugs and their respective harms. As you read his ideas, consider how he debates and rejects legalizers' perspectives.

As you wrestle with this debate, consider what is meant by "harm." Think about who, if anyone, is currently being harmed the most, and how, by the war. Who might be harmed if drugs are allowed to be sold openly and legally? Would Blacks and other minorities be helped if the drug war were ended?

YES

Thomas Szasz

BLACKS AND DRUGS:
CRACK AS GENOCIDE

Crack is genocide, 1990's style.

—Cecil Williams

No one can deny that, in the tragicomedy we call the War on Drugs, blacks and Hispanics at home and Latin Americans abroad play leading roles: They are (or are perceived to be) our principal drug abusers, drug addicts, drug traffickers, drug counselors, drug-busting policemen, convicts confined for drug offenses, and narco-terrorists. In short, blacks and Hispanics dominate the drug abuse market, both as producers and as products.

I am neither black nor Hispanic and do not pretend to speak for either group or any of its members. There is, however, no shortage of people, black and white, who are eager to speak for them. Which raises an important question, namely: Who speaks for black or Hispanic Americans? Those persons, black or white, who identify drugs—especially crack—as the enemy of blacks? Or those, who cast the American state—especially its War on Drugs—in that role? Or neither, because the claims of both are absurd oversimplifications and because black Americans—like white Americans—are not a homogeneous group but a collection of individuals, each of whom is individually responsible for his own behavior and can speak for himself?

BLACK LEADERS ON DRUGS

For the mainline black drug warrior, illegal drugs represent a temptation that African-Americans are morally too enfeebled to resist. This is what makes those who expose them to such temptation similar to slaveholders depriving their victims of liberty. After years of sloganeering by anti-drug agitators, the claim that crack enslaves blacks has become a cliché, prompting the sloganeers to escalate their rhetoric and contend that it is genocide.

From Thomas Szasz, *Our Right to Drugs: The Case for a Free Market* (Praeger, 1992). Copyright © 1992 by Thomas Szasz. Reprinted by permission of Greenwood Publishing Group, Inc., Westport, CT. Notes omitted.

Crack as Genocide, Crack as Slavery

The assertion that crack is genocide is a powerful and timely metaphor we ought to clarify, lest we get ourselves entangled in it. Slavery and genocide are the manifestations and the results of the use of force by some people against some other people. Drugs, however, are inert substances unless and until they are taken into the body; and, not being persons, they cannot literally force anyone to do anything. Nevertheless, the claim that black persons are "poisoned" and "enslaved" by drugs put at their disposal by a hostile white society is now the politically correct rhetoric among black racists and white liberals alike. For example, *New York Times* columnist A. M. Rosenthal "denounces even the slightest show of tolerance toward illegal drugs as an act of iniquity deserving comparison to the defense of slavery." Of course, people who want to deny the role of personal agency and responsibility often make use of the metaphor of slavery, generating images of people being enslaved not only by drugs but also by cults, gambling, poverty, pornography, rock music, or mental illness. Persons who use drugs may, figuratively speaking, be said to be the "victims" of temptation, which is as far as one can reasonably carry the rhetoric of victimology. However, this does not prevent Cecil Williams, a black minister in San Francisco, from claiming,

> The crack epidemic in the United States amounts to genocide.... The primary intent of 200 years of slavery was to break the spirit and culture of our people.... Now, in the 1990's, I see substantial similarities between the cocaine epidemic and slavery.... Cocaine is foreign to African-American culture. We did not create it; we did not produce it; we did not ask for it.

If a white person made these assertions, his remarks could easily be interpreted as slandering black people. Being enslaved is something done to a person against his will, while consuming cocaine is something a person does willingly; equating the two denigrates blacks by implying that they are, en masse, so childish or weak that they cannot help but "enslave" themselves to cocaine. Williams's remark that cocaine is foreign to black culture and hence destructive compounds his calumny. Rembrandt's art, Beethoven's music, and Newton's physics are also foreign to black culture. Does that make them all evils similar to slavery?

Another black minister, the Reverend Cecil L. Murray of Los Angeles, repeats the same theme but uses different similes. He refers to drugs as if they were persons and asserts that "drugs are *literally* killing our people." Like other anti-drug agitators, Murray is short on facts and reasoning, and long on bombast and scapegoating. He excoriates proposals to legalize drugs, declaring, "This is a foul breach of everything we hold sacred. To legalize it, to condone it, to market it—that is to put a healthy brand on strychnine.... [W]e cannot make poison the norm."

By now, everyone knows that cigarettes kill more people than illegal drugs. But the point needs to be made again here. "Cigarette smoking," writes Kenneth Warner, a health care economist, "causes more premature deaths than do all of the following together: acquired immunodeficiency syndrome, heroin, alcohol, fire, automobile accidents, homicide, and suicide." Many of the conditions Warner lists affect blacks especially adversely. Both smoking and obesity are unhealthy ("poisonous") but "legal" (not prohibited by the criminal law), yet neither is regarded as the "norm."

Up With Hope, Down With Dope

The Reverend Jesse Jackson is not only a permanent presidential candidate, but is also A. M. Rosenthal's favorite drug warrior. Jackson's trademark incantation goes like this: "Up with hope, down with dope." Better at rhyming than reasoning, Jackson flatly asserts—no metaphor here, at least none that he acknowledges— that "drugs are poison. Taking drugs is a sin. Drug use is morally debased and sick." Poison. Sin. Sickness. Jackson the base rhetorician refuses to be outdone and keeps piling it on: "Since the flow of drugs into the U.S. is an act of terrorism, antiterrorist policies must be applied.... If someone is transmitting the death agent to Americans, that person should face wartime consequences. The line must be drawn."

It certainly must. The question, however, is this: Where should we draw it? I believe we ought to draw it by categorizing free trade in agricultural products (including coca, marijuana, and tobacco) as good, and dumping toxic wastes on unsuspecting people in underdeveloped countries as bad; by recognizing the provision of access to accurate pharmacological information as liberating drug education, and rejecting mendacious religiomedical bombast as lamentable political and racial demagogy.

Mayor Marion Barry as Drug Hero

In former days, moral crusaders— especially men of the cloth—thundered brimstone and hellfire at those who succumbed to temptation, typically of the flesh. Why? Because in those benighted pre-Freudian days, moral authorities held people responsible for their behavior. Not any more. And certainly not Jesse Jackson vis-à-vis prominent blacks who use illegal drugs. Foreign drug traffickers are responsible for selling cocaine. Washington, D.C., Mayor Marion Barry is not responsible for buying and smoking it. After the mayor was properly entrapped into buying cocaine and was videotaped smoking it, Jackson pontificated, "Now all of America can learn from the mayor's problems and his long journey back to health." A remarkable disease, this illegal drug use, U.S.A, anno Domini 1990: Caused by being arrested by agents of the state; cured by a "program" provided by agents of the state; its course a "journey"; its prognosis —known with confidence even by priest-politicians without any medical expertise —a return "back to health."

Shamelessly, Jackson used Barry's arrest as an occasion not only for sanctifying the defendant (as if he were accused of a civil rights violation) but also for promoting his own political agenda. A priori, the defendant was a good and great man, "entering the Super Bowl of his career." His accuser—the U.S. government—was, a priori, an evil "political system that can only be described as neocolonial." While thus politicizing drugs, Jackson impudently inveighs against his own practice. "Circumstances like these," he babbles, "remind us that the war on drugs... should not be politicized. It is primarily a moral crusade, about values and about health and sickness." Having unburdened himself of his pearls of wisdom about politics, moral values, and sickness and health, Jackson comes to his main point: "Behind these gruesome statistics lies the powerlessness of the people who live in the shadow of a national government from which they are structurally excluded. Now more than ever, it is time to escalate the effort to gain statehood and self-government for the district"—and elect Jesse Jackson senator-for-life-or-until-elected-president. Should we not expect political self-government to be preceded by personal self-government, as it normally is in progressing from disfranchised childhood to enfranchised adulthood? Jackson's envy of and thirst for the power of whites is clear enough. His contention that blacks in Washington, D.C., sell, buy, and use illegal drugs because they are "powerless" is thus but another instance of a drug warrior's fingering a scapegoat in the guise of offering an explanation.

Is Jackson, one of our most prominent anti-drug agitators, trying to protect black Americans from drugs or is he trying to promote his own career? Unlike the Black Muslims committed to an ideology of self-help, self-reliance, and radical separatism, Jackson is playing on the white man's turf, trying to gain power by the "enemy's" methods and rules. The War on Drugs presents him, as it presents his white counterparts, with the perfect social problem: Here is an issue on which Jesse Jackson can join—on common ground, shoulder to shoulder—not only such eminent white liberal-democrats as Mario Cuomo and Kitty Dukakis, but also such eminent white conservative-Republicans as Nancy Reagan and William Bennett. Indeed, on what other issue besides drugs could Jesse Jackson and Nancy Reagan —one a black militant struggling up the social ladder, the other a white conservative standing on its top rung—agree? As pharmarcological agents, dangerous drugs may indeed be toxic for the body anatomic of the individuals who use them; but as a propaganda tool, dangerous drugs are therapeutic for the body politic of the nation, welding our heterogeneous society together into one country and one people, engaged in an uplifting, self-purifying, moral crusade.

THE WAR ON DRUGS: A WAR ON BLACKS

A Martian who came to earth and read only what the newspaper headlines say about drugs would never discover an interesting and important feature of America's latest moral crusade, namely, that its principal victims are black or Hispanic. (I must add here that when I use the word *victim* in connection with the word *drug*, I do not refer to a person who chooses to use a drug and thus subjects himself to its effects, for good or ill. Being his own poisoner—assuming the drug has an ill effect on him—such a person is a victim in a metaphoric sense only. In the conventional use of the term, to which I adhere, a literal or real victim is a person unjustly or tragically deprived of his life, liberty, or property, typically by other people—in our case, as a result of the criminalization of the free market in drugs.)

However, were the Martian to turn on the television to watch the evening news, or look at a copy of *Time* or *Newsweek*, he would see images of drug busts and read stories about drug addicts and drug treatment programs in which virtually all of the characters are black or Hispanic. Occasionally, some of the drug-busting policemen are white. But the drug traffickers, drug addicts, and drug counselors are virtually all black or Hispanic.

Carl Rowan, a syndicated columnist who is black, finally spoke up. "Racist stereotypes," he correctly pointed out, "have crippled the minds of millions of white Americans." Then, rather selectively, Rowan emphasized that "white prejudice on this point has produced a terrible injustice," but chose to remain discreetly silent about the fact that black leaders are the shock troops in this anti-black drug war. "Blacks," complained Rowan, "are being arrested in USA's drug wars at a rate far out of proportion to their drug use." According to a study conducted by *USA Today*, blacks comprise 12.7 percent of the population and make up 12 percent of those who "regularly use illegal drugs"; but of those arrested on drug charges in 1988, 38 percent were blacks.

Other studies indicate that blacks represent an even larger proportion of drug law violators/victims. For example, according to the National Institute on Drug Abuse (NIDA, the leading federal agency on drug abuse research), "Although only about 12% of those using illegal drugs are black, 44% of those who are arrested for simple possession and 57% of those arrested for sales are black." Another study, conducted by the Washington-based Sentencing Project, found that while almost one in four black men of age 20–29 were in jail or on parole, only one in sixteen white men of the same age group were. Clarence Page dramatized the significance of these figures by pointing out that while 610,000 black men in their twenties are in jail or under the supervision of the criminal justice system, only 436,000 are in college. "Just as no one is born a college student," commented Page, "no one is born a criminal. Either way, you have to be carefully taught."

Page does not say who is teaching blacks to be criminals, but I will: The economic incentives intrinsic to our drug laws. After all, although black Americans today are often maltreated by whites, and are in the main poorer than whites, they were *more maltreated and were even poorer* fifty or a hundred years ago, yet fewer young black males chose a criminal career then than do now. This development is far more dangerous for all of us, black and white, than all the cocaine in Columbia. "Under the nation's current approach," a feature report in the *Los Angeles Times* acknowledges, "black America is being criminalized at an astounding rate." Nevertheless, the black community enthusiastically supports the War on Drugs. George Napper, director of public safety in Atlanta, attributes this attitude to "black people... being more conservative than other people. They say: 'To hell with rights. Just kick ass and take names.'" Father George Clements, a Catholic priest who has long been in the forefront of the struggle against drugs in Chicago's black communities, exemplifies this posture: "I'm all for whatever tactics have to be used. If that means they are trampling on civil liberties, so be it." The black leadership's seemingly increasing contempt for civil liberties is just one of the disastrous consequences of drug prohibition. The drug war's impact on poor and poorly educated blacks is equally alarming and tragic. Instead of looking to the free market and the rule of law for self-advancement, the War on Drugs encourages them to look to a race war— or a lottery ticket—as a way out of their misfortune.

Drug Prohibition: Pouring Fuel on the Fire of Racial Antagonism

Clearly, one of the unintended consequences of drug prohibition—far more dangerous to American society than drugs—has been that it has fueled the fires of racial division and antagonism. Many American blacks (whose views white psychiatrists would love to dismiss as paranoid if they could, but happily no longer can) believe that the government is "out to get them" and the War on Drugs is one of its tools: A "popular theory [among blacks] is that white government leaders play a pivotal role in the drug crisis by deliberately making drugs easily available in black neighborhoods." Another consequence of our drug laws (less unintended perhaps) has been that while it is no longer officially permissible to persecute blacks qua blacks, it is permissible to persecute them qua drug law violators. Under the pretext of protecting people—especially "kids"—from dangerous drugs, America's young black males are stigmatized en masse as drug addicts and drug criminals. The possibility that black youths may be more endangered by society's drug laws than by the temptation of drugs surely cannot be dismissed out of hand. It is an idea, however, that only those black leaders who have shaken off the shackles of trying to please their degraders dare to entertain. Thus we now find the Black Muslim minister Louis Farrakhan articulating such a view, much as the martyred Malcolm X did a quarter of a century ago. "There is," says Farrakhan, "a war being planned against black youth by the government of the United States under the guise of a war against drugs." I suspect few educated white persons really listen to or hear this message, just as few listened to or heard what Malcolm X said. And of those who hear it, most dismiss it as paranoid. But paranoids too can have real enemies.

The U.S. Customs Service acknowledges that, to facilitate its work in spotting drug smugglers, the service uses "drug courier" and "drug swallower" profiles developed in the 1970s. Critics have charged that "one characteristic that most of those detained have in common is their race. 'The darker your skin, the better your chances,' said Gary Trichter, a Houston defense lawyer who specializes in such cases." In a ruling handed down on April 3, 1989, the Supreme Court endorsed the government's use of drug profiles for detaining and questioning airline passengers. Although the Court's ruling addressed only airports, the profiles are also used on highways, on interstate buses, and in train stations. In addition, the Customs Service is authorized to request the traveler, under penalty of being detained or not allowed to enter the country, to submit to an X-ray examination to determine if he has swallowed a condom containing drugs. "In Miami, of 101 X-rays, 67 found drugs. In New York, of 187 X-rays, 90 yielded drugs. In Houston . . . 60 people were X-rayed [and] just 4 were found to be carrying drugs." Although the profiles have proved to be of some value, this does not justify their use unless one believes that the government's interest in finding and punishing people with illegal drugs in their possession deserves more protection than the individual's right to his own body.

What do the statistics about the people stopped and searched on the basis of drug profiles tell us? They reveal, for example, that in December 1989 in Biloxi, Mississippi, of fifty-seven stops on Interstate 10, fifty-five involved Hispanic or black people. On a stretch of the New Jersey Turnpike where less than 5 percent of the traffic involved cars with out-of-state license plates driven by black males, 80 percent of the arrests fitted that description. Topping the record for racially discriminatory drug arrests is the drug-interdiction program at the New York Port Authority Bus Terminal, where 208 out of 210 persons arrested in 1989 were black or Hispanic. Still, the anti-drug bureaucrats insist that "the ratio of arrests reflected a 'reality of the streets,' rather than a policy of racial discrimination."

However, in January 1991 Pamela Alexander, a black judge in Minnesota, ruled that the state's anti-crack law—which "calls for a jail term for first-time offenders convicted of possessing three grams of crack, but only probation for defendants convicted of possessing the same amount of powdered cocaine" —discriminated against blacks and was therefore unconstitutional. Her ruling focuses on the fact that crack cocaine and powdered cocaine are merely two different forms of cocaine, and that blacks tend to use the former, and whites the latter. The law thus addresses a difference in customs, not a difference in drug effects. "Drug policy," Judge Alexander concluded, "should not be set according to anything less than scientific evidence." Unfortunately, this is a very naive statement. There is no scientific basis for any of our "drug policies"—a term that, in this context, is a euphemism for prohibiting pharmaceutical and recreational drugs. Warning people about the risks a particular drug poses is the most that science can be made to justify.

In any case, science has nothing to do with the matter at hand, as the contention of the drug enforcers illustrates. Their rejoinder to Judge Alexander's ruling is that "crack is different." In what way? "The stuff is cheap and ... affordable to kids in the school yard who can't afford similar amounts of powdered cocaine." Behind this pathetic argument stand some elementary facts unfamiliar to the public and denied by the drug warriors. Simply put, crack is to powdered cocaine as cigarettes are to chewing tobacco. Smoking introduces drugs into the body via the lungs; snorting and chewing, via the nasal and buccal mucosae. Different classes tend to display different preferences for different drugs. Educated persons (used to) smoke cigarettes and snort cocaine; uneducated persons chew tobacco and smoke crack. (This generalization is rapidly becoming obsolete. In the United States, though much less in Europe, Asia, and Latin America, smoking cigarettes is becoming a lower-class habit.) These facts make a mockery of the Minnesota legislators' disingenuous denunciation of Judge Alexander's decision: "The one thing we never contemplated was targeting members of any single minority group." It remains to be seen whether the Minnesota Supreme Court, to which the case was appealed, will uphold punishing crack smokers more severely than cocaine snorters.

The enforcement of our drug laws with respect to another special population—namely, pregnant women—is also shamefully racist. Many state laws now regard the pregnant woman who uses an illegal drug as a criminal—not because she possesses or sells or uses a drug, but because she "delivers" it to her fetus via the umbilical cord. Ostensibly aimed at protecting the fetus, the actual enforcement of these laws lends further support to the assumption that their real target is the unwed, inner-city, black mother. Although, according to experts, drug use in pregnancy is equally prevalent in white middle-class women, most women prosecuted for using illegal drugs while pregnant have been poor members of racial minorities. "Researchers found that about 15 percent of both the white and the black women used drugs ... but that the black women were 10 times as likely as whites to be reported to the authorities."

Drugs and Racism

How do the drug warriors rationalize the racism of the War on Drugs? Partly by ignoring the evidence that the enforcement of drug laws victimizes blacks disproportionately compared to whites; and partly by falling back on a time-honored technique of forestalling the charge by appointing a respected member of the victimized group to a high position in the machinery charged with enforcing the persecutory practice. This is what former drug czar William Bennett did when he picked Reuben Greenberg, a black Jew, as his favorite drug cop. What has Greenberg done to deserve this honor? He chose to prosecute as drug offenders the most defenseless members of the black community. "The tactics Greenberg developed in Charleston [South Carolina]," explained *Time* magazine, "are targeted on the poorest of the poor—the residents of public-housing projects and their neighbors.... The projects were 'the easiest place to start, because that's where the victims are.'" Perhaps so. But, then, it must be safer—especially for a black Jewish policeman in South Carolina—to go after blacks in inner-city housing projects than after whites in suburban mansions.

The evidence supports the suspicion that the professional pushers of drug programs pander precisely to such racial prejudices, with spectacularly hypocritical results. Consider the latest fad in addictionology: a racially segregated drug treatment program for blacks. Because the program is owned by blacks, is operated by blacks for blacks, and offers a service called "drug treatment," its owner-operators have been able to pass it off as a fresh "culturally specific" form of therapy. If whites were to try to do this sort of thing to blacks, it would be decried as racist segregation. When black "for-

mer drug abusers" do it to fellow blacks, the insurance money pours in: Soon after opening, the clinic called Coalesce was handling three hundred patients at $13,000 a head per month—not bad pay for treating a nonexistent illness with a nonexistent treatment.

BLACK MUSLIMS ON DRUGS

Mainstream American blacks are Christians, who look for leadership to Protestant priest-politicians and blame black drug use on rich whites, capitalism, and South American drug lords. Sidestream American blacks are Muslims, who look for leadership to Islamic priest-politicians and maintain that drug use is a matter of personal choice and self-discipline.

The Black Muslim supporters of a free market in drugs (though they do not describe their position in these terms) arrive at their conclusion not from studying the writings of Adam Smith or Ludwig von Mises, but from their direct experience with the American therapeutic state and its punitive agents decked out as doctors and social workers. As a result, the Black Muslims regard statist-therapeutic meddling as diminishing the person targeted as needing help, robbing him of his status as a responsible moral agent, and therefore fundamentally degrading; and they see the medicalization of the drug problem—the hypocritical defining of illegal drug use as both a crime and a disease, the capricious law enforcement, the economic incentives to transgress the drug laws, and the pseudotherapeutic drug programs—as a wicked method for encouraging drug use, crime, economic dependency, personal demoralization, and familial breakdown. I have reviewed the enduring Black Muslim principles and policies on drugs, as developed by Malcolm X, elsewhere. Here I shall summarize only what is necessary to round out the theme I developed in this [selection].

Black Muslims demand, on moral and religious grounds, that their adherents abstain from all self-indulgent pleasures, including drugs. Accordingly, it would be misleading to speak of a Black Muslim approach to the "treatment of drug addiction." If a person is a faithful Black Muslim he cannot be an addict, just as if he is an Orthodox Jew he cannot be a pork eater. It is as simple as that. The Muslim perspective on drug use and drug avoidance is—like mine—moral and ceremonial, not medical and therapeutic. Of course, this does not mean that we come to all the same conclusions.

Malcolm X: Triumph Through Resisting Temptation

Malcolm X's passion for honesty and truth led him to some remarkable drug demythologizings, that is, assertions that seemingly fly in the face of current medical dogmas about hard drugs and their addictive powers. "Some prospective Muslims," wrote Malcolm, "found it more difficult to quit tobacco than others found quitting the dope habit." As I noted, for Muslims it makes no difference whether a man smokes tobacco or marijuana; what counts is the habit of self-indulgence, not the pharmacomythology of highs or kicks. Evidently, one good mythology per capita is enough: If a person truly believes in the mythology of Black Muslimism—or Judaism, or Christianity—then he does not need the ersatz mythology of medicalism and therapeutism.

The Muslims emphasize not only that addiction is evil, but also that it is deliberately imposed on the black man by the white man. "The Muslim program began with recognizing that color and addiction have a distinct connection. It is no accident that in the entire Western Hemisphere, the greatest localized concentration of addicts is in Harlem." The monkey on the addict's back is not the abstraction of drug addiction as a disease, but the concrete reality of Whitey. "Most black junkies," explains Malcolm, "really are trying to narcotize themselves against being a black man in the white man's America." By politicizing personal problems (defining self-medication with narcotics as political oppression), the Muslims neatly reverse the psychiatric tactic of personalizing political problems (defining psychiatric incarceration as hospitalization).

Because for Muslims drug use—legal or illegal—is not a disease, they have no use for pretentious drug treatment programs, especially if they consist of substituting one narcotic drug for another (methadone for heroin). Instead, they rely on breaking the drug habit by expecting the drug user to quit "cold turkey." The ordeal this entails helps to dramatize and ritualize the addict's liberation from Whitey. "When the addict's withdrawal sets in," explains Malcolm, "and he is screaming, cursing and begging, 'Just one shot, man!' the Muslims are right there talking junkie jargon to him, 'Baby, knock that monkey off your back! ... Kick Whitey off your back!'" Ironically, what Black Muslims tell their adherents is not very different from what white doctors told each other at the beginning of this century. In 1921, writing in the *Journal of the American Medical Association*, Alfred C. Prentice, M. D.—a member of the Committee on Narcotic Drugs of the

American Medical Association—rejected "the shallow pretense that drug addiction is a 'disease'... [a falsehood that] has been asserted and urged in volumes of 'literature' by self-styled 'specialists.'"

Malcolm X wore his hair crew-cut, dressed with the severe simplicity and elegance of a successful Wall Street lawyer, and was polite and punctual. Alex Haley describes the Muslims as having "manners and miens [that] reflected the Spartan personal discipline the organization demanded." While Malcolm hated the white man—whom he regarded as the "devil"—he despised the black man who refused the effort to better himself: "The black man in the ghettoes... has to start self-correcting his own material, moral, and spiritual defects and evils. The black man needs to start his own program to get rid of drunkenness, drug addiction, prostitution."

This is dangerous talk. Liberals and psychiatrists need the weak-willed and the mentally sick to have someone to disdain, care for, and control. If Malcolm had his way, such existential cannibals masquerading as do-gooders would be unemployed, or worse. Here, then, is the basic conflict and contradiction between the Muslim and methadone: By making the Negro self-responsible and self-reliant, Muslimism eliminates the problem and with it the need for the white man and the medicine man; whereas by making the white man and the doctor indispensable for the Negro as permanent social cripple and lifelong patient, medicalism aggravates and perpetuates the problem.

Malcolm understood and asserted—as few black or white men could understand or dared to assert—that white men want blacks to be on drugs, and that most black men who are on drugs want to be on them rather than off them. Freedom and self-determination are not only precious, but arduous. If people are not taught and nurtured to appreciate these values, they are likely to want to have nothing to do with them. Malcolm X and Edmund Burke shared a profound discernment of the painful truth that the state wants men to be weak and timid, not strong and proud. Indeed, perhaps the only thing Malcolm failed to see was that, by articulating his views as he did, he was in fact launching a religious war against greatly superior forces. I do not mean a religious war against Christianity. The religious war Malcolm launched was a war against the religion of Medicine—a faith other black leaders blindly worship. After all, blacks and whites alike now believe, as an article of faith, that drug abuse is an illness. That is why they demand and demonstrate for "free" detoxification programs and embrace methadone addiction as a cure for the heroin habit. Malcolm saw this, but I am not sure he grasped the enormity of it all. Or perhaps he did and that is why in the end, not long before he was killed, he rejected the Black Muslims as well—to whom, only a short while before, he gave all the credit for his resurrection from the gutter. He converted, one more time, to Orthodox Islam. Then he was murdered.

Do Drug Prohibitionists Protect Blacks?

Not surprisingly, drug prohibitionists systematically ignore the Black Muslim position on drugs. Neither bureaucratic drug criminalizers nor academic drug legalizers ever mention Malcolm X's name, much less cite his writings on drugs. The fact that Louis Farrakhan, the present leader of the Nation of Islam, continues to support Malcolm X's position on drugs does not help to make that position more acceptable to the white establishment. In characteristically statist fashion, instead of seeing drug laws as racist, the drug prohibitionists see the absence of drug laws as racist. If "the legalizers prevail"—James Q. Wilson, a professor of management and public policy at UCLA, ominously predicts—

> then we will have consigned hundreds of thousands of infants and hundreds of neighborhoods to a life of oblivion and disease. To the lives and families destroyed by alcohol we will have added countless more destroyed by cocaine, heroin, PCP, and whatever else a basement scientist can invent. Human character is formed by society.... [G]ood character is less likely in a bad society.

Virtually everything Wilson asserts here is false. Liberty is the choice to do right or wrong, to act prudently or imprudently, to protect oneself or injure oneself. Wilson is disingenuous in selecting alcohol and drugs as the "destroyers" of people. And as for his implying that our present prohibitionist mode of managing drugs has promoted the formation of "good character"—the less said, the better.

Wilson's argument brings us back full circle to the genocidal image of drugs, suggested here by a prominent white academic rather than a black priest-politician. As I observed before, this view casts the individual in a passive role, as victim. But if there are injured victims, there must be injuring victimizers. Wilson knows who they are: us. But he is wrong. Opportunity, choice, temptation do not constitute victimization. Wilson affronts the supporters of liberty by so categorizing them.

Finally, Wilson's explanation leaves no room for why some blacks succeed in not being consigned to what he revealingly calls "a life of oblivion and disease." Nor does Wilson consider the dark possibility that there might, especially for white Americans, be a fate worse than a few thousand blacks selling and using drugs. Suppose every black man, woman, and child in America rejected drugs, chose to emulate Malcolm X, and became a militant black separationist. Would that be better for American whites, or for the United States as a nation?

NO

James A. Inciardi

AGAINST LEGALIZATION OF DRUGS

THE PRO-LEGALIZATION ISSUES AND CONTENDERS

The drug legalization debate emerged in both generic and specific configurations. In its most generic adaptation, it went something like this. First, the drug laws have created evils far worse than the drugs themselves—corruption, violence, street crime, and disrespect for the law. Second, legislation passed to control drugs has failed to reduce demand. Third, you should not prohibit that which a major segment of the population is committed to doing; that is, you simply cannot arrest, prosecute, and punish such large numbers of people, particularly in a democracy. And specifically in this behalf, in a liberal democracy the government must not interfere with personal behavior if liberty is to be maintained. . . .

Thomas S. Szasz and the control of conduct   Thomas S. Szasz is a Hungarian-born psychiatrist who emigrated to the United States in 1938 and studied medicine at the University of Cincinnati. Trained in psychiatry at the University of Chicago, he became a well-known critic of his profession. Szasz has written that "mental illness" is a mythological concept used by the state to control deviants and thereby limit freedom in American society. In his view, the conditions comprising mental illness are social and moral problems, not medical ones. He repeatedly warns against replacing a theological worldview with a therapeutic one. Moreover, he is an uncompromising libertarian and humanist who has argued against involuntary psychiatric examination and hospitalization, and who believes that the psychoanalytic relationship should be free of coercion and control. . . .

During the 1970s, relying on the postulates and assertions that he had applied to mental illness, Szasz became the most outspoken critic of the medical or "disease" model of addiction. His primary concern with the disease model is that it diminishes an individual's responsibility for his or her dysfunctional or antisocial behavior. He also argues that the concept of addiction as a disease places undue emphasis on medical authority in determining how

From James A. Inciardi, "Against Legalization of Drugs," in Arnold S. Trebach and James A. Inciardi, *Legalize It? Debating American Drug Policy* (American University Press, 1993). Copyright © 1993 by American University Press. Reprinted by permission. Notes and references omitted.

society should manage what is actually an individual violation of legal and social norms.

On the matter of whether society should attempt to control, and hence "prohibit" the use of certain substances, he offers the following:

The plain historical facts are that before 1914 there was no "drug problem" in the United States; nor did we have a name for it. Today there is an immense drug problem in the United States, and we have lots of names for it. Which came first: "the problem of drug abuse" or its name?... My point is simply that our drug abuse experts, legislators, psychiatrists, and other professional guardians of our medical morals have been operating chicken hatcheries; they continue—partly by means of certain characteristic tactical abuses of our language—to manufacture and maintain the "drug problem" they ostensibly try to solve (Szasz 1974).

What he was suggesting is something that nominalists have been saying for centuries: that a thing does not exist until it is imagined and given a name. For Szasz, a hopeless believer in this position, the "drug problem" in the United States did not exist before the passage of the Harrison Act in 1914, but became a reality when the behavior under consideration was *labeled* as a problem. Stated differently, he argues that the drug problem in America was created in great part by the very policies designed to control it.

For Szasz, the solution to the drug problem is simple. Ignore it, and it will no longer be a problem. After all, he maintained, there is precedent for it:

... Our present attitudes toward the whole subject of drug use, drug abuse, and drug control are nothing but the re-

flections, in the mirror of "social reality," of our own expectations toward drugs and toward those who use them; and that our ideas about and interventions in drug-taking behavior have only the most tenuous connection with the actual pharmacological properties of "dangerous drugs." The "danger" of masturbation disappeared when we ceased to believe in it: when we ceased to attribute danger to the practice and to its practitioners; and ceased to call it "self-abuse" (Szasz 1974).

What Szasz seems to be suggesting is that heroin, cocaine, and other "dangerous drugs" be legalized; hence, the problems associated with their use would disappear. And this is where he runs into difficulty, for his argument is so riddled with faulty scholarship and flagrant errors of fact that he lost credibility with those familiar with the history of the American drug scene.

Szasz's libertarian-laissez-faire position has continued into the 1990s. He perseveres in his argument that people should be allowed to ingest, inhale, or inject whatever substances they wish. And it would appear from his comments that he is opposed to drug regulation of any type, even by prescription....

Arnold S. Trebach and harm reduction
Perhaps most respected in the field of drug-policy reform is Arnold S. Trebach....

Briefly, his proposals for drug-policy are the following:

1. Reverse drug-policy funding priorities....

2. Curtail AIDS: Make clean needles available to intravenous drug addicts....

3. Develop a plan for drug treatment on demand, allow Medicaid to pay for the

poor, and expand the variety of treatment options available....

4. Stop prosecutions of pregnant drug users....

5. Make medical marijuana available to the seriously ill....

6. Appoint a commission to seriously examine alternatives to prohibition....

Although my objections and alternatives are discussed later, let me just say that Trebach has experienced a "conversion" of sorts in recent years. There was a time when he denied endorsing the legalization of drugs....

The Debate's Supporting Cast and Bit Players

An aspect of the drug-policy debates of the second half of the 1980s was a forum awash with self-defined experts from many walks of life.

The bit players The "bit players" were the many who had a lot to say on the debate, but from what I feel were not particularly informed positions. They wrote books, or they published papers, but they remained on the sidelines because either no one took them seriously, their work was carelessly done, or their arguments were just not persuasive....

A rather pathetically hatched entry to the debate was Richard Lawrence Miller's book, *The Case for Legalizing Drugs* (1991).... Perhaps most misleading in the book is the list of "benefits" of using illicit drugs. I'll cite but one example to provide a glimpse of the author's approach:

Heroin can calm rowdy teenagers— reducing aggression, sexual drive, fertility, and teen pregnancy—helping ado-

lescents through that time of life (Miller 1991, 153).

I have a teenage daughter, so I guess I'll have to remember that if she ever gets rowdy. Enough!

Cameos and comic relief ...Such well-known personages as conservative pundit William F. Buckley, Jr., Nobel laureate economist Milton Friedman, former Secretary of State George P. Shultz, journalist Anthony Lewis, *Harper's* editor Lewis H. Lapham, and even Washington, D. C., Mayor Marion Barry came forward to endorse legalization. The "legalizers" viewed the support of these notables as a legitimation of their argument, but all had entered the debate from disturbingly uninformed positions. With the exception of Marion Barry, and I say this facetiously, none had any first-hand experience with the issues....

ARGUING AGAINST LEGALIZATION

... While there are numerous arguments *for* legalization, there are likely an equal or greater number *against*.

Some Public Health Considerations

Tomorrow, like every other average day in the United States, about 11,449.3 babies will be born, 90 acres of pizza will be ordered, almost 600,000 M&M candies will be eaten, and some 95 holes-in-one will be claimed. At the same time, 171 million bottles of beer will be consumed, and almost 1.5 billion cigarettes will be smoked (Ruth 1992). In 1965, the annual death toll from smoking-related diseases was estimated at 188,000. By the close of the 1980s that figure had more than doubled, to 434,000, and it is expected to increase throughout the 1990s (Centers for Disease Control 1990, 1991b). And these figures do not include the almost 40,000 nonsmokers who die each year from ailments associated with the inhalation of passive smoke.

... [I]t is estimated that there are 10.5 million alcoholics in the United States, and that a total of 73 million adults have been touched by alcoholism (*Alcoholism and Drug Abuse Weekly*, 9 October 1991, 1). Each year there are some 45,000 alcohol-related traffic fatalities in the United States (Centers for Disease Control 1991a), and thousands of women who drink during pregnancy bear children with irreversible alcohol-related defects (Steinmetz 1992). Alcohol use in the past year was reported by 54 percent of the nation's eighth graders, 72 percent of tenth graders, and 78 percent of twelfth graders, and almost a third of high school seniors in 1991 reported "binge drinking." ... [T]he cost of alcohol abuse in the United States for 1990 has been estimated at $136.31 billion (*Substance Abuse Report*, 15 June 1991, 3).

Sophism, legalization, and illicit drug use Keep the above data in mind, and consider that they relate to only two of the *legal* drugs. Now for some reason, numerous members of the pro-legalization lobby argue that if drugs were to be legalized, usage would likely not increase very much, if at all. The reasons, they state, are that "drugs are everywhere," and that everyone who wants to use them already does. But the data beg to differ. For example,... 56 percent of high school seniors in 1991 had never used an illicit drug in their lifetimes, and 73 percent had never used an illicit drug other than marijuana in their lifetimes. ... [T]he absolute numbers

in these age cohorts who have never even *tried* any illicit drugs are in the tens of millions. And most significantly for the argument that "drugs are everywhere," half of all high school students do not feel that drugs are easy to obtain.

Going further,... most people in the general population do not use drugs. Granted, these data are limited to the "general population," which excludes such hard-to-reach populations as members of deviant and exotic subcultures, the homeless, and others living "on the streets," and particularly those in which drug use rates are highest. However, the data do document that the overwhelming majority of Americans do not use illicit drugs. This suggests two things: that the drug prohibitions may be working quite well; and that there is a large population who might, and I emphasize might, use drugs if they were legal and readily available....

An interesting variety of sophist reasoning pervades segments of the pro-legalization thesis. It is argued over and over that drugs should be legalized because they don't really do that much harm.... The legalizers use... data to demonstrate that not too many people actually have adverse encounters with heroin, cocaine, and other illicit drugs, as compared with the hundreds of thousands of deaths each year linked to alcohol and tobacco use.... But interestingly, it is never stated that proportionately few people actually use illicit drugs, and that the segment of the population "at risk" for overdose or other physical complications from illegal drug use is but an insignificant fraction of that at risk for disease and death from alcohol and tobacco use.

The problems with illegal drugs Considerable evidence exists to suggest that the legalization of drugs could create behavioral and public health problems that would far outweigh the current consequences of drug prohibition. There are some excellent reasons why marijuana, cocaine, heroin, and other drugs are now controlled, and why they ought to remain so.…

Marijuana. There is considerable misinformation about marijuana. To the millions of adolescents and young adults who were introduced to the drug during the social revolution of the 1960s and early 1970s, marijuana was a harmless herb of ecstasy. As the "new social drug" and a "natural organic product," it was deemed to be far less harmful than either alcohol or tobacco (see Grinspoon 1971; Smith 1970; Sloman 1979). More recent research suggests, however, that marijuana smoking is a practice that combines the hazardous features of both tobacco and alcohol with a number of pitfalls of its own. Moreover, there are many disturbing questions about marijuana's effect on the vital systems of the body, on the brain and mind, on immunity and resistance, and on sex and reproduction (Jones and Lovinger 1985).

One of the more serious difficulties with marijuana use relates to lung damage.… Researchers at the University of California at Los Angeles reported… in 1988 that the respiratory burden in smoke particulates and absorption of carbon monoxide from smoking just one marijuana "joint" is some *four times greater* than from smoking a single tobacco cigarette.… [M]arijuana deposits four times more tar in the throat and lungs and increases carbon monoxide levels in the blood fourfold to fivefold.

… [A]side from the health consequences of marijuana use, recent research on the behavioral aspects of the drug suggests that it severely affects the social perceptions of heavy users. Findings from the Center for Psychological Studies in New York City, for example, report that adults who smoked marijuana daily believed the drug helped them to function better—improving their self-awareness and relationships with others (Hendin et al. 1987). In reality, however, marijuana had acted as a "buffer," enabling users to tolerate problems rather than face them and make changes that might increase the quality of their social functioning and satisfaction with life. The study found that the research subjects used marijuana to avoid dealing with their difficulties, and the avoidance inevitably made their problems worse, on the job, at home, and in family and sexual relationships.

… [W]hat has been said about cocaine also applies to crack, and perhaps more so. Crack's low price (as little as $2 per rock in some locales) has made it an attractive drug of abuse for those with limited funds. Its rapid absorption brings on a faster onset of dependence than is typical with other forms of cocaine, resulting in higher rates of addiction, binge use, and psychoses. The consequences include higher levels of cocaine-related violence and all the same manifestations of personal, familial, and occupational neglect that are associated with other forms of drug dependence.…

Heroin. A derivative of morphine, heroin is a highly addictive narcotic, and is the drug historically associated with addiction and street crime. Although heroin overdose is not uncommon, unlike alcohol, cocaine, tobacco, and many prescription drugs, the direct physiological damage caused by heroin use tends to be minimal. And it is for this reason that the protagonists of drug legalization include heroin in their arguments. By making heroin readily available to users, they argue, many problems could be sharply reduced if not totally eliminated, including: the crime associated with supporting a heroin habit; the overdoses resulting from unknown levels of heroin purity and potency; the HIV and hepatitis infections brought about by needle-sharing; and the personal, social, and occupational dislocations resulting from the drug-induced criminal lifestyle.

The belief that the legalization of heroin would eliminate crime, overdose, infections, and life dislocations for its users is for the most part delusional. Instead, it is likely that the heroin-use lifestyle would change little for most addicts regardless of the legal status of the drug, an argument supported by ample evidence in the biographies and autobiographies of narcotics addicts, the clinical assessments of heroin addiction, and the drug abuse treatment literature. And to this can be added the many thousands of conversations I have had over the past 30 years with heroin users and members of their families.

The point is this. Heroin is a highly addicting drug. For the addict, it becomes life-consuming: it becomes mother, father, spouse, lover, counselor, and confessor. Because heroin is a short-acting drug, with its effects lasting at best four to six hours, it must be taken regularly and repeatedly. Because there is a more rapid onset when taken intravenously, most heroin users inject the drug. Because heroin has depressant effects, a portion of the user's day is spent in a semi-stupefied state. Collectively, these attributes result in a user more concerned with drug-taking and drug-seeking than health, family, work, relationships, responsibility, or anything else.

The pursuit of pleasure and escape ... [R]esearch by professors Michael D. Newcomb and Peter M. Bentler of the University of California at Los Angeles has documented the long-term behavioral effects of drug use on teenagers (Newcomb and Bentler 1988). Beginning in 1976, a total of 654 Los Angeles County youths were tracked for a period of eight years. Most of these youths were only occasional users of drugs, using drugs and alcohol moderately at social gatherings, whereas upwards of 10 percent were frequent, committed users. The impact of drugs on these frequent users was considerable. As teenagers, drug use tended to intensify the typical adolescent problems with family and school. In addition, drugs contributed to such psychological difficulties as loneliness, bizarre and disorganized thinking, and suicidal thoughts. Moreover, frequent drug users left school earlier, started jobs earlier, and formed families earlier, and as such, they moved into adult roles with the maturity levels of adolescents. The consequences of this pattern included rapid family break-ups, job instability, serious crime, and ineffective personal relationships. In short, frequent drug use prevented the acquisition of the coping mechanisms that are part of maturing; it blocked teenagers' learning of interpersonal skills and general emotional development.

... [A]lthough we have no explicit data on whether the numbers of addicts and associated problems would increase if drugs were legalized, there are reasons to believe that they would, and rather dramatically. First, the number of people who actually use drugs is proportionately small. Second, the great majority of people in the United States have never used illicit drugs, and hence, have never been "at risk" for addiction. Third, because of the drug prohibition, illicit drugs are *not* "everywhere," and as a result, most people have not had the opportunity to even experiment with them. Fourth, alcohol *is* readily available, and the numbers of people who have been touched by alcoholism are in the dozens of millions.

Given this, let's take the argument one step further. There is extensive physiological, neurological, and anthropological evidence to suggest that we are members of a species that has been honed for pleasure. Nearly all people want and enjoy pleasure, and the pursuit of drugs—whether caffeine, nicotine, alcohol, opium, heroin, marijuana, or cocaine—seems to be universal and inescapable. It is found across time and across cultures (and species). The process of evolution has for whatever reasons resulted in a human neurophysiology that responds both vividly and avidly to a variety of common substances. The brain has pleasure centers—receptor sites and cortical cells—that react to "rewarding" dosages of many substances....

If the legalization model were of value, then ... the narcotic would just be there—attracting little attention. There would be minimal use, addiction, and the attendant social and public health problems—as long as the drug's availability was not restricted and legislated against.

... [C]onsider Poland. For generations, Poles have cultivated home-grown poppies for the use of their seeds as flavoring in breads, stews, pretzel sticks, cookies, cakes, and chocolates. During the early 1970s, many Polish farmers began transforming their poppy straw into what has become known as *jam, compote,* or "Polish heroin." Then, many Poles began using heroin, but the practice was for the most part ignored. By the end of the 1970s heroin use in Poland had escalated significantly, but still the situation was ignored. By late 1985, at a time when the number of heroin users was estimated at 600,000 and the number of heroin-dependent persons was fixed at 200,000, the Polish government could no longer ignore what was happening. The number of overdose deaths was mounting, and the range of psychosocial and public health problems associated with heroin use was beginning to affect the structure of the already troubled country. By 1986, feeling that heroin use had gotten out of hand, the Communist government in Poland placed controls on the cultivation of poppy seeds, and the transformation of poppy straw into heroin was outlawed....

Although the events in Poland have not been systematically studied, what is known of the experience suggests that introducing potent intoxicants to a population can have problematic consequences. Moreover, the notion that "availability creates demand" has been found in numerous other parts of the world, particularly with cocaine in the Andean regions of South America (see Inciardi 1992, 222).

The Legacy of Crack Cocaine
The great drug wars in the United States have endured now for generations, although the drug legalization debates have less of a history—on again, off again since the 1930s, with a sudden burst of energy at the close of the 1980s. But as the wars linger on and the debates abide, a coda must be added to both of these politically charged topics. It concerns crack cocaine, a drug that

has brought about a level of human suffering heretofore unknown in the American drug scene. The problem with crack is not that it is prohibited, but rather, the fact that it exists at all.... The chemistry and psychopharmacology of crack, combined with the tangle of socioeconomic and psychocultural strains that exist in those communities where the drug is concentrated, warrant some consideration of whether further discussion of its legality or illegality serves any purpose. Focusing on crack as an example, my intent here is to argue that both the "drug wars" and "harm reduction effort" are better served by a shifting away from the drug legalization debate.

Crack cocaine in the United States ... For the inner cities across America, the introduction of crack couldn't have happened at a worse time. The economic base of the working poor had been shrinking for years, the result of a number of factors, including the loss of many skilled and unskilled jobs to cheaper labor markets, the movement of many businesses to the suburbs and the Sun Belt, and competition from foreign manufacturers. Standards of living, health, and overall quality of life were also in a downward direction, as consequences of suburbanization and the shrinking tax bases of central cities, combined with changing economic policies at the federal level that shifted the responsibility for many social supports to the local and private sectors. Without question, by the early to mid–1980s there was a growing and pervasive climate of hopelessness in ghetto America. And at the same time, as HIV and AIDS began to spread through inner-city populations of injectable drug users and their sex partners and as funding for drug abuse treatment declined, the production of coca and cocaine in South America reached an all-time high, resulting in high-purity cocaine at a low price on the streets of urban America. As I said, crack couldn't have come to the inner city at a worse time....

I've been doing street studies in Miami, Florida, for more years than I care to remember, and during that time I've had many an experience in the shooting galleries, base houses, and open-air drug and prostitution markets that populate the local drug scene. None of these prepared me, however, with what I was to encounter in the crack houses. As part of a federally funded street survey and ethnography of cocaine and crack use, my first trip to a crack house came in 1988. I had gained entrée through a local drug dealer who had been a key informant of mine for almost a decade. He introduced me to the crack house "door man" as someone "straight but OK." After the door man checked us for weapons, my guide proceeded to show me around.

Upon entering a room in the rear of the crack house (what I later learned was called a "freak room"), I observed what appeared to be the forcible gang-rape of an unconscious child. Emaciated, seemingly comatose, and likely no older than 14 years of age, she was lying spread-eagled on a filthy mattress while four men in succession had vaginal intercourse with her. Despite what was happening, I was urged not to interfere. After they had finished and left the room, another man came in, and they engaged in oral sex.

Upon leaving the crack house sometime later, the dealer/informant explained that she was a "house girl"—a person in the employ of the crack house owner. He gave her food, a place to sleep, some cigarettes and cheap wine, and all the crack she wanted in return for her providing sex—any type and amount of sex—to his crack house customers.

That was my first trip to a crack house. During subsequent trips to this and other crack houses, there were other scenes: a woman purchasing crack, with an infant tucked under her arm—so neglected that she had maggots crawling out of her diaper; a man "skin-popping" his toddler with a small dose of heroin, so the child would remain quietly sedated and not interrupt a crack-smoking session; people in various states of excitement and paranoia, crouching in the corners of smoking rooms inhaling from "the devil's dick" (the stem of the crack pipe); arguments, fist fights, stabbings, and shootings over crack, the price of crack, the quantity and quality of crack, and the use and sharing of crack; any manner and variety of sexual activity—by individuals and/or groups, with members of the opposite sex, the same sex, or both, or with animals, in private or public, in exchange for crack. I also saw "drug hounds" and "rock monsters" (some of the "regulars" in a crack house) crawling on their hands and knees, inspecting the floors for slivers of crack that may have dropped; beatings and gang rapes of small-time drug couriers—women, men, girls, and boys—as punishment for "messing up the money"; people in convulsions and seizures, brought on by crack use, cocaine use, the use of some other drug, or whatever; users of both sexes, so dependent on crack, so desperate for more crack, that they would do anything for another hit, eagerly risking the full array of sexually transmitted diseases, including AIDS; imprisonment and sexual slavery, one of the ultimate results of crack addiction....

Many crack users engage in sexual behaviors with extremely high frequency. However, to suggest that crack turns men into "sex- crazed fiends" and women into "sex-crazed whores," as sensationalized media stories imply, is anything but precise. The situation is far more complex than that.

... Medical authorities generally concede that because of the disinhibiting effects of cocaine, its use among new users does indeed enhance sexual enjoyment and improve sexual functioning, including more intense orgasms (Weiss and Mirin 1987; Grinspoon and Bakalar 1985). These same reports maintain, however, that among long-term addicts, cocaine decreases both sexual desire and performance.

Going further, the crack-sex association involves the need of female crack addicts to pay for their drug. Even this connection has a pharmacological component— crack's rapid onset, extremely short duration of effects, and high addiction liability combine to result in compulsive use and a willingness to obtain the drug through any means.... Prostitution has long been the easiest, most lucrative, and most reliable means for women to finance drug use (Goldstein 1979).

The combined pharmacological and sociocultural effects of crack use can put female users in severe jeopardy. Because crack makes its users ecstatic and yet is so short-acting, it has an extremely high addiction potential. Use rapidly becomes compulsive use. Crack acquisition thus becomes enormously more important than family, work, social responsibility, health, values, modesty, morality, or self-respect....

A benefit of its current criminalization is that since it *is* against the law, it doesn't have widespread availability, so proportionately few people use it.

So where does all of this take us? My point is this. Within the context of reversing the human suffering that crack has helped to exacerbate, what purpose is served by arguing for its legalization? Will legalizing crack make it less available, less attractive, less expensive, less addictive, or less troublesome? Nobody really knows for sure, but I doubt it.

Drugs-Crime Connections

For the better part of this century there has been a concerted belief that addicts commit crimes because they are "enslaved" to drugs, that because of the high prices of heroin, cocaine, and other illicit chemicals on the black market, users are forced to commit crimes in order to support their drug habits. I have often referred to this as the "enslavement theory" of addiction (Inciardi 1986, 147–49; Inciardi 1992, 263–64)....

Research since the middle of the 1970s with active drug users in the streets of New York, Miami, Baltimore, and elsewhere has demonstrated that enslavement theory has little basis in reality, and that the contentions of the legalization proponents in this behalf are mistaken (see Inciardi 1986, 115–43; Johnson et al. 1985; Nurco et al. 1985; Stephens and McBride 1976; McBride and McCoy 1982). All of these studies of the criminal careers of heroin and other drug users have convincingly documented that while drug use tends to intensify and perpetuate criminal behavior, it usually does not initiate criminal careers. In fact, the evidence suggests that among the majority of street drug users who are involved in crime, their criminal careers were well established prior to the onset of either narcotics or cocaine use....

POSTSCRIPT

... [L]et me reiterate the major points I have been trying to make.

The arguments *for* legalization are seemingly based on the fervent belief that America's prohibitions against marijuana, cocaine, heroin, and other drugs impose far too large a cost in terms of tax dollars, crime, and infringements on civil rights and individual liberties. And while the overall argument may be well-intended and appear quite logical, I find it to be highly questionable in its historical, sociocultural, and empirical underpinnings, and demonstrably naive in its understanding of the negative consequences of a legalized drug market. In counterpoint:

1. Although drug-prohibition policies have been problematic, it would appear that they have managed to keep drugs away from most people. High school and general population surveys indicate that most Americans don't use drugs, have never even tried them, and don't know where to get them. Thus, the numbers "at risk" are dramatically fewer than is the case with the legal drugs. Or stated differently, there is a rather large population who might be at risk if illicit drugs were suddenly available.

2. Marijuana, heroin, cocaine, crack, and the rest are not "benign" substances. Their health consequences, addiction liability, and/or abuse potential are considerable.

3. There is extensive physiological, neurological, and anthropological evidence to suggest that people are of a species that has been honed for pleasure. Nearly all people want and enjoy pleasure, and the pursuit of drugs—whether caffeine, nicotine, alcohol, opium, heroin, marijuana, or cocaine—seems to be uni-

versal and inescapable. It is found across time and across cultures. Moreover, history and research has demonstrated that "availability creates demand."

4. Crack cocaine is especially problematic because of its pharmacological and sociocultural effects. Because crack makes its users ecstatic and yet is so short-acting, it has an extremely high addiction potential. *Use* rapidly becomes *compulsive use....*

5. The research literature on the criminal careers of heroin and other drug users have convincingly documented that while drug use tends to intensify and perpetuate criminal behavior, it usually does not initiate criminal careers.

6. There is also a large body of work suggesting that drug abuse is overdetermined behavior. That is, physical dependence is secondary to the wide range of influences that instigate and regulate drug-taking and drug-seeking. Drug abuse is a disorder of the whole person, affecting some or all areas of functioning. In the vast majority of drug offenders, there are cognitive problems, psychological dysfunction is common, thinking may be unrealistic or disorganized, values are misshapen, and frequently there are deficits in educational and employment skills. As such, drug abuse is a response to a series of social and psychological disturbances. Thus, the goal of treatment should be "habilitation" rather than "rehabilitation." Whereas *rehabilitation* emphasizes the return to a way of life previously known and perhaps forgotten or rejected, *habilitation* involves the client's initial socialization into a productive and responsible way of life.

7. The focus on the war on drugs can be shifted. I believe that we do indeed need drug enforcement, but it is stressed far too much in current policy. Cut it in half, and shift those funds to criminal justice-based treatment programs.

8. Drug control should remain within the criminal justice sector for some very good reasons. The Drug Use Forecasting (DUF) program clearly demonstrates that the majority of arrestees in urban areas are drug-involved. Moreover, recent research has demonstrated not only that drug abuse treatment works, but also that coerced treatment works best. The key variable most related to success in treatment is "length of stay in treatment," and those who are forced into treatment remain longer than volunteers. By remaining longer, they benefit more. As such, compulsory treatment efforts should be expanded for those who are dependent on drugs and are involved in drug-related crime.

9. Since the "war on drugs" will continue, then a more humane use of the criminal justice system should be structured. This is best done through treatment in lieu of incarceration, and corrections-based treatment for those who do end up in jails and prisons....

American drug policy as it exists today is not likely to change drastically anytime soon. Given that, something needs to be kept in mind. While the First Amendment and academic freedom enable the scholarly community to continue its attack on American drug policy, verbal assault and vilification will serve no significant purpose in effecting change. Calls for the legalization or decriminalization of marijuana, heroin, cocaine, and other illicit drugs accomplish little more than to further isolate the legalizers from the policy-making enterprise.

Finally, there is far too much suffering as the result of drug abuse that is not being addressed. Many things warrant discussion, debate, and prodding on the steps of Capitol Hill and the White House lawn. More drug abuse treatment slots, a repeal of the statutes designed to prosecute pregnant addicts and prohibit needle-exchange programs, the wider use of treatment as an alternative to incarceration—all of these are worthy of vigorous consideration and lobbying. But not legalizing drugs. It is an argument that is going nowhere.

POSTSCRIPT

Is the Drug War Harming Blacks?

For some (such as Szasz) the drug war is only part of a larger war on individual freedom. Blacks, according to this reasoning, are simply a convenient conduit for establishing greater legal, medical, and psychological control over citizens. The media and politicians are successful in linking Blacks and crime, crime and drugs, and drugs and Blacks. This makes a war on drugs and the alleged concomitant loss of basic freedoms for all of us more palpable. Szasz implies that few people understand this other than the medical and criminal justice establishments, especially the former. Moral do-gooders, some Black leaders, and criminological scholars, in supporting the drug war and claims of Black genocide, unwittingly acquiesce to the charade.

To Szasz, Inciardi's position of calling for treatment over incarceration is dangerous semantics and conceptual surrender to the medical experts, who Szasz sees as grabbing a monopoly on the issue. That is, to define drug use as an illness in need of treatment simply reinforces medical hegemony and maintains the myth that individuals who make drug-related choices are sick and in need of help.

Although Inciardi agrees with Szasz that Blacks have been discriminated against in drug arrests, he also feels that arrests do help Black communities. Naturally, differential racial arrest rates, if undeserved, should be remedied. For Inciardi, the solution is more rehabilitation programs for everyone. He insists that the drug problem is real and that it is not simply a matter of labeling, as Szasz suggests.

Works that are relevant to this issue include "Differential Punishing of African Americans and Whites Who Possess Drugs," by R. Alexander, Jr., and J. Gyamerah, *Journal of Black Studies* (September 1997); *Making Crime Pay: Law and Order in Contemporary American Politics* by Katherine Beckett (Oxford University Press, 1997); and "Race and Criminal Justice," in Steven R. Donziger, ed., *The Real War on Crime* (HarperPerennial, 1996). An excellent source that looks at the media connection is D. Rome's "Stereotyping by the Media: Murders, Rapists, and Drug Addicts," in Coramae R. Mann and Marjorie S. Zatz, eds., *Images of Color, Images of Crime* (Roxbury, 1998). Also see "A Get-Tough Policy That Failed," by John Cloud, *Time* (February 1, 1999) and "Drug War Disarray Up Close," *The Washington Times* (March 20, 1999). More neutral accounts can be found in *Webs of Smoke: Smugglers, Warlords, Spies, and the History of the International Drug Trade* by Kathryn Meyer and Terry Parssinen (Rowman & Littlefield, 1998) and *Drug Crazy: How We Got into This Mess and How We Can Get Out* by Mike Gray (Random House, 1998).

CONTRIBUTORS
TO THIS VOLUME

EDITOR

RICHARD C. MONK is a professor of criminal justice at Coppin State College in Baltimore, Maryland. He received a Ph.D. in sociology from the University of Maryland in 1978, and he has taught sociology, criminology, and criminal justice at Morgan State University, San Diego State University, and Valdosta State College. He has received two NEH fellowships, and he coedited the May 1992 issue of the *Journal of Contemporary Criminal Justice,* which dealt with race, crime, and criminal justice. Among his edited works are *Baltimore: A Living Renaissance* (Historic Baltimore Society, 1982) and *Structures of Knowing* (University of America Press, 1986), which partially deals with theories and research methods related to ethnic minorities. He coedited a special issue entitled "Police Training and Violence" for the *Journal of Contemporary Criminal Justice* (August 1996) and coauthored two articles on issues in philosophy of science for the *Journal of Social Pathology* (Fall 1995 and Winter 1997). Professor Monk's research article "Some Unanticipated Consequences of Women Guarding Men in Prison" was published in Nijole Benokraitis, ed., *Subtle Sexism: Current Practice and Prospects for Change* (Sage Publications, 1998). He is also the editor of *Taking Sides: Clashing Views on Controversial Issues in Crime and Criminology* (Dushkin/McGraw-Hill), now in its fifth edition. He is currently completing a coauthored book on theory and policies in crime and crime control.

STAFF

Theodore Knight   List Manager
David Brackley   Senior Developmental Editor
Juliana Poggio   Developmental Editor
Rose Gleich   Administrative Assistant
Brenda S. Filley   Production Manager
Juliana Arbo   Typesetting Supervisor
Diane Barker   Proofreader
Lara Johnson   Design/Advertising Coordinator
Richard Tietjen   Publishing Systems Manager

AUTHORS

ROBERT APONTE is an assistant professor of sociology in the James Madison College at Michigan State University in East Lansing, Michigan, and a research associate at the Julian Samora Research Institute.

DAVID A. BELL is a former reporter and researcher for *The New Republic.*

MAITRAYEE BHATTACHARYYA is an editor and a researcher at the Institute for Research on the African Diaspora in the Americas and the Caribbean (IRADAC).

DEREK BOK is president emeritus at Harvard University and the 300th Anniversary University Professor in the Kennedy School of Government. He is the author of *The State of the Nation: Government and the Quest for a Better Society, 1960–1995* (Harvard University Press, 1998).

WILLIAM G. BOWEN is president of the Andrew W. Mellon Foundation. He is coauthor, with Derek Bok, of *The Shape of the River: Long-Term Consequences of Considering Race in College and University Admissions* (Princeton University Press, 1998).

PETER BRIMELOW is senior editor at *Forbes* and *National Review* magazines. He is the author of *Alien Nation: Common Sense About America's Immigration Disaster* (Random House, 1995).

CHRISTOPHER R. BROWNING teaches at Pacific Lutheran University. He is the author of *Ordinary Men: Reserve Police Battalion 101 and the Final Solution in Poland* (HarperCollins, 1993).

JOHN SIBLEY BUTLER is a professor of sociology and management at the University of Texas at Austin. He is the author of *Entrepreneurship and Self-Help Among Black Americans: A Reconsideration of Race and Economics* (SUNY Press, 1991).

PAUL BUTLER is an associate professor at the George Washington University Law School.

LINDA CHAVEZ, a political commentator, policy analyst, and author, is the John M. Olin Fellow of the Manhattan Institute for Policy Research in Washington, D.C., and chairperson of the National Commission on Migrant Education. Her articles have appeared in such publications as *Fortune,* the *Wall Street Journal,* and the *Los Angeles Times.*

DAVID COLE is a professor at Georgetown University Law Center and a volunteer staff attorney for the Center for Constitutional Rights.

OLGA IDRISS DAVIS is an assistant professor of speech communication at Kansas State University in Manhattan, Kansas. A Rockefeller Humanities Fellow for summer 1997, she conducted research on a project entitled *Piecing Ourselves Together: The Rhetoric of Coalition-Building in Black Women's Slave Narratives.*

DINESH D'SOUZA, a former senior domestic policy analyst for the Reagan administration, is the John M. Olin Research Fellow at the American Enterprise Institute in Washington, D.C. He is the author of *The End of Racism: Principles for a Multiracial Society* (Free Press, 1995).

JEFF FERRELL is an associate professor of criminal justice at Northern Arizona University in Flagstaff, Arizona. He is the author of *Crimes of Style: Urban Graffiti and the Politics of Criminology* (Garland, 1993).

DANIEL JONAH GOLDHAGEN teaches political science at Harvard University. He is the author of *Hitler's Willing Executioners: Ordinary Germans and the Holocaust* (Alfred A. Knopf, 1996).

H. L. GOLDSTEIN is a freelance writer living in Baltimore, Maryland.

EDMUND W. GORDON is the John M. Musser Professor of Psychology Emeritus at Yale University and a professor of psychology at City College of New York. He is also the director of the Institute for Research on the African Diaspora in the Americas and the Caribbean (IRADAC).

MARK S. HAMM is a professor of criminology at Indiana State University in Terre Haute, Indiana. He is the author of *American Skinheads: The Criminology and Control of Hate Crime* (Praeger, 1993).

SHEILA E. HENRY is affiliated with the School of Arts and Sciences at National University in Costa Mesa, California. Her research interests include ethnic identity, the African diaspora, ethnic inequality, and historical sociology.

JAMES A. INCIARDI is director of the Center for Drug and Alcohol Studies at the University of Delaware in Newark, Delaware, and an adjunct professor in the Comprehensive Drug Research Center at the University of Miami School of Medicine in Miami, Florida.

JOSEPH P. KALT is codirector of the Harvard Project on American Indian Economic Development in the Kennedy School of Government at Harvard University.

RANDALL KENNEDY is a professor at Harvard Law School.

SUSAN LEDLOW is a faculty associate for the University Program for Faculty Development at Arizona State University in Tempe, Arizona. She was also involved with teacher training in bilingual education progams for the University of Arizona's Mountain State Multifunctional Resource Center for eight years.

GLENN C. LOURY is a professor of economics at Boston University in Boston, Massachusetts. He has been actively involved in public debate and analysis of the problems of racial inequality and social policy toward the poor in the United States, which is reflected in his publication *Achieving the Dream* (Heritage Foundation, 1990).

CORAMAE RICHEY MANN is a professor of criminal justice at Indiana University in Bloomington, Indiana. Her publications include *Female Crime and Delinquency* (University of Alabama Press, 1984) and *Unequal Justice: A Question of Color* (Indiana University Press, 1993).

DENNIS R. MARTIN is former president of the National Association of Chiefs of Police in Arlington, Virginia.

ROBERT K. MERTON is an adjunct professor at Rockefeller University, a resident scholar at the Russell Sage Foundation, and a professor emeritus at Columbia University, all located in New York City. His publications include *The Sociology of Science: Theoretical and Empirical Investigations* (University of Chicago Press, 1973).

HENDRIK MILLS is a Montana writer and a schoolteacher with extensive experience on Indian reservations.

ANN OAKLEY is a professor at the University of London Institute of Education. She is coeditor, with Juliet Mitchell, of

Who's Afraid of Feminism? Seeing Through the Backlash (New Press, 1997).

JON REYHNER is an associate professor in the Department of Curriculum and Instruction at Eastern Montana College, where he teaches education and Native American studies. His publications include *Teaching American Indian Students* (University of Oklahoma, 1992).

KEITH B. RICHBURG is the Southeast Asia correspondent for the *Washington Post*. He is the author of *Out of America: A Black Man Confronts Africa* (Basic Books, 1997).

EUGENE F. RIVERS III is the founder and pastor of Azusa Christian Community and a Harvard Divinity School guest lecturer.

PAUL RUFFINS is executive editor of *Crisis* magazine.

ARTHUR M. SCHLESINGER, JR., is the Albert Schweitzer Professor of the Humanities at the City University of New York and the author of *The Cycles of American History* (Houghton Mifflin, 1986).

JACK G. SHAHEEN is a journalist, a former professor of mass communications at Southern Illinois University in Edwardsville, Illinois, and a recipient of two Fulbright-Hayes Lectureship Grants.

THOMAS SOWELL is a Senior Fellow of the Hoover Institution at Stanford University. He has taught economics at a number of universities, including Brandeis University, and he is the author of several books, including *Conquests and Cultures* (Basic Books, 1998).

BRENT STAPLES writes editorials for the *New York Times*.

THOMAS SZASZ is a psychiatrist, a psychoanalyst, and a professor in the Department of Psychiatry at the State University of New York's Upstate Medical Center at Syracuse, New York. His publications include *Our Right to Drugs: The Case for a Free Market* (Praeger, 1992).

RONALD TAKAKI is a professor of ethnic studies at the University of California, Berkeley. A member of the American Historical Association, his publications include *From Different Shores: Perspectives on Race and Ethnicity in America*, 2d ed. (Oxford University Press, 1994).

JONATHAN B. TAYLOR directs American Indian projects at the Economics Resource Group, Inc., in Cambridge, Massachusetts.

WILLIAM WILBANKS is a professor of criminal justice at Florida International University in Miami, Florida. He has published more than 50 book chapters and journal articles on issues of race and crime, homicide, and addiction, and he is the author of 6 books, including *The Myth of a Racist Criminal Justice System* (Brooks/Cole, 1987).

WALTER E. WILLIAMS is the John M. Olin Distinguished Professor of Economics at George Mason University in Fairfax, Virginia. He writes a weekly syndicated column that is carried by approximately 100 newspapers, and he is the author of *South Africa's War Against Capitalism* (Greenwood Press, 1989).

LAWRENCE WRIGHT is a staff writer for the *New Yorker* magazine and the author of *Twins: And What They Tell Us About Who We Are* (John Wiley, 1997).

INDEX